MASTERING **STREET**

PHOTOGRAPHY

BRIAN LLOYD DUCKETT

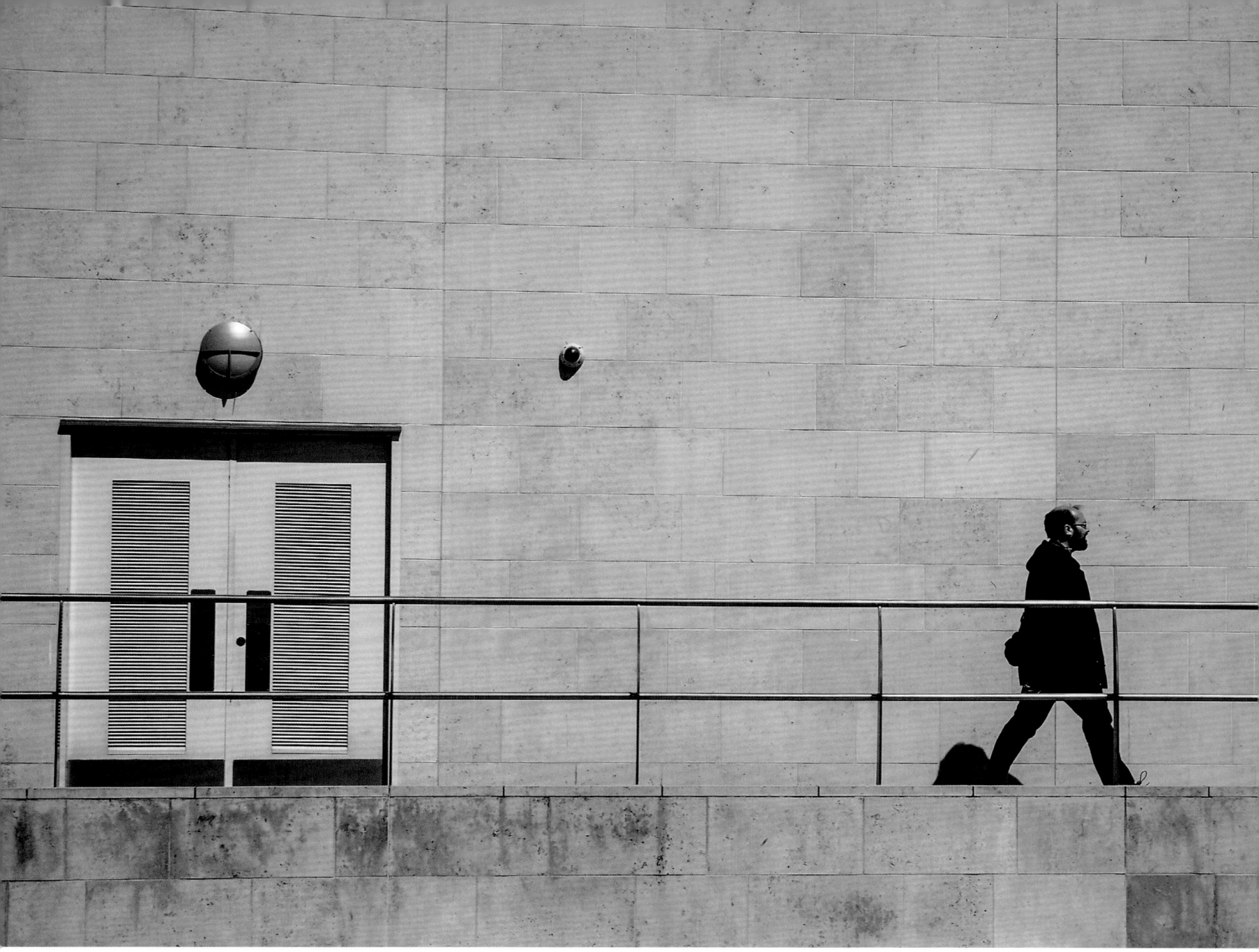

Above: Street photography is an all-encompassing genre that can include portraiture, architecture, and candidly observed moments of life unfolding around us.

Focal length: 50mm

Aperture: f/10

Shutter speed: 1/2500 sec.

ISO: 400

MASTERING **STREET**
PHOTOGRAPHY

BRIAN LLOYD DUCKETT

UPDATED EDITION

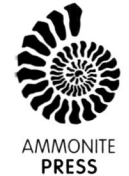

AMMONITE
PRESS

This edition published 2025 by
Ammonite Press
an imprint of GMC Publications Ltd, Castle Place,
166 High Street, Lewes, East Sussex, BN7 1XU, UK.
www.ammonitepress.com

First published 2016; reprinted 2017, 2019, 2020

ISBN 978-1-78145-499-2

The EEA authorised representative is Authorised Rep Compliance Ltd.
Ground Floor, 71 Baggot Street Lower, Dublin, DO2 P593, Ireland.
www.arccompliance.com

A catalog record of this book is available from the British Library.

Editor: Chris Gatcum
Publisher: Jason Hook
Designer: Robin Shields

Typeface: Helvetica Neue
Color reproduction by GMC Reprographics
Printed in China

Contents

Introduction	6

Chapter 1

Equipment	12
Analog Or Digital?	14
Digital Cameras	16
Shooting Film	20
Lenses	22
Accessories	26
Other Essentials	28

Chapter 2

Technical Skills	30
Exposure	32
Focus	36
Composition	40
Raw Or JPEG?	52
Shooting For Color	54
Shooting For Black & White	56
Low Light	58
Assignment 1: Alone	62
Assignment 2: It's All A Blur	64

Chapter 3

Inspiration	66
Finding & Developing Your Style	68
Develop A Project Mentality	70
Color Or Black & White?	74
What To Shoot	76
Where To Shoot	94
Assignment 3: Juxtaposition	104
Assignment 4: Objects	106

Chapter 4

On Location	108
Planning A Shoot	110
Working Safely	114
Developing Observational Skills	115
How To Be Invisible	116
Conquer Your Fear	120
Timing	126
Assignment 5: Up Close & Personal	130
Assignment 6: Where I Live	132

Chapter 5

Legal & Ethical Issues	134
Shooting On The Streets	136
Photographing Children	144
Cultural Issues	145
Red Lines	146
Copyright	147

Chapter 6

Postproduction	152
The Integrity Of The Image	154
Image-Editing Software	156
Cropping	160
Editing Raw Images	162
Converting To Monochrome	164
Fine Tuning In Photoshop	166

Glossary	170
Useful Websites	172
Index	173
Acknowledgments	176

Introduction

For well over a century, photographers have been recording life on the streets—in the raw and as it happens. Often witty, sometimes provocative, and occasionally disturbing, street photography can stir the emotions like no other photographic genre.

From the early, grainy, black-and-white efforts of the likes of Henri Cartier-Bresson and Robert Doisneau, to the bold, colorful, 21st-century work of Bruce Gilden, street photography has been telling the story of life as it unfolds—compelling, unpredictable, unstaged, and often unforgiving.

It is one of the few fields of photography that does not require huge amounts of expensive kit, exotic locations, or complex technical skills. In that sense—and with such low barriers to entry—street photography is more of an art than a science, which can be enjoyed by anyone, irrespective of the depth of their photographic knowledge or the quality of their equipment.

But it is perhaps not as easy as it sounds: we need to distinguish between street photography and pictures taken on a street.

So what's the difference and why does it matter? It's really all about intention and approach: street photography is a distinct genre with a focus on capturing candid, unposed moments that reflect life in the public realm. It emphasizes storytelling, composition, and spontaneity, aiming to capture the human condition, urban life, or humorous juxtapositions. A good street image isn't about where it's taken but how it frames a moment.

On the other hand, photography taken on the street is a broader term that simply refers to any kind of photography that happens to be taken in a street setting. The street is merely a backdrop rather than an integral part of the image's meaning. Essentially, most (but not all) street photography happens on the street, but not all photography on the street is street photography.

We have probably all seen street photographs that fall into the "so what?" category: pictures of random people in random places, doing nothing in particular. Do you really want to look at a picture of someone's uncle coming out of a hardware store? Is it interesting? Is it art? Could you do better? You decide.

Across the following chapters we will combine established, tried-and-trusted techniques with some new ways of working, helping to build your confidence and develop your skills. We will explore the tradecraft of street photography—from how to work effectively in the field, through to the technical essentials such as composition, light, focus, and postproduction.

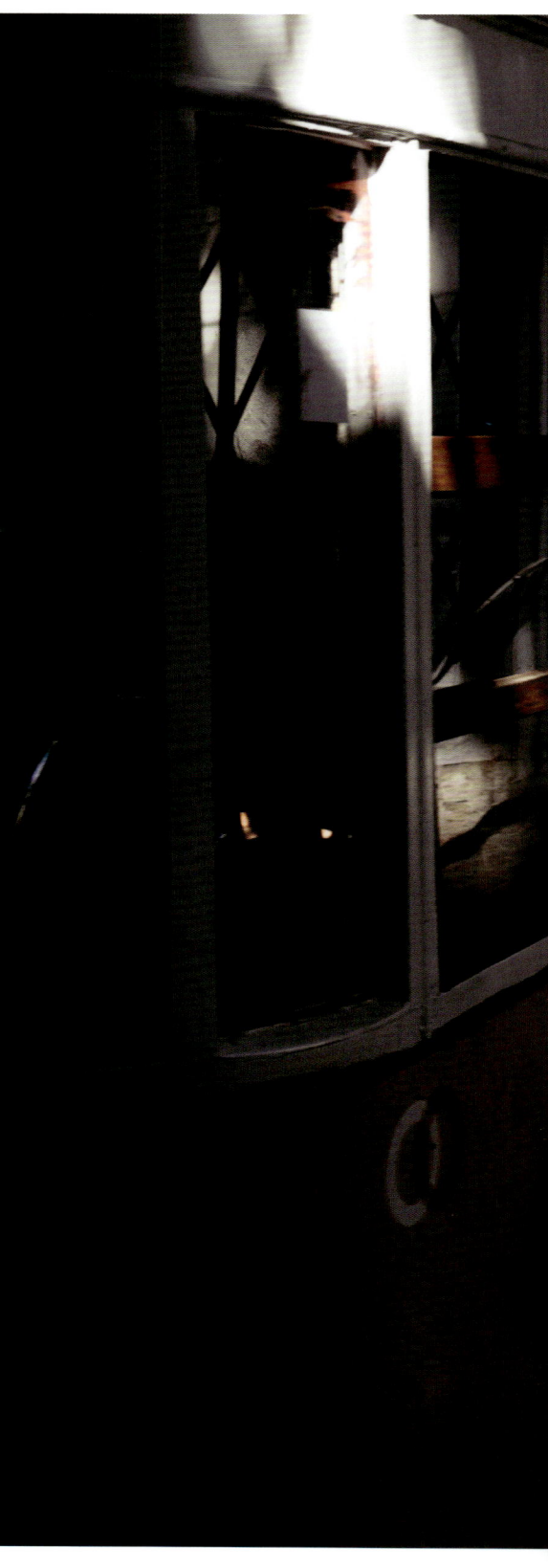

Right: Street photography doesn't necessarily mean candid pictures of people; images can be more "poetic," reflecting mood, feeling, or atmosphere.

Focal length: 40mm

Aperture: f/4.8

Shutter speed: 1/320 sec.

ISO: 400

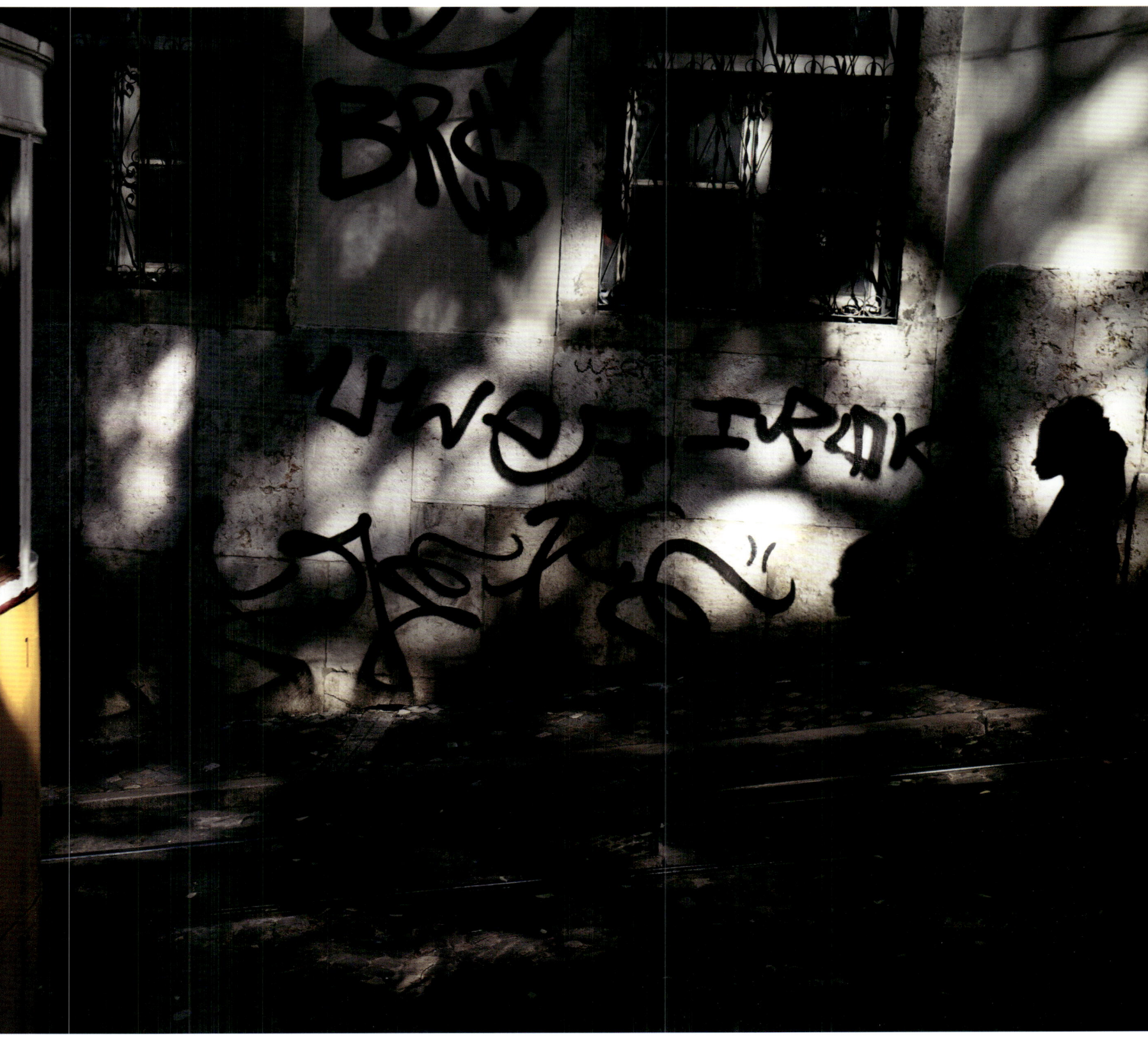

Street Photography: A Brief History

It is worth briefly exploring the history of street photography, not only to compile a list of the people who have helped define the art, but also to help us assess the current state of play.

Louis-Jacques-Mandé Daguerre took what is thought to be the first street photograph in the late 1830s—a view taken from his studio window of the Boulevard du Temple in Paris. Although this is probably the first example of the genre, it was not to become a common feature in Daguerre's work. It wasn't until the turn of the century that street photography became recognized as a genre in its own right, thanks mainly to the work of Eugène Atget, who captured the streets of his home city, Paris, France. Interestingly, people didn't figure prominently in much of his work.

At around the same time, Paul Martin started to photograph the streets of London with a concealed camera, probably signaling the start of the candid style of street photography we recognize and practice today.

Fast-forward 40 years or so and we see the birth of the "decisive moment," as coined by Henri Cartier-Bresson, a photographer whose poetic style documented the lives of real people in street settings. This phrase, now embedded deep into the psyche of most street photographers, was explained by Cartier-Bresson: "*To me, photography is the simultaneous recognition, in a fraction of a second, of the significance of an event as well as of a precise organization of forms which give that event its proper expression.*"

Proving the point that you don't need masses of gear in order to be a great street photographer, Cartier-Bresson worked almost exclusively with a battered Leica and a 50mm standard (or, occasionally, a 35mm wide-angle) lens.

Below: Like the pioneering work of Eugène Atget, street photographs don't necessarily have to include people; this is what we might call "street still life."

Focal length: 85mm

Aperture: f/4

Shutter speed: 1/250 sec.

ISO: 2000

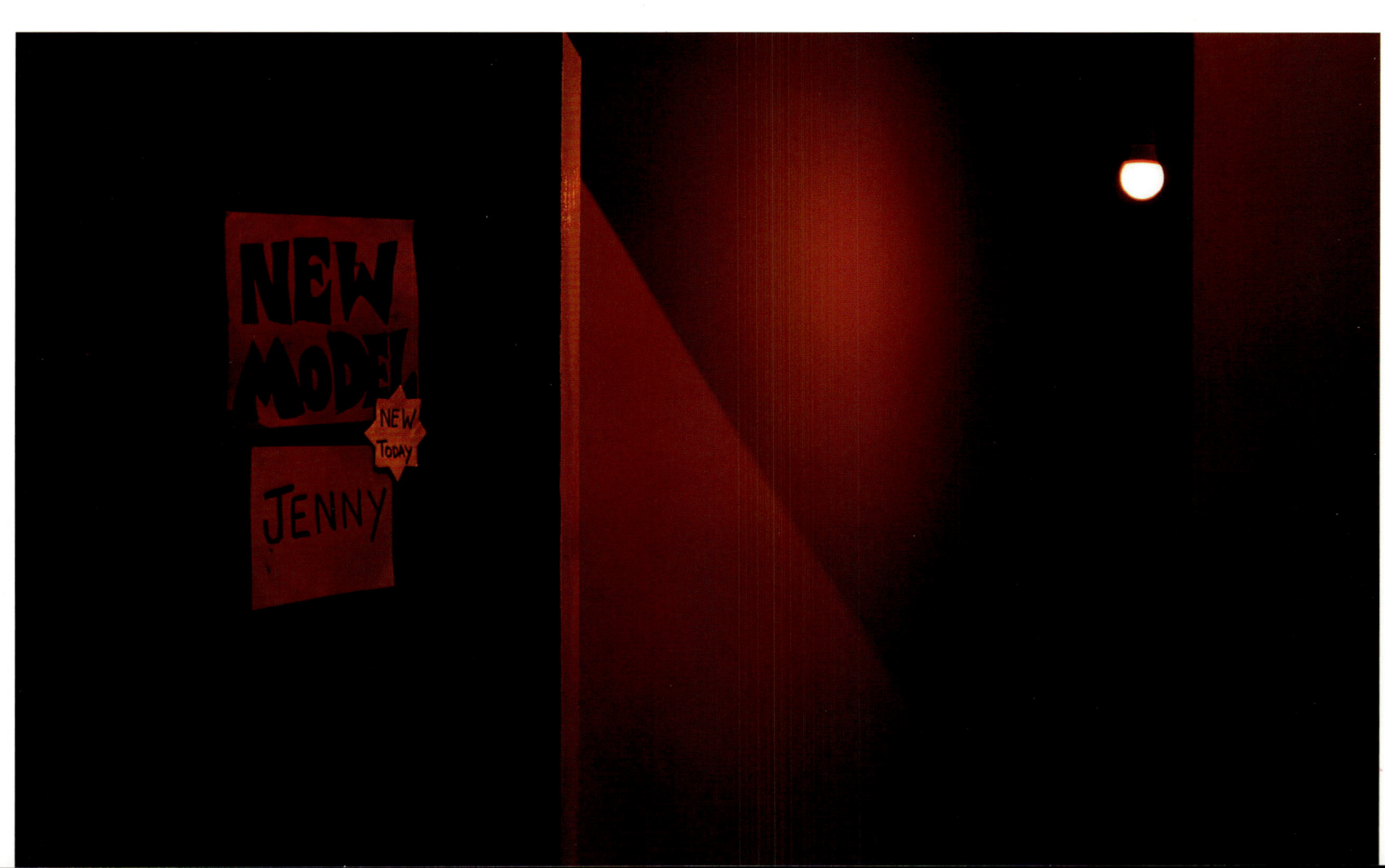

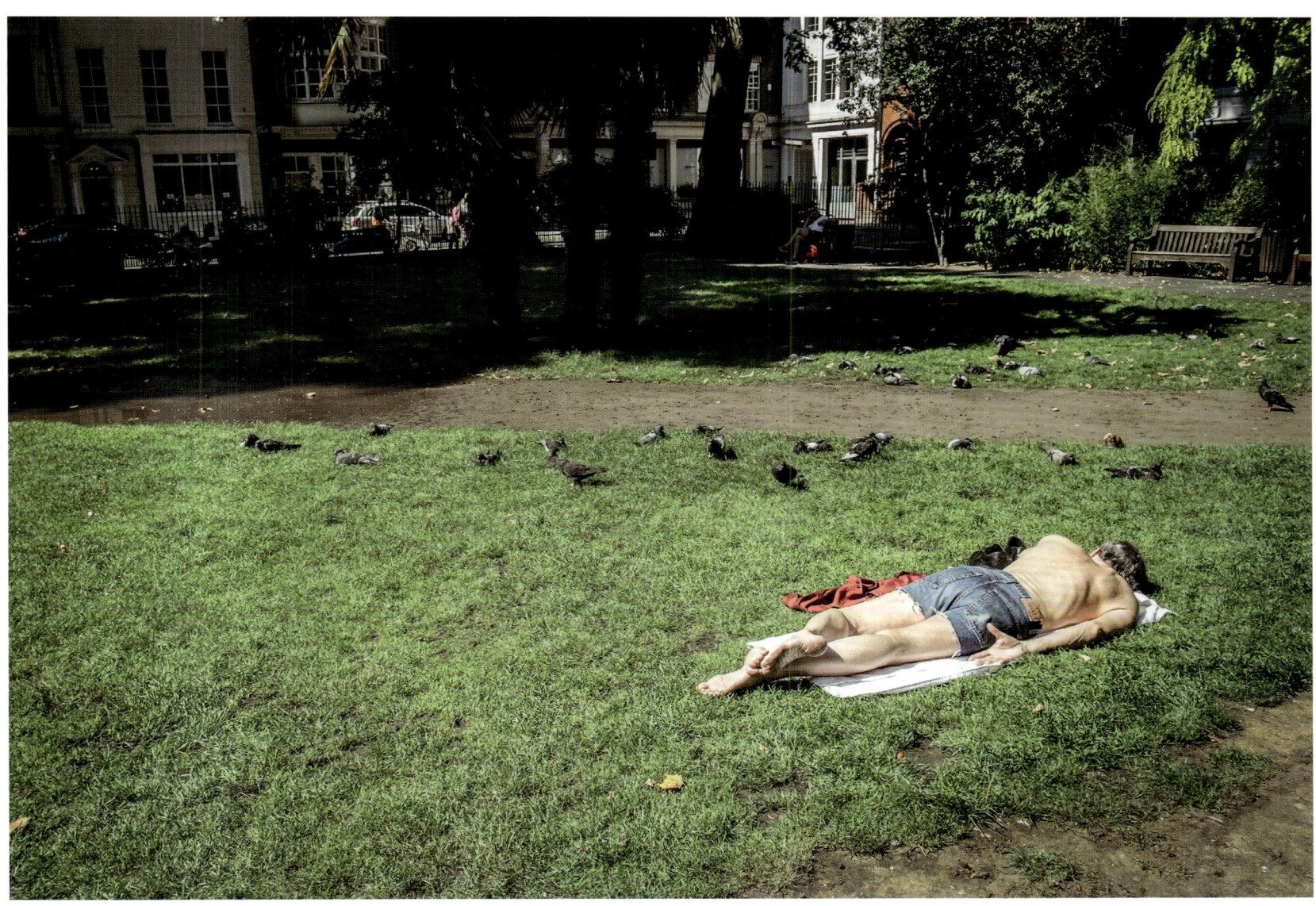

Recent Masters

The art advanced pretty swiftly from the 1950s up to the present day, notably due to the work of masters such as Robert Frank, Vivian Maier, Saul Leiter, Joel Meyerowitz, Garry Winogrand, Lee Friedlander, Bruce Gilden, and Martin Parr. Explore the work of these photographers and try to understand how they saw the world through their lens. As artists, we can do ourselves a favor by taking inspiration from others.

Above: Find a style of photography that you enjoy looking at and which motivates you to keep going; work on that style and let it become your signature. For example, some photographers—such as Martin Parr—have become known for their use of vivid colors.

Focal length: 28mm

Aperture: f/8

Shutter speed: 1/25 sec.

ISO: 200

"In photography, the smallest thing can be a great subject. The little human detail can become a leitmotiv."

—Henri Cartier-Bresson

Street Photography Today

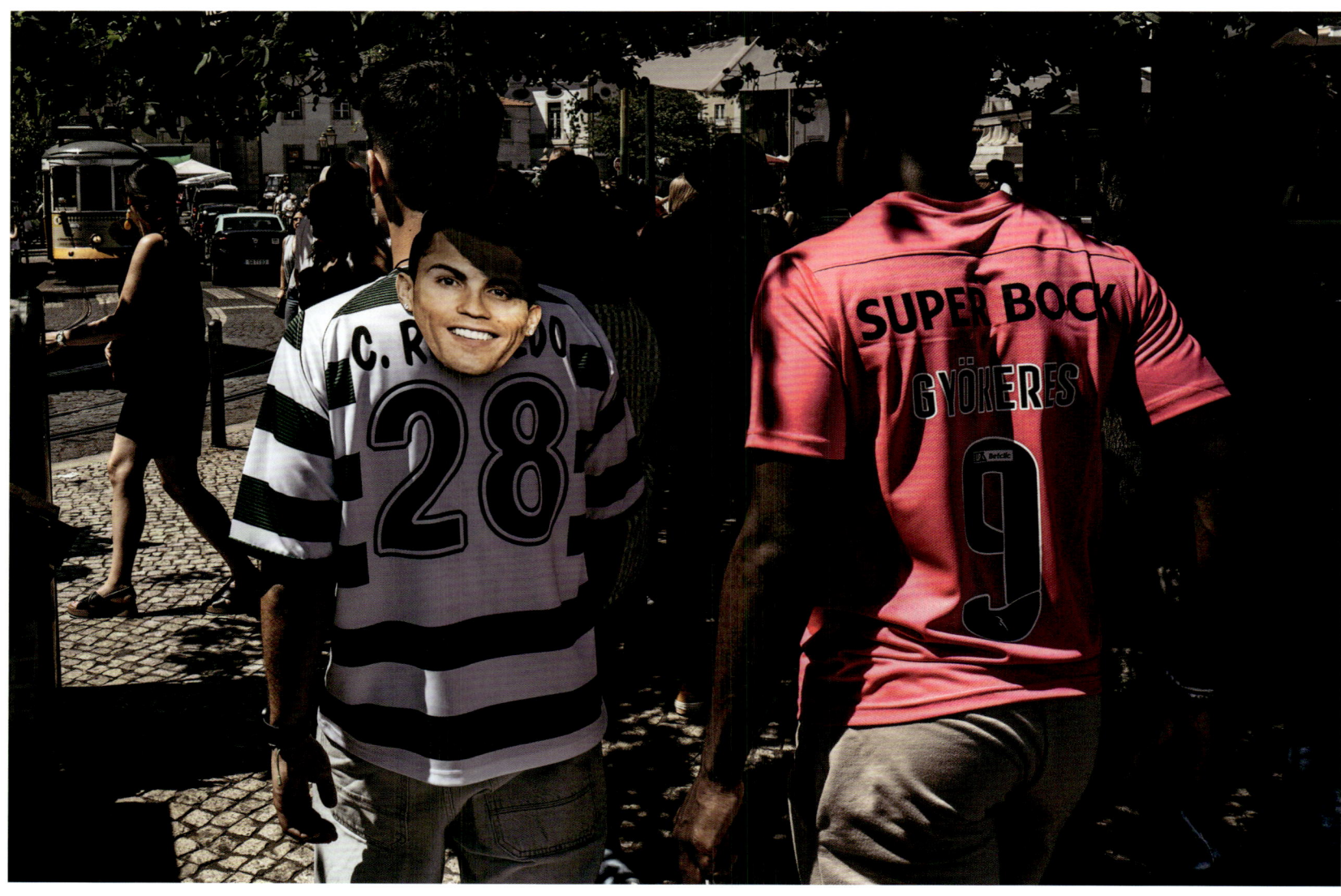

The term "street photography" is all encompassing and it means different things to different people. For a picture to qualify as a street photograph, does it have to be taken on a street? Is it essential that people feature in the shot? Does it have to be candid? Must it be in black and white? Is the decisive moment a crucial ingredient? I would suggest that the answer to each of these questions is "No," although this will always be a matter for debate.

As with any art form, there is a danger that street photography could reach a point where nothing new is happening. Bruce Gilden was certainly a pusher of boundaries with his "machine gun" style, but where has that led us? That style has advanced the art up to a point, but it has also bred a generation of photo-plagiarists. Sure, there's nothing wrong with being inspired by a distinctive style, but there is a limit to how many close-ups of strangers the world wants to see.

Be inspired, sure, but also let street photography challenge you and stretch your creativity. With the minimum of kit, some good technique, and a strong sense of purpose, get out there and just do it. Hit the streets, be patient, and the magic will eventually happen.

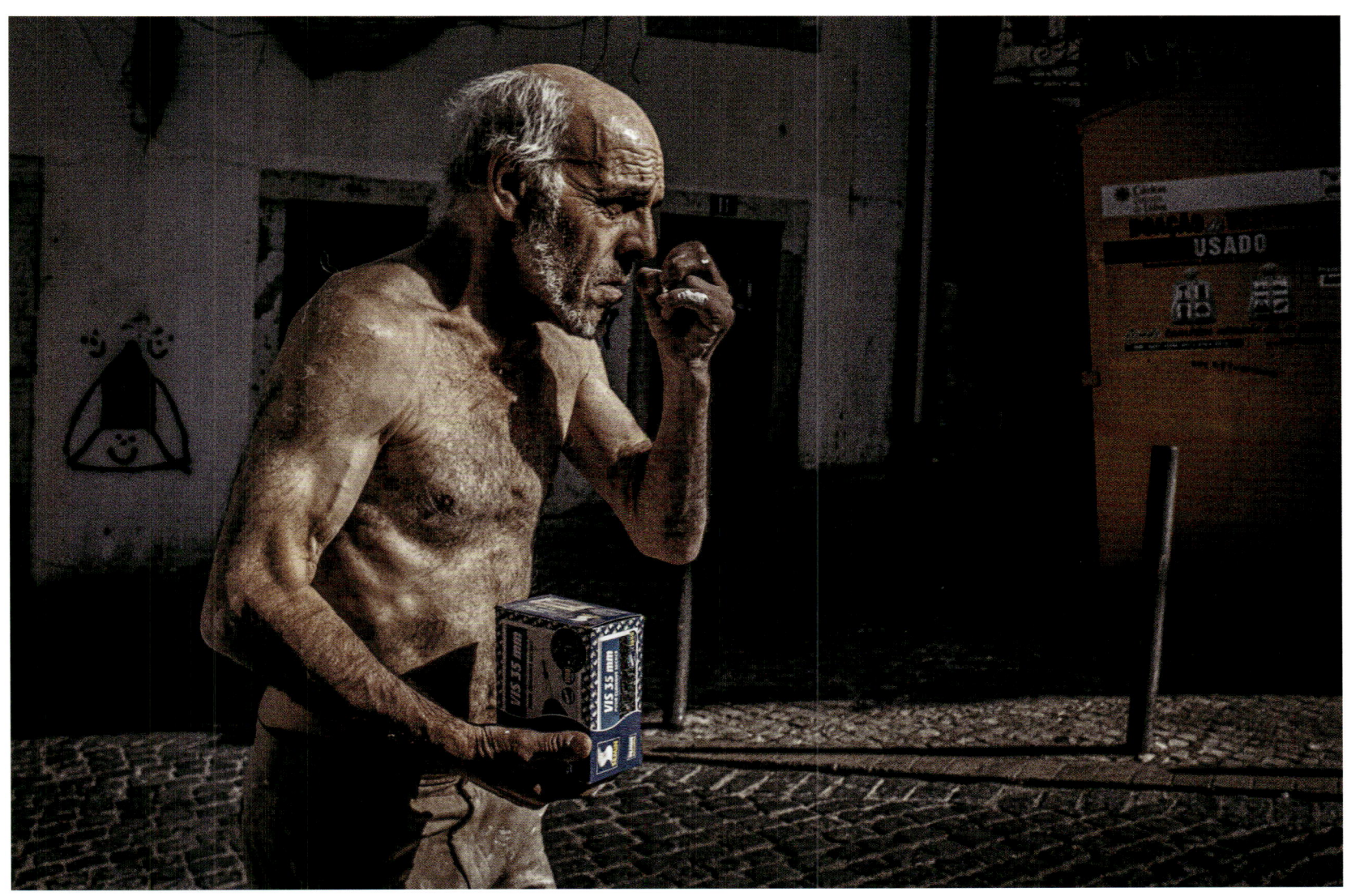

Left: Always look out for the "unusual in the usual"—it's great if your image causes the viewer to do a double take.

Focal length: 43mm

Aperture: f/10

Shutter speed: 1/500 sec.

ISO: 160

Above: If you work quickly and quietly, it's likely that people won't notice you taking their picture. While this guy was going about his business, the camera was raised at the last minute and he didn't notice.

Focal length: 35mm

Aperture: f/11

Shutter speed: 1/680 sec.

ISO: 640

"The only interesting answers are those which destroy the questions."

—*Susan Sontag*

Chapter 1
Equipment

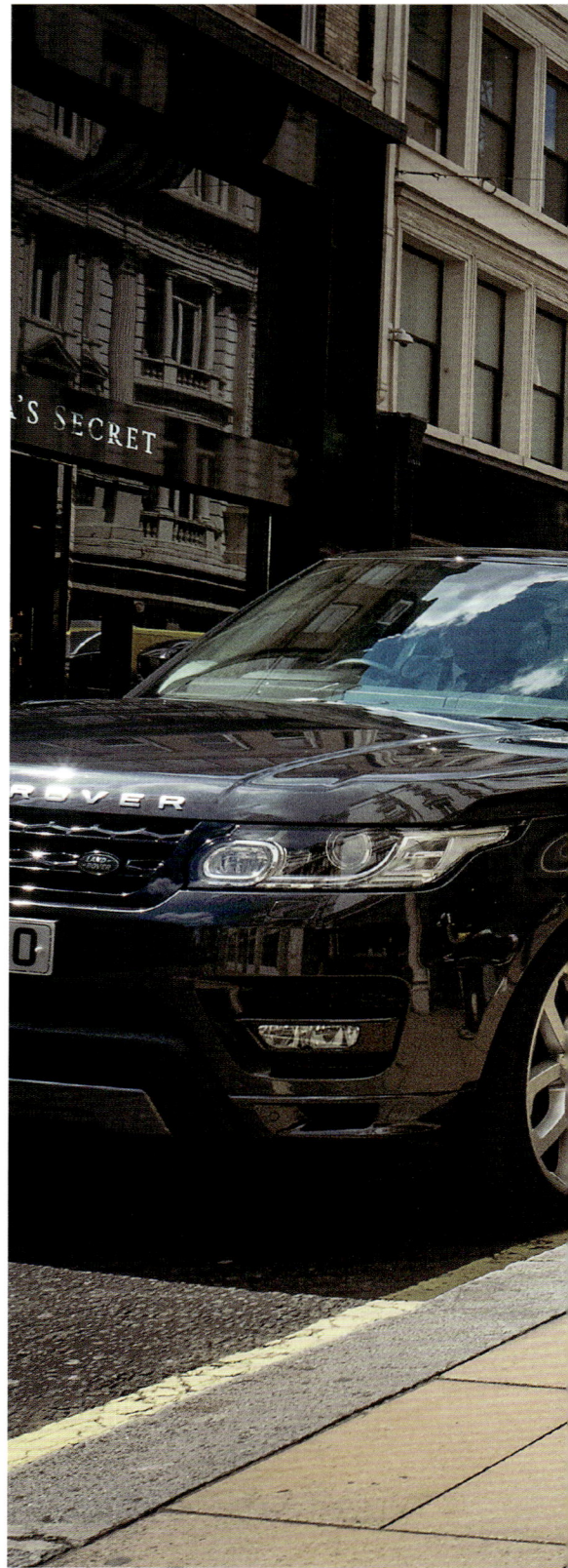

One of the great things about street photography is its accessibility and low-cost entry point. Less is most definitely more, and you certainly don't need a bag full of expensive gear to be a great street photographer. In fact, some of the best street photography you will ever see will probably have been taken on a battered old 35mm rangefinder camera, or perhaps even on a smartphone. When it comes to planning a shooting expedition, you really don't need to carry much in the way of lenses and accessories—as a general rule, if it won't fit into a small shoulder bag, you're carrying too much!

Right: Try to get comfortable with a "one camera, one lens" approach. If you practice a lot with the same combination you'll find that you can work quickly and instinctively. This means you won't need to look through the viewfinder, which can save valuable seconds.

Focal length: 24mm

Aperture: f/7.1

Shutter speed: 1/3200 sec.

ISO: 1000

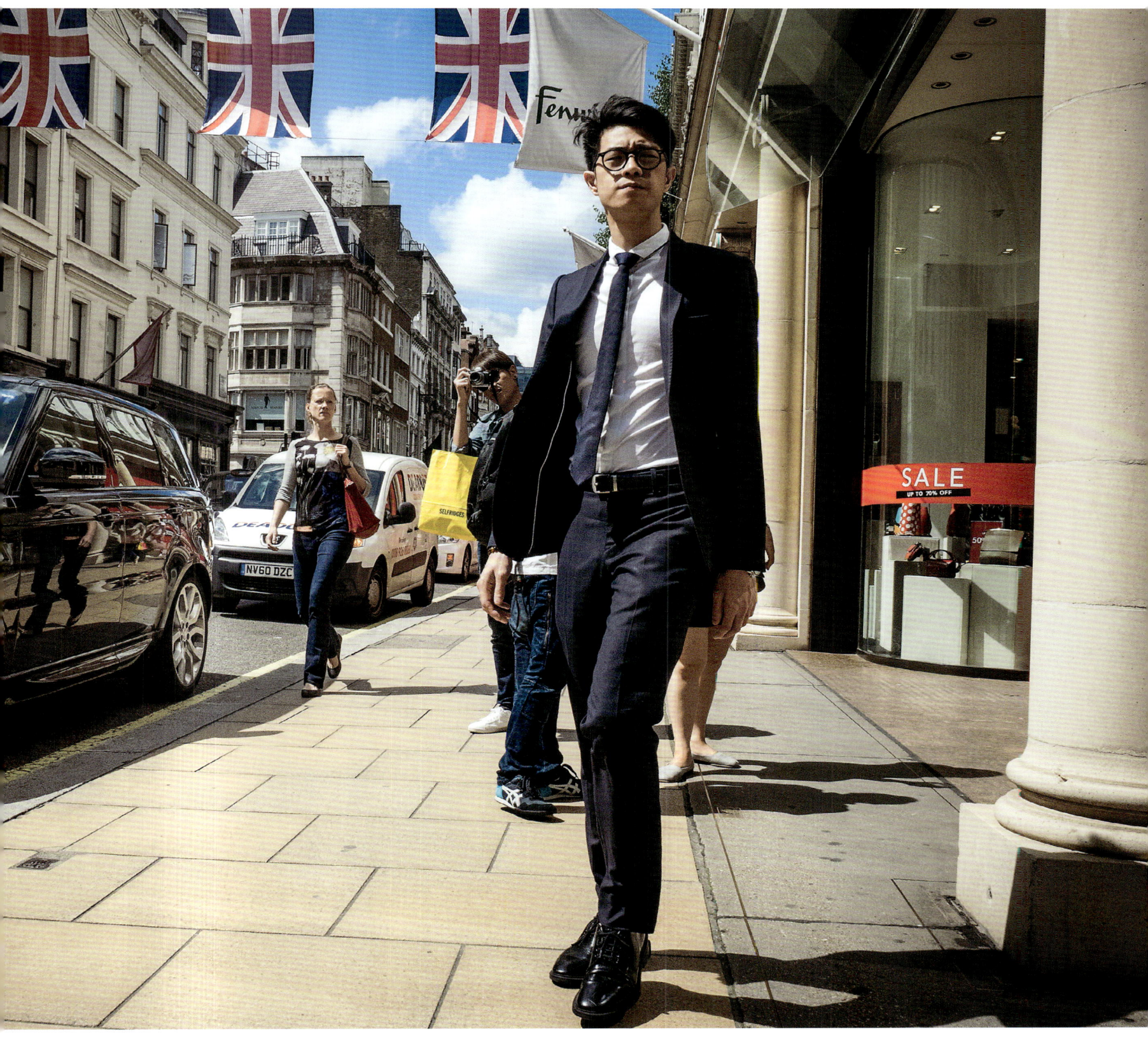

Analog Or Digital?

One of the most fundamental decisions is whether to use analog or digital equipment, and this is a recurring topic for debate among street photographers. Everyone has their own view on this and every street photographer you meet will discuss the merits of their chosen platform.

However, while the decision is a very intensely personal one, you need to put aside emotion and consider some of the practicalities. There is no doubt that film has a certain look and feel, particularly for people who have been brought up using film cameras. But can it stand up to its more sophisticated digital cousin?

Film is now more popular than it has been for many years and, rather like vinyl in the music world, it's enjoying a renaissance. One of the great things about shooting on film—particularly in low light—is grain. There is something more aesthetically pleasing about grain than digital noise, and many photographers would say that the texture added by a little grain adds to the mood of a shot (especially in monochrome). There's also a strong argument which says that film is better at faithfully recording highlights, and that it blends light and color more effectively. Others would say that the experience of using a film camera slows you down and makes you think—*really* think—about what you are doing because every frame counts (and costs).

However, while there are still valid reasons for shooting film, it's easy to see why digital is dominant. For street photographers, compactness, convenience, cost, and speed of use are critical and it is digital technology that is most likely to bring us these benefits.

PRO	DIGITAL	PRO	FILM
+	Cameras are compact and light	+	Equipment can be far cheaper
+	Low running costs	+	Less reliant on batteries
+	Quiet or silent operation	+	Reliability and durability
+	Greater margin for error	+	Slows you down and makes you think about every shot
+	Can change settings easily	+	Romantic appeal
+	Allows experimentation while shooting	+	The excitement of waiting to see the results
+	Abundance of learning materials and resources		
+	See results immediately		
+	Shoot with very high ISO		
CON		CON	
-	High upfront cost of kit	-	Film and processing can be expensive
-	Empty batteries can leave you stranded	-	Gear is often noisy and heavy
-	A corrupt memory card can lead to days or weeks of lost work	-	Reduced latitude for getting it wrong
-	Tendency to shoot too much—the "spray and pray" mentality	-	Film is bulky to carry
-	Too easy to accidentally delete work	-	Often a long wait to see the results
		-	Grain at high ISO
		-	Can't vary ISO mid-shoot

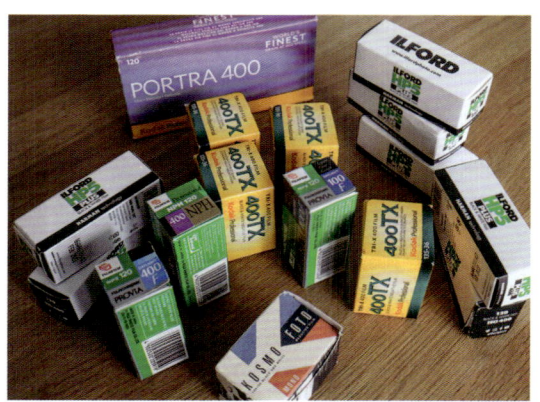

Above: If you're shooting film, you'll need to carry plenty of rolls around with you. It's also worth remembering that you can't easily switch between color and black and white unless you have more than one camera.

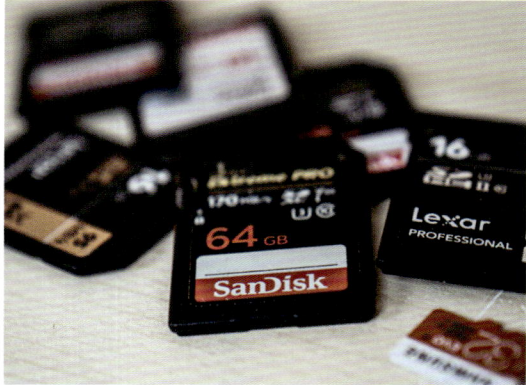

Above: Memory cards are more portable than film, but make sure you have enough of them: it's better to use a number of smaller capacity cards than one large card—losing a card with a whole day's (or week's) shooting on it can be catastrophic!

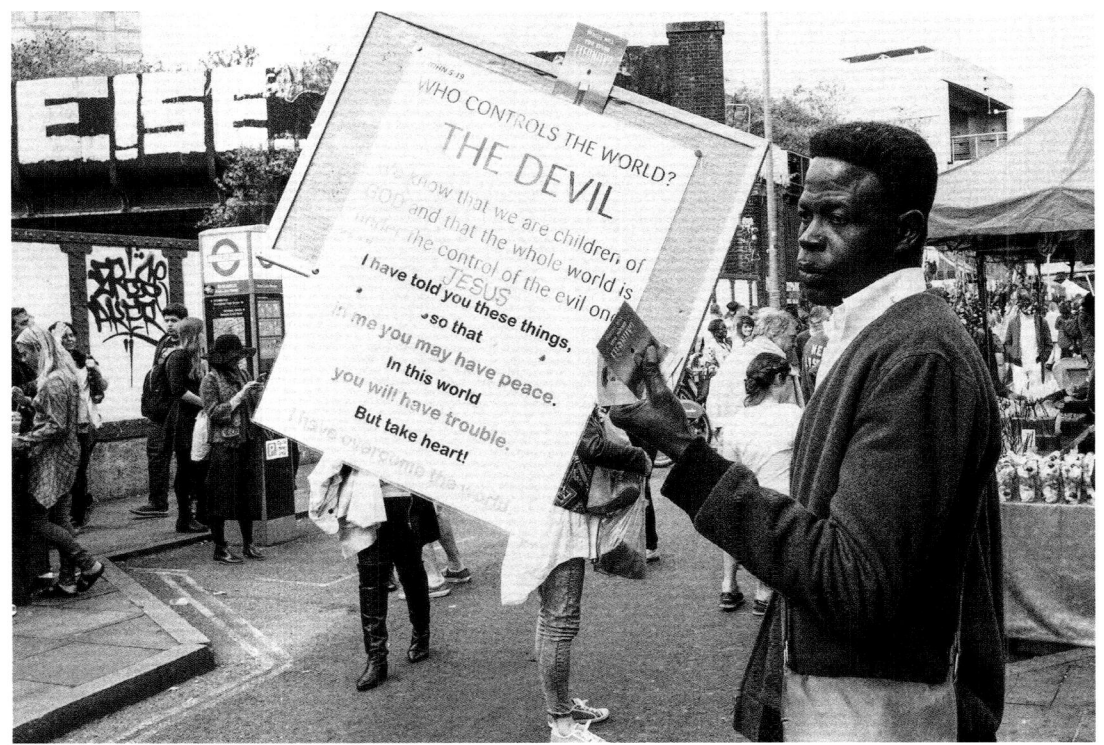

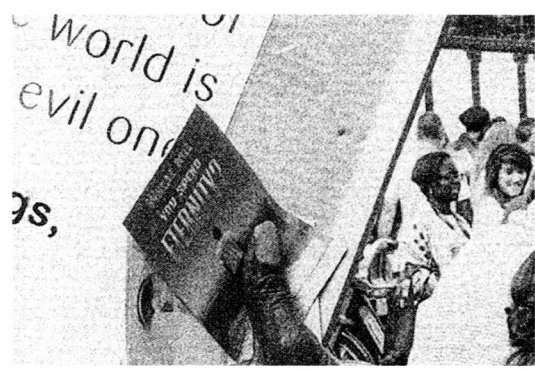

Left & Above: The grain in fast film adds a gritty texture to images. As the grain structure is random, it is not unpleasant—some people actually like to see grain, as they feel it adds atmosphere.

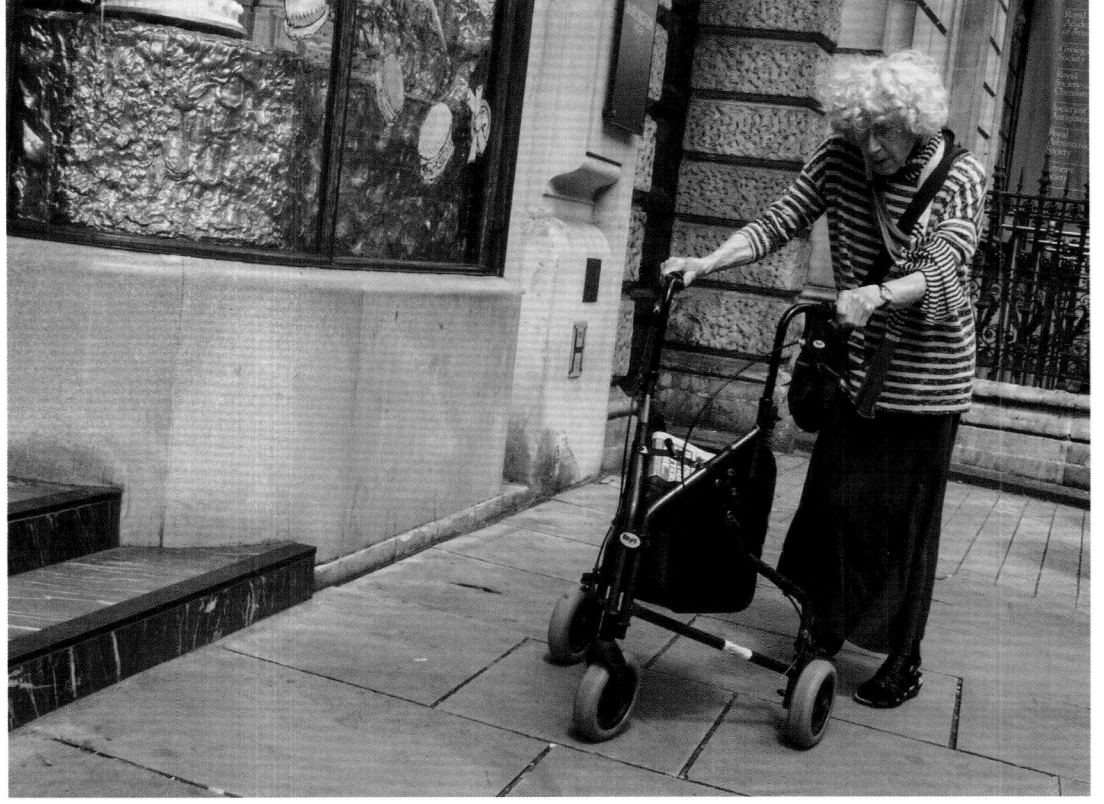

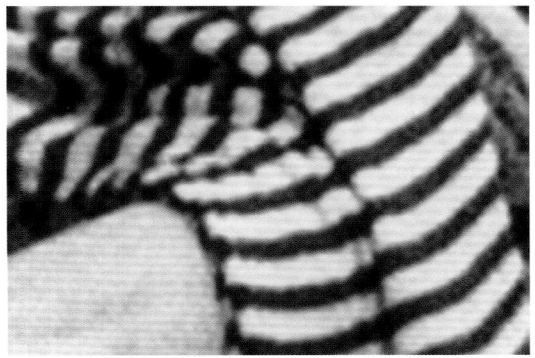

Left & Above: Compared to film, digital images are much cleaner, with regular pixels replacing grain at the heart of the image. However, unlike grain, the pixel structure of an image rarely adds atmosphere, so digital noise is usually seen as something that's best avoided.

Digital Cameras

If you are shooting digitally, your choice of camera will probably be based on three principal factors:

1 Portability (size and weight)
2 Speed of use
3 Budget

Street photography is all about spending time out and about, often for extended periods and in all weathers. It is also about speed, immediacy, comfort, and discretion. With this in mind, the ideal camera is one that is small, light, quiet, easy to use, and unobtrusive. DSLRs, digital rangefinder cameras, compacts, and smartphones can all meet those criteria to a greater or lesser degree, but which is best for you?

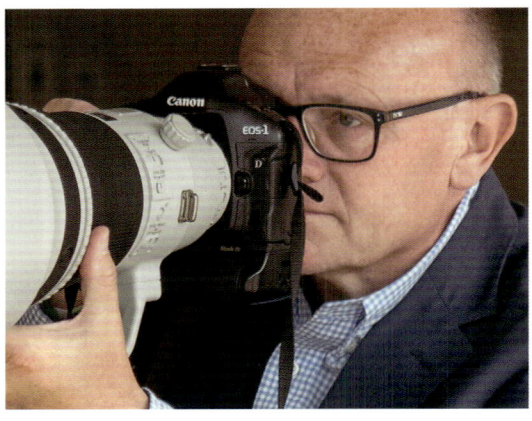

Above: Most DSLRs will produce great images, but with one of these over your shoulder, you'll always look like a photographer—or, even worse, a pro photographer! With a smaller camera, you'll look less serious and will be perceived as less of a threat.

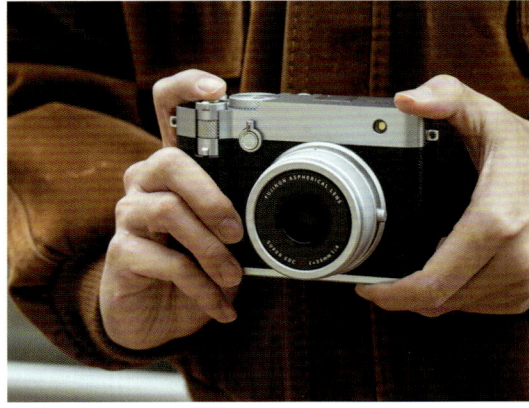

Above: Mirrorless compacts often have a fixed wide-angle lens, which is perfect for getting close and bringing a sense of intimacy and energy to your shots.

DSLR Cameras

Let's start with the upside. DSLRs come in all shapes and sizes, and are often thought of as being more durable and reliable than their smaller counterparts. They are also part of a much bigger system, which opens up a huge world of lenses and accessories.

The downside is that DSLRs tend to be bulkier, less discreet, noisier, and heavier than a lot of other cameras, and this reduces their appeal for use in street photography. However, if you already own a DSLR, don't let this put you off—this is one of a few genres where pretty much any camera can do a great job.

Right: You often need to work quickly in order to catch people in an unguarded moment. When choosing a camera, think about its handling characteristics and speed of operation: a bulky DSLR is generally far less maneuverable than a digital compact or mirrorless camera.

Focal length: 28mm
Aperture: f/8
Shutter speed: 1/800 sec.
ISO: 100

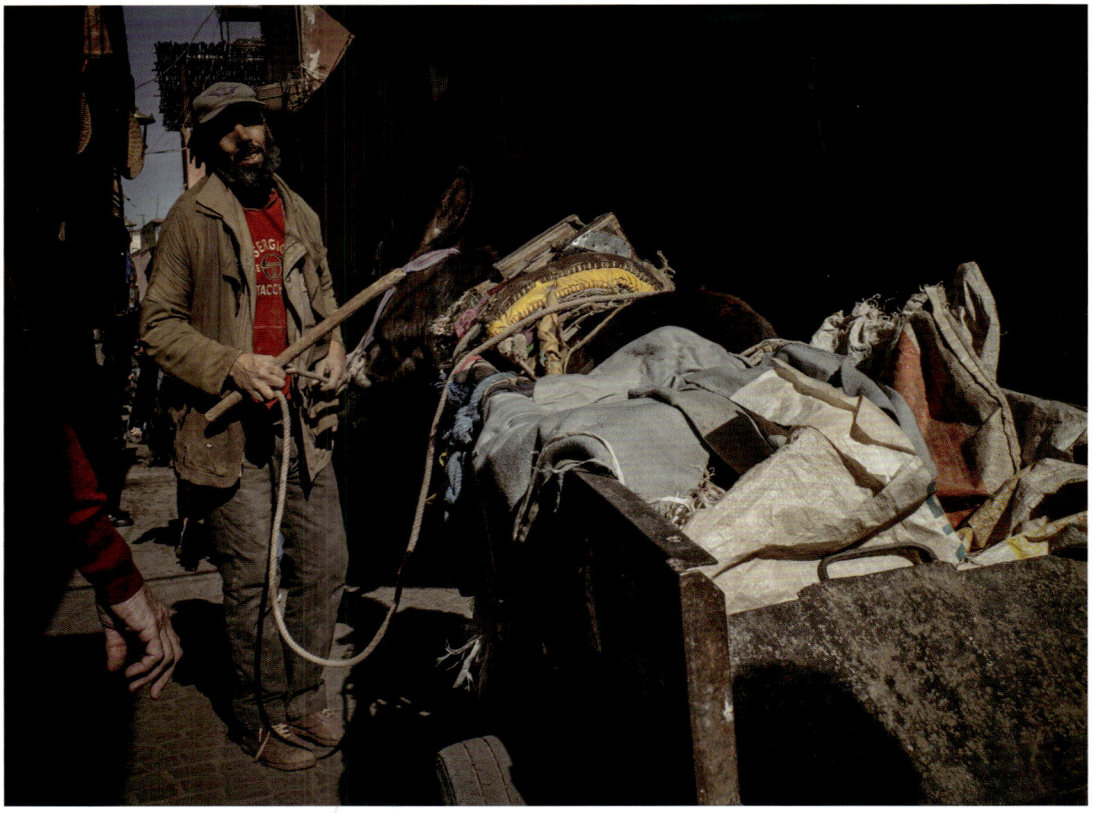

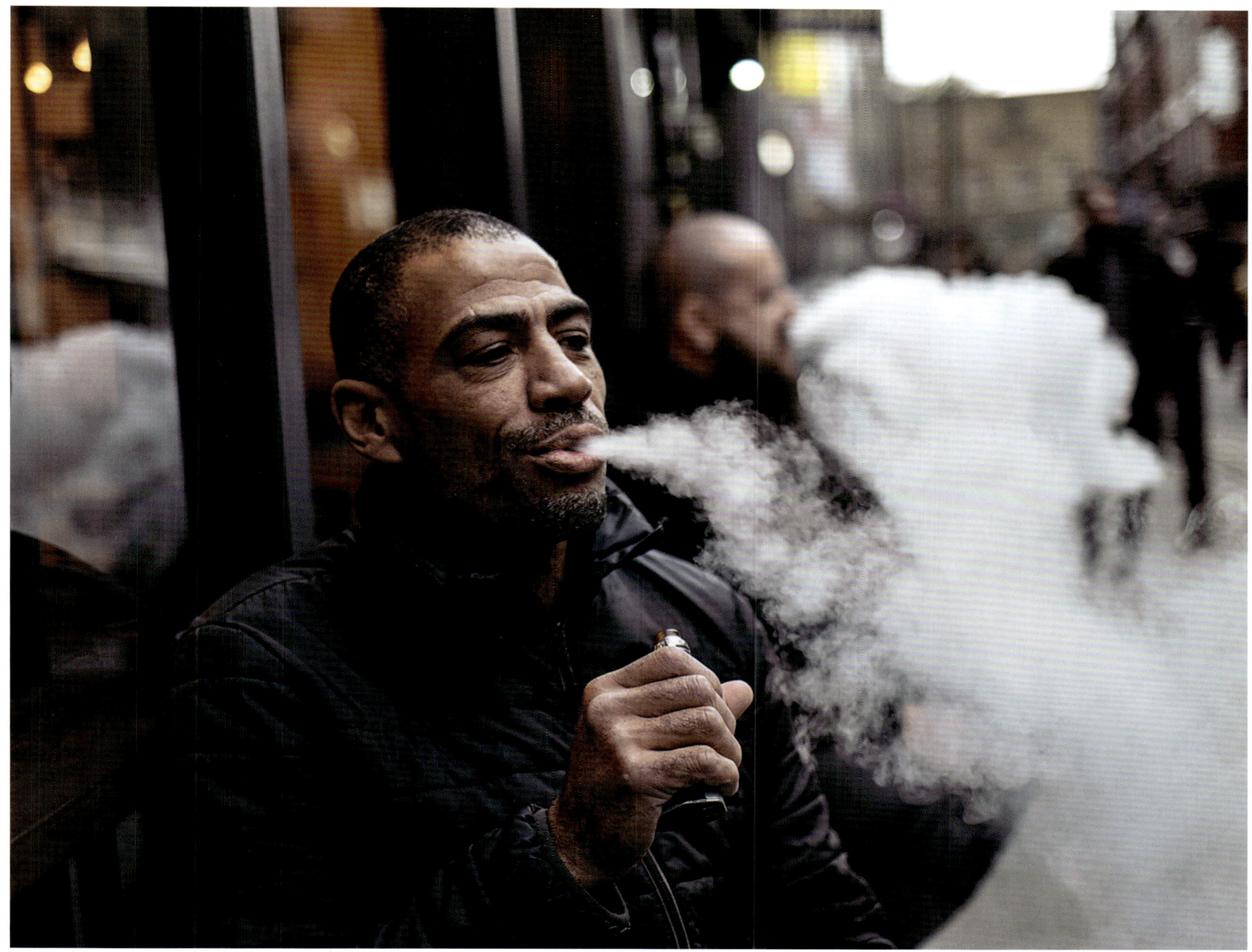

Mirrorless Cameras

Mirrorless cameras—and particularly digital rangefinders—have come of age in recent years and are the cameras mostly associated with contemporary street photography. They usually have large sensors and offer superb image processing capability, but are compact and light, so will fit into a jacket pocket or small bag.

The digital rangefinder style camera has become almost the default camera of choice for street photographers, with a light, compact body and often a touch of "old school" appeal. Some manufacturers, such as Leica, Fujifilm, and Ricoh, have deliberately targeted the street photography world with hugely capable mirrorless offerings.

Above: Digital rangefinder style cameras allow you to shoot from the hip more easily, especially if the camera has an articulated screen.

Focal length: 50mm

Aperture: f/1.4

Shutter speed: 1/280 sec.

ISO: 400

Small Compact Cameras

Digital compacts are usually pocketable, relatively cheap to buy, and will allow you to point and shoot in one of their (usually plentiful) automatic modes. Armed with a compact you will look more like a tourist than a proper photographer, which can mean you're perceived as less of a nuisance or threat when using one on the streets. The best compacts for street photography tend to be those with a fixed, rather than a zoom, lens; these tend to provide better image quality and are faster to use. A compact is the ideal camera to have with you at all times, but it is probably not going to be your go-to camera for street photography.

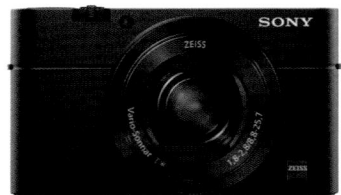

Above: You may find the lack of manual control frustrating with a digital compact, but cameras like this are so small and light you can have one with you at all times, so there's no excuse for missing that once in a lifetime shot!

Smartphones

The ubiquitous iPhone (and its Windows and Android equivalents) has brought street photography within everyone's reach. Combined with photo sharing-sites such as Instagram and Flickr, these devices have led to a revolution in street photography and are partly responsible for its dramatic rise in popularity.

Smartphones are small and light, always with you and always on, and are capable of capturing, editing, and sharing an image within seconds, without the need for a computer or expensive software. But perhaps their biggest attraction is their ability to be used covertly—the shutter on some phones can be released from a button on the earphone cable.

	DSLR	MIRRORLESS / CSC	COMPACT	SMARTPHONE
SPEED OF OPERATION	Medium to fast	Fast	Medium	Medium to fast
SIZE & WEIGHT	Often bulky & heavy	Small/light	Small/light	Very small/light
ABILITY TO USE COVERTLY	Poor	Good	Very good	Excellent
OVERALL CONVENIENCE	Medium	Excellent	Good	Excellent: it's always with you
MANUAL OPERATION	Yes	Yes	Sometimes	No
IMAGE QUALITY	Very high	Very high	Medium	Low to medium
ISO RANGE	Excellent	Excellent	Medium	Poor
LOW LIGHT CAPABILITY	Excellent	Excellent	Medium	Poor
ABILITY TO CHANGE LENSES	Yes	Yes	No	No
SYSTEM EXPANDABILITY	Excellent: access to large system of lenses & accessories	Good: increasing popularity has led to more options	None	None
BATTERY LIFE	Excellent	Good	Excellent	Poor
MEGAPIXEL COUNT	High to very high	High	Medium	Low
EASE OF SHARING	Fair: some models are Wi-Fi enabled	Good: cameras increasingly have Wi-Fi	Medium	Excellent: via the phone network or Wi-Fi
COST	High to very high	Moderate to high	Low to moderate	Low to moderate

Above: When choosing a camera for street photography, work out what features are most important to you. In this grid, the features are ranked in order of importance to street photographers.

Right: The quality of the images being produced by smartphones gets better all the time. Pictures can be edited on the fly, with some neat effects added using the device's built-in apps and filters. This picture was quickly converted to monochrome and the contrast was boosted before sharing it on social media.

Focal length: 68mm

Aperture: f/2.2

Shutter speed: 1/17 sec.

ISO: 40

The main disadvantage is image quality. While most pictures look fine on the small screen of an iPhone, they do not stand up to scrutiny when viewed on a much larger screen or printed at any size above Letter/A4; in this respect, their application can be limited.

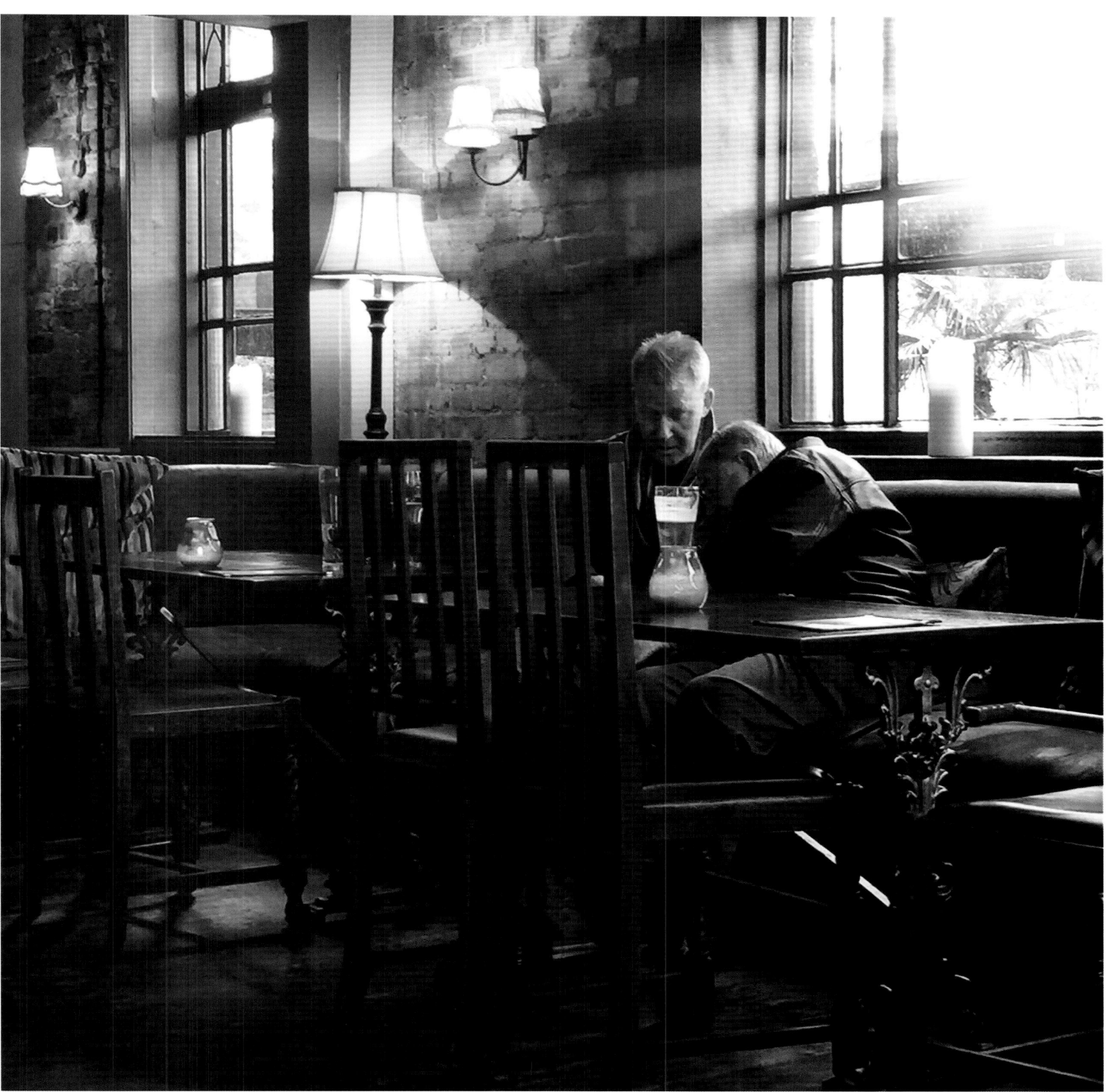

Shooting Film

Rather like the resurgence of vinyl records, film has undergone a revival in recent years. This is due to a combination of increased sales of "toy" cameras; an interest in all things vintage; the teaching of film techniques on university and college courses; and, of course, the increasing popularity of street photography, which has a longstanding association with film.

Although color film photography still has a following, it is not as popular as black and white—the majority of street photographers using film shoot in black and white, which is often thought of as being more arty and original. Black-and-white film is also relatively cheap to buy and is convenient to have processed (and is easy enough to process yourself).

Shooting film can also be a highly rewarding experience, and even the equipment offers a feel-good factor: nothing feels more wonderfully tactile than a solid, metallic, well-engineered film camera from the 1960s or '70s.

Film Cameras

If you have never used film, try it! You can buy an old 35mm SLR or rangefinder camera for the price of a couple of bottles of wine and it could open up a whole new creative seam for you:

- A rangefinder camera, whether it's a prized Leica or a tough old Russian model, is ideal for street photography. Armed with a lens of around 35mm and some ISO 400 film you will feel like one of the street photography heroes of yesteryear.

- A 35mm SLR—again equipped with a wide-angle lens, can be a rather heavy and noisy beast—thanks to a large dose of mirror clatter. However, these cameras are in plentiful supply, usually come complete with a lens or two, and

often have built-in TTL metering. For your first foray into film-based street photography, this is a good starting point.

- There are plenty of traditional medium-format cameras around, from Hasselblads to Mamiya TLRs, and in many ways they are great to work with. Loaded with 120 roll film, you will have only 10–12 exposures to play with, so every shot must count. Consequently, these cameras will slow you down and really make you think; you may think this is counterintuitive as far as street shooting goes, but it offers quite a visceral experience. Twin-lens reflex (TLR) medium-format camera models are useful for street photography because the viewfinder is usually held at waist level, which makes covert shooting easy; Vivian Maier took many thousands of iconic pictures in the 1950s and '60s with a Rolleiflex TLR.

- Although they are as much fashion items as they are cameras, "toy" cameras, such as the Lomo LC-A and Holga, are worth a mention. They produce retro, vintage-looking images, and are often used by street photographers. Although they are not the most sophisticated cameras, they have a large following around the world and have produced some outstanding work (even if some of it is perhaps technically lacking).

Tip

Look at online auction sites, camera stores selling pre-owned equipment, and even yard sales or flea markets for an old medium-format TLR camera and you can put yourself in the shoes of a street photographer in 1950s Chicago.

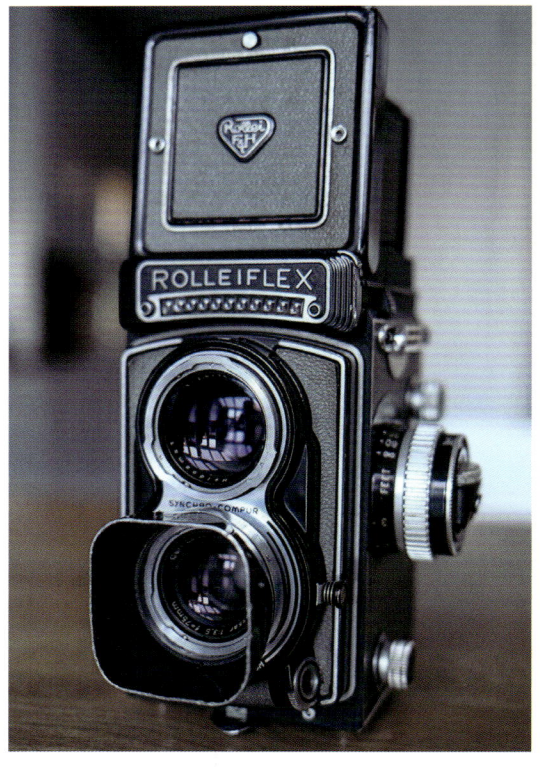

Above: Medium-format TLRs offer superb image quality and will introduce you to a whole new way of shooting; models such as this can also be bought very cheaply.

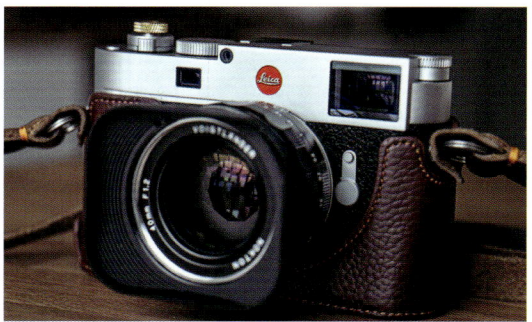

Above: You would be extremely lucky to find a pre-owned Leica rangefinder, but film cameras are in plentiful supply. If you're going to invest money in film gear, spend most of it on lenses, as virtually any reliable camera body will do a good job. However, a camera like this will hold its value well.

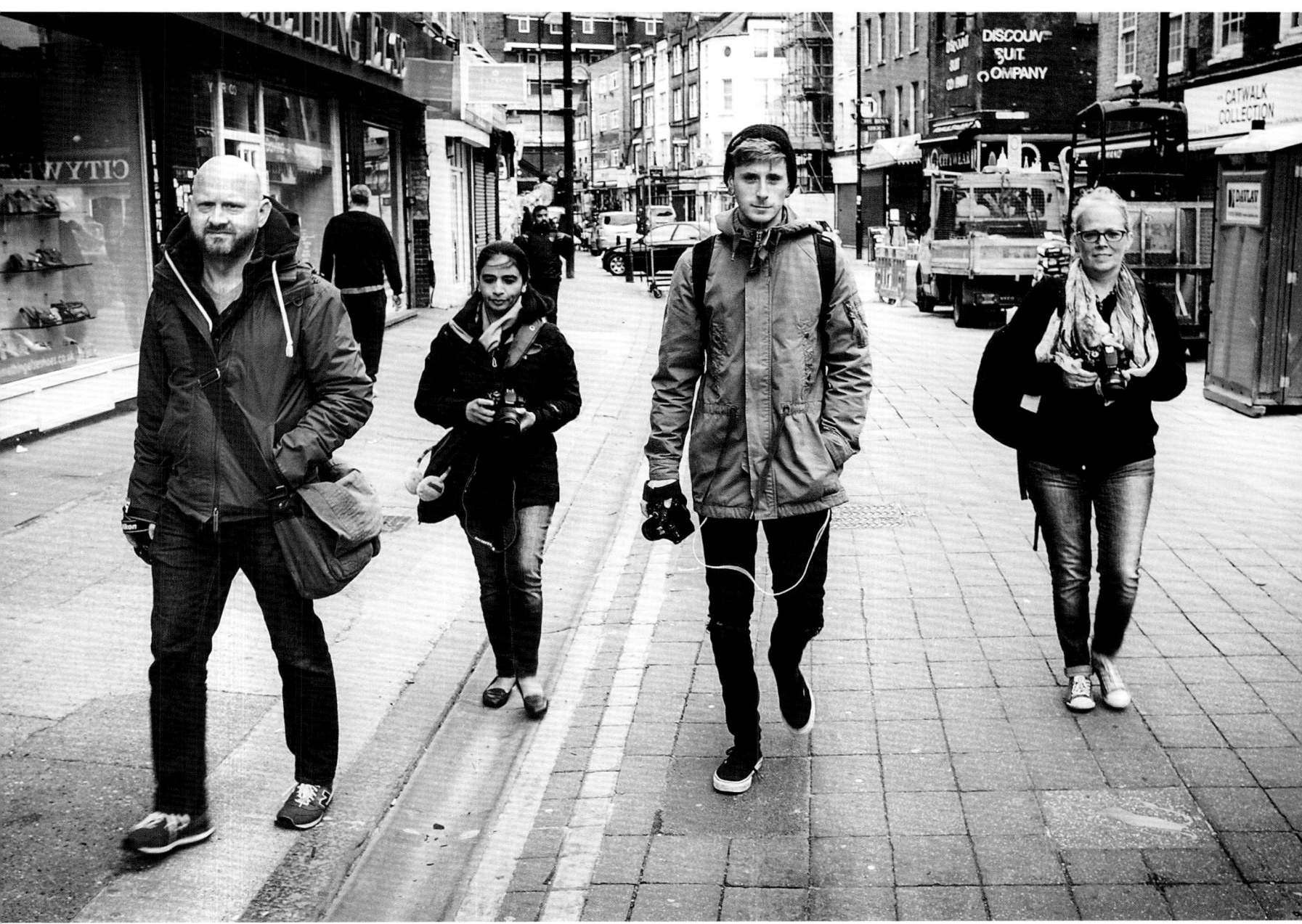

Above: This picture of a group of street photographers was shot on a 35mm Leica using Kodak Tri-X film, and printed on high-contrast paper.

Focal length: 28mm

Aperture: f/8

Shutter speed: 1/125 sec.

ISO: 400

Lenses

Still working on the basis that less is more, you are unlikely to need more than one or two (or, at the very most, three) lenses for street photography. In the following chapters you will read about the need to get close to your subjects, to shoot with plenty of depth of field, and to incorporate meaningful context—the type of lens that will best help you achieve this is a prime wide-angle lens.

Why Use A Prime Lens?

A prime lens has a fixed focal length, such as 28mm, 50mm, or 200mm, which is preferable to a zoom for a number of reasons. For a start, the process of using a zoom to frame (and often to constantly re-frame) your shot can waste valuable seconds. In the process, you can easily lose the spontaneity of a shot or—worse—miss the opportunity altogether.

Secondly, the image quality from a prime lens usually exceeds that of a zoom by some margin. In a world in which we often have to make other compromises over image quality, getting maximum sharpness and detail out of the lens gives us a head start.

Thirdly, as they have fewer glass elements, fewer moving parts, and less electronic circuitry, prime lenses tend to be smaller, lighter, quieter, and more reliable than zooms. They also tend to have a wider maximum aperture (although for a lot of your street photography you will likely be shooting in the region of f/8–f/11, so ultra-fast lenses aren't essential).

Finally (and perhaps most importantly), you will become a better street photographer if you spend time becoming intimately acquainted with just one focal length. Once you completely understand its capabilities and characteristics, you will find you can shoot more quickly, more spontaneously, and more accurately, without thinking too much about framing or composition;

you will start to "see" like this lens and will understand how it describes the world before you even look through the viewfinder.

So why is this latter point important? As we will discuss later, street photography is all about speed, so you want to be ready to capture that elusive decisive moment without having to worry too much about where your lens is pointing. By practicing with your favorite lens, you will instinctively know not only what edge-to-edge coverage you are achieving, but also the vertical angle at which the lens needs to be held in order to get the desired composition—all without looking through the viewfinder.

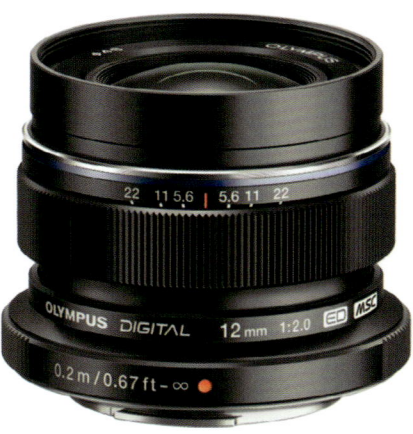

What About Zooms?

Although it is not a strong one, there is a case for zoom lenses in street photography. If you are on a tight budget, you can combine several focal lengths into one small package, and this will save you money, as well as space. However, zoom lenses are usually bulkier and heavier than primes, and are less covert.

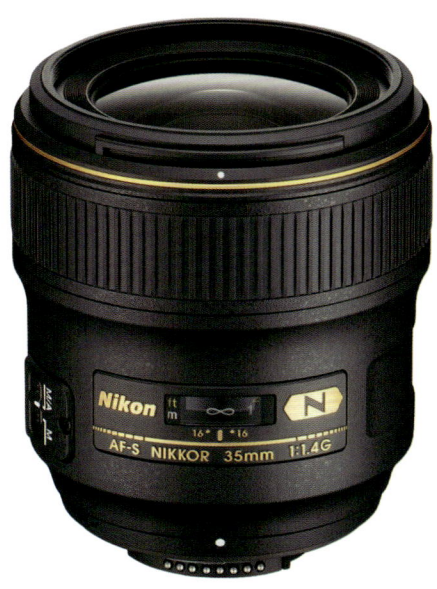

Left & Above: In general, a prime, wide-angle lens with a focal length of around 24–35mm (on a full-frame camera) is preferable to a zoom lens, as it allows you to work quicker and more intuitively.

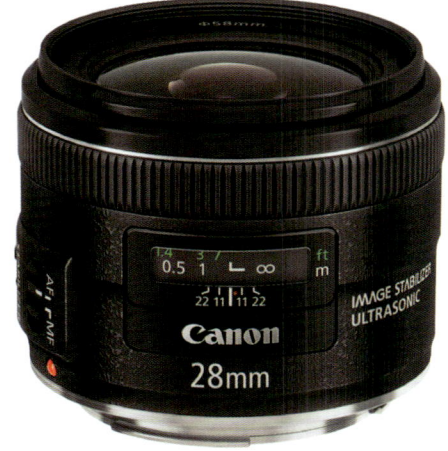

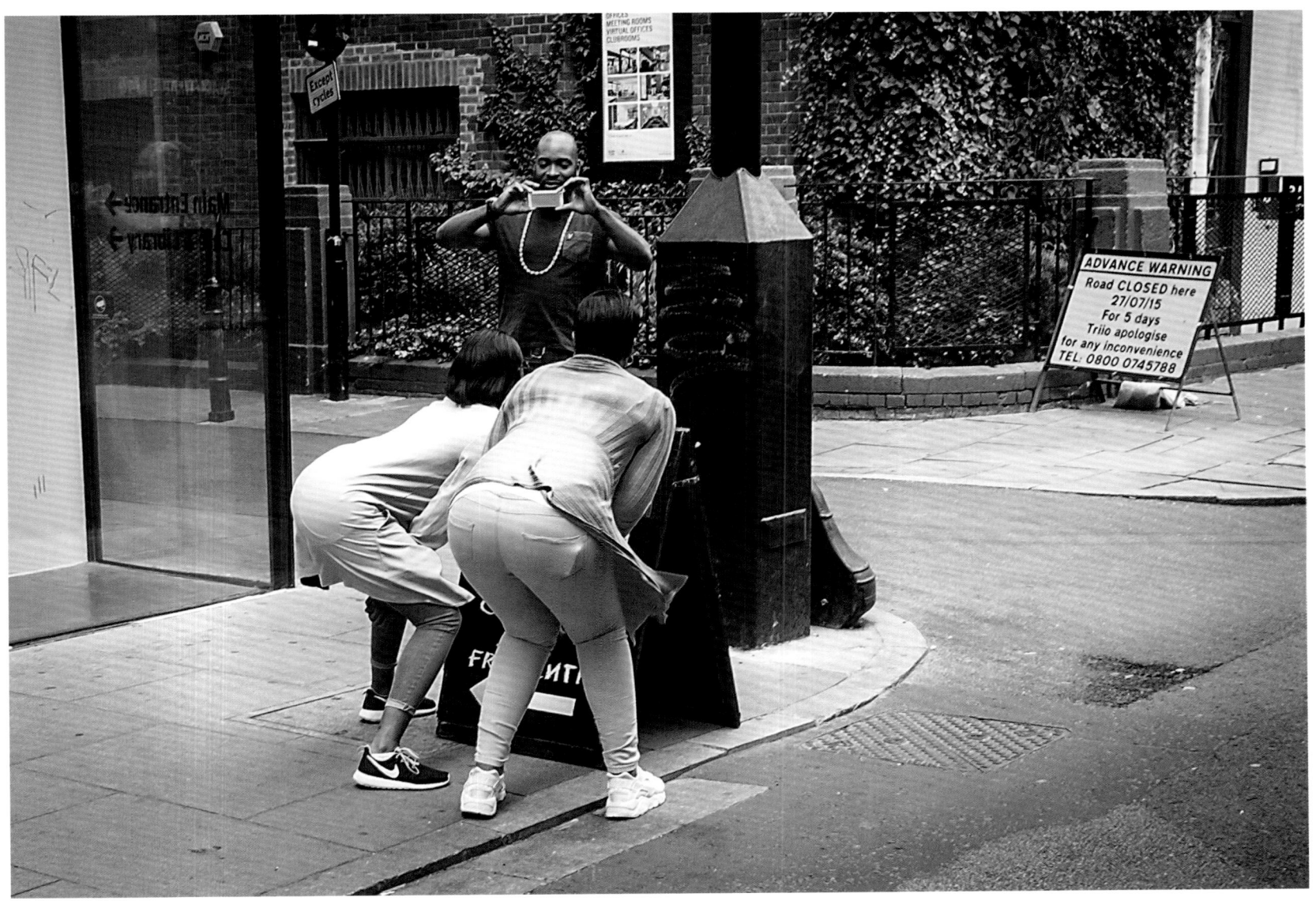

Above: Zoom lenses allow you to tweak your composition on the move, but this can mean you miss the moment; prime lenses are quicker and simpler.

Focal length: 28mm

Aperture: f/11

Shutter speed: 1/20 sec.

ISO: 200

Focal Length

In street photography context is often important. It is of little use to shoot a lovely crisp headshot from a distance, using a 300mm lens, when any interesting or relevant background (or foreground) is excluded from the composition. In street photography we really do need to know what's going on: Who is the subject waving to? What is he laughing at? Why is she shaking her fist? The only way we'll know this is if we have context.

If you look at some of the work of the great street photographers—Robert Frank, Vivian Maier, and William Klein are all good examples—you will see how they manage to get close to their subjects while incorporating enough of the background to provide context.

They have only been able to do this by using a wide-angle lens. A wide-angle lens with a focal length of between 24mm and 35mm (in full-frame terms) will take you to the heart of the story, getting you close to the action and producing a sense of involvement that will come across in the final image. If you don't have access to prime lenses, a zoom lens that covers these focal lengths should serve you well.

Crop Factor

You should always consider your camera's crop factor when choosing a lens. If you are using a camera with an APS-C sensor, your frame will be smaller than that of 35mm film and the images will be magnified or enlarged—typically by a factor of 1.4–1.6x if the camera has an APS-C-sized sensor, or 2x with Micro Four Thirds cameras. This means that a 28mm focal length will behave more like a 35mm lens on a camera with a 1.5x crop sensor (typically an APS-C format sensor), or 56mm on a Micro Four Thirds model.

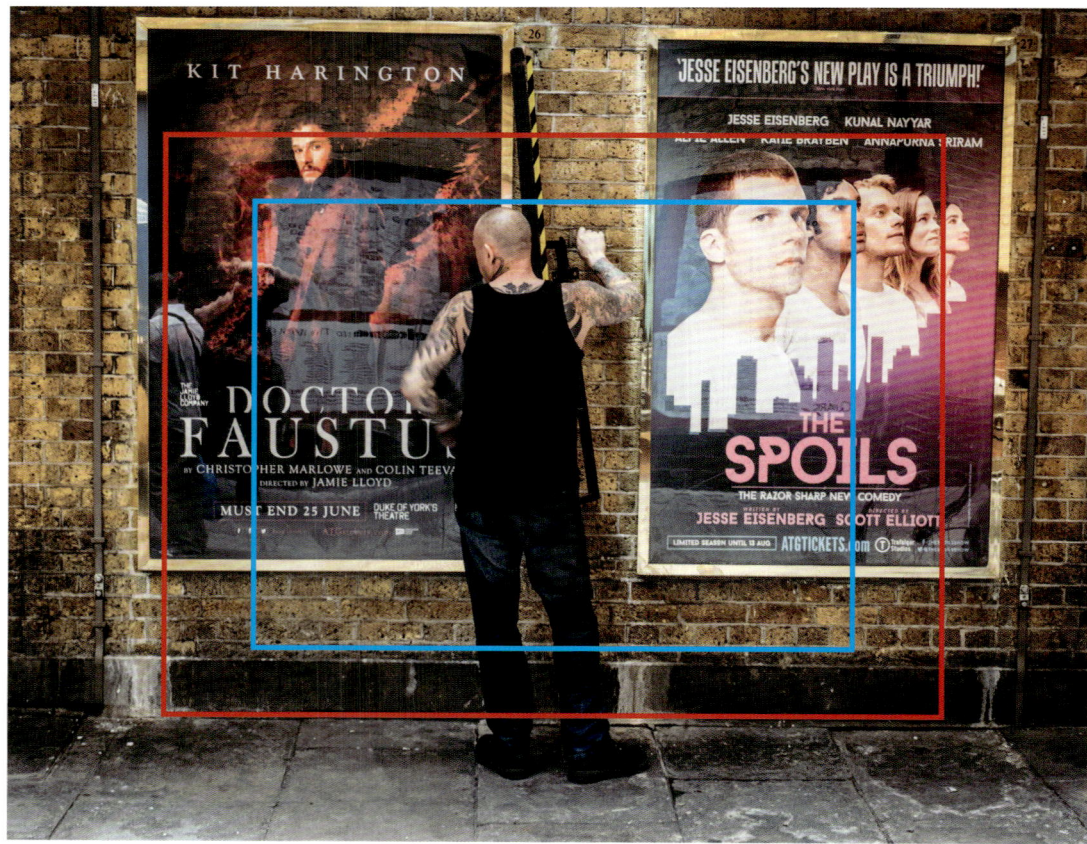

Above: The crop factor that applies to a camera's sensor will effectively narrow the angle of view of the lens you are using. This image was taken using a 50mm focal length on a full-frame camera. However, on a camera with an APS-C-size sensor, the same focal length would have recorded the smaller area indicated by the red frame; on a Micro Four Thirds camera, the lens would have seen the area within the blue frame.

Focal length: 50mm

Aperture: f/13

Shutter speed: 1/20 sec.

ISO: 1000

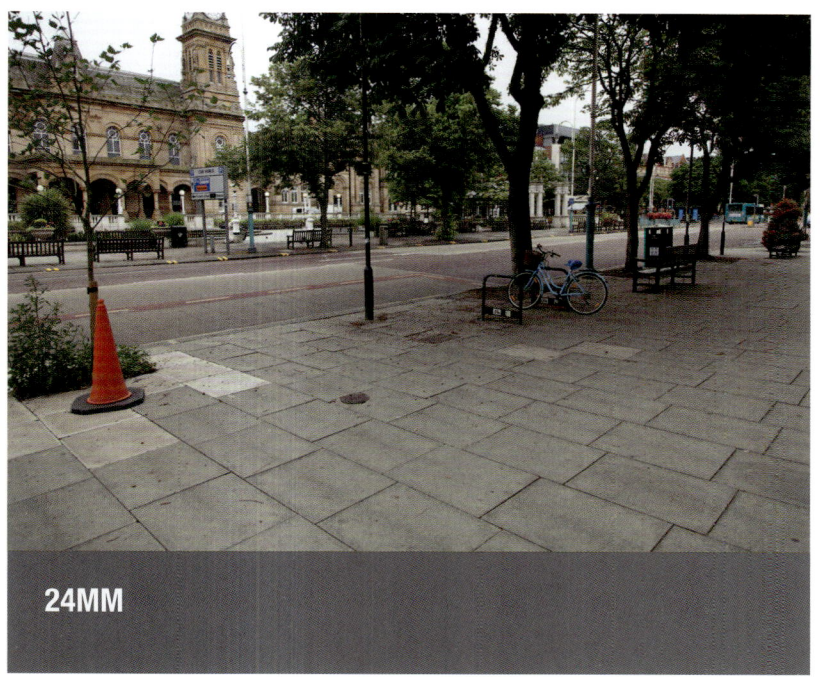

24MM

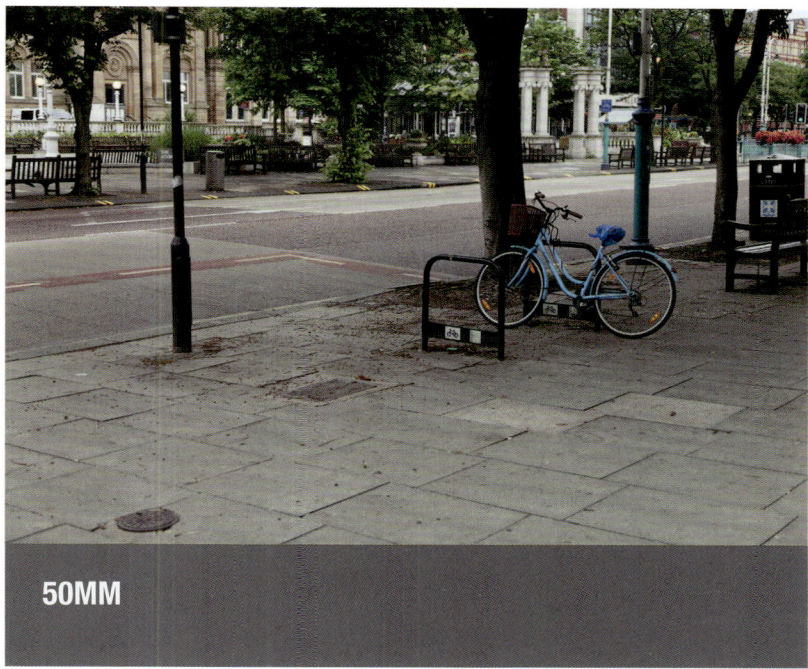

50MM

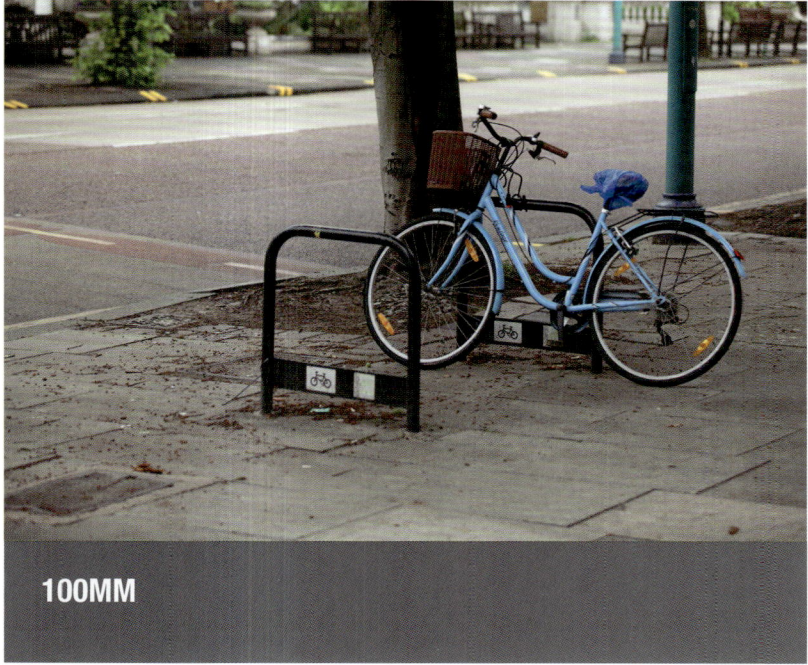

100MM

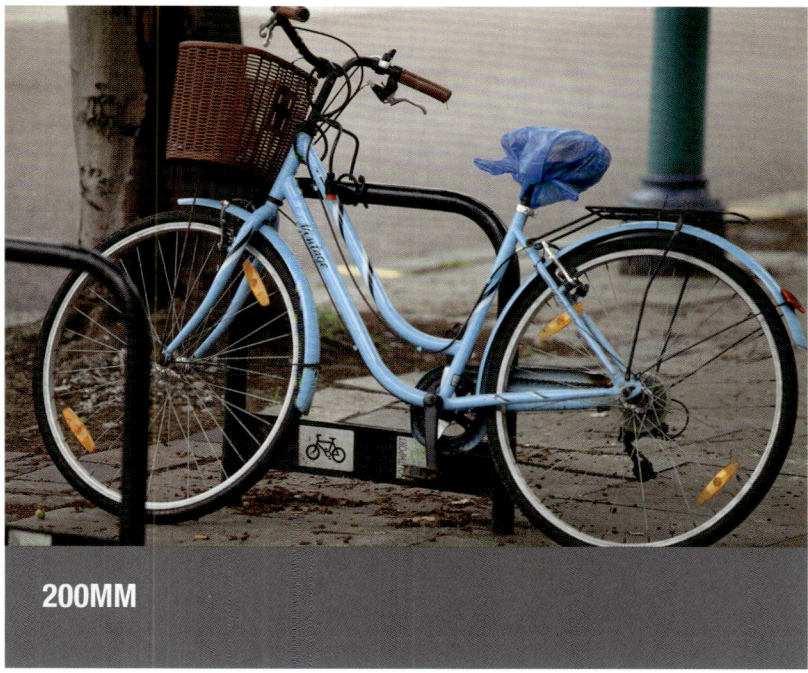

200MM

Above: These images show a range of focal lengths from 24mm to 200mm. Most street photographers shoot somewhere between 28mm and 50mm, which allows for a significant amount of background—context—to be included in the shot.

Accessories

In The Bag

It's a good idea to take as little kit out with you as possible, which means leaving bulky items such as a tripod, flash, and extra lenses at home. A typical camera bag might therefore consist of the following:

1. Shoulder bag
2. Lightweight tripod
3. Camera with one (ideally wide-angle) lens
4. Additional lens
5. Spare batteries
6. ID cards and business cards
7. Lens cloth
8. Memory cards
9. Notebook and pen
10. Sunscreen
11. Earphones
12. Rubber bands for batteries

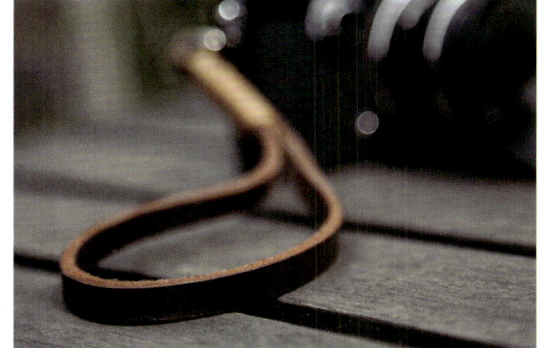

Camera Strap

Many street photographers use a wrist strap with their camera, as it allows the camera to be kept out of sight, somewhere near their hip. Look for a sturdy, secure strap—ones made of parachute cord (paracord) are very durable and will lock onto the wrist should the camera slip.

However, other photographers prefer a neck strap, which allows the camera to be kept at midriff level, giving a shorter distance to travel between camera and eye. If you decide to use a neck strap, it's a good idea to avoid the strap that comes with your camera—it will probably have garish branding that instantly identifies you as a photographer with something potentially valuable around your neck.

Whichever version of strap you prefer, spend time getting used to it so that the camera feels like an extension of your hand.

Above: A wrist strap enables you to keep your camera out of sight and constantly to hand, ready for action.

Flash

Flash is unnecessary for most street photography, unless you are going for a direct, in your face approach in the style of, say, Bruce Gilden. Although flash can add vibrancy, a sense of urgency, and a grittiness to an image, it often takes away the honesty and the real life quality of a scene, as well as adding an unwelcome distraction.

Tripod

Your three-legged friend is great for landscapes and architectural work, but is a hindrance for most street photography. With the excellent low-light performance of modern digital cameras, it's possible to shoot night scenes with acceptable shutter speeds—often 1/30 second and faster.

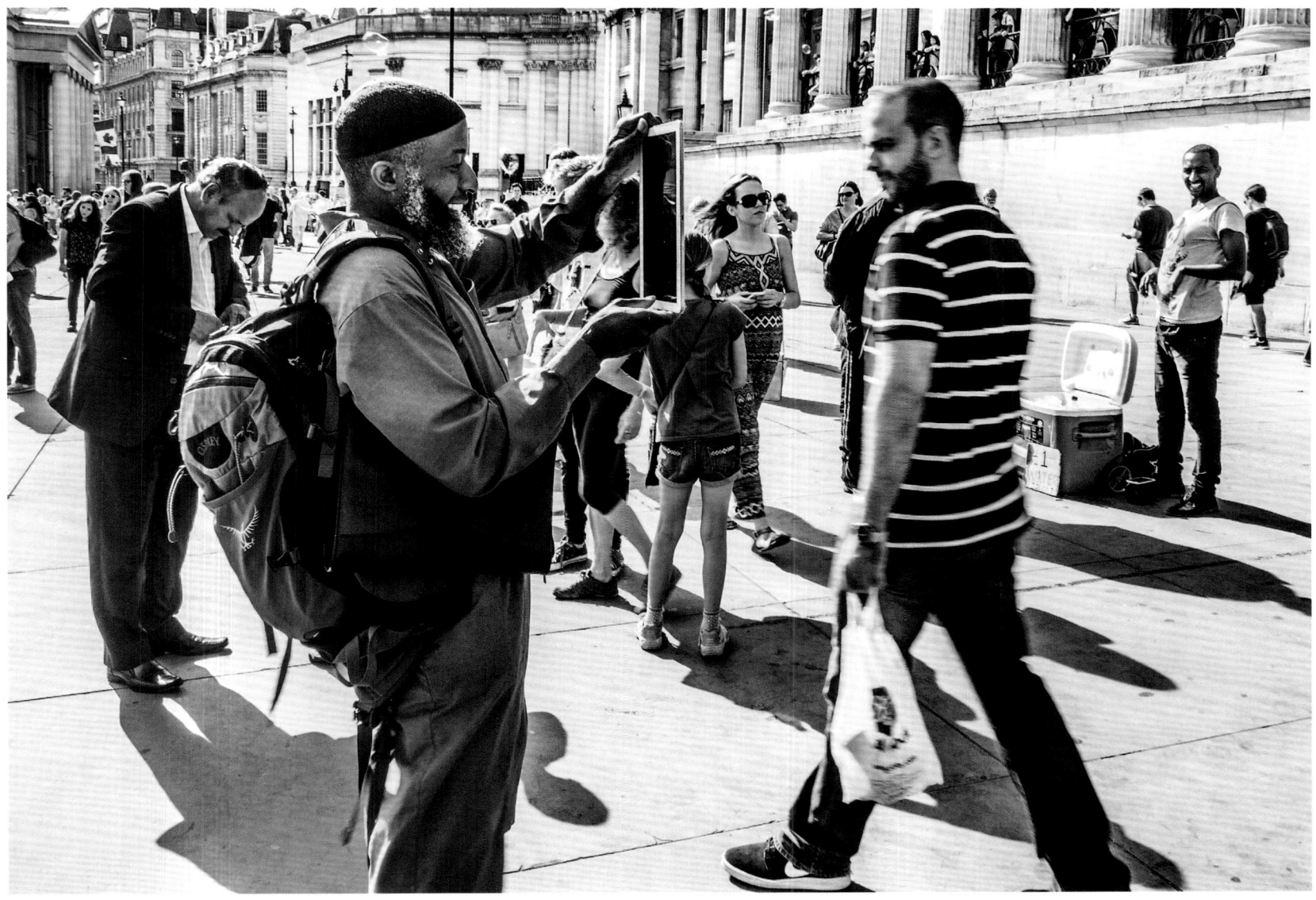

Bags

Your bag should be small, comfortable, and—ideally—not look like a camera bag. As you will be carrying a fairly minimal amount of kit around with you, you really don't need anything more than a shoulder bag or sling, or, alternatively, a very small backpack. Another good reason for using a small bag is that photographers tend to fill the bag they are using (regardless of its size) with more gear than they need, just in case. Having a smaller bag means you won't fall into this trap quite so easily, but if in doubt, leave it out!

Bear in mind that you could be on the move for the best part of a day, so comfort should be your prime consideration. As you will often need to react quickly to a situation, the ease and speed of access is another important factor—in this regard, a shoulder bag is often preferable.

Above: For street photography, a shoulder bag is preferable to a backpack because of its accessibility; and the less your bag looks like a photographer's bag, the better!

Other Essentials

Memory Cards

Make sure you never run out of memory card capacity, especially if you are shooting Raw and JPEG files simultaneously, as memory cards can quickly fill up. It is worth buying the fastest cards you can afford so the write speed is not compromised when you are shooting continuously. However, remember that any card can fail, losing data in the process, so rather than putting all your day's shoot on a single, high-capacity memory card, consider using a number of smaller-capacity cards instead.

If you are shooting film, take as much film stock as you are comfortable carrying; you'll be surprised how much you can use in a day on the streets.

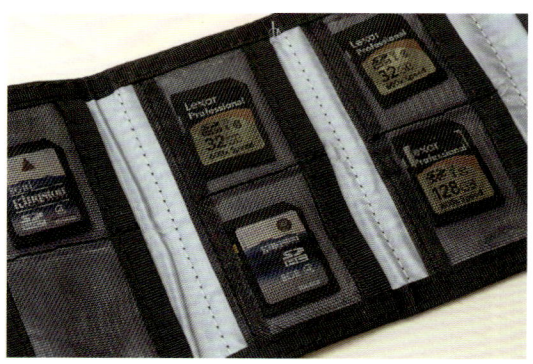

Above: Keep your camera's memory cards in a dry, dustproof place—a case like this is ideal.

Batteries

Don't underestimate how much battery power you will need on a day's shoot. In cold weather, keep your batteries as warm as is possible, preferably in an insulated pouch or in an inside pocket.

OTHER THINGS TO HAVE IN YOUR BAG

Even small bags tend to have numerous pockets, and although it's best to keep the weight of your equipment down as much as possible, there are some essential items to carry with you:

- **Notebook** and **pen**. To make notes about subjects, locations, and techniques
- **Model release forms**. It's always worth having a couple of these in your bag for when you get a shot that may be marketable (see chapter five for more on the legal aspects of street photography).
- **Lens cloth**. For wiping clean your camera and lens(es).
- **Chamois leather**. To dry the outside of your camera if the weather is really bad.
- **Rubber bands**. These can be used to help you identify drained batteries.
- **Water bottle**. It's surprising how quickly you will become dehydrated when pounding the streets, so always carry water.
- **ID cards** and/or **business cards**.
- **Sunscreen** and/or **lip salve**.

Tip

There's nothing more frustrating than missing a shot because you've just put a drained battery back in your camera. A simple way to avoid this is to wrap an elastic band around any spent batteries, which will act as a simple visual indicator that the battery is empty.

CLOTHING

The key thing with your clothing is to blend in, prepare for the worst, and not to dress like a photographer! Here are a few tips to help you:

- Wear dark colors: you won't be as noticeable.
- Wear a system of layers that can be adjusted quickly according to the conditions.
- A hat will keep your head warm and dry, and will help make you less approachable (see pages 116–119).
- Comfortable shoes are essential. You don't want to abandon your shoot because of sore or tired feet, so don't underestimate how far you will walk in a day on the streets!
- Keep a foldable waterproof jacket in your bag (or possibly a disposable plastic poncho) in case the weather changes.

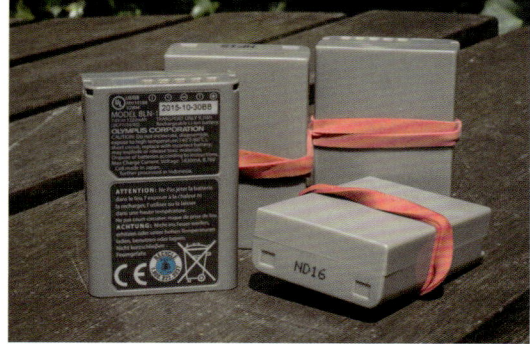

Above: Wrapping an elastic band around a drained battery will save you inadvertently putting it back into the camera.

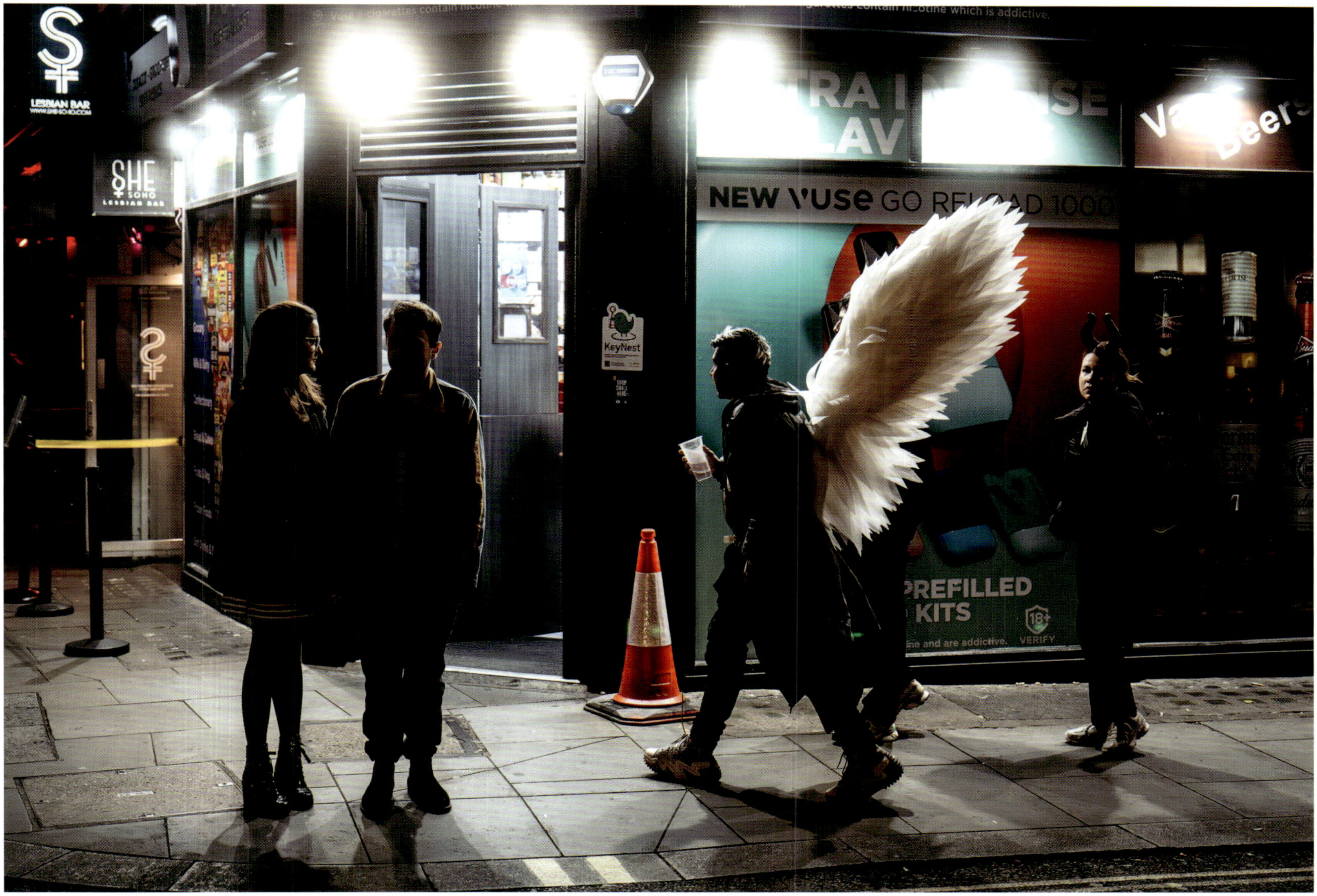

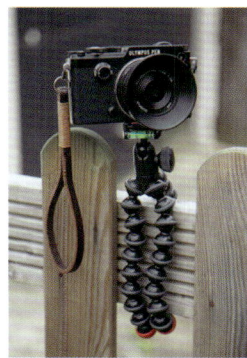

Left: It may be worth keeping a small tripod in your bag if you are planning to shoot at night. Designs like this can be wrapped around railings or other street furniture and will hold a small camera steady when you need to use a slow shutter speed.

Above: Shooting after dark is perfectly feasible without a tripod; a combination of a high ISO and a fast lens should see you through.

Focal length: 43mm

Aperture: f/2

Shutter speed: 1/250 sec.

ISO: 2000

Chapter 2
Technical Skills

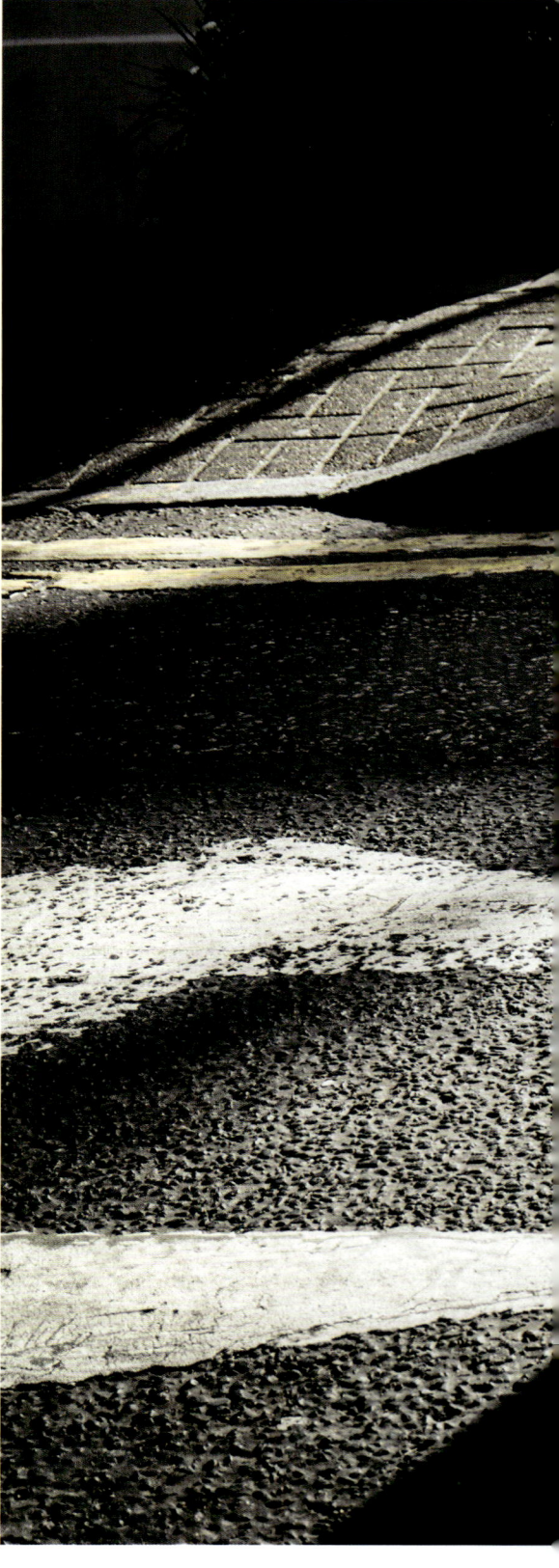

From a technical point of view, street photography is not a difficult subject to master and, in many respects, the art is more important than the science. Introducing too many technical hurdles can inhibit a street photographer's creative vision, their movement, and their speed of operation, so a simple, pared-down approach works best: as with many technical subjects, the "KISS" principle applies (Keep It Simple, Stupid!).

However, a firm grasp of some fundamental principles is important. By setting up your camera in a certain way, you will be ready to go, and free to concentrate on getting the picture, rather than worrying about your exposure or focus.

Right: Street photography is less about the technicalities of photography and more about observing and recording life around you. In this way, composition and "seeing" images is of greatest importance.

Focal length: 35mm
Aperture: f/4
Shutter speed: 1/450 sec.
ISO: 100

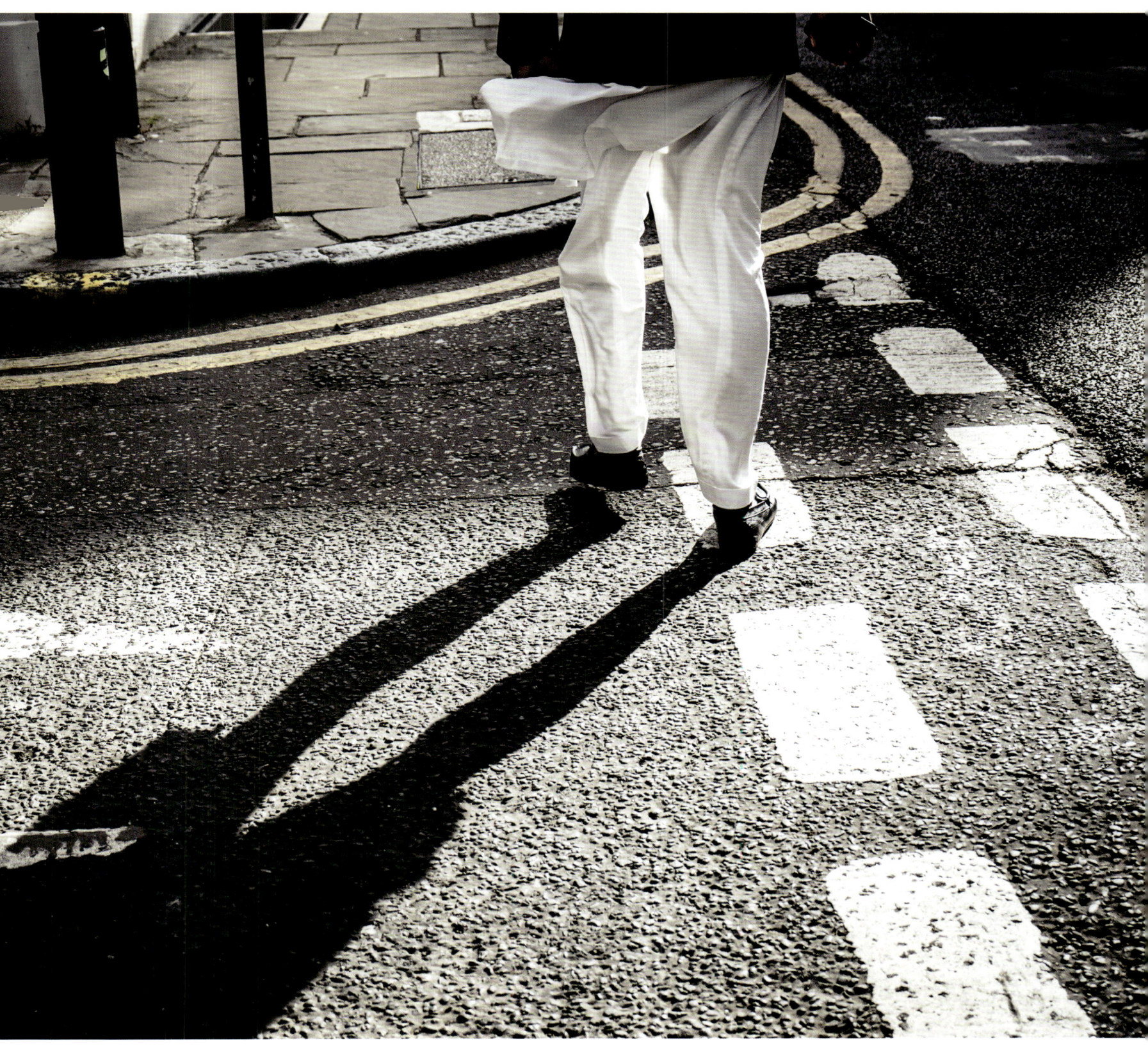

Exposure

Street photography is often fast paced and spontaneous, with little time to agonize over exposure modes or light readings. The key is to get the shot and if—in the heat of the moment—you don't have time to achieve an absolutely perfect exposure, all is not necessarily lost, especially if you're shooting Raw. That said, it is still better to get the exposure right in-camera, and only resort to postproduction techniques to rescue the situation if necessary.

Working on the premise that you want to achieve a correctly exposed and sharp image, you should consider how the three key elements of exposure work together: aperture, shutter speed, and ISO. The ideal settings for most street photography are a combination of a high ISO, fast shutter speed, and small aperture. Let's look at why this may be the case.

Aperture & Depth Of Field

In most forms of street photography you will want to have a deep depth of field to ensure that most of what you see through the viewfinder is in focus—so the subject is in focus, as well as the areas in front of it and behind it. The simple thing to remember here is that the larger the f/number, the smaller the aperture, and the greater the depth of field. In most situations, an aperture of around f/8 (or, if the light is bright, f/11) should be your go-to setting.

WHEN YOU MAY NEED A WIDE DEPTH OF FIELD:
When all the elements in the frame are central to the composition or content of the image and you want everything to be in focus.

WHEN YOU MAY NEED A SHALLOW DEPTH OF FIELD:
When you want to isolate the main subject from its background, removing any unwanted or distracting elements.

ISO

It is generally agreed that a sharp image (without any hint of camera shake, and with the main element of the shot in focus) is paramount. The best way to achieve this is to use as fast a shutter speed as possible, and this is achieved by selecting a high ISO setting.

Whereas conventional photographic teaching suggests that ISO is the last setting you should adjust, in street photography it is the *first*—and it needs to be high. In street photography, high ISO is your friend and should be the anchor for all the exposure settings that follow. This may sound counterintuitive, as high ISO settings increase noise, but imaging technology has moved at such a fast pace that most modern cameras avoid any discernible noise at higher levels. Some photographers even say that a little noise adds to the ambience!

To maximize the potential of your ISO settings, try the following:
- Set your ISO to Auto
- In your menu, set the auto ISO range from 200 to 3,200
- Set the minimum shutter speed to 1/250 sec.

Provided you have a reasonable amount of light to work with, this will help guarantee a fast shutter speed; when the camera needs more light, it will take it from the ISO rather than compromising the shutter speed with an unacceptably low value.

Shutter Speed

Street photography is a dynamic discipline in which either the photographer or the subject is often moving, so it is important to freeze movement and/or avoid camera shake. If you are using Aperture Priority mode and have set a combination of a high ISO and a moderately small aperture, the camera will (in most situations) set a fast shutter speed for you.

What do we mean by a fast shutter speed? The faster the better! In reasonably bright daylight conditions, a shutter speed of at least 1/250 sec. is usually achievable—anything higher is a bonus!

However, sometimes you will want to set a slow shutter speed to create a sense of movement, usually by deliberately enhancing blur. You can achieve this by setting Shutter Priority mode and dialing in the shutter speed yourself. I'd suggest using a start point of around 1/5 sec., but the precise shutter speed required will depend on the speed and direction of movement of the subject.

Right: When you're photographing a moving subject, combining Aperture Priority mode with a high ISO will encourage the camera to set a fast shutter speed. This will ensure you freeze any movement and avoid blur.

Focal length: 35mm
Aperture: f/7.1
Shutter speed: 1/60 sec.
ISO: 1000

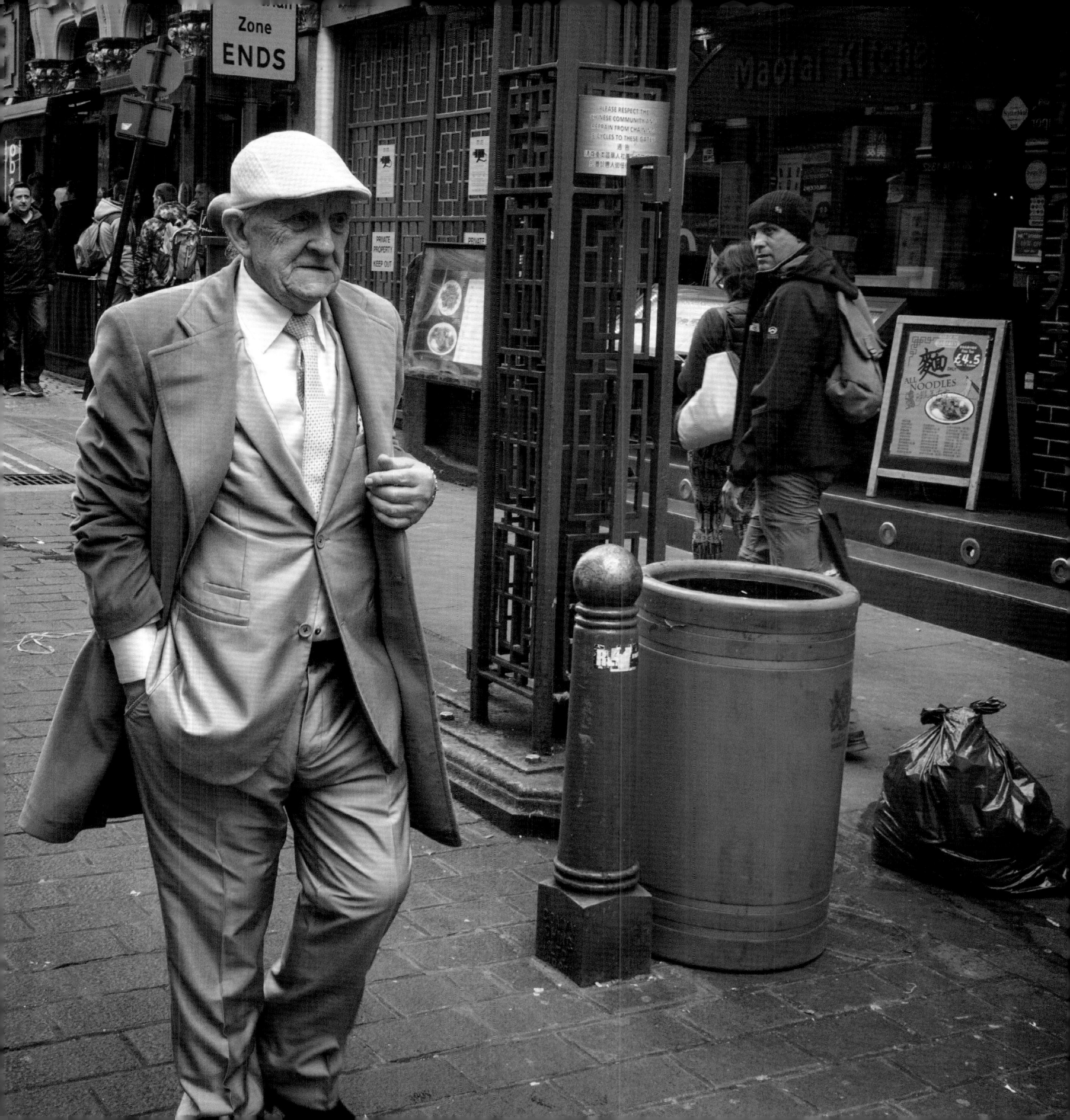

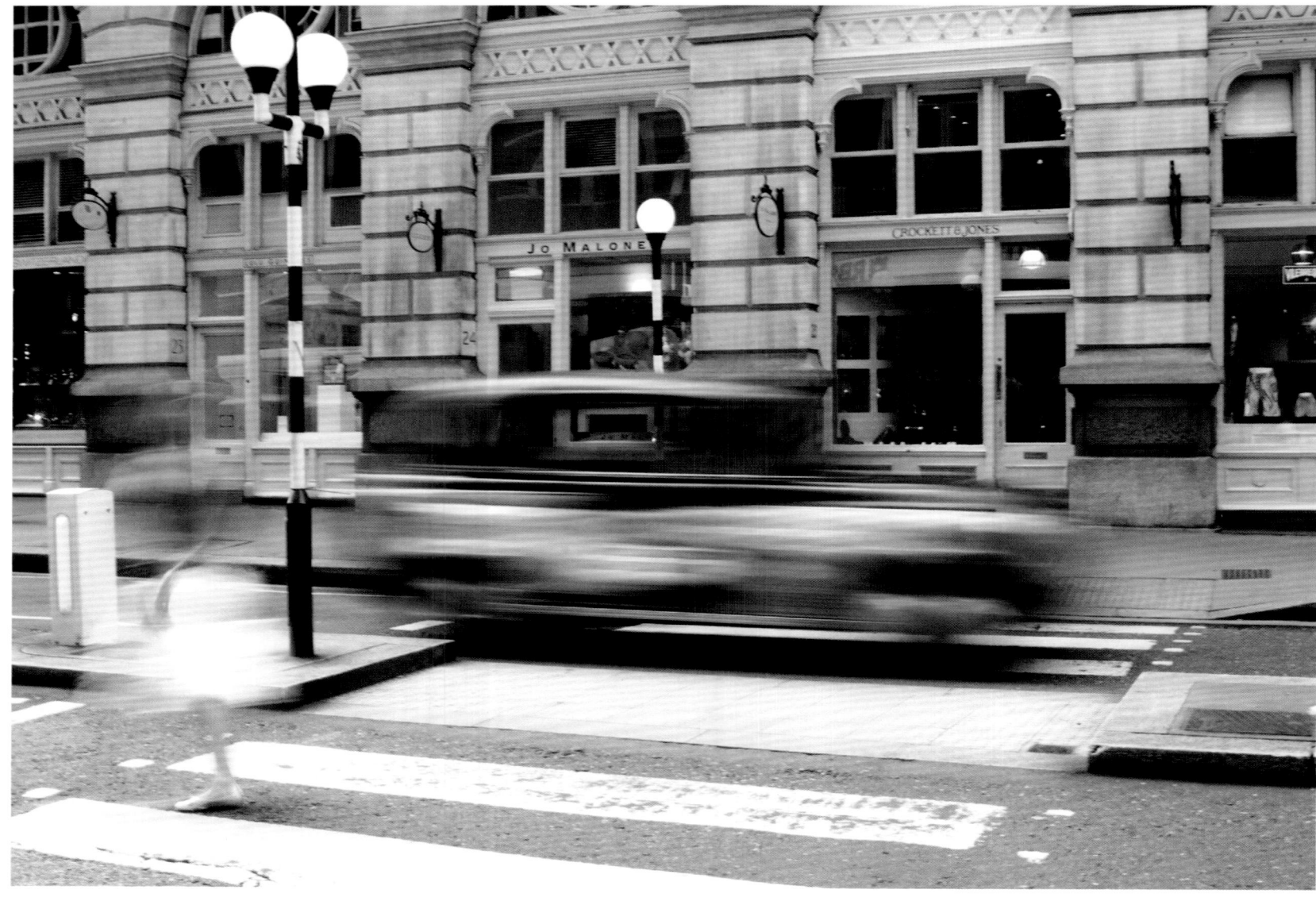

Above: A shutter speed of around 1/5 sec. can produce some great creative effects, such as this ghostly figure on a pedestrian crossing.

Focal length: 35mm

Aperture: f/22

Shutter speed: 1/5 sec.

ISO: 100

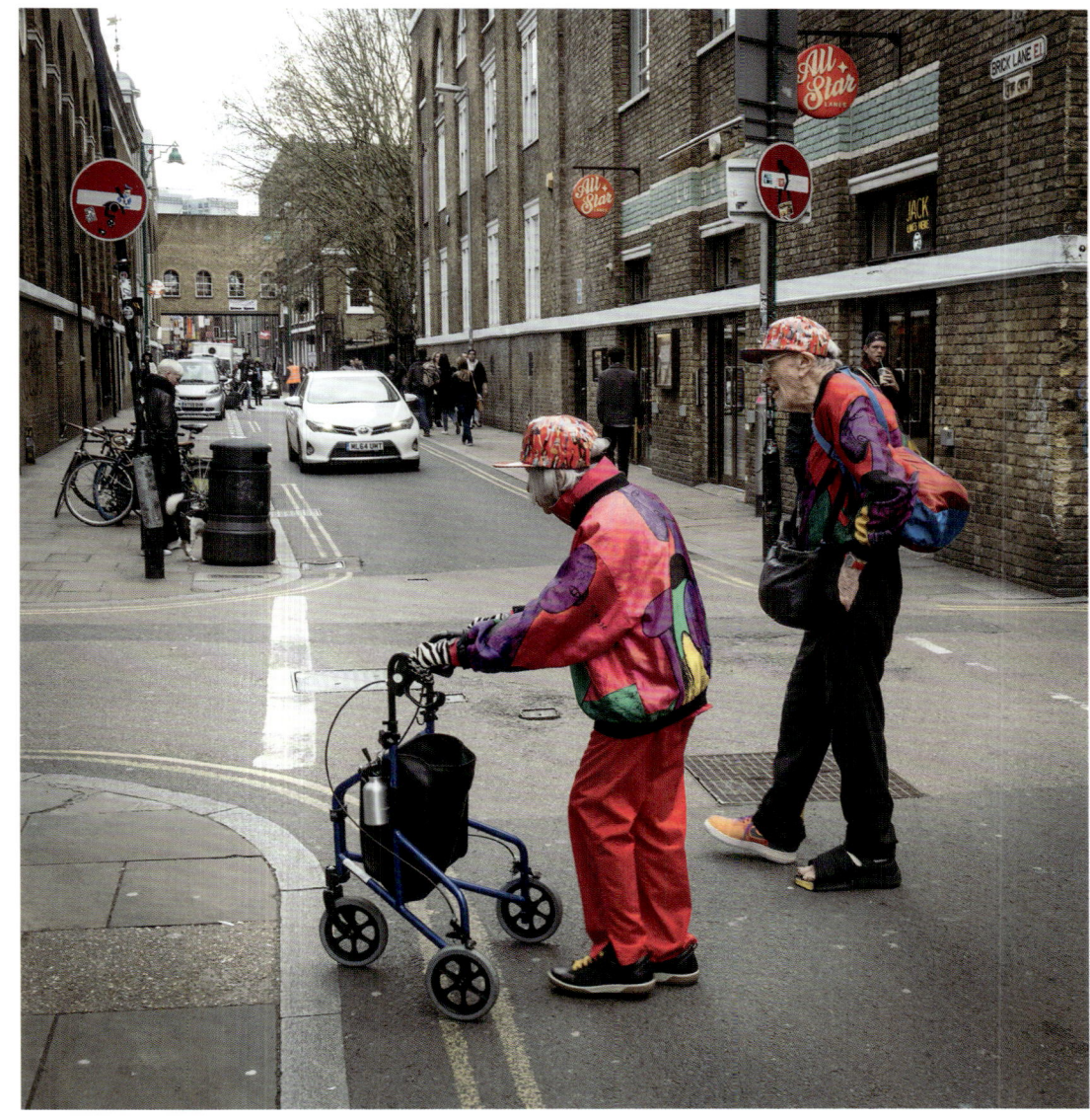

Above: Even if there is relatively little movement, it is usually a good idea to aim for as fast a shutter speed as possible. Although this couple was moving slowly, any blur would have ruined the picture.

Focal length: 35mm

Aperture: f/9

Shutter speed: 1/200 sec.

ISO: 1000

Manual Exposure

With the accuracy and ease of automatic exposure, you may be thinking why bother with manual? However, some photographers swear by it and this chapter would not be complete without a brief overview.

There's no doubt that using manual exposure feels pure (it's about as basic as photography gets), but it can take too much valuable thinking time to set the exposure accurately, and this is a major drawback in a discipline where reaction times are often critical.

On the plus side, shooting manually can help you understand light. Because it slows you down, it makes you more reflective and considerate, and forces you to make assumptions and calculations about the direction, quality, and intensity of the light. For students of photography, this is an essential part of the learning process, but for street photographers who have a reasonable grasp of the basics, manual exposure is ultimately a hindrance.

Focus

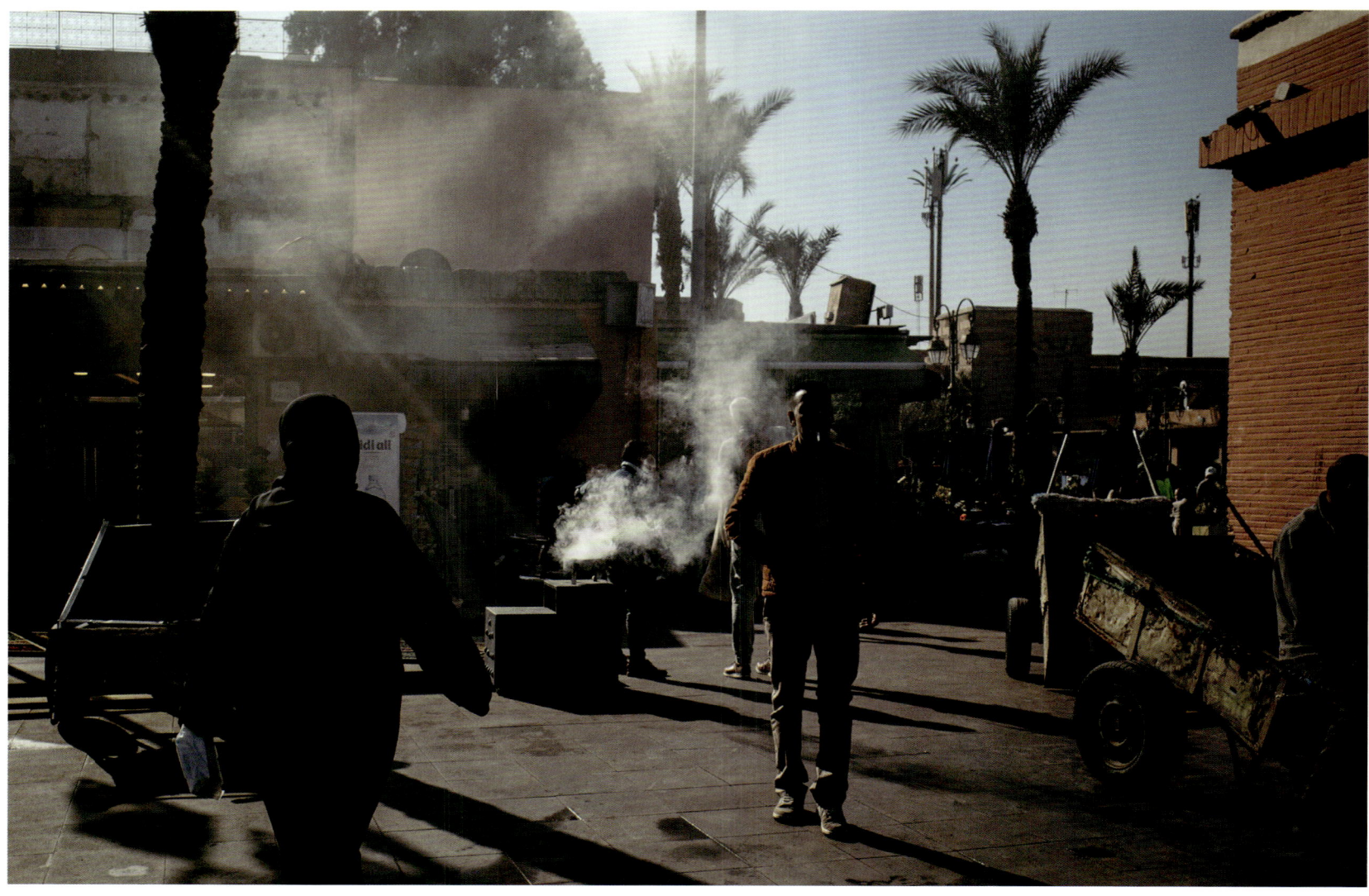

Perhaps one of the most vexing questions for street photographers is whether to use manual focus or autofocus. While there is no right or wrong answer (and personal preference has a part to play), it has long been acknowledged that manual focus rules. Why could that be so? Well, the principal reason is that speed is generally critical. If you are presented with an opportunity that seriously tests your reaction speed, the critical moment may well have been lost by the time an

autofocus lens has hunted and found the right point of focus. There's also the danger that in the heat of the moment your AF system will miss the correct point of focus completely, leaving you with a blurred image.

This doesn't mean that you have to set your lens to manual focus then guess the distance and hope for the best—instead, you need to learn to "zone focus." Zone focusing refers to pre-focusing your lens at a specific distance and using a fairly

small aperture. Depending on the focal length you are using, the depth of field would give you a zone of sharpness for your subjects to be in.

For example, if you were focusing at 8ft (2.5m) with a 35mm lens, and set the aperture at f/8, the depth of field would extend from roughly 5–15ft (1.5–4.5m). Knowing that everything within this zone would be sufficiently in focus, you could shoot quickly and spend those valuable split seconds getting the composition right.

Left: When a subject is moving toward or away from you, zone focusing will help you get it right—most of the time.

Focal length: 28mm

Aperture: f/8

Shutter speed: 1/800 sec.

ISO: 200

How To Zone Focus

There is an old adage—"f/8 and be there"—which pretty much sums up the basis for zone focusing. Here's how it works:

1 Choose an appropriate aperture. On a bright day, use f/11 or f/16; in darker conditions set f/8. Let's assume for now that you have set the aperture at f/16.

2 Guess at the likely range of shooting distances. Let's assume this is somewhere in the region of 5–10ft (1.5–3m).

3 Look at the depth of field markings on your lens barrel and set the focusing scale so that your guessed distances sit within the depth of field marks for the aperture you are using. You will now see which distances will be in focus for your chosen aperture.

4 When set up in this way, your camera effectively becomes a snapshot camera: you don't have to worry about getting the focus right, you just point and shoot when your subject is within your focus zone.

Bear in mind, though, that this is not an absolute rule—the depth of field will depend on your camera's sensor size, the distance to the subject, focal length, and aperture.

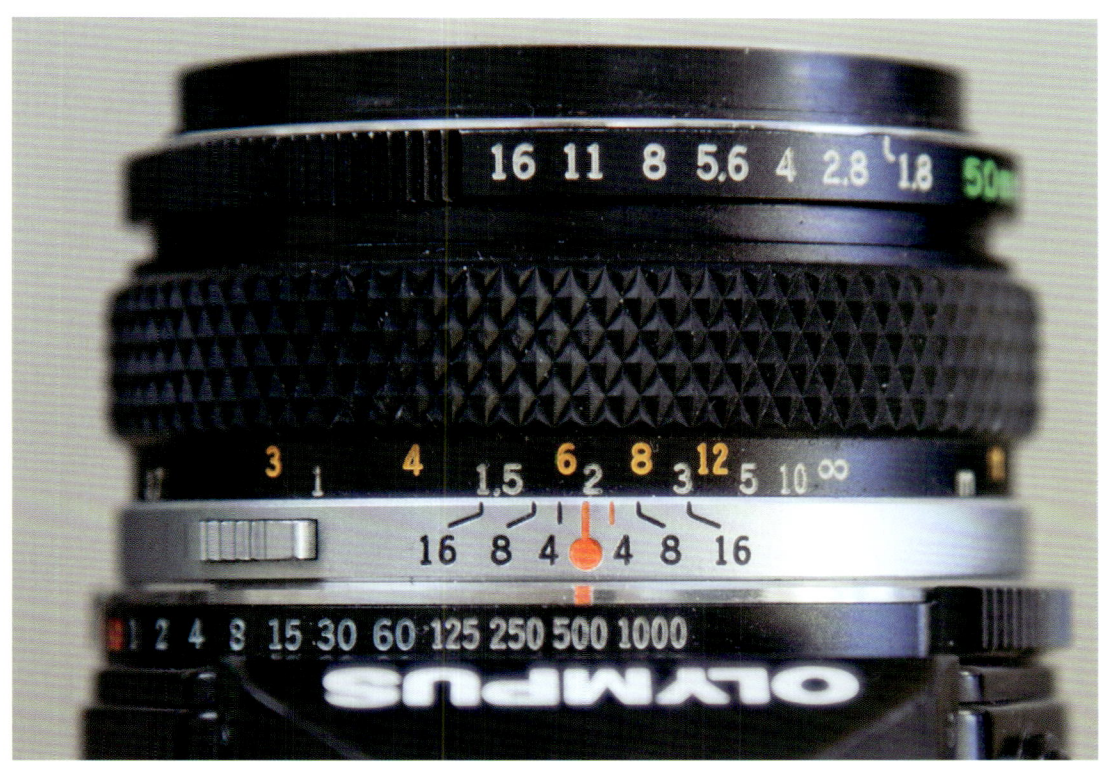

The Case For Autofocus

Although it's useful, there are difficulties with manual focusing. For a start, the viewfinder on many modern digital cameras doesn't show a large enough image for accurate manual focusing. Also, manual focus lenses are designed to have a long focus "throw" (the amount of rotation needed to go from minimum focus to infinity), which allows for precise focus adjustments. Modern AF lenses have a much shorter throw, and combined with the smaller viewfinder this can make manual focusing tricky. A further problem with many modern lenses is their lack of depth of field markings, which makes it difficult to be accurate with your focusing decisions. In this regard, autofocus can often be an easier (and more precise) option.

Above: Most traditional lenses (and many modern ones) have markings to aid zone focusing. In this picture of a 50mm standard lens you can see that by using an aperture of f/16 and setting the focus at around 6ft (2m), everything from 5–10ft (1.5–3m) would be in focus. With a wide-angle lens, this zone would be much wider.

Tip

Many cameras have an AF assist light. If yours does, turn it off. If you are trying to be invisible, having a bright light shine out of the front of your camera tends to give the game away!

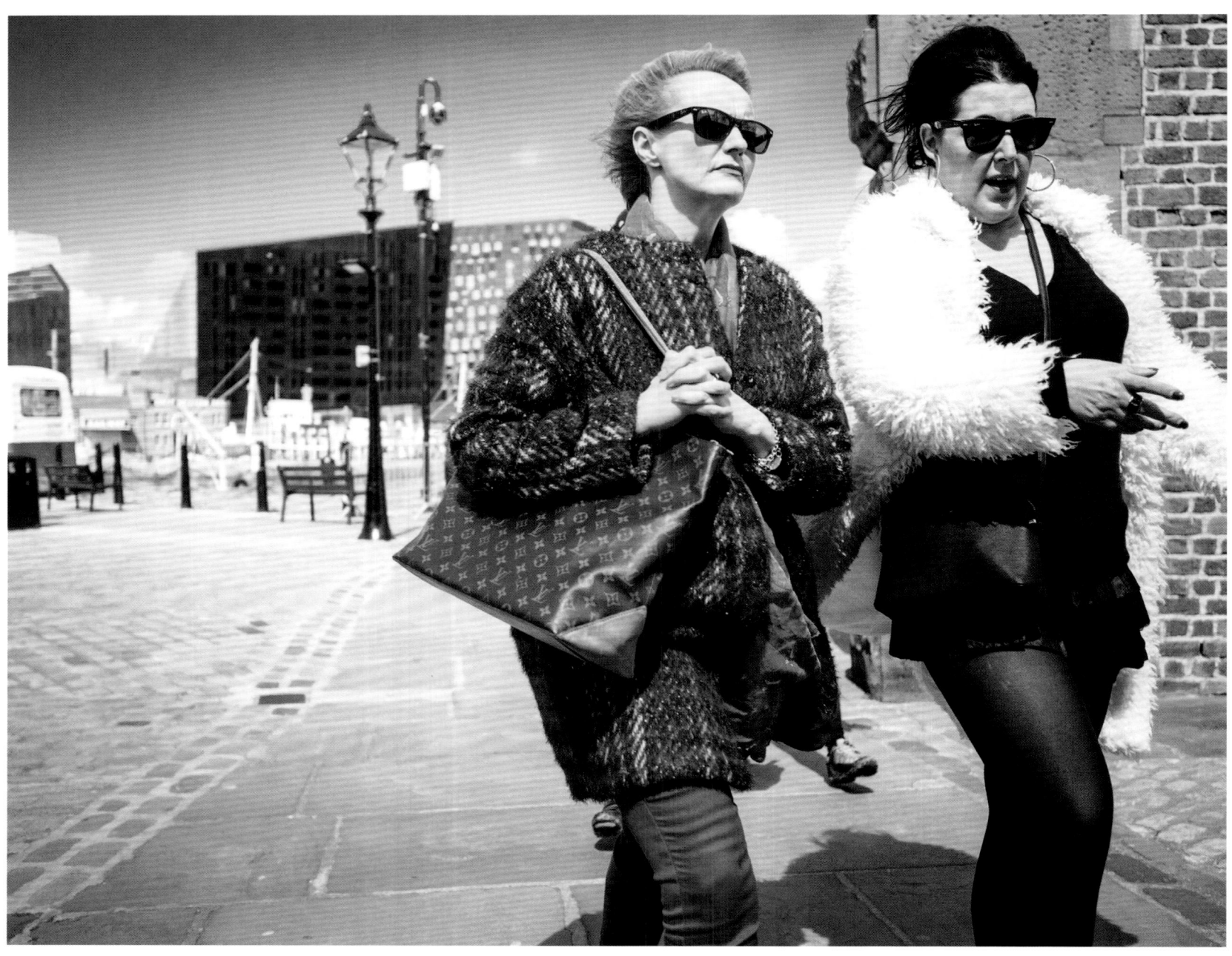

Above: When a subject is moving quickly toward you, the camera's AF system can easily let you down. In a case like this, zone focusing offers a wide margin for error, resulting in a sharp image.

Focal length: 28mm

Aperture: f/11

Shutter speed: 1/160 sec.

ISO: 100

"Sharpness is a bourgeois concept."

—Henri Cartier-Bresson

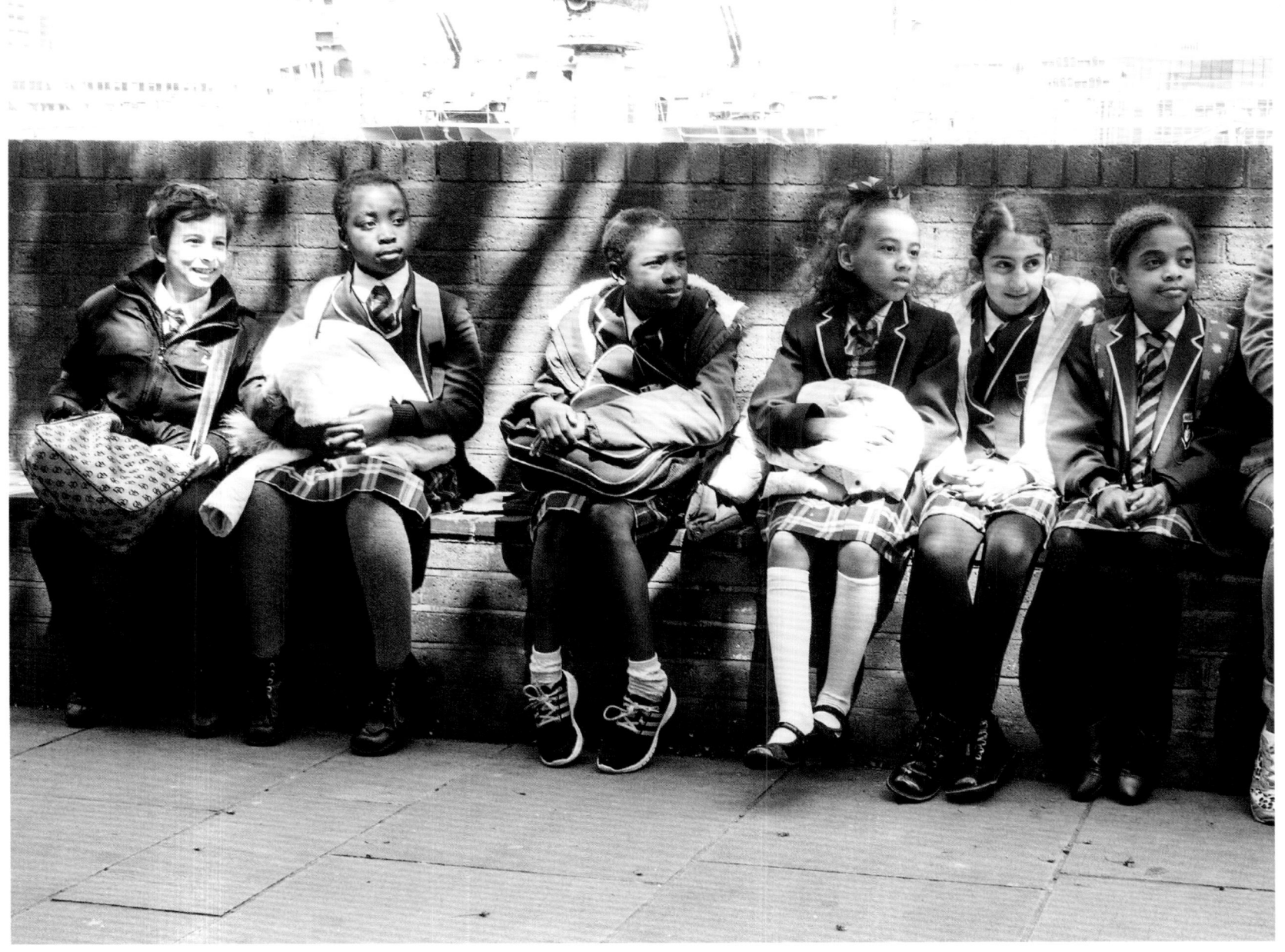

Above: If all the elements in the frame are on the same plane, depth of field becomes less of an issue and you can open up the aperture if you need to.

Focal length: 35mm

Aperture: f/5.6

Shutter speed: 1/400 sec.

ISO: 1250

Composition

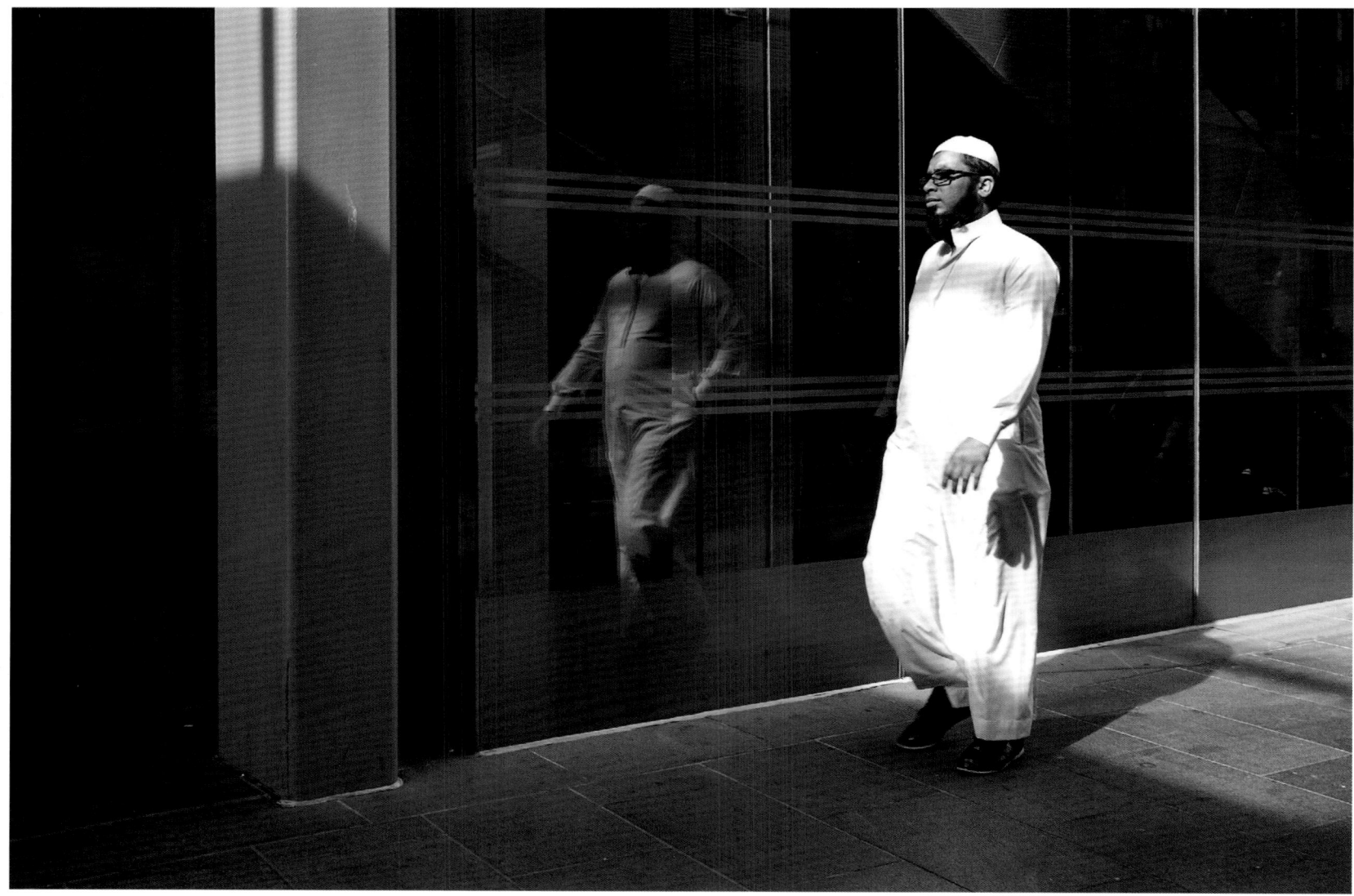

Composition is concerned with how we position the various elements within the frame, and it is at the heart of street photography. There are various compositional techniques that will help you draw attention to the most important elements in your frame and to create an image that is pleasing to the eye. Much has been written about compositional theory, but if ever there was a genre in which such rules can be easily broken, it is street photography— we often call it the jazz of photography!

The world of street photography is often fluid and dynamic, which can leave little or no time to pay much attention to composition, other than, perhaps, where the main subject is positioned within the frame. There are occasions, however, when you will have time to compose with rather more deliberation. This is when you should consider using some time-honored techniques to help give your pictures the "wow" factor.

Above: A combination of a dark background and a sunny foreground will always create the potential for an image that "pops" due to its contrast.

Focal length: 27mm

Aperture: f/9

Shutter speed: 1/300 sec.

ISO: 1600

Pre-Visualization

It was the landscape photographer Ansel Adams who brought us the concept of pre-visualization, which is about seeing the final image and knowing what it will look like before firing the shutter. The ability to pre-visualize an image is an important skill for street photographers, although unlike landscape photographers we do not have the luxury of time or reflection—we will often need to act quickly and instinctively.

Taking a great street shot is not just a question of looking—it's about really seeing. It's about taking in not only the overall composition and balance, but also the detail and the narrative. As far as pre-visualization goes, that's a lot to consider in a very short space of time, but you should persevere: it is an instinctive skill that will develop over time and with practice.

Composing Quickly

When you're shooting "on the fly," with things happening quickly around you, composition can easily disappear out of the window. However, by following some of the camera set-up techniques discussed previously, you should be in a state of readiness and able to concentrate on getting the picture, rather than thinking about focus or exposure. These three simple rules will help you compose your shots quickly when under pressure:

1 **Compose in your head first**. Frame the picture in your mind well before the camera comes up to eye level. This isn't something you'll master over a weekend, but using a focal length of around 35–50mm will mean your camera's field of vision is close to that of the human eye, which will help you visualize what will be in the frame. Get to know one lens really well and practice using only that lens.

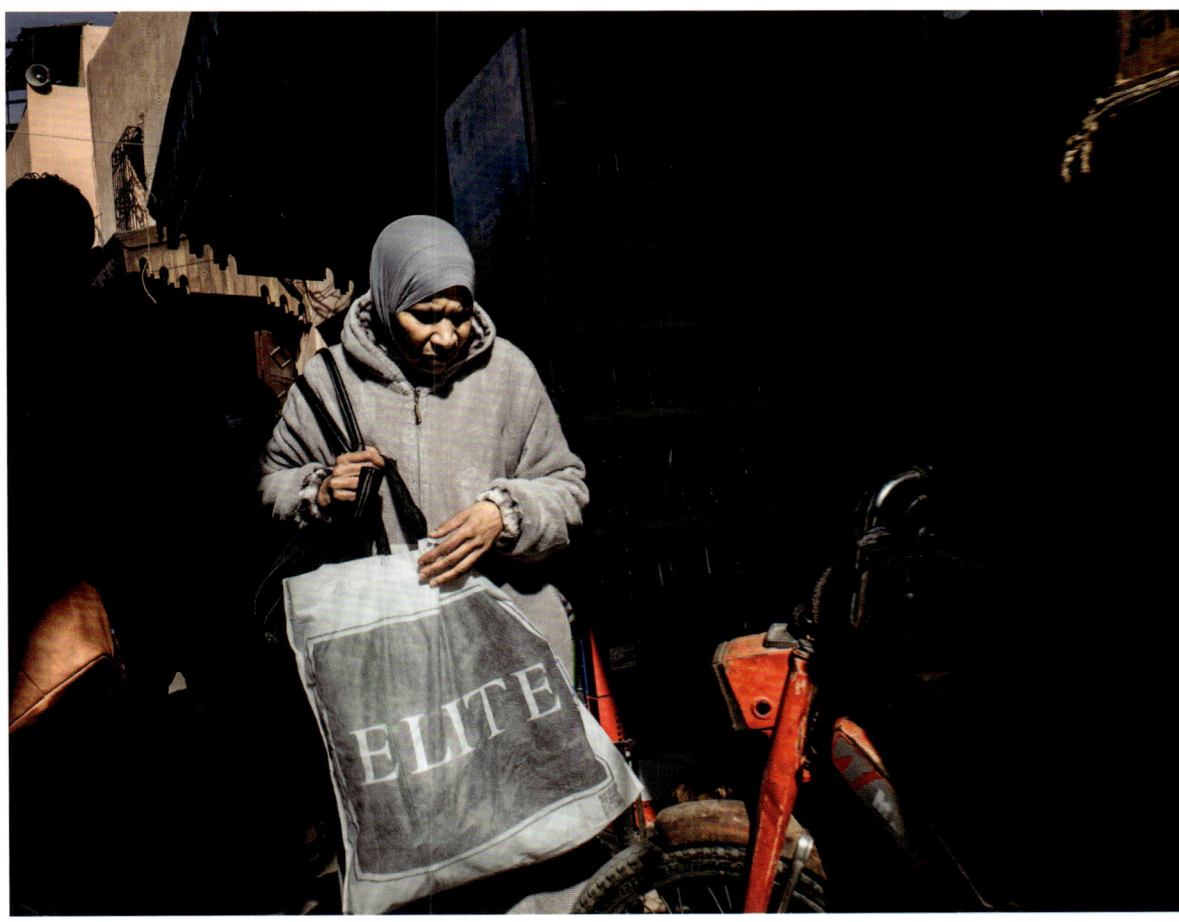

2 **Don't zoom**. Zooming delays composition. If you use a prime lens you will find you "see" the desired image more quickly and don't waste valuable seconds framing and re-framing. If you only have a zoom lens, try putting tape over the barrel to prevent you zooming.

3 **Stand still**. However tempting it may be to keep moving while you take a picture, don't. Stand still! It is usually possible to pause for a brief moment in order to steady yourself; if you are moving slowly to start with, there's less chance of you being noticed.

Above: You need to think and act quickly when shooting a moving subject. If you spend too long thinking "shall I or shan't I?" and then zooming or adjusting settings, you'll almost certainly miss the moment. Get into the habit of shooting first and worrying about it later!
Focal length: 28mm
Aperture: f/8
Shutter speed: 1/160 sec.
ISO: 100

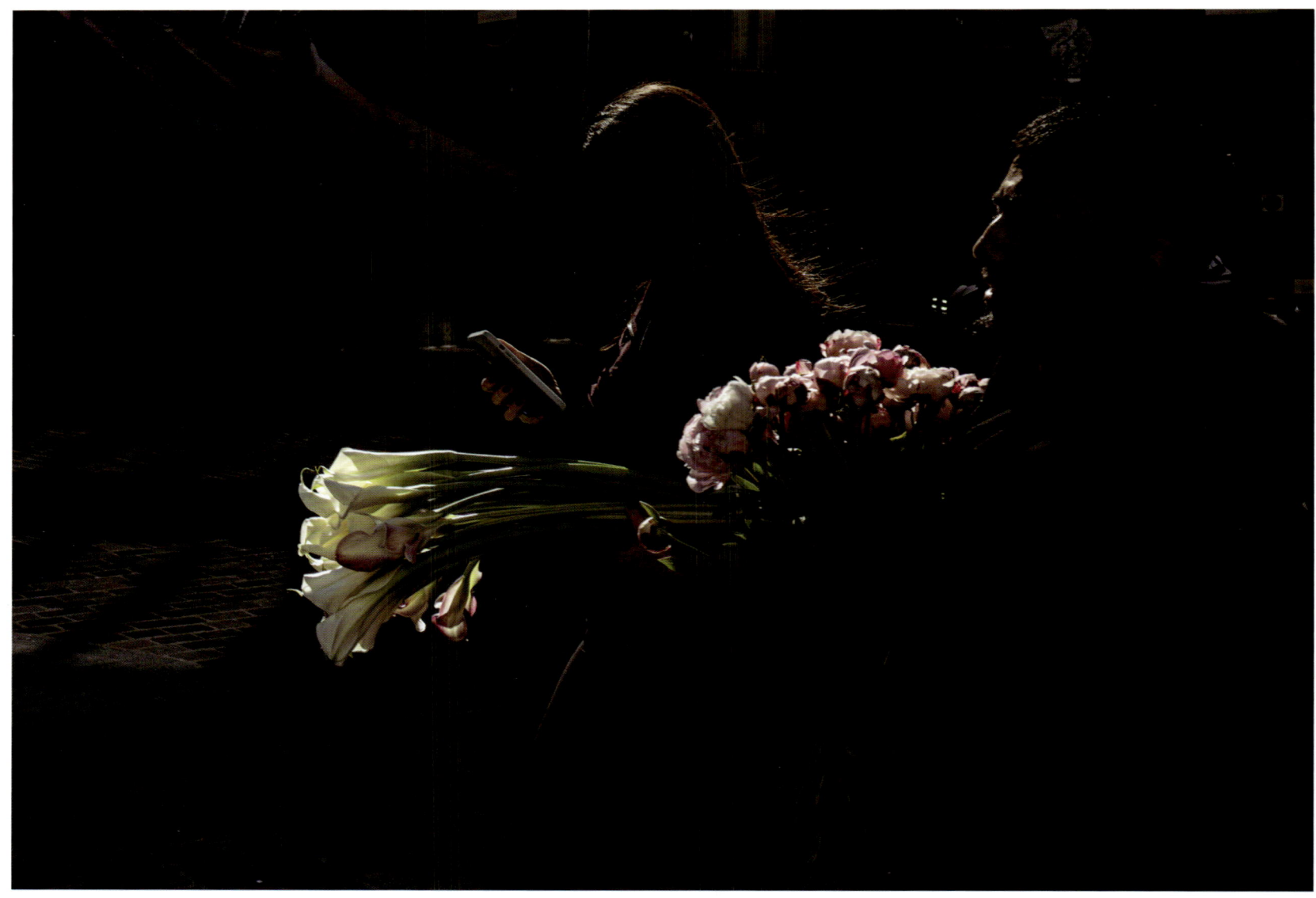

Portrait Or Landscape?

Perhaps your first compositional consideration when framing an image is whether to shoot in a horizontal (landscape) format or a vertical (portrait) one. There is no right or wrong answer: do whatever is aesthetically most suitable in the circumstances. It could be the case, for example, that images presented in portrait orientation form a key component in your personal style, as in the case of the great Saul Leiter. This doesn't mean that you need to rigidly follow one direction or the other—it's just something to be conscious of.

Bear in mind, however, that the human eye naturally sees the world in a landscape orientation, and when pictures are viewed on a screen, they are also usually viewed landscape—except, of course, in the case of smartphones.

Often, you won't know which style works best until you are viewing the images on a big screen, with the benefit of time to reflect; for this reason it is always worth shooting a scene both ways (assuming you have the time) so you can make the decision later on.

Above: When the subject matter is arranged in a linear fashion, sometimes only a landscape composition will work.

Focal length: 35mm

Aperture: f/8

Shutter speed: 1/500 sec.

ISO: 100

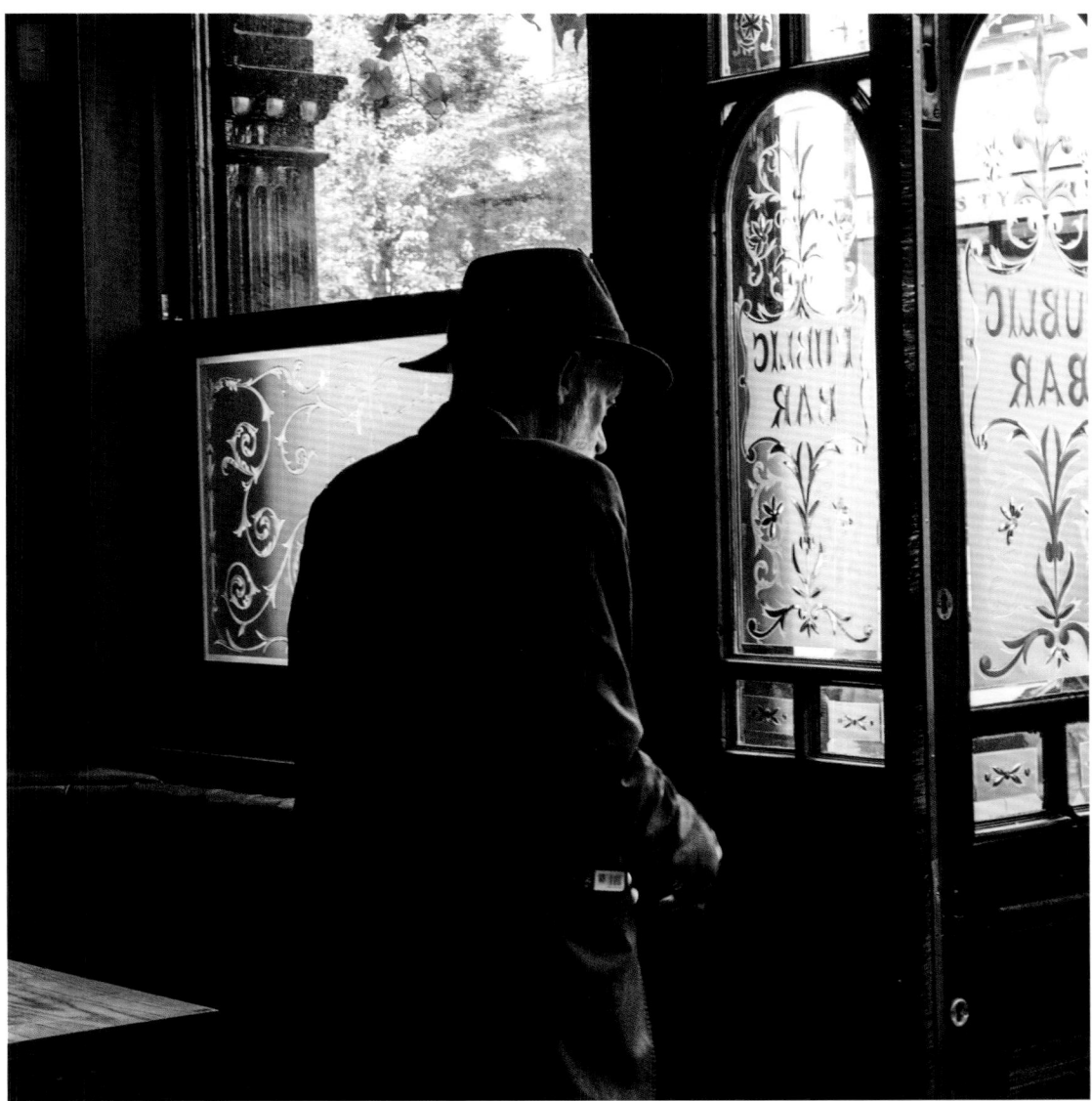

What About Square?

The square format was introduced by Rollei in 1929, but fell out of fashion as the rectangular 35mm film frame with its 3:2 aspect ratio became prevalent. However, the square has recently undergone a revival, due in no small part to the rise in popularity of Instagram. To many people there is something visually pleasing—some would say exquisite—about a square image, as unlike an oblong frame, a square maintains a natural sense of balance.

It is worth experimenting with square images, but make sure there is space around the main subject to allow it to "breathe." Some digital cameras will allow you to set a square aspect ratio and crop your images accordingly, but others require you to pre-visualize a square outcome and crop the image yourself during postproduction. For inspiration, look at some of the work of Lee Friedlander, Robert Doisneau, and Diane Arbus—all of whom used the square to good effect.

Above: Sometimes you'll look at an image in both portrait and landscape orientations, then decide that it just "speaks to you" as a square.

Focal length: 33mm

Aperture: f/10

Shutter speed: 1/110 sec.

ISO: 3200

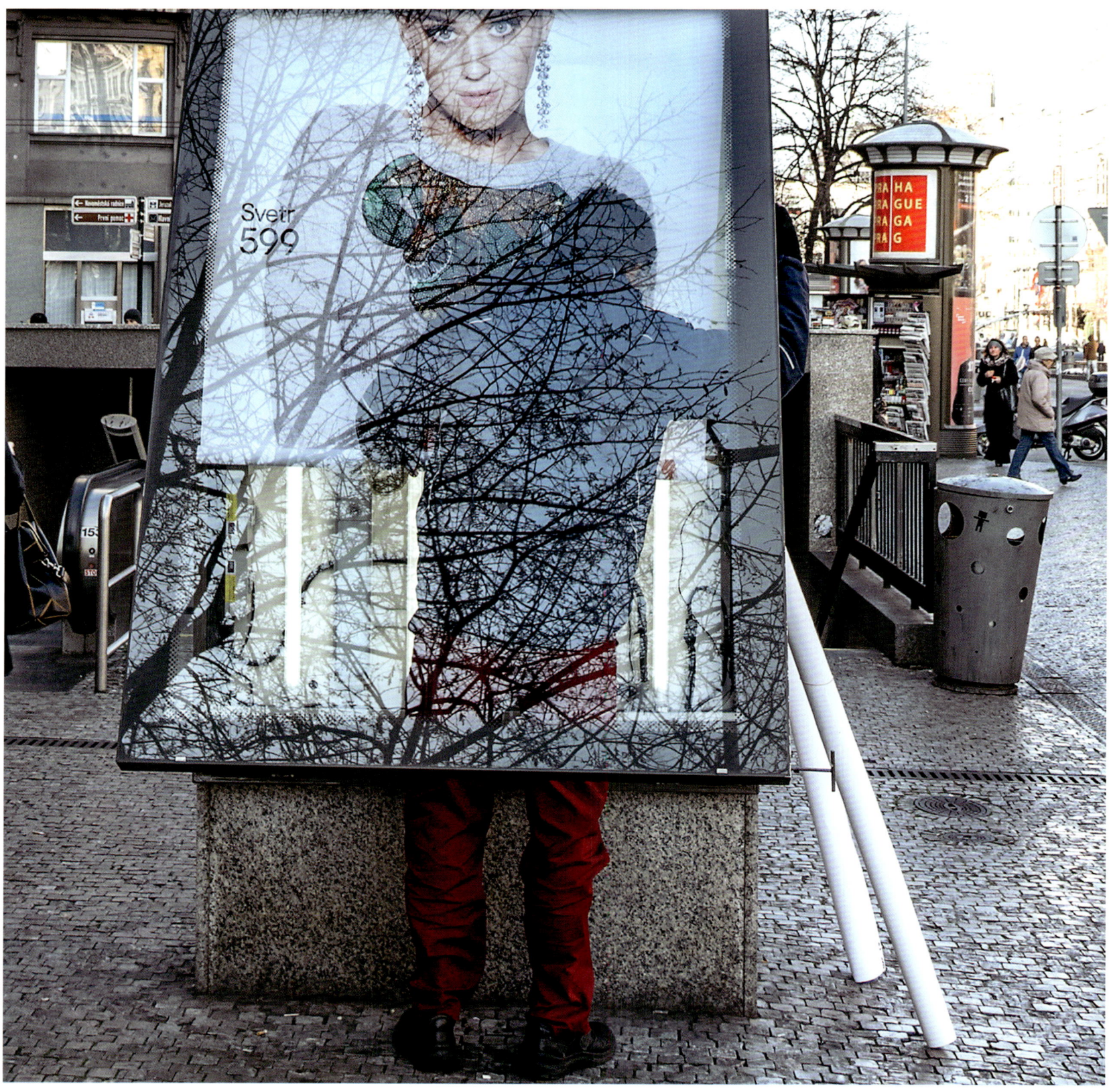

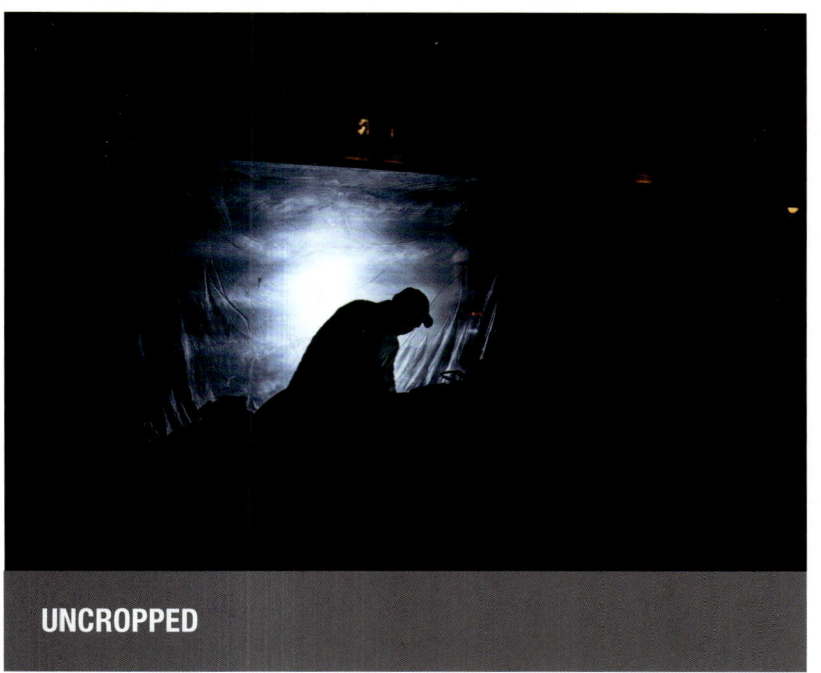

UNCROPPED

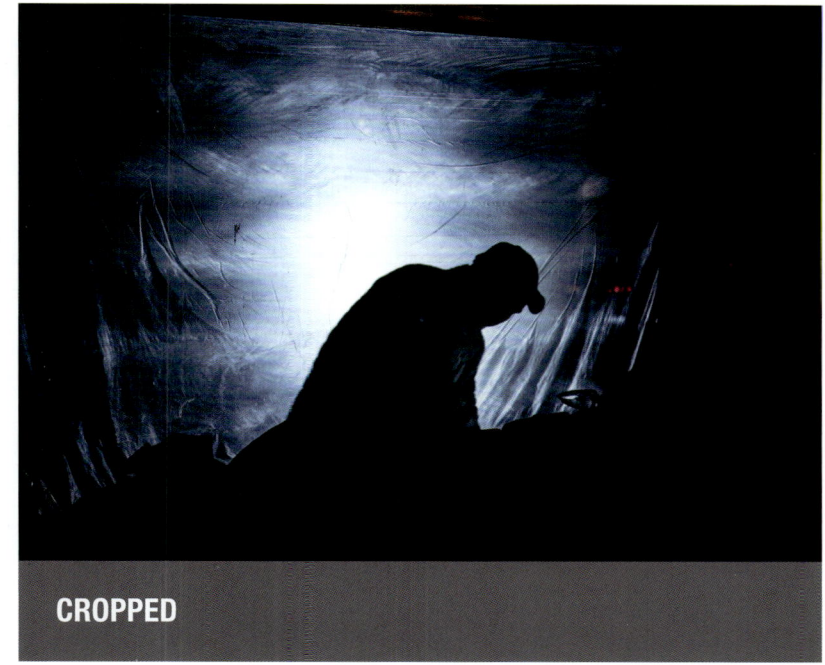

CROPPED

Is Cropping Allowed?

There are many so-called rules about street photography, but "never crop" is perhaps the most frequently quoted. So, should we crop our images?

If you believe Henri Cartier-Bresson, the answer is a resounding "*No.*" In fact, Cartier-Bresson used a black border, created by enlarging the negative holder in the enlarger, to prove that his images were not cropped. He said: "*If you start cutting or cropping a good photograph, it means death to the geometrically correct interplay of proportions. Besides, it very rarely happens that a photograph which was feebly composed can be saved by reconstruction of its composition under the darkroom's enlarger; the integrity of vision is no longer there.*"

Was he right? In a small way he may have been, but a little judicious cropping to enhance the composition of an image can be effective and is perfectly acceptable. Of course, we should do our best to ensure the composition is right in the camera, but that is not always easy to achieve when working quickly and under pressure. Cropping to improve the visual balance of the image, or to straighten wonky vertical or horizontal lines is perfectly acceptable, provided you keep the original aspect ratio consistent.

Beware, however, that frequent cropping can turn you into a lazy photographer, careless about composition and without enough serious consideration about how an image might look. The "I can always crop it later" mentality is an easy trap to fall into and one you should avoid; use cropping as a creative choice rather than a lazy afterthought.

Left: A square crop can be used to good effect if you need to eliminate irrelevant or distracting elements. Here, the attention needed to be on the man in the red pants and the woman in the poster; cropping to a square eliminated some distracting background at either side.

Focal length: 35mm

Aperture: f/5.6

Shutter speed: 1/200 sec.

ISO: 200

Above left & Above: The uncropped version of this image (above left) had too much unnecessary dark background. The cropped version (above right) is a more balanced and meaningful composition with less negative space.

Focal length: 43mm

Aperture: f/2

Shutter speed: 1/500 sec.

ISO: 500

Tip

Try the Cartier-Bresson approach and spend a month without cropping *any* of your images, no matter how tempted you may be. Analyze the results and watch as your compositional skills improve!

"Visualization is the single most important factor in photography."

—*Ansel Adams*

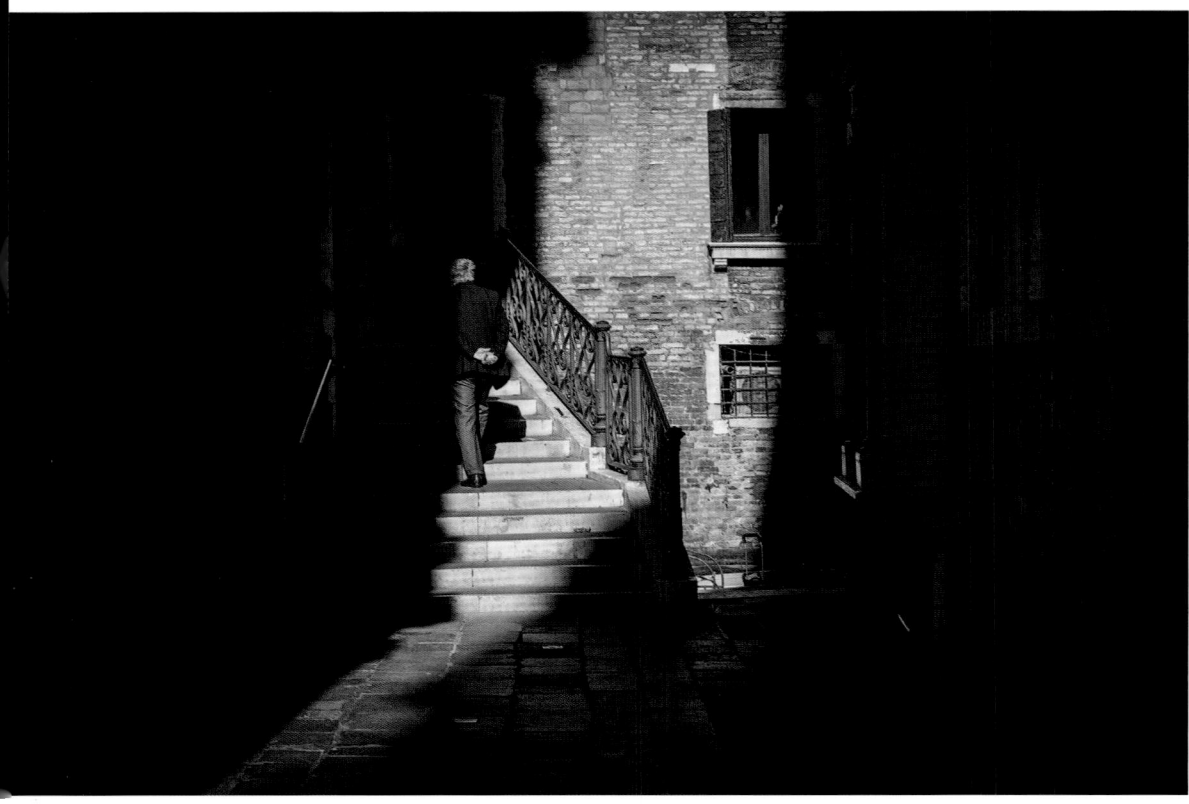

Leading Lines

Leading lines are one of the pillars of compositional theory. You don't (usually) want the viewer's eye constantly scanning the image and looking for a focal point, so you can sometimes use the concept of leading lines to focus attention on what is important: they give the viewer directions as to where to look. Think of them as visual signposts.

A leading line can be created by fixed elements such as a pathway, railway line, a row of trees, or the geometric lines of a building, but you can also find coincidental leading lines in the form of hand gestures, arrows, information on posters, or even the direction in which someone's eyes are looking. Lines can be straight or curved and they can be pointing at any angle, but the point is that they direct the eye to the subject; lines can be particularly effective if they enter your image from the bottom left or right corner, or run symmetrically from the sides to the center.

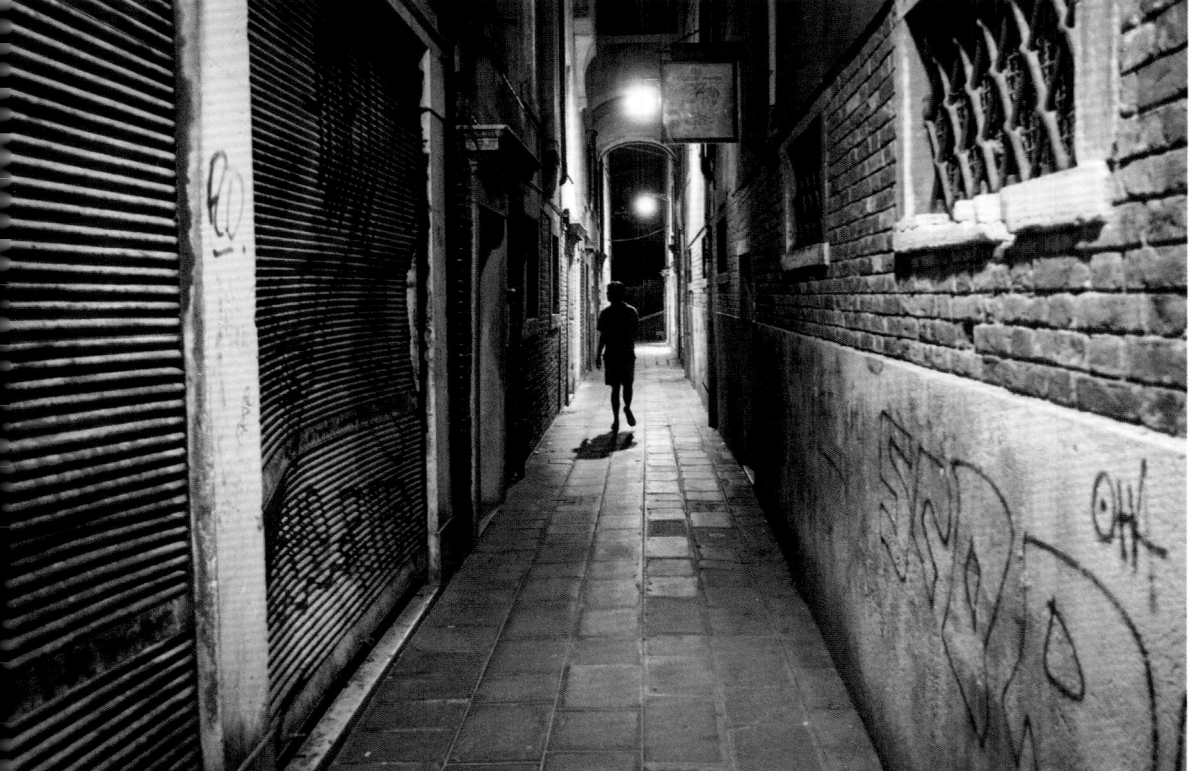

Above left: A staircase is a great way to use leading lines —you just need to get a person in the right position.
Focal length: 50mm
Aperture: f/8
Shutter speed: 1/600 sec.
ISO: 800

Left: The lines of the walls, together with the lights at the end of this alleyway, draw the eye toward the boy.
Focal length: 75mm
Aperture: f/2
Shutter speed: 1/25 sec.
ISO: 6400

Rule Of Thirds

While the rule of thirds is a nice to have rather than an essential ingredient, it can enhance a composition. The idea is that you imagine your frame is divided into equal thirds using two lines, both horizontally and vertically. Where these lines intersect is where you place your point of interest (as marked in red on the diagram opposite).

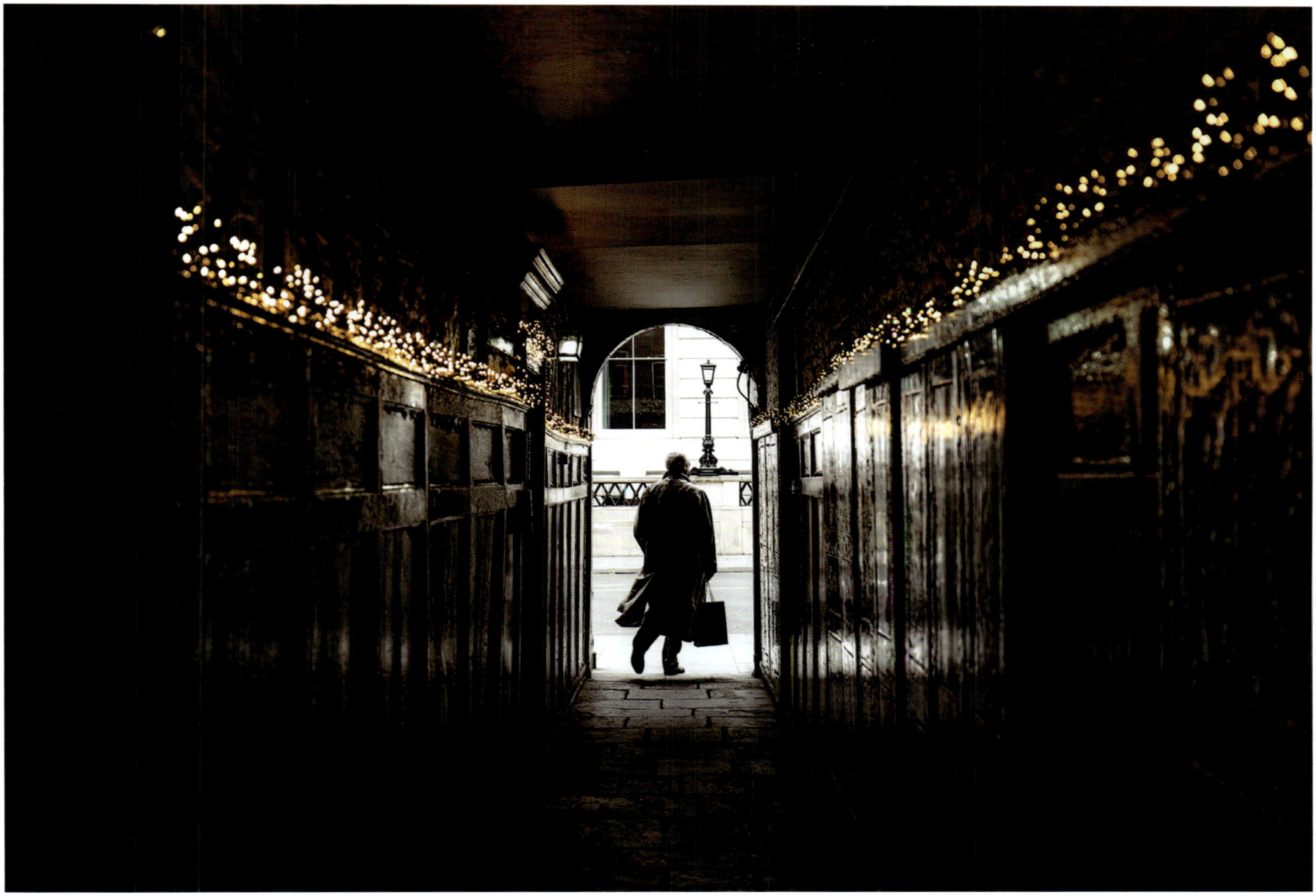

Studies have shown that when viewing an image, the human eye goes directly to one of these intersection points, rather than to the center of the frame. So, by placing your point of interest at an intersection, the image becomes more balanced and will allow the viewer to interact with it more readily (and for longer).

If you don't manage to apply the rule of thirds at the capture stage, it can usually be applied by cropping your image during postproduction. Because of this possibility, when you are shooting spontaneously it pays to leave some space around the subject for cropping.

Above & Right: The leaning lines of the lights combined with the door frame draw the eye toward the figure. To apply the rule of thirds, mentally divide the frame into nine equal blocks (as shown below right). The lines—and the points at which they intersect—indicate where your point(s) of interest should be positioned.

Focal length: 43mm

Aperture: f/3.5

Shutter speed: 1/60 sec.

ISO: 100

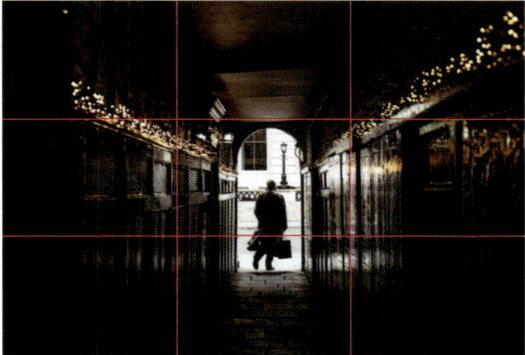

Symmetry

Flying directly in the face of the rule of thirds is symmetry. Symmetry can help catch the viewer's attention, while creating a relaxing sense of balance and ease. In street photography, it can be incredibly powerful and it is one of those visual tools that instantly grabs attention and creates a sense of order, balance, and beauty amid the chaos of urban life.

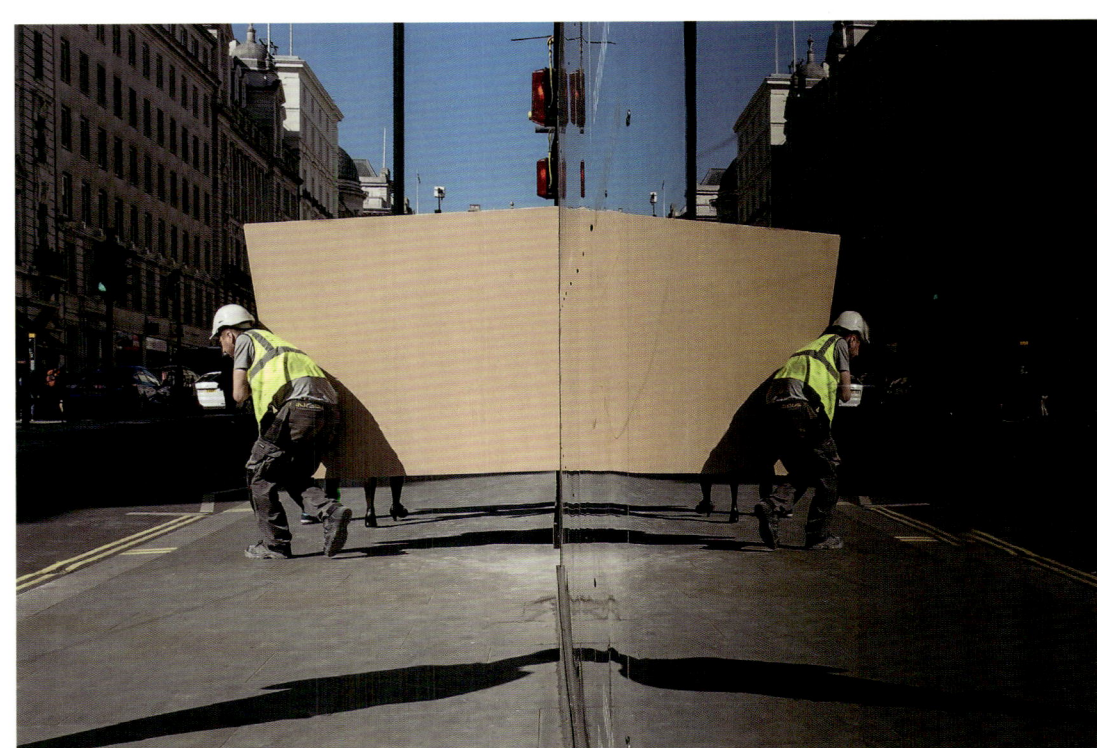

Right: The built environment contains many reflections—and these can give us interesting symmetrical effects, particularly where there are strong lines or obvious contrasts between tones.

Focal length: 28mm

Aperture: f/8

Shutter speed: 1/480 sec.

ISO: 400

HOW TO CAPTURE SYMMETRY
• Use a grid on your viewfinder to align elements precisely.
• Look up and down, not just straight ahead: ceilings, floors, and reflections often hide great symmetrical frames.
• Shoot wide and crop later if needed for perfect alignment.
• Wait for the right moment: the right subject won't always present itself immediately and you may need to wait—for example, for someone to walk into the exact center of your frame.

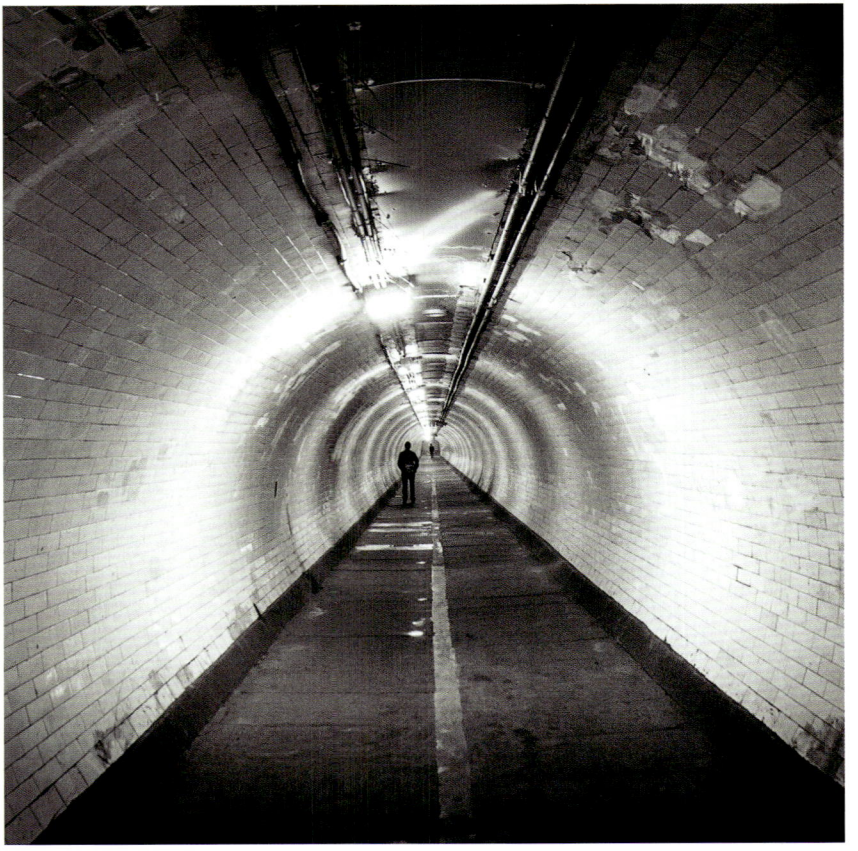

Right: A symmetrical image with a distant vanishing point can make a strong composition.

Focal length: 24mm

Aperture: f/4.5

Shutter speed: 1/20 sec.

ISO: 400

Using Layers

Layers are important because they can add volume and depth to an image. The easiest way to uncerstand layers is to think of your image as having a foreground, a middleground, and a background—these are your three principal layers and here's how they work together:

- **Foreground:** this is the closest element to the camera and it could be anything you like: a person, window frame, fence, or an automobile, for example. The foreground layer adds context and dimensionality and it can be in or out of focus.
- **Middleground:** this is usually where your main subject is placed and is often the area of sharpest focus and attention.
- **Background:** this should complement the main subject, rather than be a distraction, and it often adds useful context. It could include architecture, signage, or other people.

Another way of looking at layers is to take a photograph *through* something, such as glass, which can provide an unusual and artistic interpretation of an everyday street scene. Sure, you can add fake layers using filters or software, but the effect will be much more powerful if you create it in-camera. Look for windows, fine curtains, plastic sheets, leaves, mesh fences— anything that offers a fine cloak on the visual pathway to the final subject (fog, drizzle, or snow can provide good natural layers). Take care with focusing and ensure that you focus on the subject, rather than the layer (unless you intend otherwise—perhaps to create an abstract of raindrops on a window). Look at the work of Saul Leiter, who was the master of this technique.

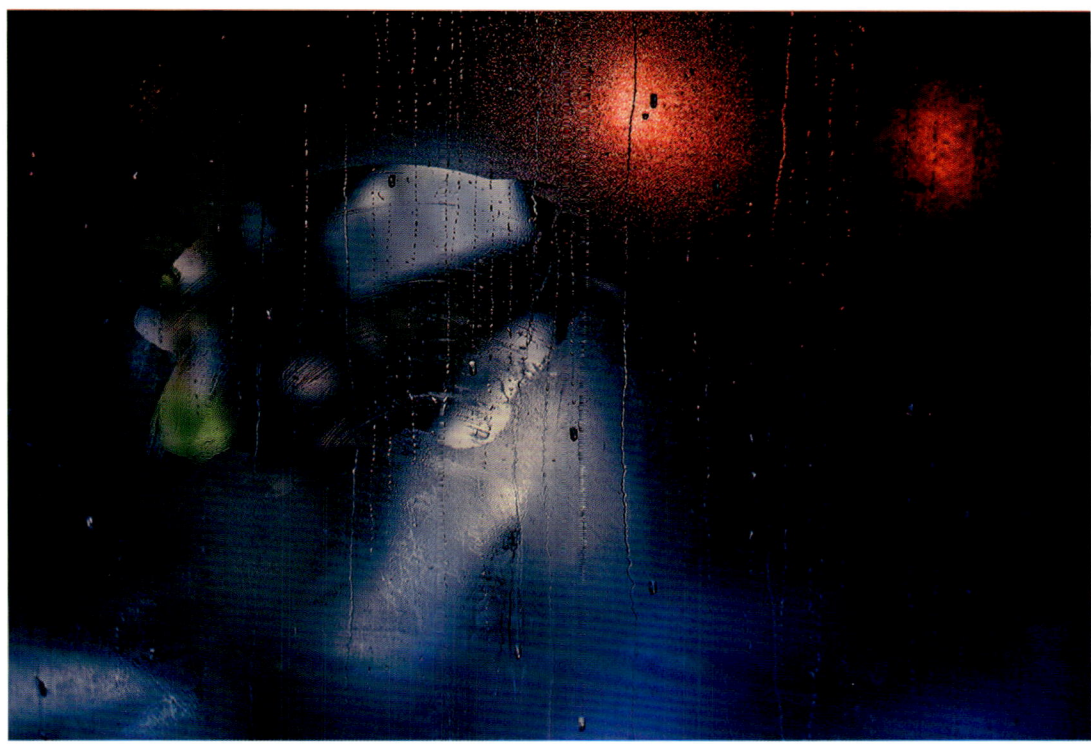

TIPS FOR SHOOTING LAYERS
- Shoot wide: use a 28mm or wider lens to capture more of the scene.
- Shoot through things: moisture on a widow, for example.
- Train your eye to spot overlapping elements.
- Pre-focus and wait for the subject to enter your frame.
- Study light and shadow for natural separations between layers.

Don't be afraid to experiment and see how the image plays out with a variety of interpretations.

Above: Natural filters, such as moisture on a window, can give a moody, atmospheric look. By focusing on the window itself, rather than the subject in the middle distance, you can create an abstract image. Try this at night when looking through a restaurant window and you can create some striking effects.

Focal length: 85mm
Aperture: f/1.2
Shutter speed: 1/180 sec.
ISO: 160

Figure-To-Ground Ratio

In psychology, figure-to-ground organization is one of the Gestalt principles and is a type of perceptual grouping that allows us to easily recognize things; in other words, it is a way of separating the figure from the background. That might sound very theoretical, but it has a simple implication for street photographers: separating the foreground interest from the background clutter.

When you next look at a photograph, ask yourself: "Can I easily understand what's going on here?" If the main subject in the frame pops out of the background and gives you a quick and clear understanding of the image, it has strong figure-to-ground ratio. A woman in a white dress against a dark wall would be a good example of this, as is a portrait with a very shallow depth of field where the background is out of focus.

How can you use this principal when you are out taking pictures on the street? Leaving aside spontaneous grab shots (where you have precious little time to react), a good starting point is to consider the background before deciding how to add the principal element(s). You should also invest a little time working the scene and hunting out the best light; this is probably the most effective way of creating strong figure to ground (and it can be achieved in the same way by using flash, although most people rarely use flash in street photography).

Bear in mind there's a compromise here. While you usually want a reasonably strong figure-to-ground ratio in your street images, you may also want to include some context that helps tell the story. A successful picture needs to have just the right balance between the two.

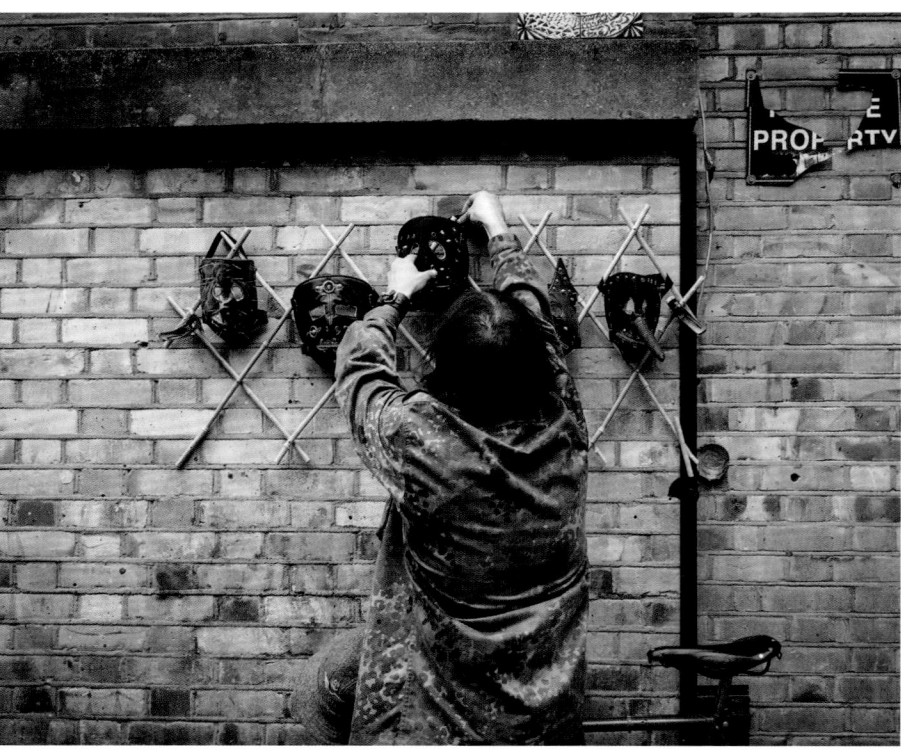

Above: This image demonstrates a weak figure-to-ground ratio. The problem is, there is little to distinguish the man from his masks and the wall, so the eye struggles to find a strong focal point.

Focal length: 24mm

Aperture: f/8

Shutter speed: 1/150 sec.

ISO: 1600

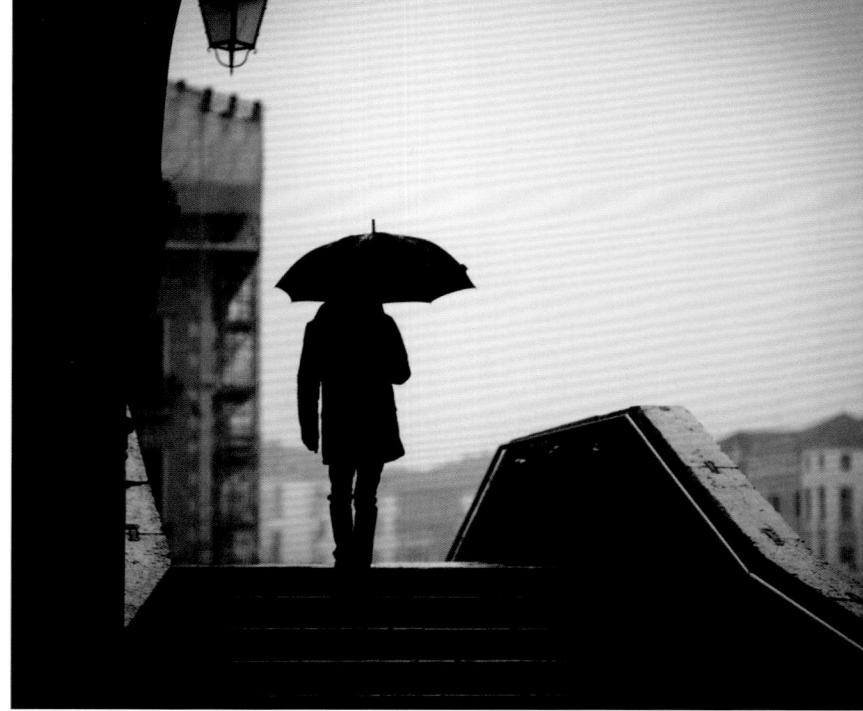

Above: A strong silhouette should really pop out of a dark background and is a good example of a strong figure-to-ground ratio.

Focal length: 40mm

Aperture: f/1.4

Shutter speed: 1/320 sec.

ISO: 125

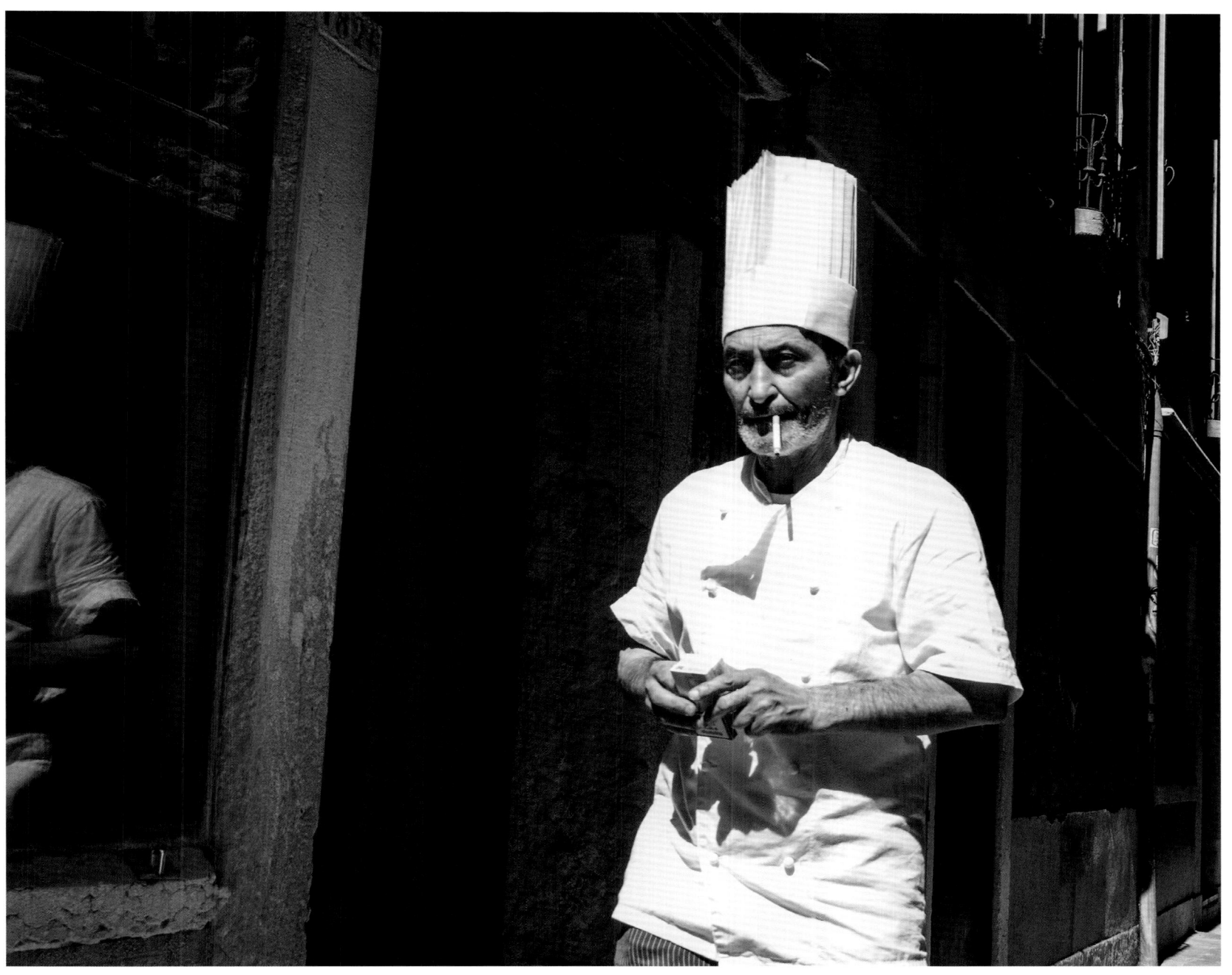

Above: Keep your eyes open for contrasty subjects that really stand out from their backgrounds, whether it's dark against light, or light against dark, such as this picture of a chef.

Focal length: 50mm

Aperture: f/8

Shutter speed: 1/400 sec.

ISO: 640

Raw Or JPEG?

One of the first critical technical decisions to make is whether to shoot Raw images or JPEGs. When you shoot in JPEG, the camera's internal software—or firmware—reads the information on the sensor, processes it, and then saves it. At this stage a little detail is lost (in the form of color and resolution), which is why JPEG is referred to as a lossy file format.

When you take a Raw photograph, it is your computer, not your camera, which processes the data. As Raw files generate lossless images, there is no degradation in image quality at this stage. Shooting in Raw will give you much more control over how your image looks and it is even possible to correct several sins that you may have committed when you took the photograph, such as adjusting the exposure.

Most modern cameras enable you to shoot both Raw files and JPEGs simultaneously, which is an approach that is often favored by street photographers. The Raw file becomes the equivalent of a digital negative, which will always remain intact, allowing you to take a more creative approach with the JPEG.

For example, if you lean toward black-and-white images, you can set your camera to produce monochrome JPEGs, while leaving the Raw file in color. This will give you a monochrome preview on your LCD screen and/or through the camera's viewfinder, allowing you to visualize the world in black and white.

Right: Raw files allow you to make adjustments without having a significant impact on image quality. This shot was taken in bright sunlight and the contrast needed to be carefully controlled, without losing the color in the subjects' hair.

Focal length: 35mm

Aperture: f/11

Shutter speed: 1/1200 sec.

ISO: 450

WHAT IS A RAW FILE?

A Raw file is not an image file per se, and it will require special software for viewing or editing. It is usually a proprietary format, with each camera manufacturer having its own format and file extension (such as Canon's .CR3, Fuji's .RAF, Leica's .DNG, Nikon's .NEF, Sony's .ARW, or Olympus' .ORF). The important factor is that a Raw file is not processed in-camera, so you will not be able to do much with it without first doing some post-processing.

WHAT IS A JPEG?

A JPEG (short for Joint Photographic Experts Group) is a file format that offers a standard method for compressing images. Because JPEGs are compressed, they are often used for storing and transmitting photographs on the web. The degree of compression can be varied, allowing a selectable trade-off between file size and image quality: the higher the compression, the smaller the file, but the lower the quality.

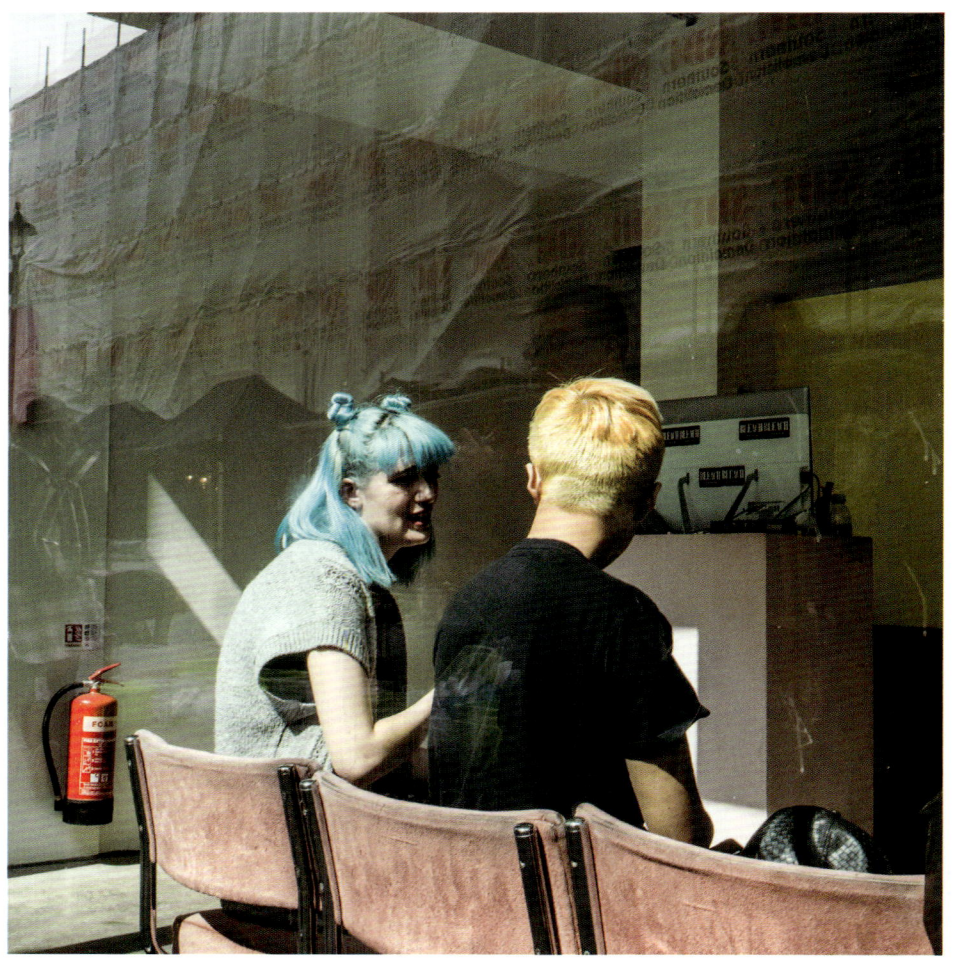

The Downside To Raw

Although there are many benefits to shooting Raw, there are a couple of factors you should be aware of. Firstly, the file sizes are considerably larger than JPEGs, so your memory cards will fill up faster and you will need more computer storage space if you intend to archive your Raw files.

It also takes longer for your camera to transfer Raw images from the sensor to the memory card.

If you are shooting using your camera's continuous burst mode you may find that your sequence comes to an abrupt halt while the camera catches up (this becomes less of an issue if you buy a fast memory card).

Perhaps the biggest issue, though, is that while you can preview your images in-camera, you won't be able to see them on a computer without specialist software, such as Adobe Camera Raw. You also won't necessarily be able to print your images, or share them online without first converting the Raw file into a JPEG or other popular file format.

Which Is Best?

If you are new to working with Raw files it is worth spending some time experimenting, so shoot Raw and JPEG simultaneously and explore the capabilities of each. Try shooting under different lighting conditions and see how the images compare. You may find that the differences are negligible with your style of

shooting, so it isn't worth spending the extra time processing Raw files.

Many street photographers do shoot in Raw, though, mainly for the flexibility it offers them further down the line. As you will often shoot in difficult conditions—perhaps in low or contrasty light, or with moving subjects—you should do all you can to maximize image quality and, with this in mind, Raw offers the best solution. If your camera allows you to record Raw and JPEG files at the same time—and you have lots of memory card capacity—it's usually a good idea to keep your options open and shoot both. If you do, invest some time in getting to know your Raw conversion software, so your efforts are well rewarded.

Below: Whichever Raw conversion software you use, explore all its capabilities—you may be surprised at just how many adjustments you can make at the Raw stage. Remember, much of the manipulation done here will not have a significant impact on image quality.

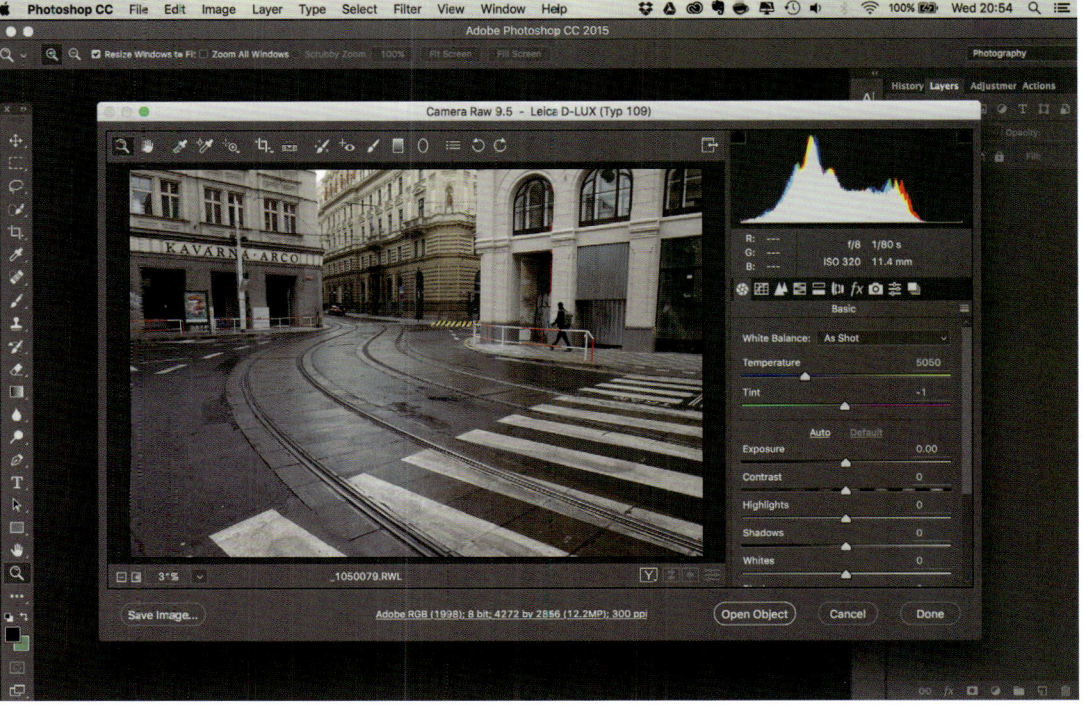

Shooting For Color

One of the most frequently asked questions among street photographers is "Do you shoot in color or black and white?" Relatively speaking, color in street photography is rare and in some circles is considered the "poor relation" to monochrome. However, that rarity value now gives color street photography an interesting edge—by shooting in color, you are immediately doing something different, which is more likely to make it stand out.

Saul Leiter first took color street photographs in 1948, which began to give the medium credibility. Others followed, and by the mid-1950s color was deemed acceptable in the genre. Fast-forward to today and you need look no further than the work of Martin Parr to see how color can be used to bring out the best—and worst—in your subjects.

Why Shoot In Color?

Most of us, whether shooting Raw or JPEG, will start with a color image, but why should you *end* up with a color image? Here are five good reasons:

- It's different. A lot of street photography is represented in black and white, so what better reason to shoot color? Following the crowd might be a safe option and may win peer group praise, but if you want to develop a strong personal style, a good starting point is to deviate from the norm.

- Sometimes only color will do. A boy dressed in bright blue, eating a banana, and standing in front of a red wall could make a stunning color image. But in black and white? Probably not.

- Color can add meaning. Color can be used to convey mood or add meaning to an image: red for danger, yellow for caution, green for nature, blue for tranquility, purple for royalty, and so on.

- To emphasize certain elements within the frame. Color can help pick out detail or bring elements together with a sense of uniformity.

- Be abstract. Use colors to create abstract art— you'll have much more fun doing it than you would in black and white.

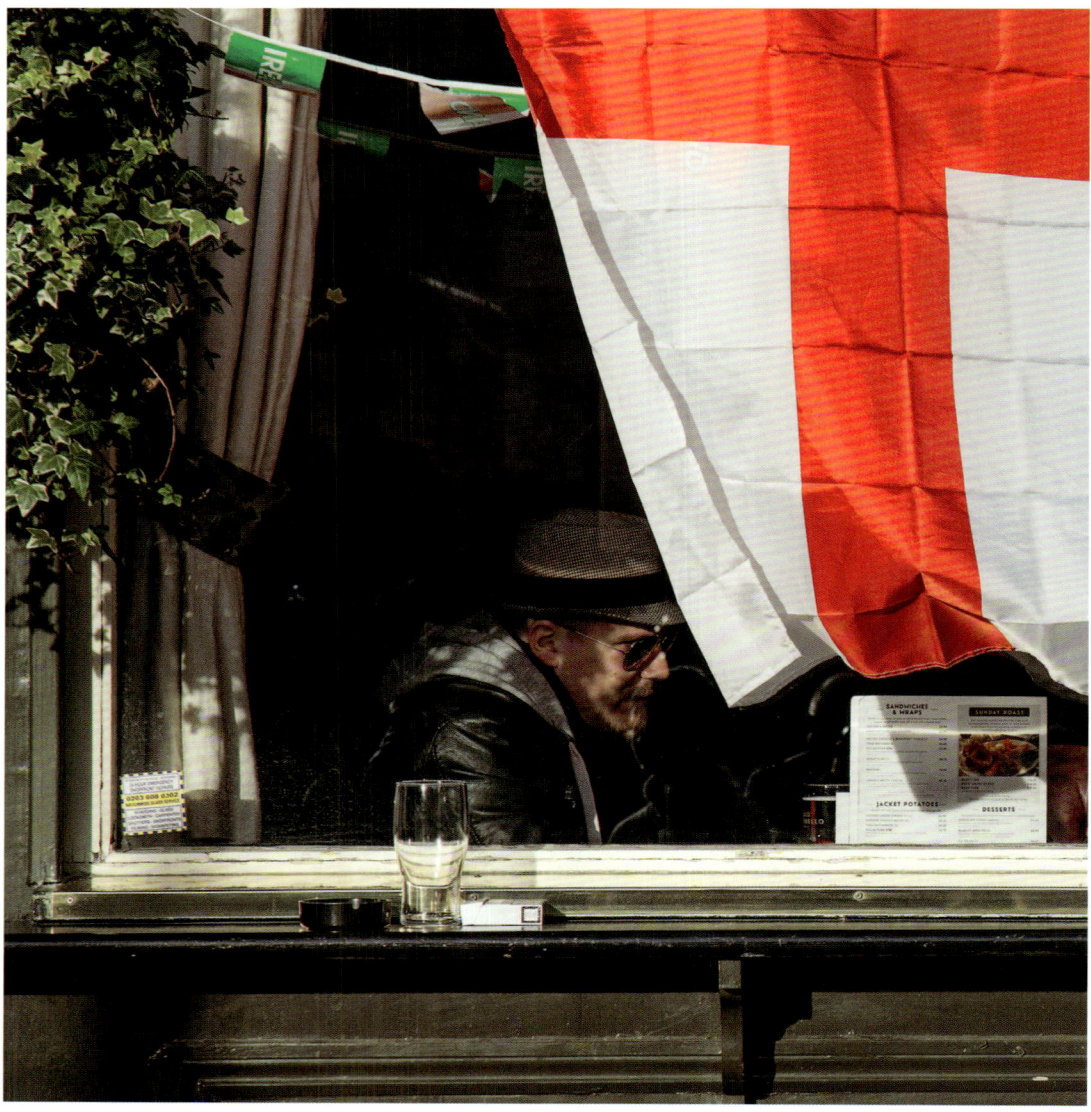

Above: A strong graphical element, such as this flag of St. George, could only work in color.

Focal length: 105mm

Aperture: f/9

Shutter speed: 1/1250 sec.

ISO: 800

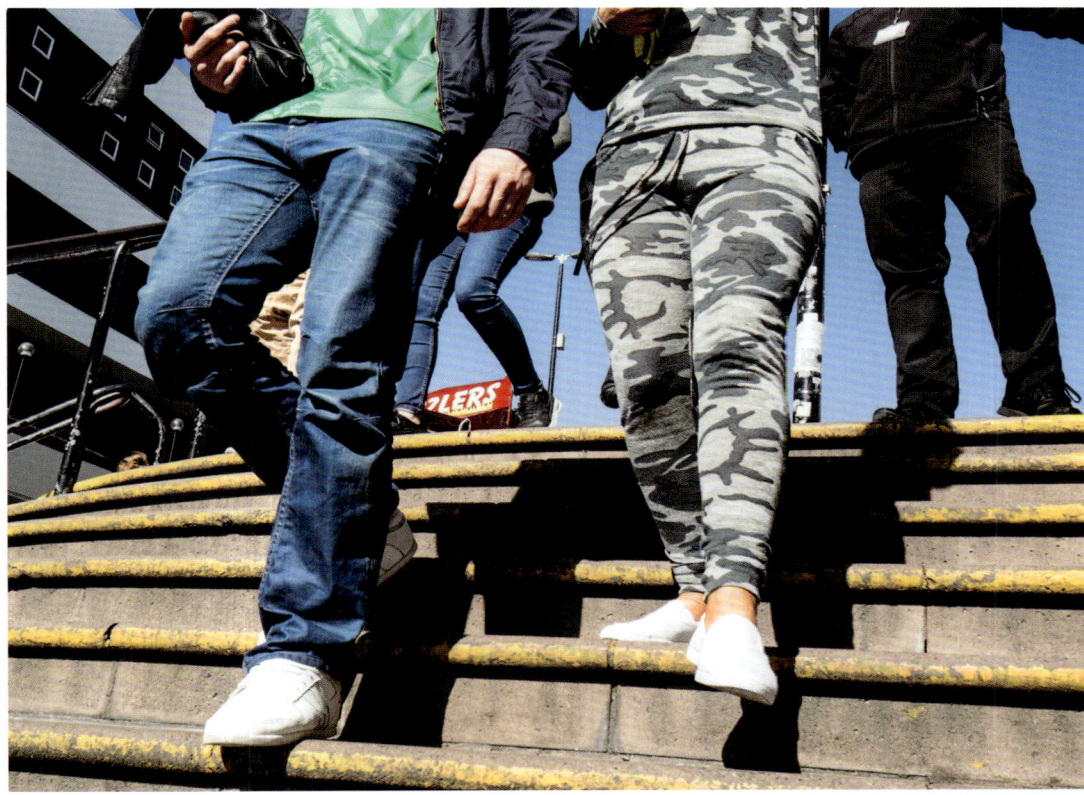

Left & Below left: Bright colors are particularly striking in strong sunlight—like this combination of primary colors and a deep blue sky. See how different—and less impactful—the image is in black and white.

Focal length: 35mm

Aperture: f/9

Shutter speed: 1/250 sec.

ISO: 1250

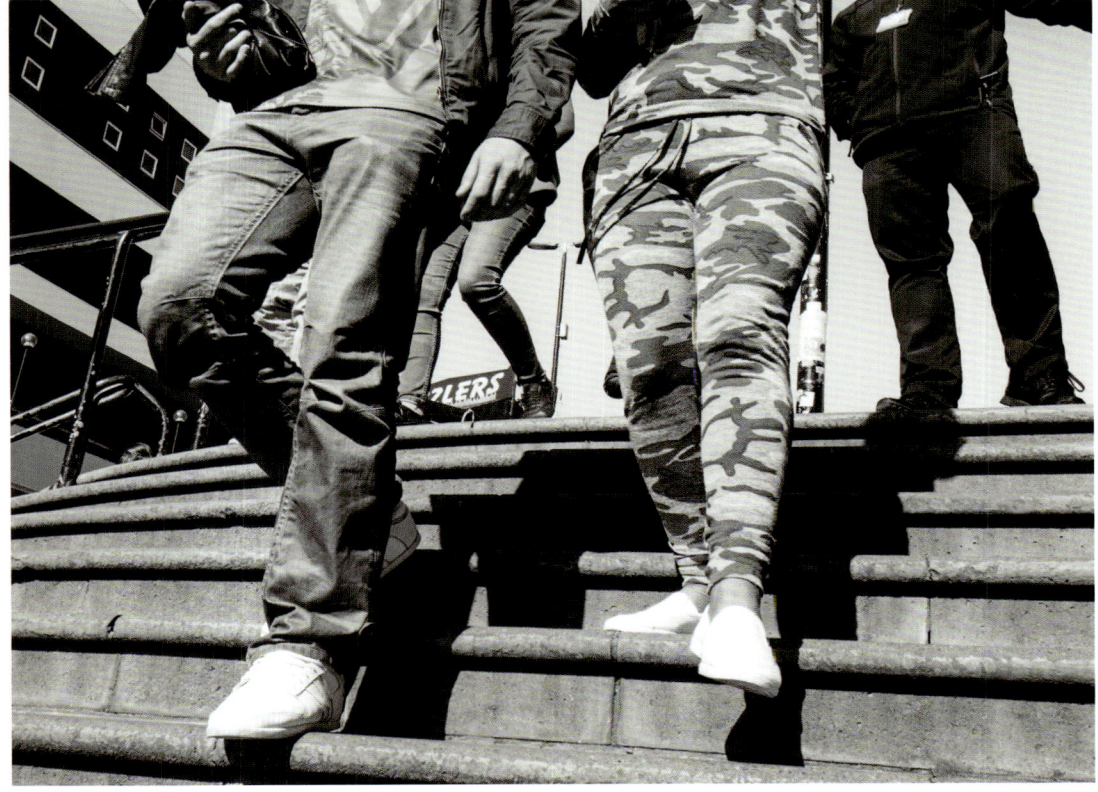

"In black and white you suggest, in color you state."

—*Paul Outerbridge*

Shooting For Black & White

Most of us will draw a natural association between street photography and black-and-white pictures. We probably consider monochrome images to have a nostalgic, vintage, or timeless quality; when we think of street photography the images that spring to mind are probably the iconic black-and-white pictures shot in the 1950s and '60s. There are many convincing reasons why street photographers tend to favor monochrome—here are a few, but why not see if you can add some of your own to the list?

• Black-and-white images offer an alternative perspective on real life; they don't reflect the world as we see it.

• Shooting in black and white can enhance the mood and atmosphere in a scene.

• There is often a timeless quality about monochrome, making it easier to recreate iconic styles from the past.

• Black-and-white photographs are often seen as more artistic and may be more credible in certain circles.

• Without the distraction of color, the content and composition tell the story.

• Monochrome can better emphasize or highlight textures and shapes.

• It may be easier to appreciate the detail in a scene in black and white; detail can be overlooked in color.

• With a black-and-white image it's easier to manage the contrast and exposure in difficult lighting situations.

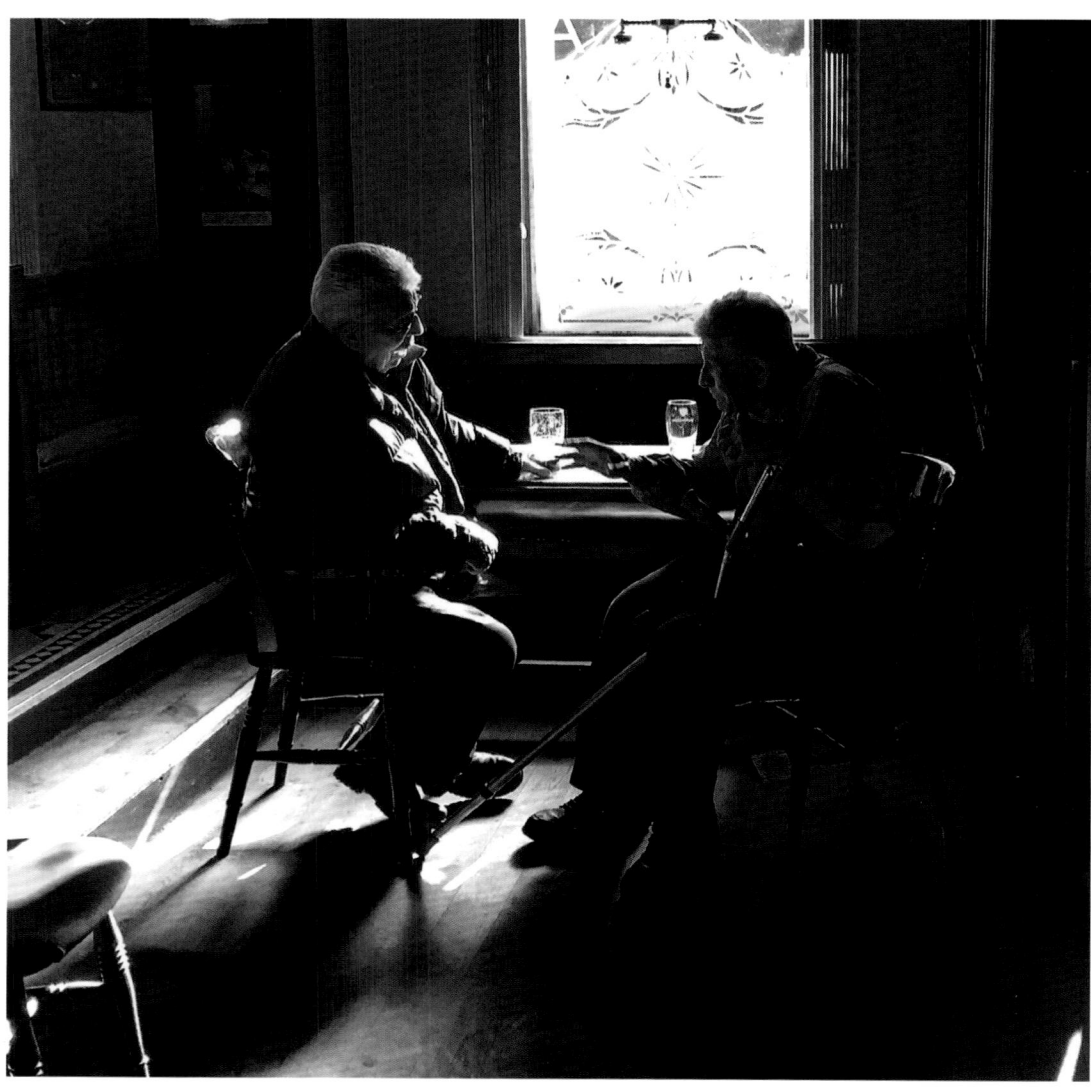

Tip

If you can't decide whether to shoot a session in black and white or color, start off with black and white (ideally capturing a Raw file and a monochrome JPEG simultaneously). Later on, if you feel that color might add to the story, use the color image.

Above: You sometimes need the power of black and white to enhance the atmosphere or mood of a scene. This recent photograph of two drinkers could easily have been taken 50 years ago.

Focal length: 40mm

Aperture: f/2.2

Shutter speed: 1/100 sec.

ISO: 50

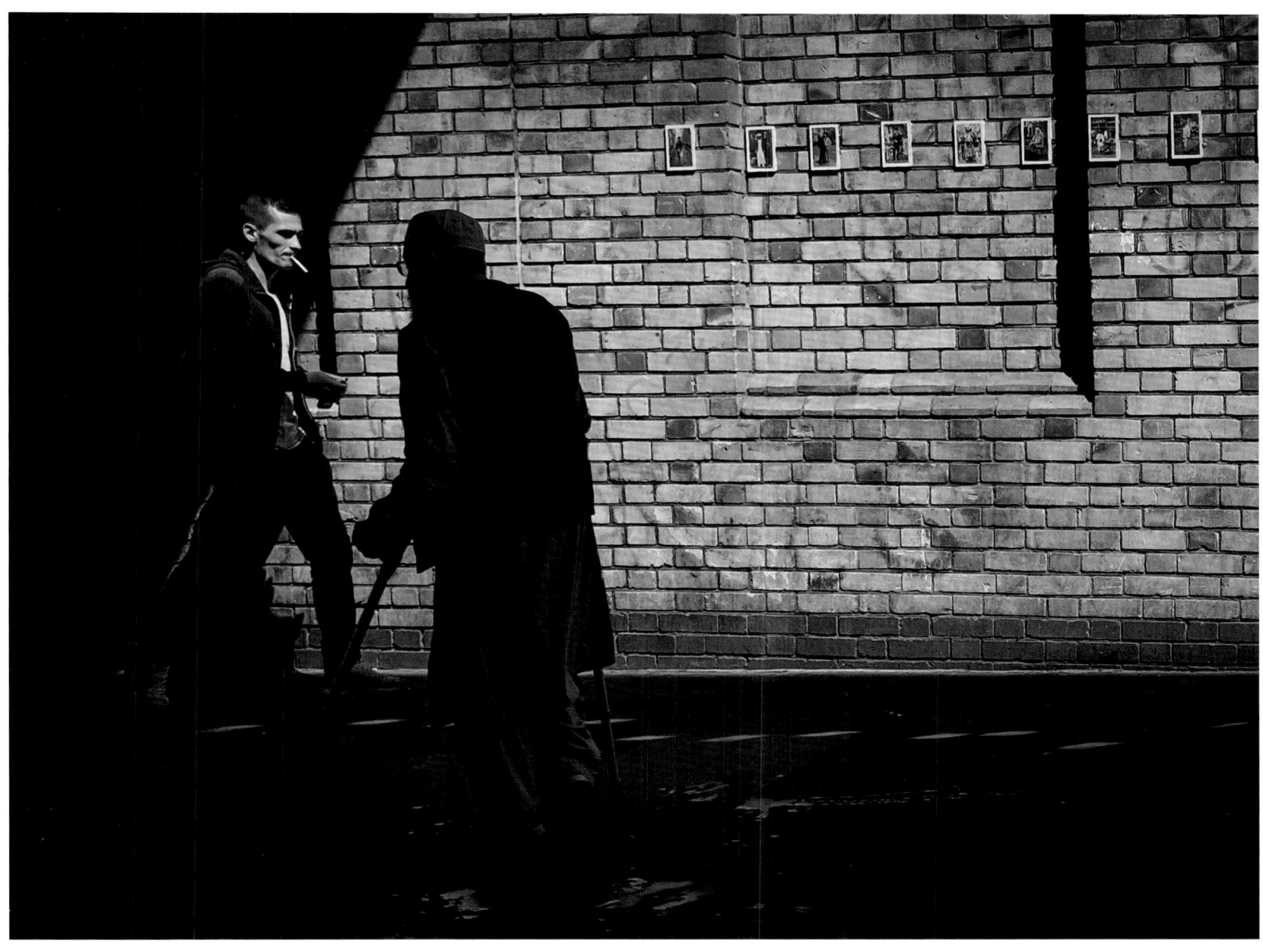

"When you photograph people in color, you photograph their clothes. But when you photograph people in black and white, you photograph their souls!"

—Ted Grant

Above: Black-and-white images are often more evocative than color shots: they invite you to question or think about their content and narrative.

Focal length: 28mm

Aperture: f/13

Shutter speed: 1/125 sec.

ISO: 5000

Low Light

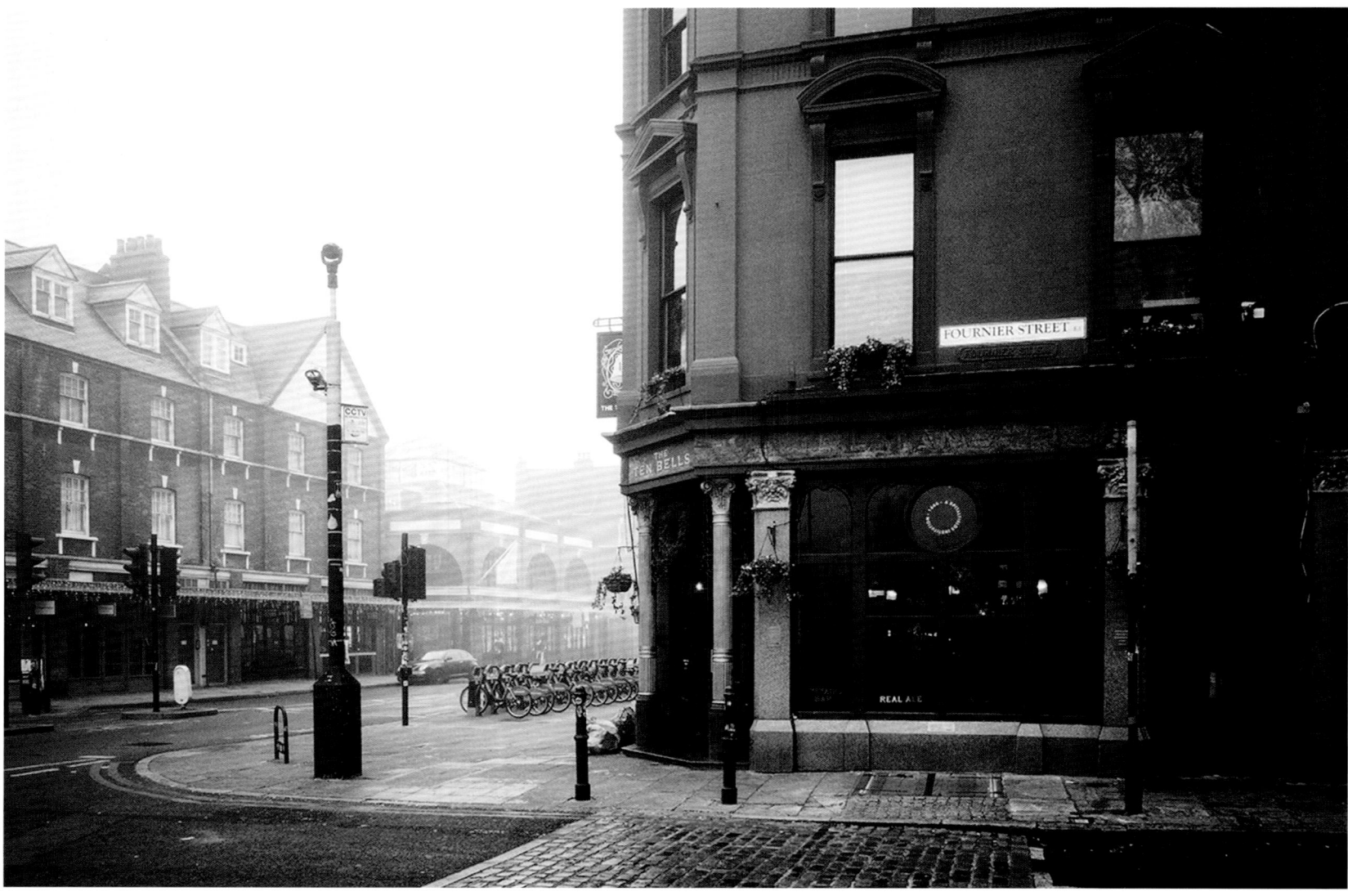

The hours between dusk and dawn can provide street photographers with some magical possibilities. Just think of all the types of interesting and colorful sources of light in any town or city: neon signs, store windows, restaurants, car and bus lights, and even the moonlight. Urban environments have a completely different complexion when viewed after dark—everything looks different and people will often behave differently as well.

Then think of the subject matter itself: people coming out of bars, getting into taxis, life through bus windows, scenes in cafés and bars, the movement of traffic—not to mention the darker side of urban life. There is enough raw material around you to make a low-light shooting expedition very worthwhile. However, you will need to deploy some techniques that are different to those you use for normal daylight shooting.

Above: Shooting in the early morning mist can add an air of mystery to a low-light scene.

Focal length: 28mm

Aperture: f/13

Shutter speed: 1/125 sec.

ISO: 5000

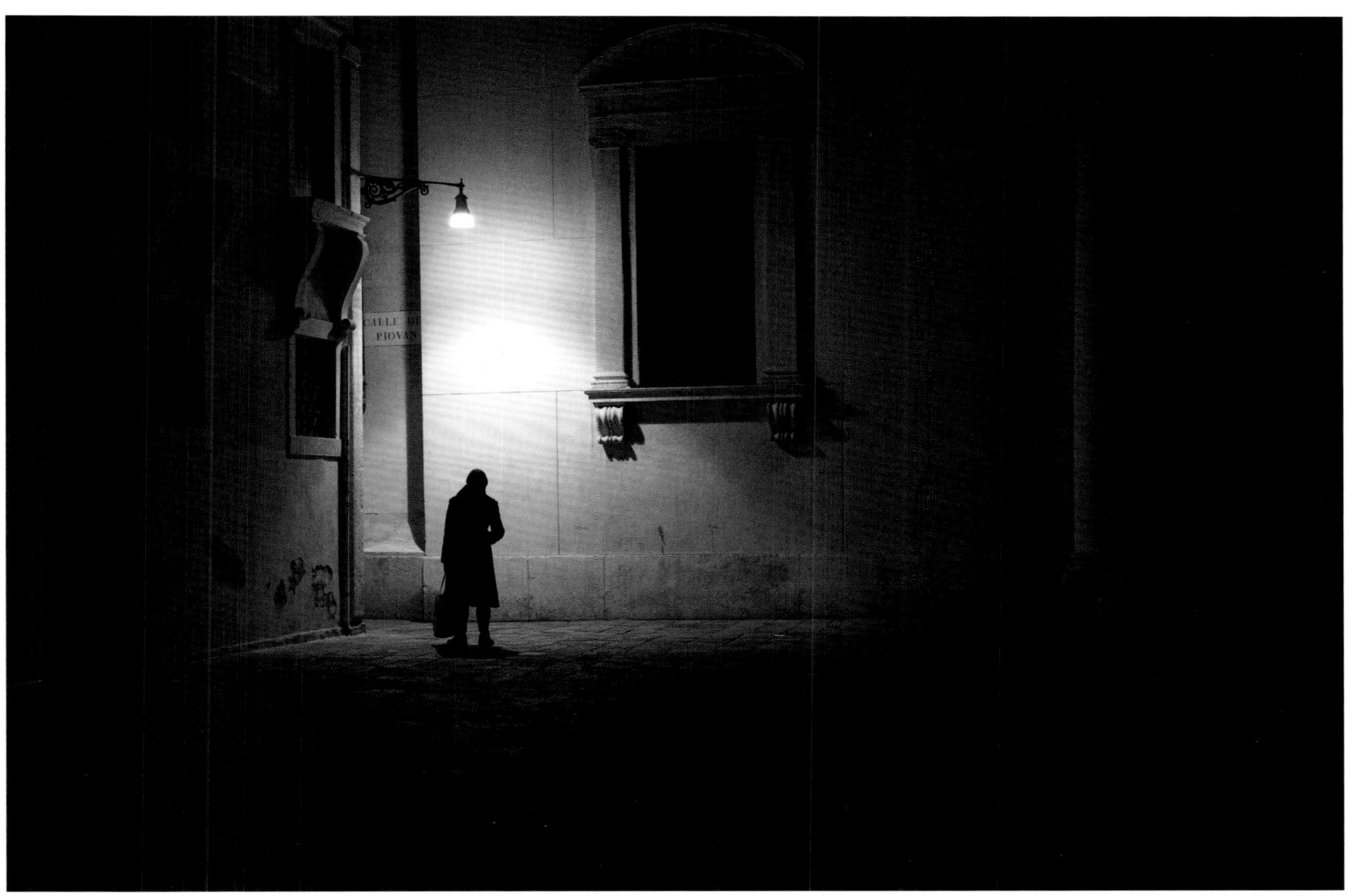

Chase The Light

As with daylight shooting, your first consideration should be the main light sources in a scene. A great starting point is to find an attractive—or good quality—light source, then stick around and observe the life that goes on around it. Like a moth, you should be drawn to the light. Once you have found your spot, look carefully at how this light reacts with your subjects. Do you need to find a better position?

While lurking in the shadows may seem a little creepy, be mindful of the fact that you probably want to shoot candidly and be unobserved. Also be aware that there may be other people lurking in the shadows with rather less honorable intentions, so keep your wits about you and always pay heed to your personal safety and to that of your gear.

Above: In situations like this, when the light sources are weak, you'll need to open up your aperture. Here it was perfectly acceptable to do so because most of the subject matter was on the same plane and depth of field wasn't required.

Focal length: 43mm
Aperture: f/3.2
Shutter speed: 1/100 sec.
ISO: 6400

Talking of shadows, think about shooting figures emerging from dark spaces, silhouetted against brighter areas; maybe aim to create an air of mystery or intrigue.

Then look at the lights themselves. Is there an opportunity for some interesting abstract work—maybe by involving car light trails or by achieving a bokeh effect by throwing colored lights shimmering in the distance completely out of focus?

Below: Always favor noise over blur by setting a high ISO value, particularly when your subject is moving. Also, don't become too obsessive about sharpness, as it will strangle your low-light creativity.

Focal length: 43mm

Aperture: f/2

Shutter speed: 1/250 sec.

ISO: 1250

Focusing

When shooting in low light, you should consider focusing manually for two reasons: firstly, with autofocus the camera will take too long to focus and will hunt for the correct focus point; secondly, it will probably need to deploy the camera's AF assist beam, which will draw attention to you unnecessarily.

The answer is to focus manually. Pre-focus on a point at which your subject is likely to be (if they are not there already) and set a small aperture that will give you a large depth of field (and therefore a margin for focusing error).

Maximum Sharpness

A sharp image is better than a blurred one, no matter how much grain or noise there is, so your priority should be to freeze the action with a sufficiently fast shutter speed. This will have an inevitable consequence on the ISO setting, which will need to be high. If possible, try to maintain an aperture in the region of f/8 (possibly f/5.6) and don't worry if you need to set what seems to be an unnaturally high ISO—a little bit of noise in a low-light street shot, particularly in black and white, can be quite atmospheric.

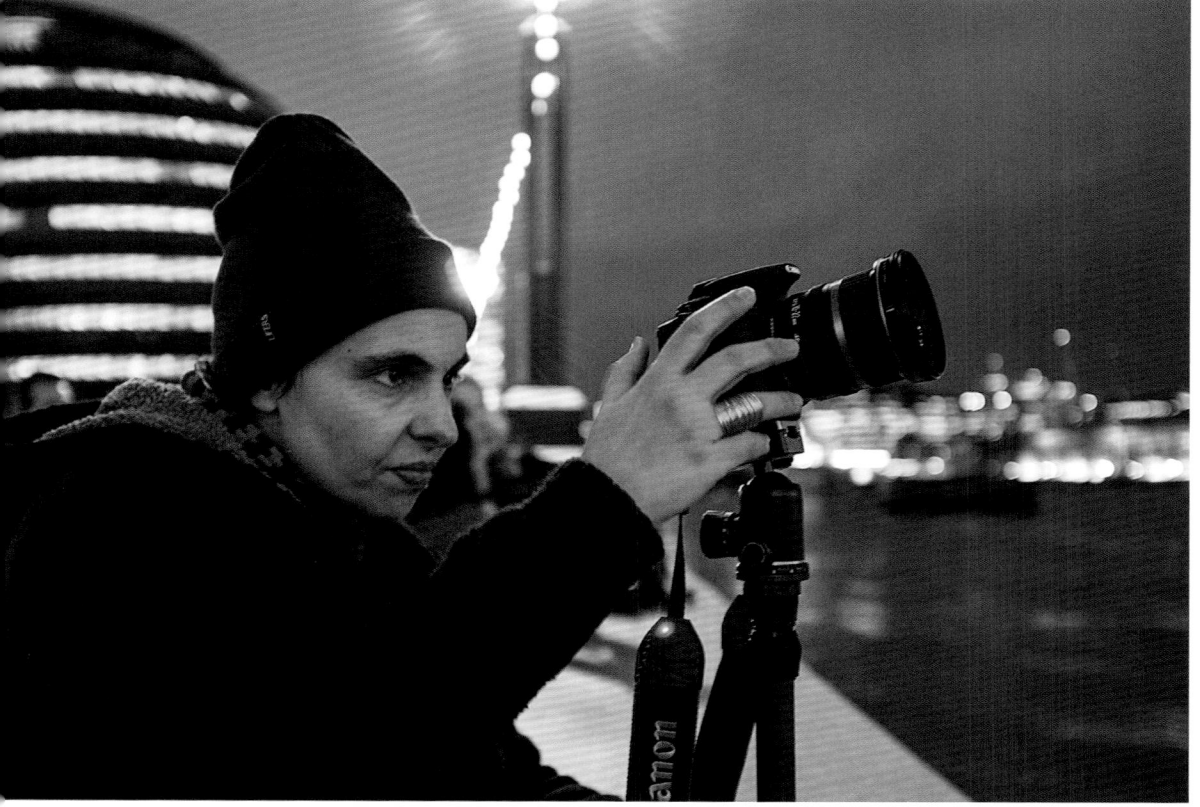

SAFETY TIPS

There's no need to feel uncomfortable when shooting at night, but you can follow some simple guidelines to keep yourself as safe as possible:

- Wear dark clothing and don't look like a photographer
- Take a friend with you
- Be inconspicuous, but not furtive
- Don't stay in one place for too long
- Don't make eye contact with anyone
- Try to keep to well-populated areas
- Take the bare minimum of kit
- Turn off your camera's LCD screen and use the viewfinder
- Turn off the AF assist beam and any camera noises, such as bleeps
- Always know your exit route
- Make sure your shoes are suitable for running!

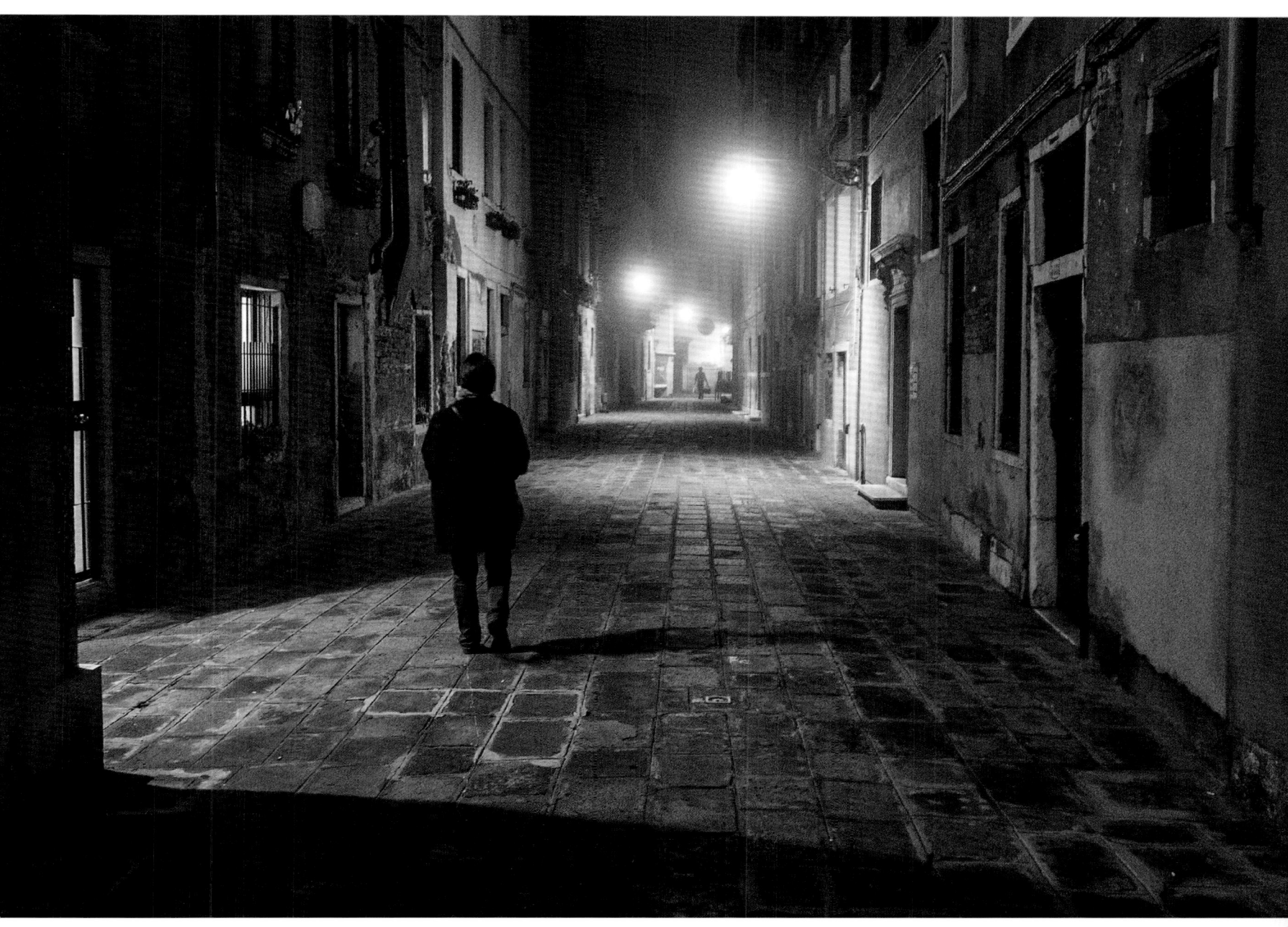

Above: A shutter speed in the region of 1/20 sec. is probably the slowest speed you should consider when shooting handheld in low light (depending on focal length). If you need more light, increase your ISO instead.

Focal length: 24mm

Aperture: f/1.7

Shutter speed: 1/20 sec.

ISO: 1600

Assignment 1: Alone

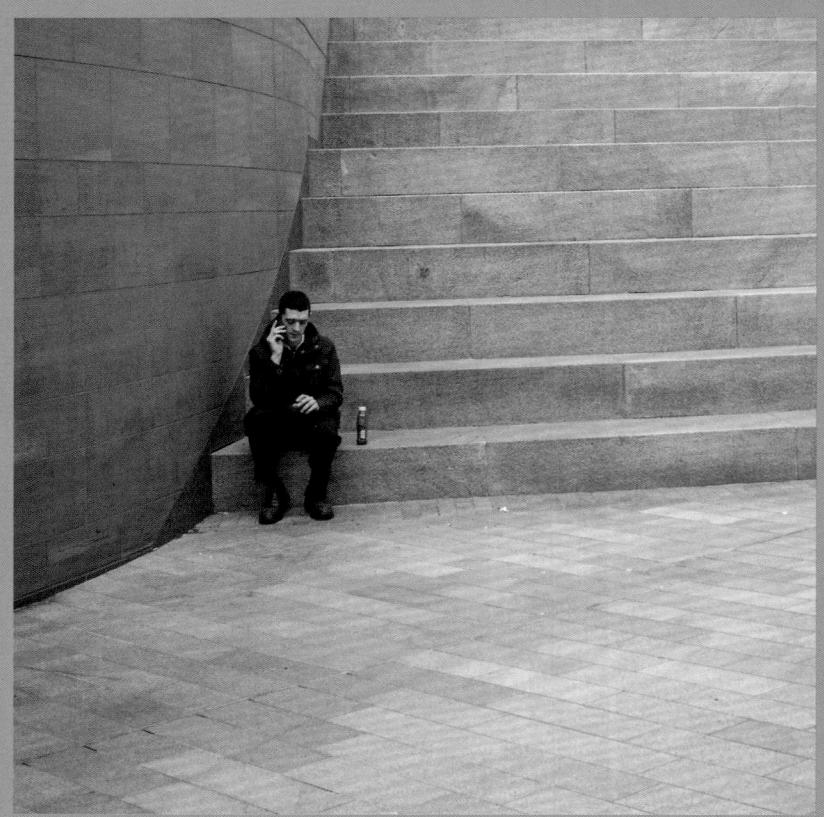

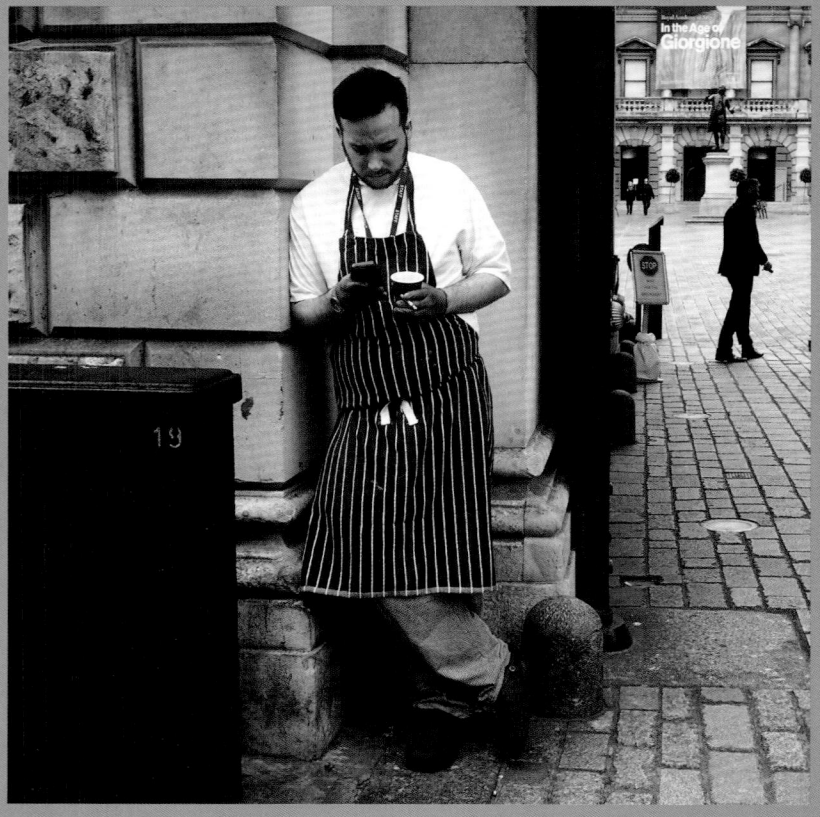

The Challenge

Despite the hustle and bustle, towns and cities can be lonely places, with people on their own and in a hurry, particularly during commuting times. People are always busy and often lost in their own worlds, interacting with nothing except a phone, tablet, newspaper, or book.

Your challenge with this assignment is to capture the loneliness and the solitude of city life: images of single people who are self-absorbed and not interacting with any outside stimulus.

LOCATION

Any busy town or city: a business district is ideal. Try early morning and late afternoon when the shadows are long and people are rushing to or from work.

Above left:

Focal length: 35mm

Aperture: f/1.8

Shutter speed: 1/1600 sec.

ISO: 1250

Above:

Focal length: 35mm

Aperture: f/8

Shutter speed: 1/100 sec.

ISO: 800

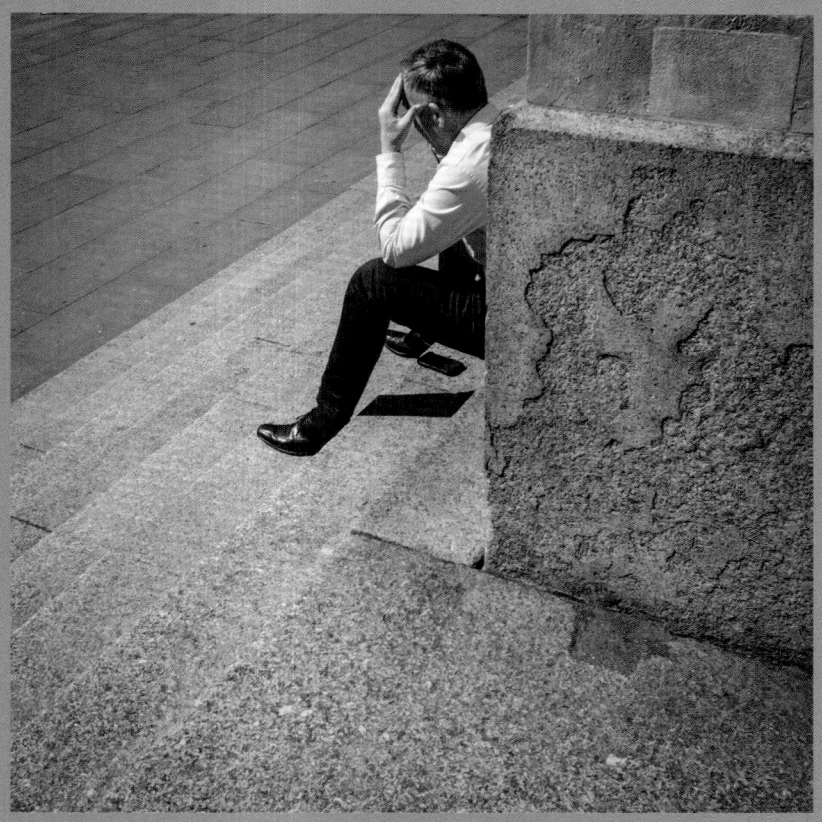

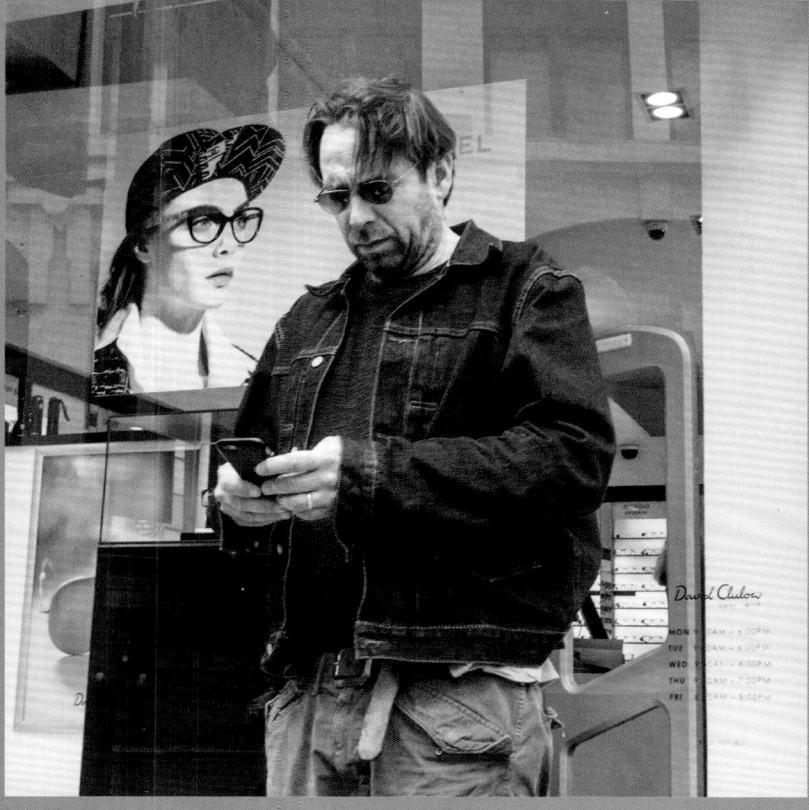

TECHNIQUES

- Try shooting this assignment in black and white, with bright whites and deep blacks.

- Look for uncluttered backgrounds to make your subject stand out; aim for a strong figure-to-ground ratio.

- Practice composing your shots around the straight lines you will almost certainly encounter in the manmade environment.

TOP TIPS

- Look for strong contrasts between light and dark tones.

- Seek out leading lines and make use of them wherever possible.

- Be wary of any horizontal and vertical lines in your images and ensure they are straight.

- Keep an eye open for people using phones or tablets. A lot of the time people are not aware of their behavior when using these devices, and often make funny gestures.

Above left:
Focal length: 35mm
Aperture: f/5
Shutter speed: 1/1000 sec.
ISO: 1250

Above:
Focal length: 35mm
Aperture: f/8
Shutter speed: 1/320 sec.
ISO: 800

Assignment 2: It's All A Blur

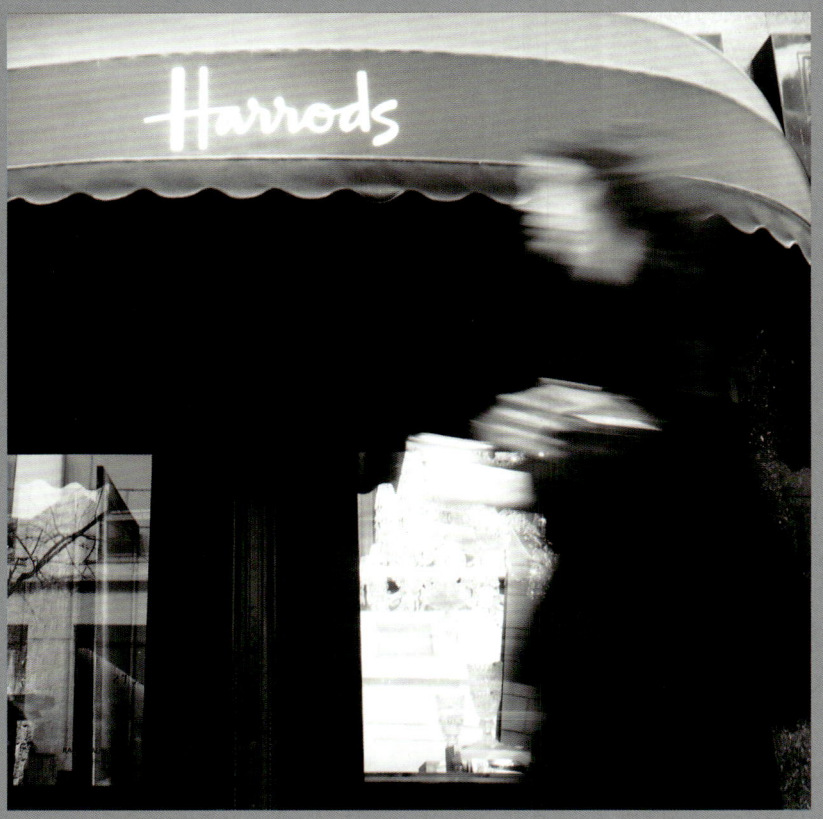

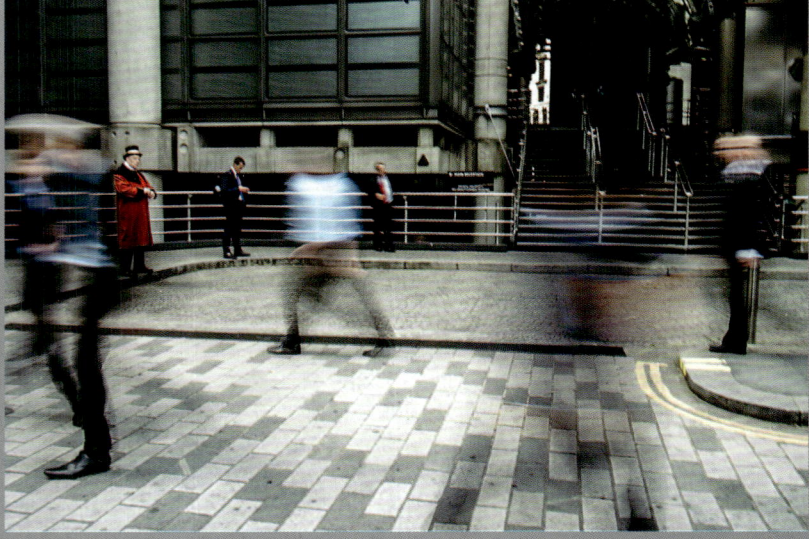

Left:

Focal length: 35mm

Aperture: f13

Shutter speed: 1/13 sec.

ISO: 800

Above:

Focal length: 28mm

Aperture: f/16

Shutter speed: 1/4 sec.

ISO: 200

The Challenge

We often associate the word "blurry" with a mistake. However, placing a blurred subject against a sharp background is regularly used in street photography to add a sense of movement and drama to an otherwise uninteresting scene.

Your challenge with this assignment is to produce a cohesive set of images following a similar theme: for example, *The Ghosts of New York City* (blurred people in NYC dressed in light clothing against a dark background), or *Soho by Night* (abstract shots of night life made by deliberately moving the camera during exposure).

LOCATION

You need a location where there is going to be some sort of moving element, whether that's people, traffic, or something else that catches your eye. Cities during rush hour are a great hunting ground, as are train and bus depots and shopping malls.

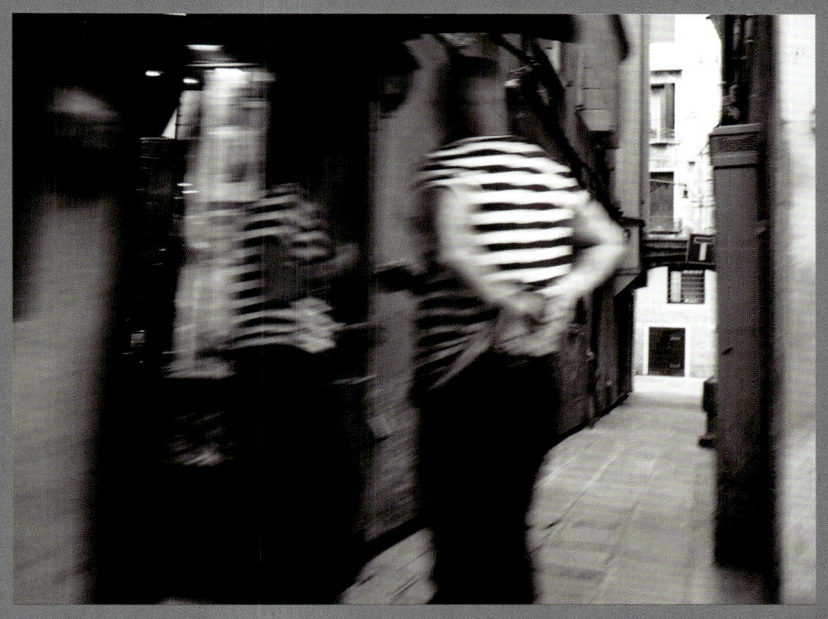

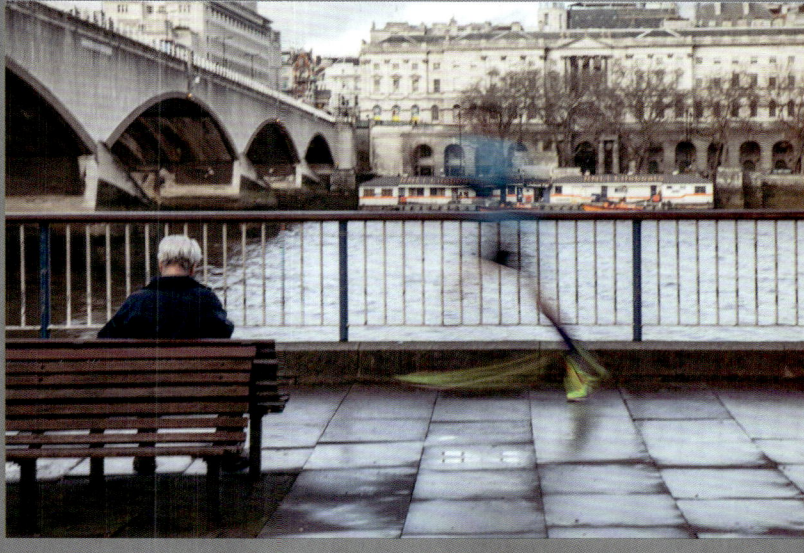

TECHNIQUES

- This assignment is all about the shutter speed. With subjects moving at varying speeds and in different directions you'll need to experiment to find the most suitable speed.

- Switch your camera to Shutter Priority mode and select a slow shutter speed in the region of 1/4–1/10 sec.

- Practice holding your camera steady while taking the picture: most street photographers don't use tripods, but for support you can try leaning against a wall or resting your camera on a ledge or railing.

- Think about the separation between subject and background; a strong figure-to-ground ratio often delivers the best results.

TOP TIPS

- With longer exposures, a small lens is best; the longer and heavier the lens, the more difficult it is to handhold your camera at speeds below 1/30 sec.

- If you're using Manual mode, don't forget to reduce the ISO to avoid overexposure.

- For a very arty, abstract image, deliberately move the camera during exposure. This works really well with bright colors, strong lines, or lights.

- Try shooting at night with car light trails or the movement of people under street lighting.

- This exercise is a process of trial and error— don't expect to get it right first time!

Above left:
Focal length: 28mm
Aperture: f/5
Shutter speed: 1/10 sec.
ISO: 800

Above:
Focal length: 70mm
Aperture: f/22
Shutter speed: 1/8 sec.
ISO: 100

Chapter 3
Inspiration

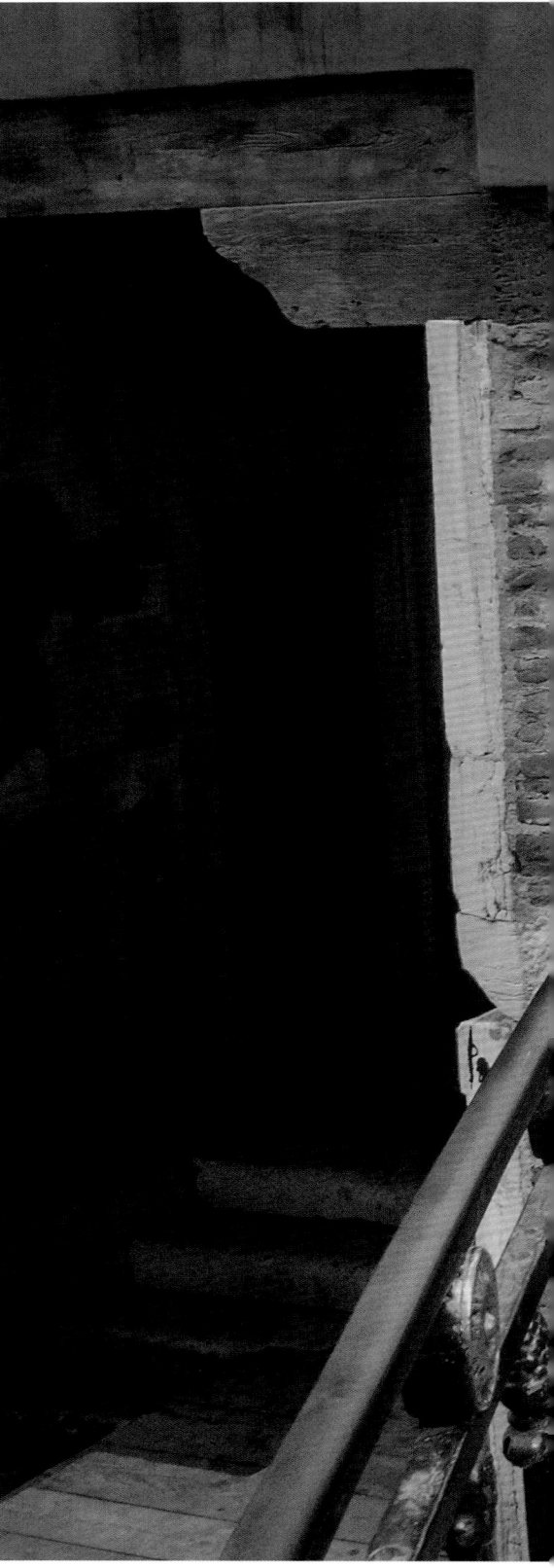

We all find inspiration for street photography in different ways; it could come from our own existing interests or passions, from other photographers, or perhaps as a result of needing to challenge ourselves and push some boundaries. A film, an exhibition or a lecture, a book, a painting, or even a dream could inspire you. There is also no shame in taking inspiration from other photographers; in fact, that's how many of the masters of street photography started out.

So what inspires you? Think about what you like or dislike, what stirs your emotions, what makes you feel happy or angry, what makes you want to press the shutter. What sort of photographs do you enjoy looking at? What sort excite you? Write down the elements you believe come together to make a good street photograph and use these as the starting point.

Right: A Venetian gondolier rubs his head in disbelief at the amount of luggage these tourists are carrying. We are often inspired by places we visit on vacation—especially charismatic cities, such as Venice, Italy.

Focal length: 28mm

Aperture: f/16

Shutter speed: 1/60 sec.

ISO: 2500

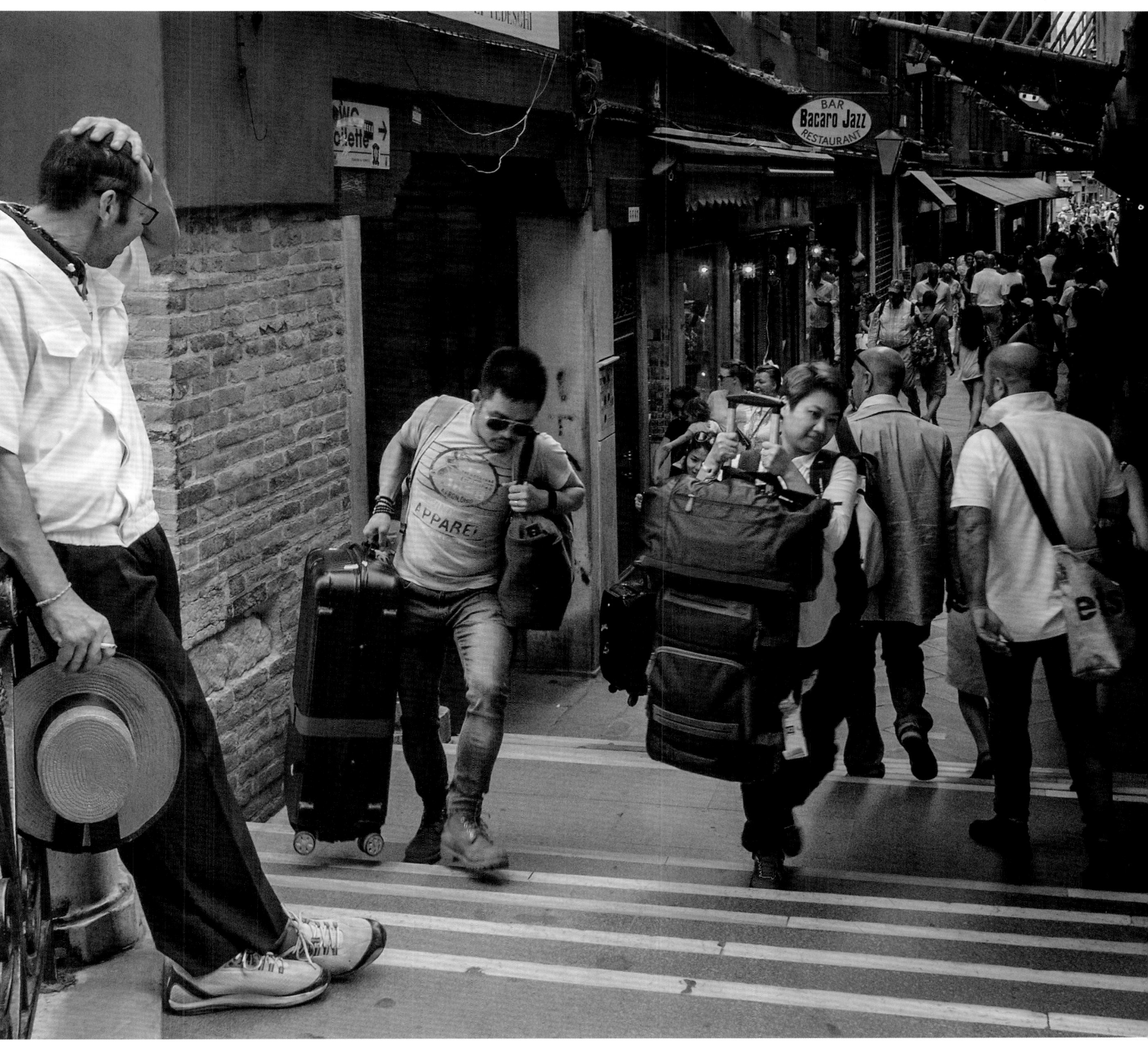

Finding & Developing Your Style

Have you ever thought, flicking through web pages, that a great deal of street photography looks the same and is lacking something? We see endless shots of strangers walking toward the camera, offering the viewer no insight or narrative. Sometimes, however, you will come across images that really stand out as "special." They contain a certain engaging element that compels you to look more deeply into them and they are probably the work of a photographer who has developed a distinctive personal style.

One issue we face is the sheer volume of street photography out there and it can be difficult to cut through the clutter to get to the really good work. In some ways, Instagram has a lot to answer for and a quick search using the hashtag #streetphotography will reveal a lot of images which are anything but street photography! This can lead to the uninitiated being sent in the wrong direction in the belief that, for example, a fluffy kitten sitting on a wall represents good street photography.

You should, therefore, think long and hard about developing your own style, which could take one of many forms. The first thing to consider is a general direction of travel, which will probably fall into one of three broad categories:

1 **An observational approach;** often witty or ironic and usually based on a "moment" (see Joel Meyerowitz, Garry Winogrand, Matt Stuart for inspiration).

2 **An aesthetic approach;** based on the visual or artistic appeal of the imagery—it could be about composition, color, atmosphere, or abstraction (see Saul Leiter, Harry Gruyaert, or Olga Karlovac for inspiration).

3 **A narrative/storytelling approach;** where the imagery is based on a compelling narrative (there is no better example than Robert Frank's seminal work, *The Americans*).

Next, and more specifically, your voice could have its foundations in the subject matter, such as people shot at close range (in the manner of Bruce Gilden). It could be based on a square format, or using vivid colors, or monochrome, or with a particular postproduction twist; you may favor a particular viewpoint, such as shooting from the hip or from above; you may like to shoot into the sun, or with strong sunlight behind you; you may choose to shoot only in the rain. Many street photographers use wit as a key element in their images and you may choose to have a humorous angle as the defining factor of your style.

You are probably getting the picture that the possibilities are endless. Some photographers have a very clear vision of their style from the outset, while for others it takes time—perhaps many years—for ideas to percolate and for a distinctive style to develop.

However, don't lose sight of the fact that street photography is all about self-expression. The images you take are for you, so they must appeal to *you*. Don't worry about what others may think—please yourself rather than following the herd!

12 STREET PHOTOGRAPHERS YOU SHOULD KNOW

Look to some of the great street photographers for ideas and inspiration. Here are 12 masters of the art to whet your appetite:

Henri Cartier-Bresson
Elliott Erwitt
Robert Frank
Lee Friedlander
Helen Levitt
Bruce Gilden
Saul Leiter
Vivian Maier
Joel Meyerowitz
Martin Parr
Garry Winogrand
Alex Webb

Right: An identifier of a photographer's style can be something as simple as producing all their work in a square format.

Focal length: 50mm
Aperture: f/8
Shutter speed: 1/400 sec.
ISO: 1000

What Makes A Good Street Photograph?

The answer depends on how you define "good." Street photography is highly subjective and what may be a good picture to one person could be dreadful to another. So, what elements could be brought into play for an image to be considered good rather than average?

The subject matter is, of course, critical. Nobody wants to see boring pictures of random strangers doing nothing in particular, or street scenes where there is very little happening. The image content itself needs to evoke some emotion, whether that's laughter, joy, anger, sadness, disbelief, or something stronger, and there has to be some emotional response from the viewer, however small. Unlike, say, landscape photography, this quality is far more important than striving for technical perfection, and street photography should make the viewer think, wonder, question, or feel something. Some of the world's greatest images are technically poor, but their power is striking.

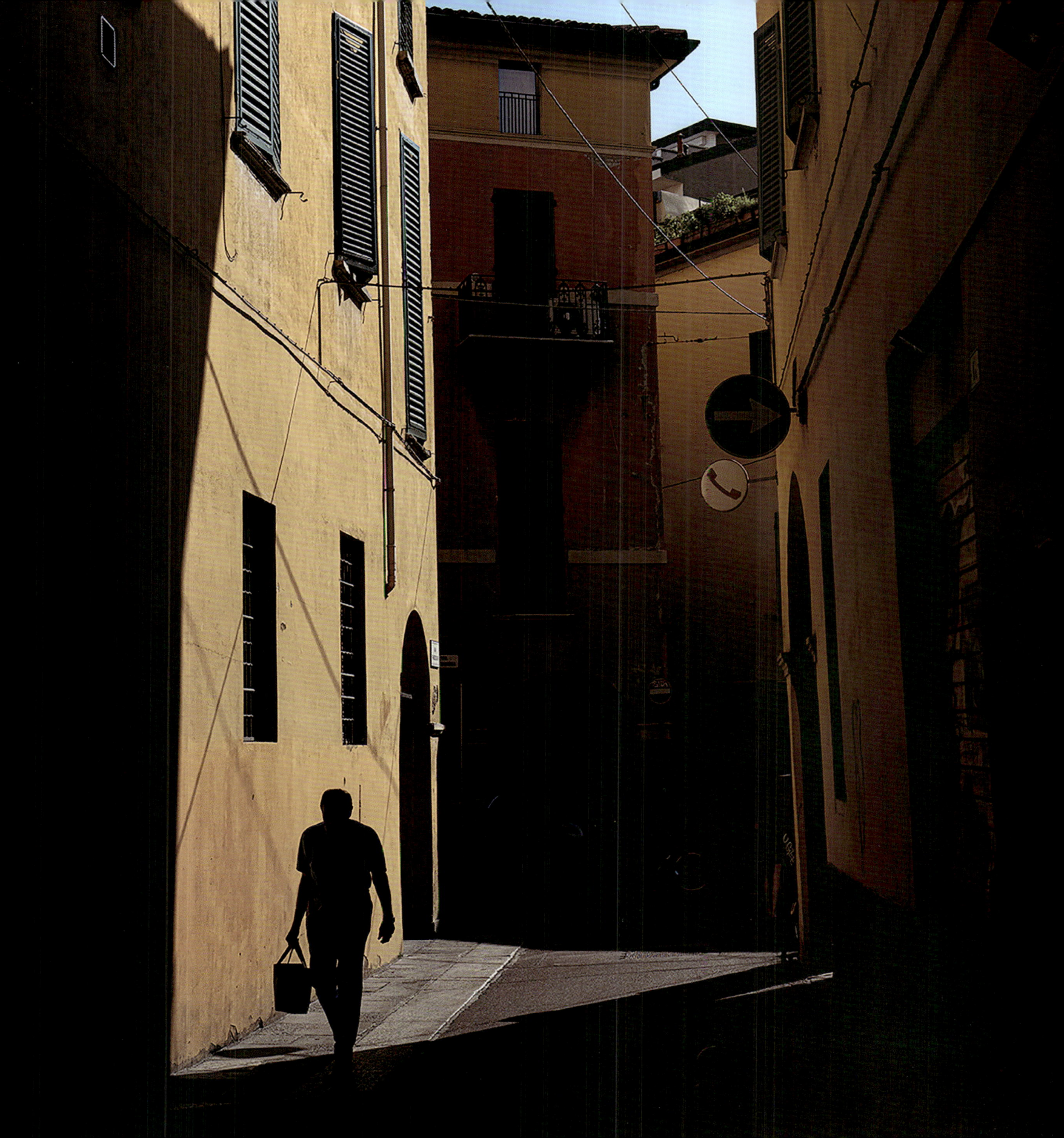

Develop A Project Mentality

Many street photographers struggle to find sufficiently interesting material to photograph and so resort to randomness. You've probably seen many thousands of street photographs on the internet that are of random people, in random places, doing random things. There is no sense of narrative, no theme, and no connection between the images; there's no "visual glue" to bind them together in any meaningful way.

Of course, that isn't always a bad thing. When you venture out onto the streets you might hope to come across what Henri Cartier-Bresson defined as the decisive moment—that split second when you get a once-in-a-lifetime opportunity for an unrepeatable shot—but those elusive moments can be few and far between. More often you will find yourself reacting quickly to what is going on around you.

However, it is worth noting that virtually all successful street photographers tend to have a project-based approach. They may have one, five, or even 10 projects on the go at any one time and they focus their mind and their creative energy into creating bodies of work that have a sense of direction and purpose: in this regard, projects are the street photographer's friend.

Above: Being easy and cheap to produce, zines are a popular way of bringing a project to life.

WHAT IS A PROJECT?

A project is a collection of images—a distinct body of work—that is generated around a specific theme. It allows you to build a strong narrative, using images to tell your story. There are three very good reasons why you should develop a project mindset:

- Projects give you focus and direction. On days when you can find little inspiration, or when there is nothing happening, they will give you the impetus to go out and shoot in a fairly organized manner.

- They can provide you with a clear end game, whether in the form of a photo book, a zine, a set of prints, an exhibition, a web gallery, or a blog. This should spur you on to produce a tangible (and worthy) body of work.

- They allow you to tell a story. While it is possible to tell a story using a single image, think about how much more powerful that story can be if it's told using a cohesive set of images that have been edited and sequenced in a logical order.

HOW LONG SHOULD A PROJECT TAKE?

How long is a piece of string? In reality, it doesn't matter how long a project takes. When you embark on a project, you won't have any idea when it will end, but you will usually know when you get there. Projects can take 10 days or 10 years to complete, so try to visualize the end result and work toward that goal. Write down ideas for general themes or specific images for your project.

WHERE DO IDEAS COME FROM?

Coming up with ideas for street photography projects may not come easily, so a good starting point is to look at what others have done in the past. I'm not suggesting you copy other photographers' ideas, simply that you look to them for inspiration.

For example, Stephen McLaren published a book entitled *The Crash* (Hoxton Mini Press, 2018), which was a study of the financial crisis that hit the City of London in 2008. While it would be impossible to undertake an identical project, you would almost certainly get some ideas and inspiration for your own project by flicking through a book like this.

Look at the work of street photographers you admire and see how they have approached projects in terms of the subject matter, the photographic techniques used, and the sequencing and editing of the work. Use your research to inspire your own project.

Another approach to projects is to explore themes in which you have an interest outside the world of photography. If, for example, you support a charity, you could find a rich seam of opportunity in the work they do. Perhaps you have an interest in sports: a behind-the-scenes look at a local sports club could make an interesting photo story. Whatever your other interests—sport, music, food, fashion, social issues, or the arts—there is plenty of raw material out there.

Finally, explore your own archive of work for ideas. Look for trends and patterns in your work and think back to what you enjoyed shooting. You may already have the makings of a project without realizing it.

SOHO LIFE PROJECT

The following five images form part of a project entitled *Soho Life*, which aims to reflect daily life in this characterful London neighborhood. For consistency, the images are all in the same (square) format and are all in black and white. The pictures will eventually form a body of work of 60 images that will be reproduced in a book.

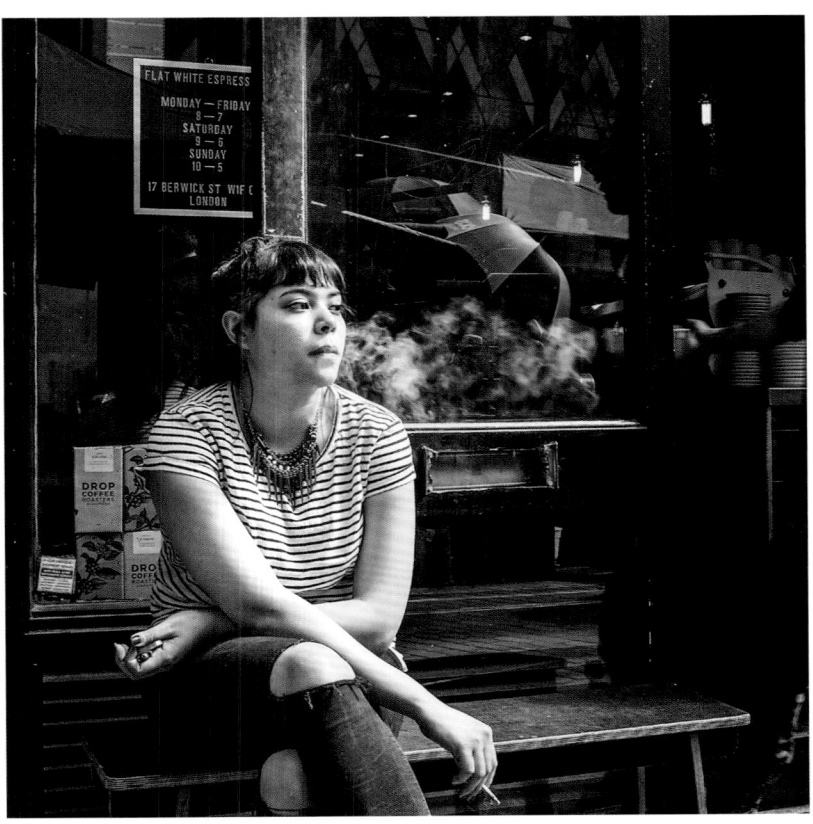

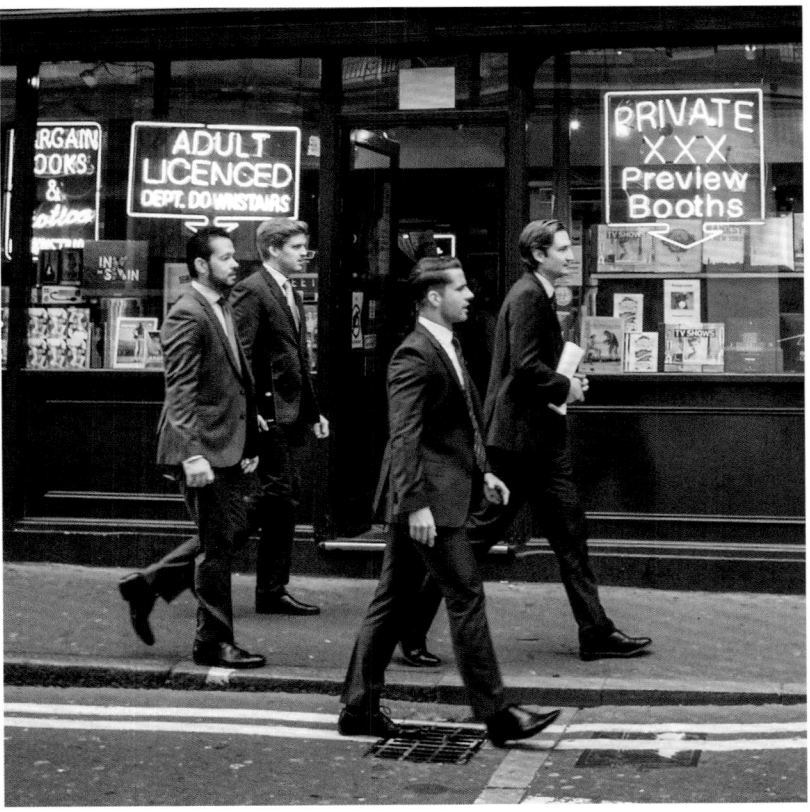

Above:

Focal length: 28mm

Aperture: f/8

Shutter speed: 1/60 sec.

ISO: 640

Above:

Focal length: 28mm

Aperture: f/8

Shutter speed: 1/170 sec.

ISO: 1600

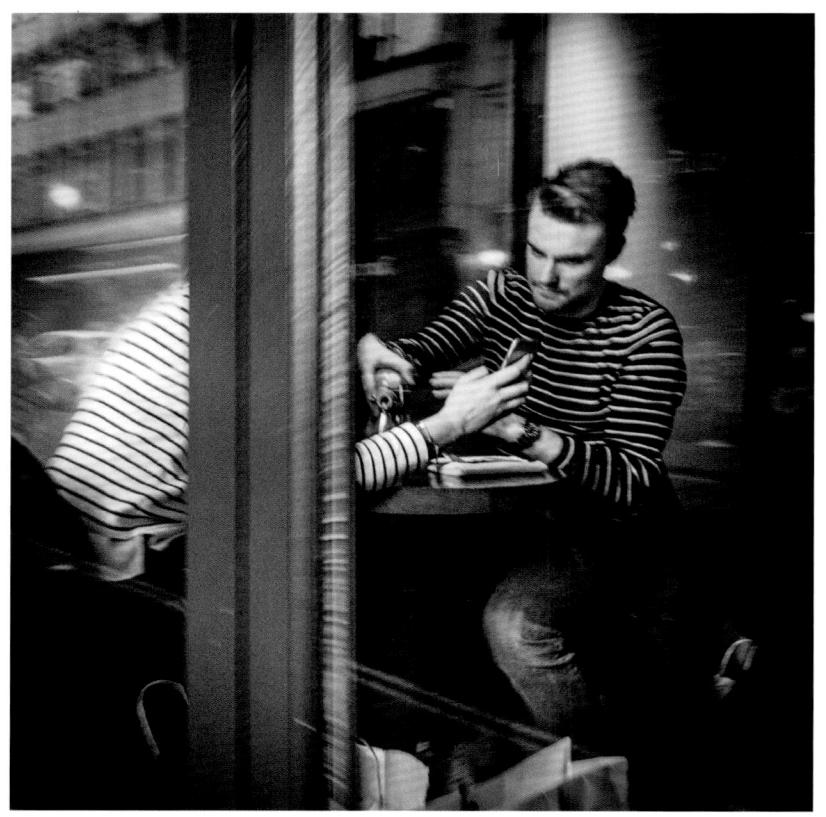

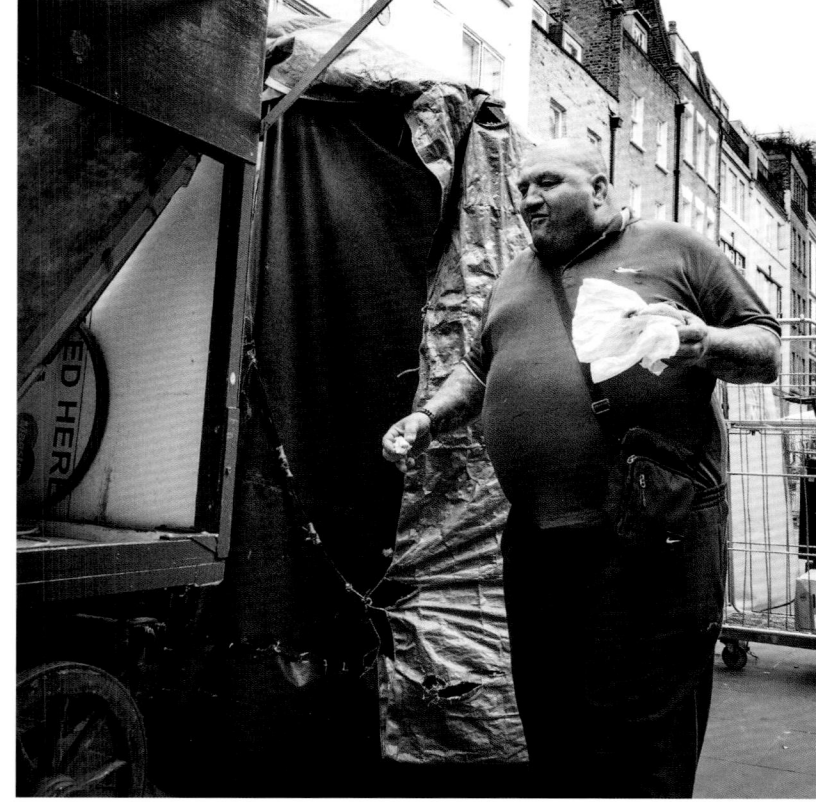

Above:
Focal length: 28mm
Aperture: f/8
Shutter speed: 1/25 sec.
ISO: 1600

Above:
Focal length: 24mm
Aperture: f/8
Shutter speed: 1/500 sec.
ISO: 1000

The Result

One of the most satisfying outcomes of a project is to allow others to see your work. There is a real sense of achievement to see photographs that you have taken in a gallery, on a website, or in the pages of a book. Here are a few ways in which you can show off your project:

- **Exhibitions**. Smaller galleries are often keen to exhibit the work of new photographers, particularly those whose work is contemporary or avant garde. Speak to the owner of your local coffee shop or restaurant; they may be very pleased to have something interesting to display on their walls—and you might even get some print sales out of it.

- **A web presence**. With web space now being so easy and cheap to set up, it is very feasible to set up a site to show or promote a specific project. Alternatively, establish the project as a standalone gallery on your existing website.

- **Self-publishing**. Online and on-demand printing has never been more accessible and, for the price of a few drinks, you can see the fruits of your labors in a zine or a printed book.

- **Traditional publishing**. While it is difficult and highly competitive to get a mainstream publisher interested in your work, it is by no means impossible. Look at the smaller publishers and pitch your project to those who have an interest in, or success with, similar work.

- **Magazines** and **newspapers**. There are many thousands of publications that regularly publish

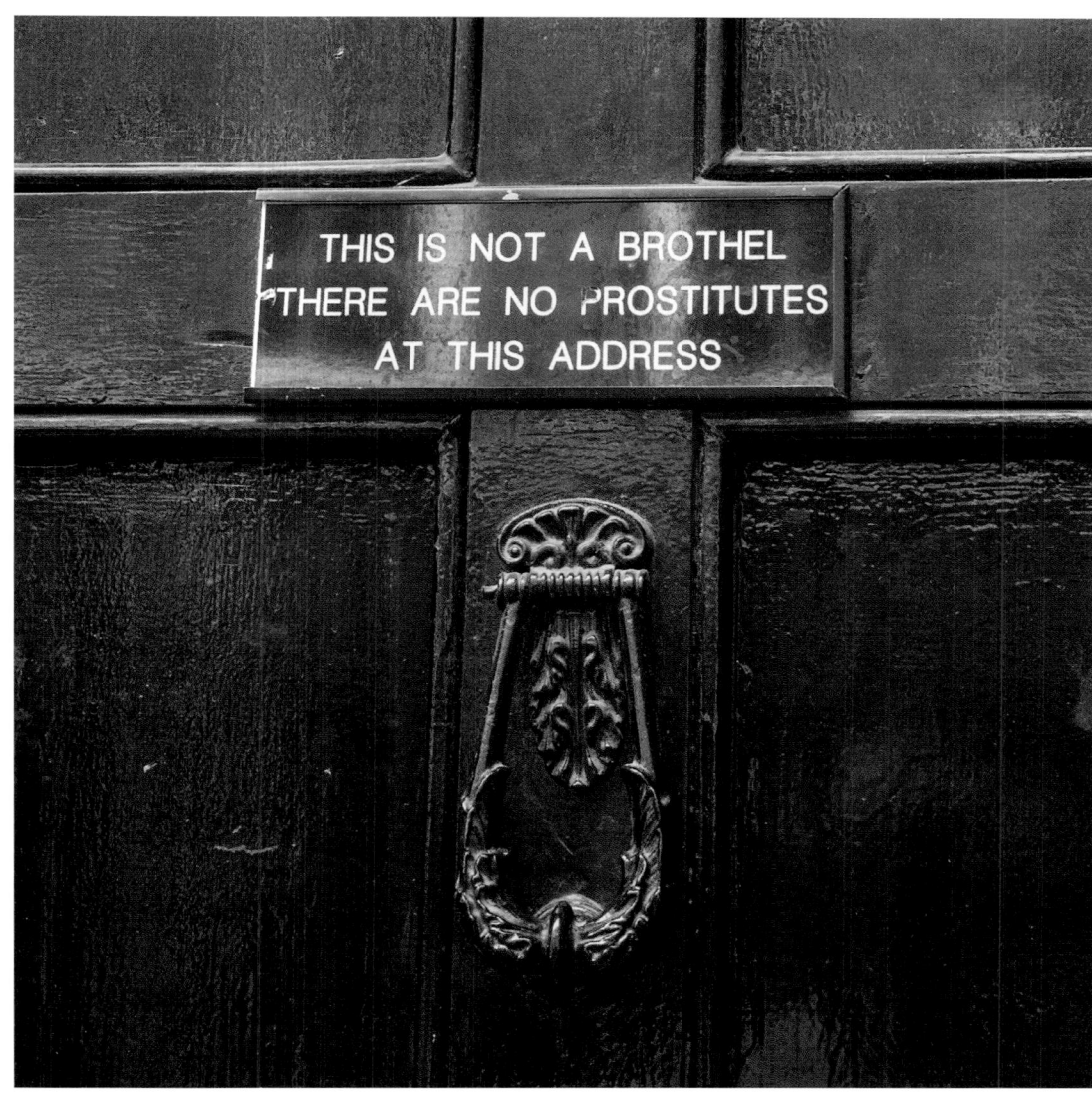

Left:
Focal length: 105mm
Aperture: f/4
Shutter speed: 1/50 sec.
ISO: 400

photographers' projects. Before pitching an idea to them, think carefully about their style, their editorial slant, and their readership, ensuring that your material is suitable.

- **Decorate your home**. What better way to show off your photography than to dedicate part of your home to it? All you need to do is paint a wall (or two) white, invest in some quality frames, and you'll soon be living in your own art gallery!

Color Or Black & White?

Look around the internet, at exhibitions, and in books about street photography, and much of the work you will see will be in black and white. In fact, when most of us think about street photography, we instinctively think "black and white." Some say that the masters of the art have brainwashed us into believing that monochrome is the only way; others, perhaps more realistically, link its popularity among street photographers to nostalgia and our desire to recreate some of the great images of the past. Some cynics would say that black and white can be a crutch for people who take poor pictures, then rescue them in postproduction.

Black and white, however, is not the only way. Color has become more acceptable since the 1970s, helped by some terrific work from the likes of Martin Parr, Jeff Mermelstein, Joel Meyerowitz, Alex Webb, and Saul Leiter. Even Vivian Maier, best known for her monochrome work, produced some striking color imagery in the 1970s and '80s.

Below: The orange tissue that forms the mannequin's head is an important part of the subject matter, as are the yellow road markings; these would be lost in monochrome.

Focal length: 28mm

Aperture: f/11

Shutter speed: 1/150 sec.

ISO: 1600

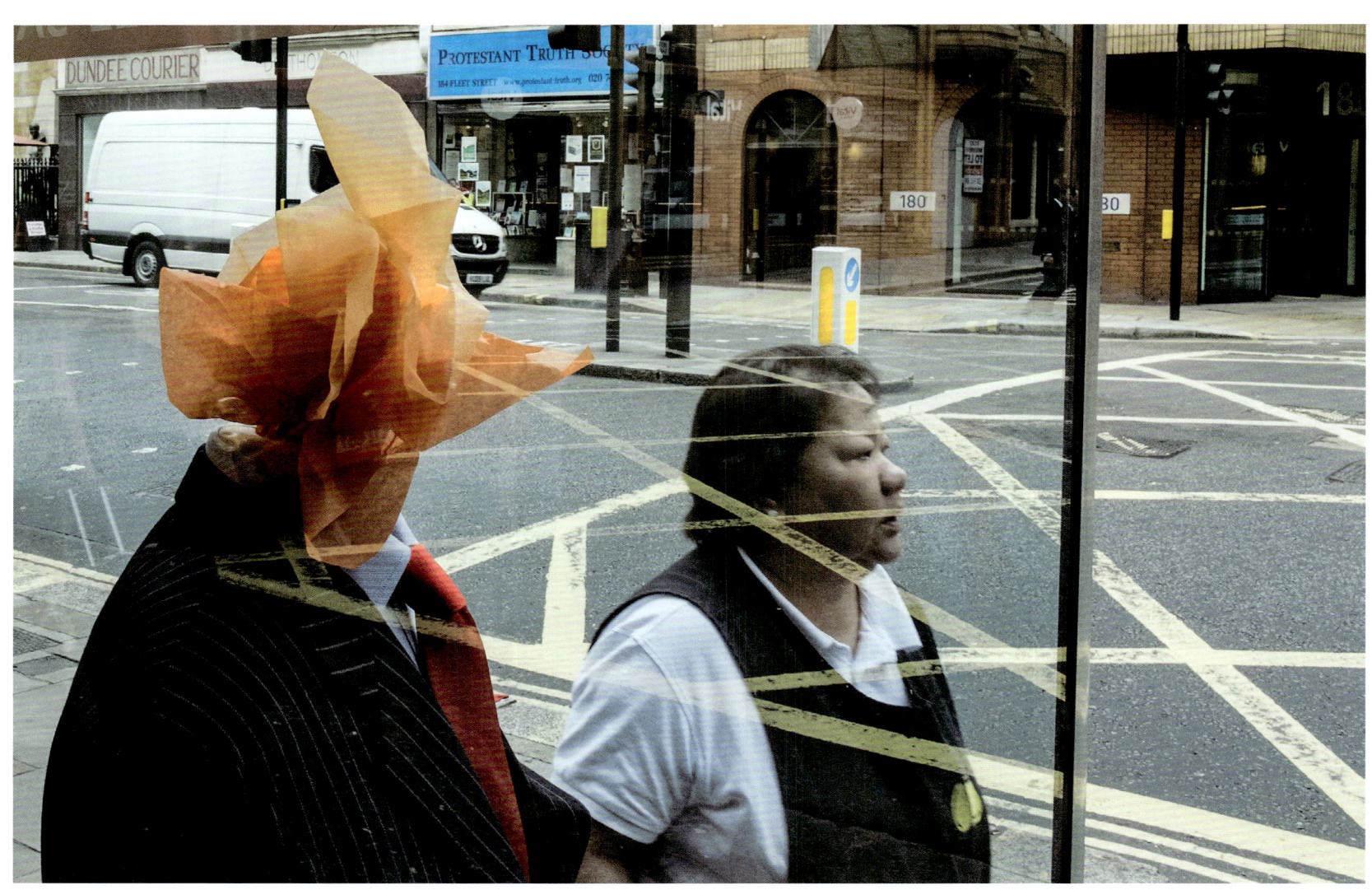

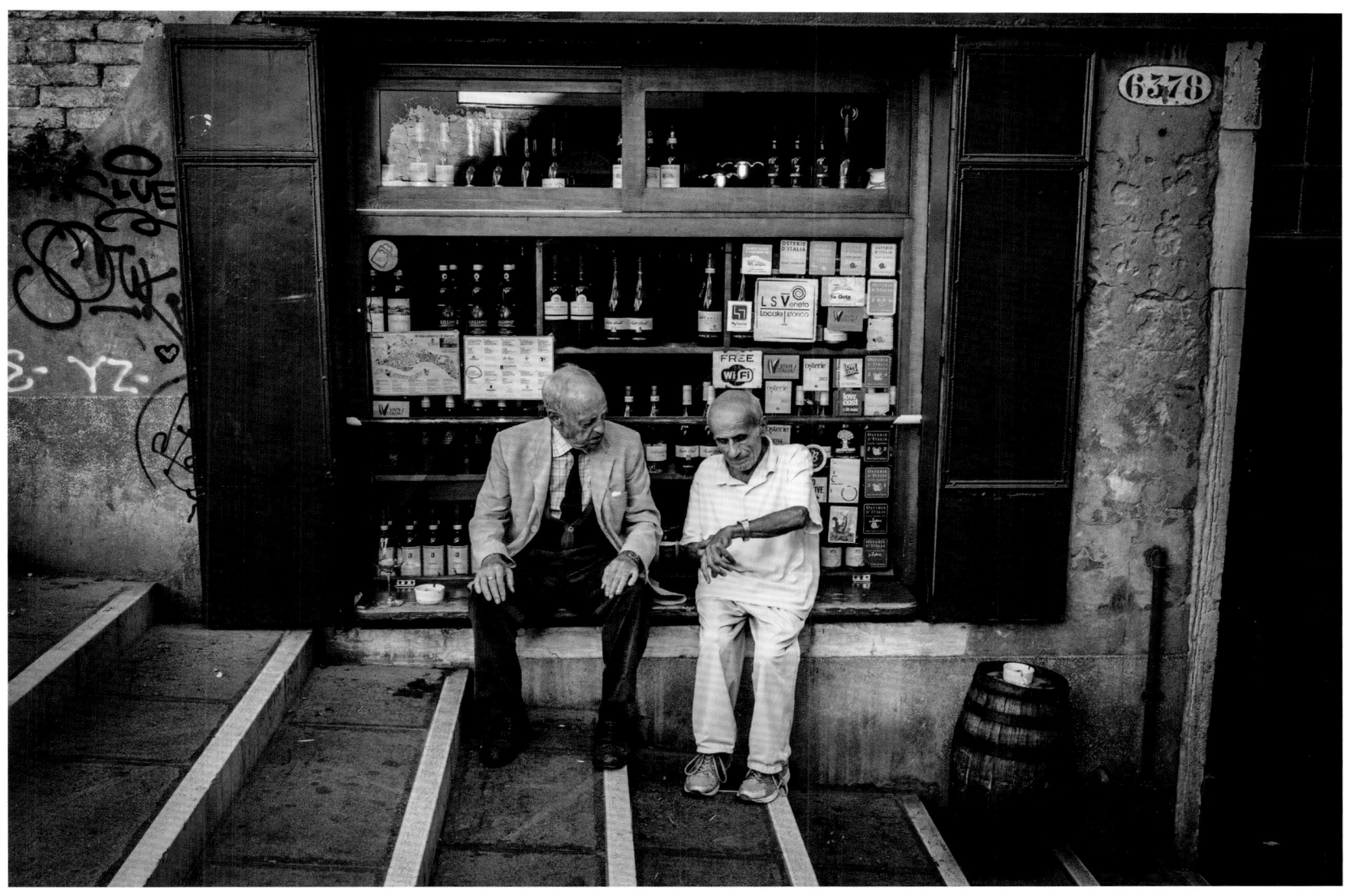

So where does that leave you? Can you shoot in color *and* black and white? Of course you can, and much depends on your personal style and what you are setting out to achieve. If you shoot Raw, the decision can be made later—some pictures will look best in color and others are made for monochrome, but you may not know which is which until you see them on a big screen. However, it is considered to be good practice to commit to either black and white or color *before* you press the shutter button—so that it's a creative choice rather than an afterthought.

While there is no reason why you shouldn't shoot in both styles, you should be wary about mixing color and monochrome in the same body of work, as it rarely looks right. Instead, spend time experimenting and start to pre-visualize your images in one style or the other.

TIP

If you shoot Raw and JPEG simultaneously, you can view the image in monochrome through the viewfinder (on a CSC) or on the camera's rear LCD (on a mirrorless camera), but will still get a high-quality (color) Raw file to process.

Above: The black-and-white treatment of this shot removed some distracting colors and invites the viewer to think about the narrative.

Focal length: 40mm

Aperture: f/11

Shutter speed: 1/160 sec.

ISO: 640

What To Shoot

Novice street photographers often set out on a mission, filled with enthusiasm and anticipation, only to be disillusioned halfway through the day because there is "nothing to shoot" It's a common problem and one that is easily banished by working on projects.

Ideally, you should have three or more projects on the go at any one time, and be constantly looking for material to fit into those project silos. Leave home with the idea of shooting project material and anything else that happens around you—which it almost certainly will—is a bonus.

Projects aside, and with well-developed observational skills and a keen eye, there is an endless supply of material to shoot in the world around us. Some scenes will unfold as you approach, while others will require you to lie in wait until several elements come together to make the shot complete. Let's start by looking at some broad subject areas.

People Close-Up

The master of the "in your face" style of street photography is undoubtedly Bruce Gilden, who gets very close to people and uses flash. The combined effect is to shock the subject into pulling a strange face. For Gilden, the grotesque somehow became the photogenic, although it left viewers with varying levels of discomfort.

However, this very overt way of operating is not for the faint-hearted, as it often leads to confrontation. If you move back a few feet, things get a lot easier. You lose the edgy, angry element, but you gain the opportunity to shoot unposed, candid images, often catching an unguarded moment when the subject is unaware of the photographer's presence.

"Most of my photos are grounded in people. I look for the unguarded moment, the essential soul peeking out, experience etched on a person's face."

—*Steve McCurry*

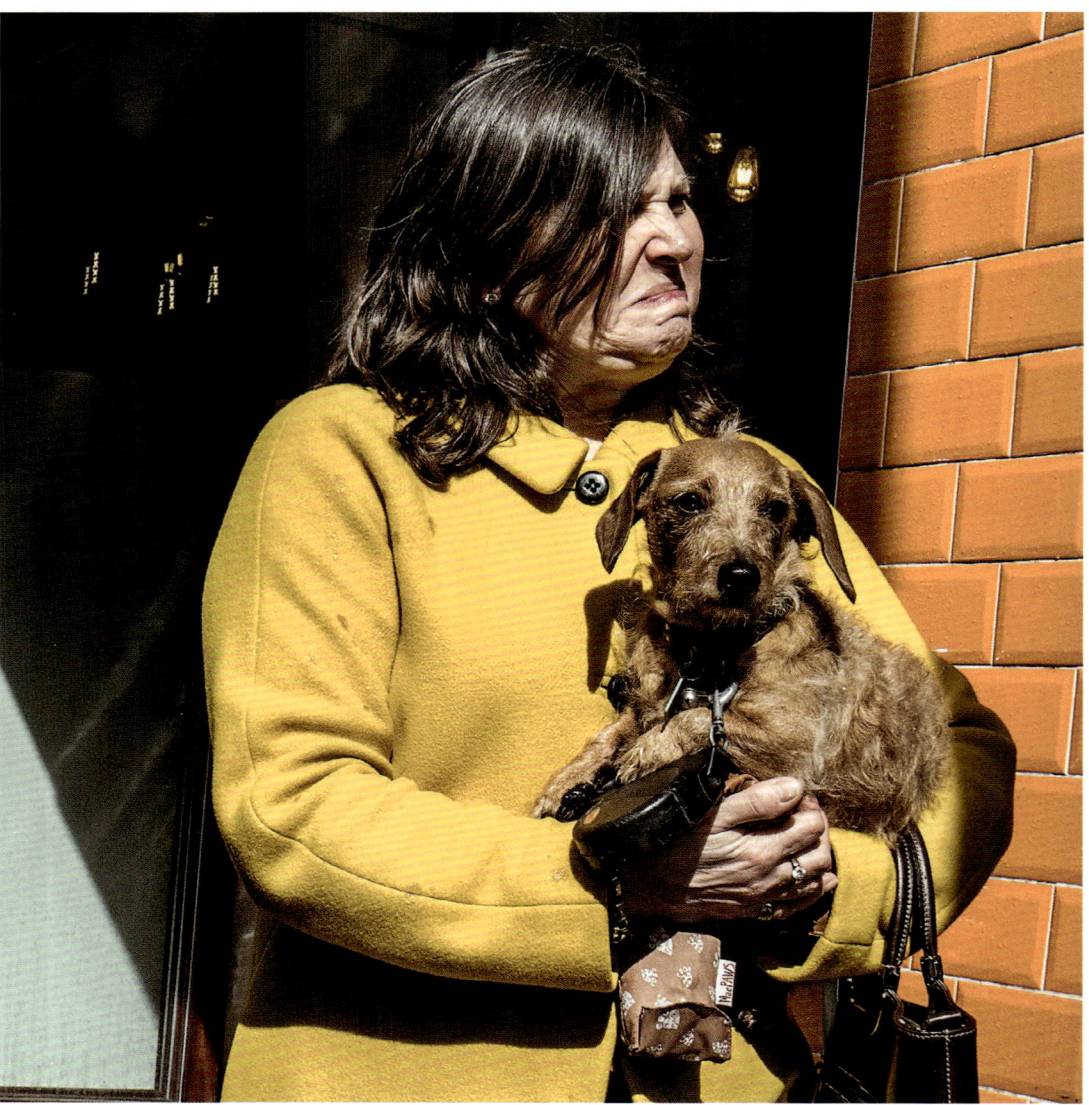

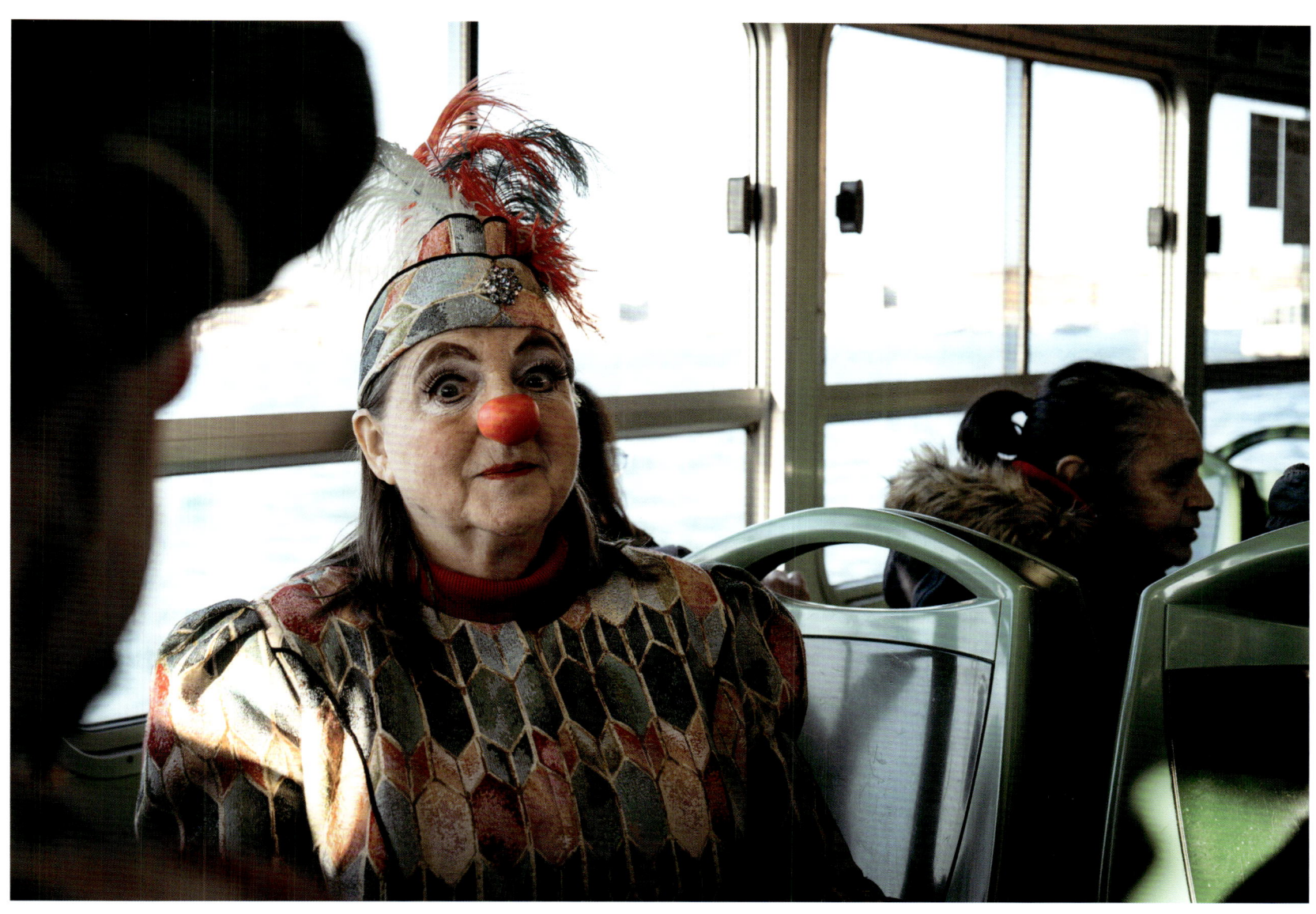

Above: If people are dressed for an event, they probably expect—and want—to be photographed. This woman was quite happy to play up to the camera.

Focal length: 43mm

Aperture: f/4

Shutter speed: 1/125 sec.

ISO 200

Left: When shooting people at close quarters, always look for some kind of expression—good or bad. Here, the woman's grimace contrasts with the dog's cute gaze.

Focal length: 35mm

Aperture: f/8

Shutter speed: 1/1600 sec.

ISC: 1000

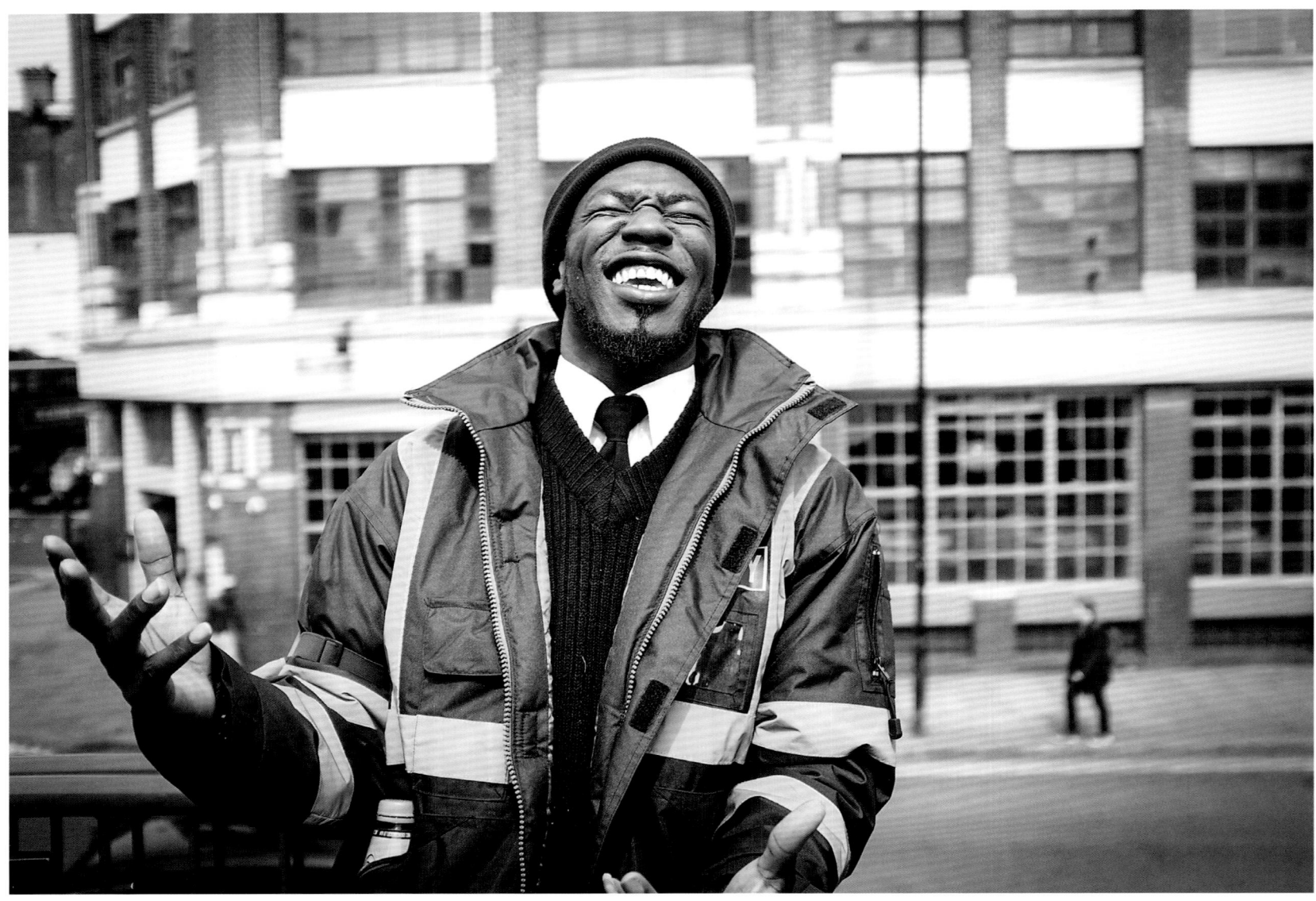

Street Portraits

Street portraits are usually considered to be posed shots of strangers on the street, and as such, perhaps should not be classed as street photography in its purest form. They are usually shot with the subject's knowledge and consent and are therefore set up.

If you intend to shoot in this style always engage with your subject first; chat to them about what you're doing, ask them some questions, and generally put them at ease. However, you may find that your most satisfying pictures of this type are taken when your subject is not expecting it and is caught unawares.

So, how do you approach people to ask if you can take their picture? It couldn't be simpler: just say "Hi, do you mind if I take your portrait?"—then take it before they have the chance to respond. There's no need for a lengthy explanation about why you want to do it, but be prepared to explain yourself if asked. It's a good idea to have a stock answer ready; this could be that you are working on a project or are completing a college course,

Above: This security guard was reluctant to pose but was quite happy to be snapped while in animated conversation.

Focal length: 35mm

Aperture: f/2

Shutter speed: 1/1000 sec.

ISO: 200

for example. Always be honest with your response as anything else will probably sound contrived or insincere. If they say "No," just smile, accept it, and move on to the next person. Generally, if you smile and look friendly and open, you'll get a positive reaction.

As a sweetener you could offer to email the subject a (low resolution) copy of the picture. Try to avoid showing them the image on your camera, though, and only ever agree to delete a frame if you feel uncomfortable or physically threatened.

Bear in mind that if you approach people to take their picture, they usually say "Yes." Most people are flattered to be considered interesting (or attractive) enough to appeal to a photographer and see it as a positive, rather than negative, experience. As photographers, we are sometimes guilty of imagining a problem that doesn't exist!

From a technical perspective, this is one area of street photography where it is a good idea to open up to a wider aperture (ideally f/2.8 or wider) in order to minimize the depth of field and give emphasis to the main subject; the person is usually of more interest than the environment they are in.

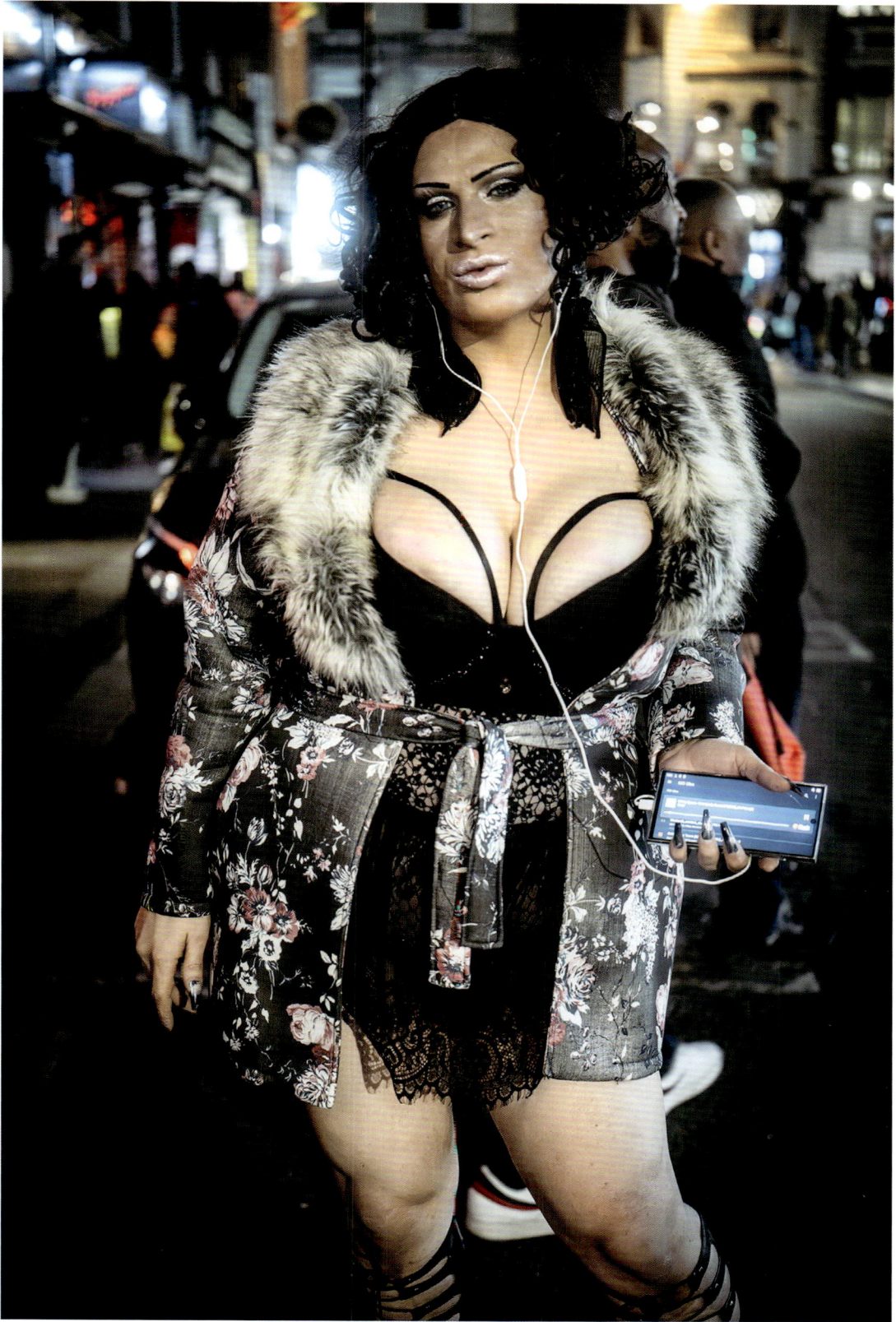

Right: Someone with a distinctive look is often happy to be photographed.

Focal length: 43mm

Aperture: f/2

Shutter speed: 1/125 sec.

ISC: 6400

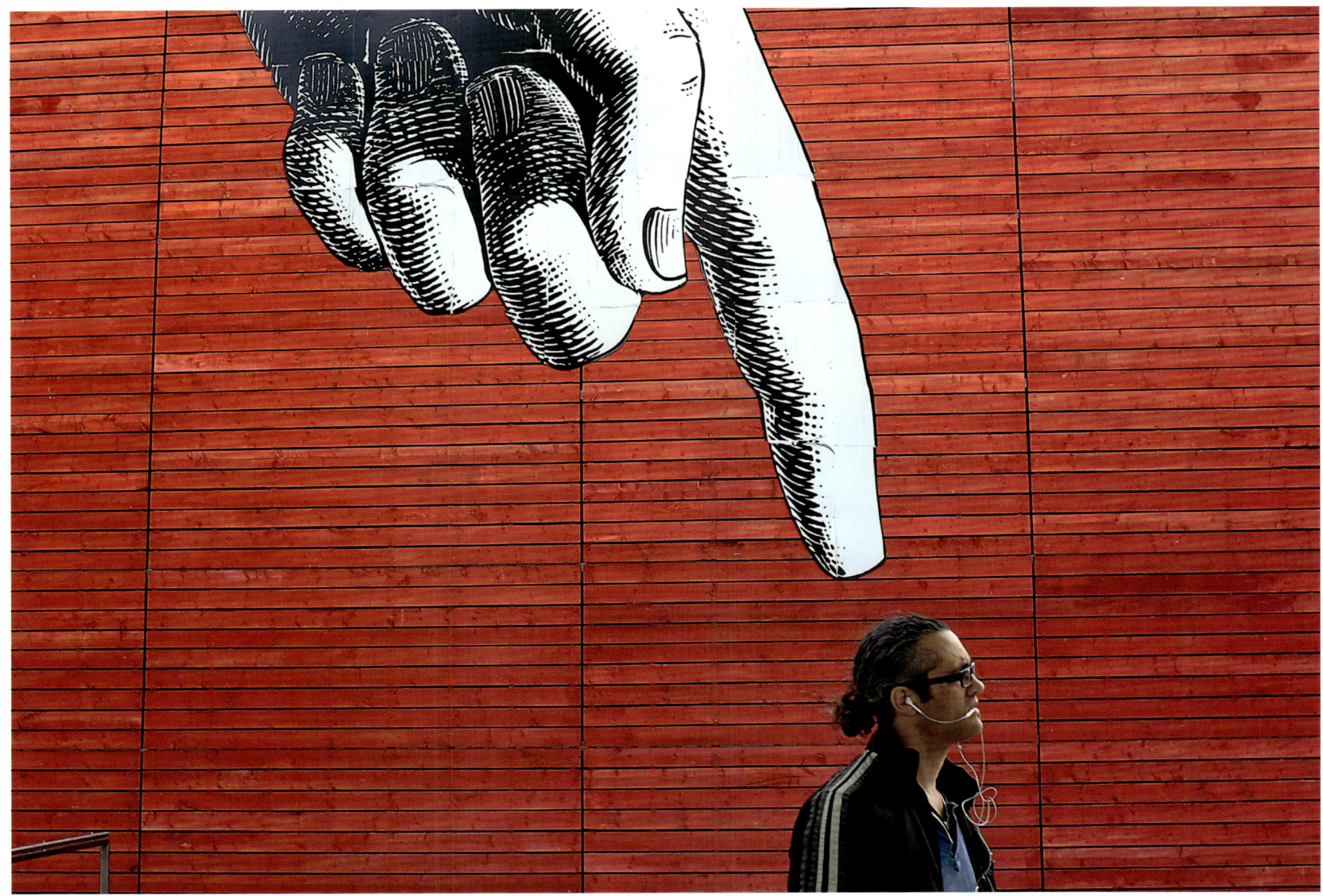

Contemporary Street Scenes

This is perhaps the bread and butter of street photography, and the area most photographers are drawn toward. These scenes can be planned or they can be shot spontaneously as a scene unfolds before your eyes. This brand of street photography is probably closest to Cartier-Bresson's take on the genre—the decisive moment, never to be repeated. People usually figure prominently in these scenes and are generally unaware they are being photographed. The image is often witty, evocative, or provocative.

So, how do you find such opportunities? What do you look for? Much of it is down to luck and being in the right place at the right time. Success comes more easily if you amble around slowly, absorbing your surroundings, being curious, and questioning every activity or situation around you; you need a keen sense of curiosity. By developing your observational skills you will start to see things that would have previously passed you by (read more on this in a later chapter). Your camera needs to be quickly accessible, switched on, and awake

in order to capture a fleeting moment; speed is of the essence with this sort of photography.

A more considered approach is the planned opportunity. You may spot the potential in a scene, but need another element to make it work. You'll take time to think about the composition and the viewpoint, and your camera will be ready for when the final element comes along. It's a good idea to find a convenient place to linger and then wait, perhaps for an hour or so, until everything falls into place. We usually refer to this as "fishing."

Left: When you see a good opportunity for a shot, find somewhere comfortable to stand, plan your composition, and wait for all the elements to come together.

Focal length: 35mm

Aperture: f/4

Shutter speed: 1/390 sec.

ISO: 200

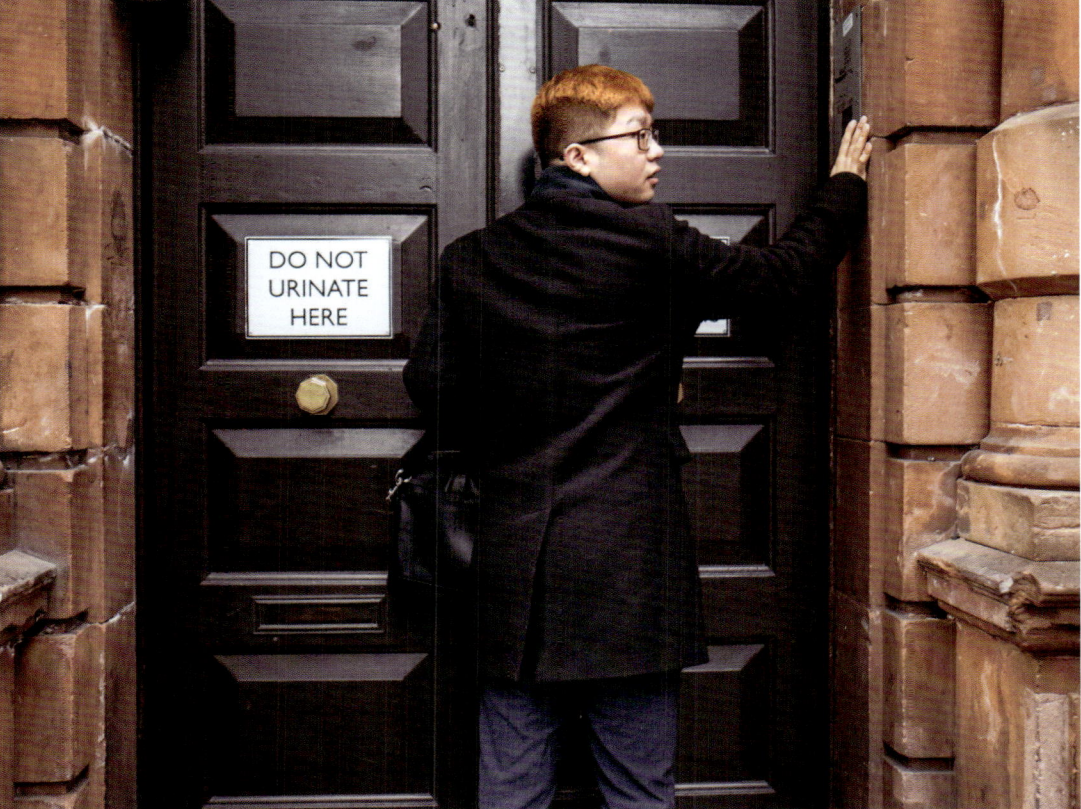

Right: It was impossible to walk past this sign without trying to use it in some way; the perfect example of a "fishing" exercise.

Focal length: 35mm

Aperture: f/1.4

Shutter speed: 1/550 sec.

ISO: 1250

Right: The written word will often provoke a reaction. In this case it was just a question of time before some inquisitive bankers arrived on the scene.

Focal length: 35mm

Aperture: f/8

Shutter speed: 1/320 sec.

ISO: 640

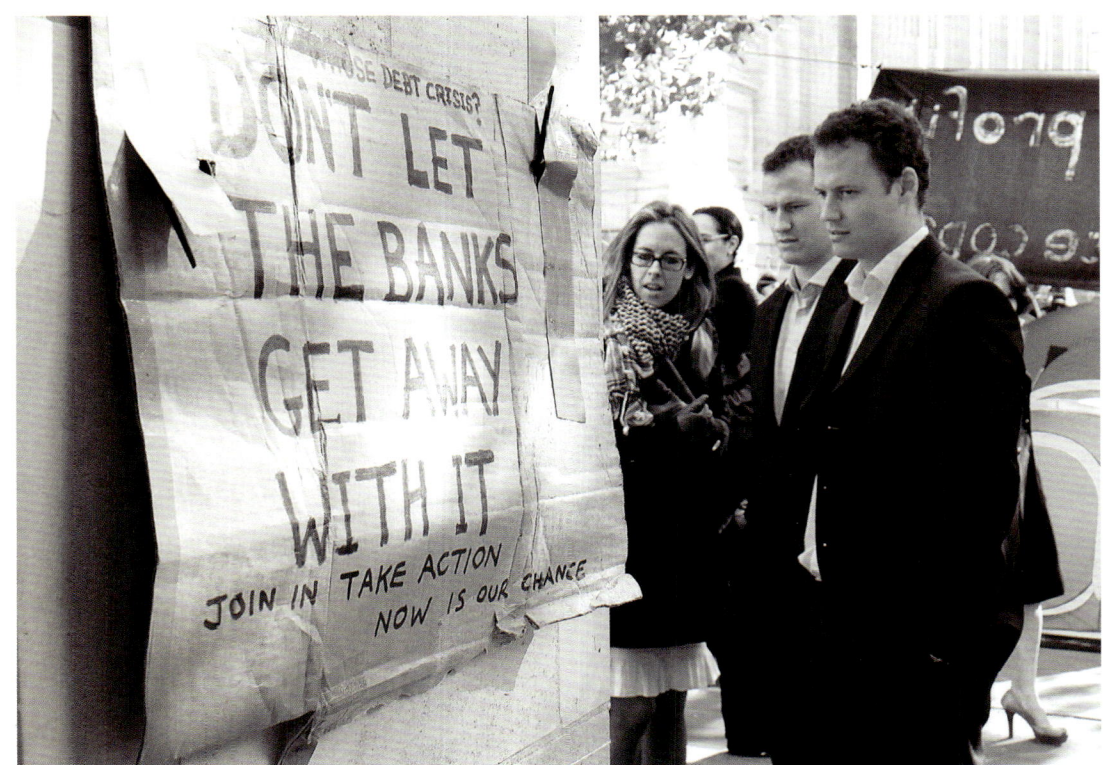

Social Documentary

Reinvented in America in the late 1950s, this more humanistic genre of street photography is used effectively to document historical events or social issues. It often paints a more sober and reflective picture of life on the streets and is sometimes associated with a drive for social or political change. Noteworthy proponents of this style include Don McCullin, Sebastião Salgado, and Martha Cooper, all of whom are worth studying for their powerful images and strong narrative.

Social documentary photography tracks a single issue over a period of time, as opposed to photojournalism's real-time coverage of news. Getting to grips with shooting social documentary street photography is challenging, not least because of the difficult and often unpredictable nature of the subject matter.

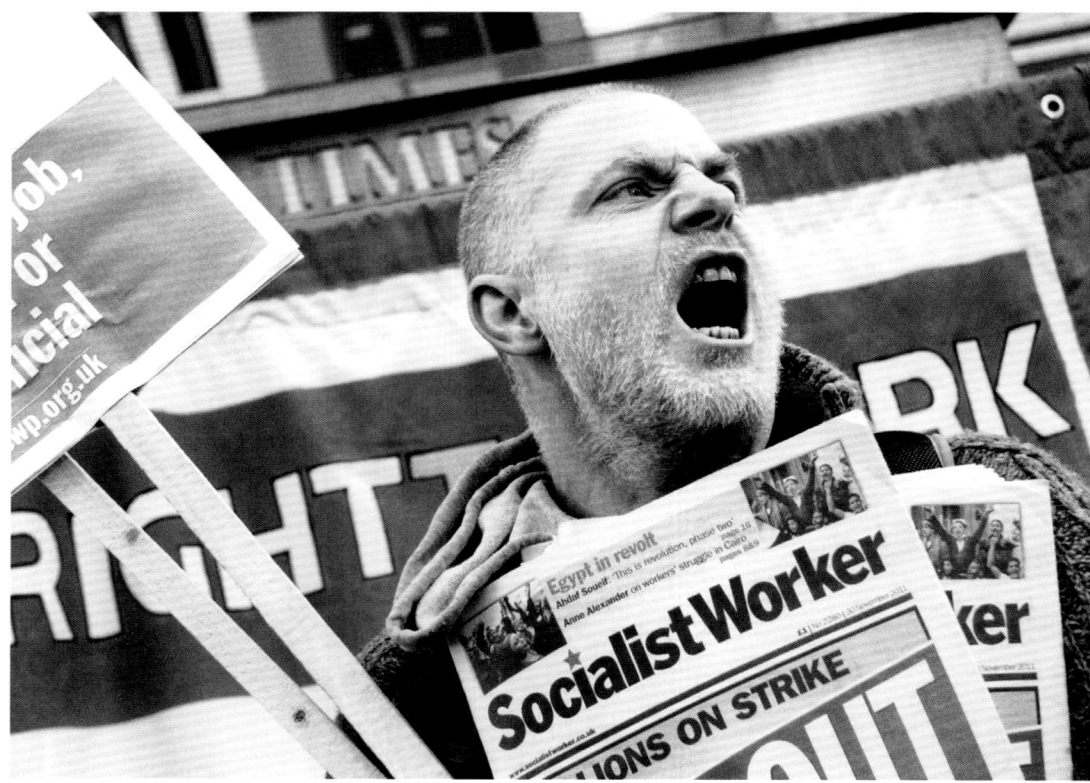

Above right: By moving in close, you can capture the emotion and anger in a scene such as this. Protests take place in most cities and they offer great opportunities for street photographers who are interested in social documentary photography.

Focal length: 50mm

Aperture: f/5.6

Shutter speed: 1/60 sec.

ISO: 400

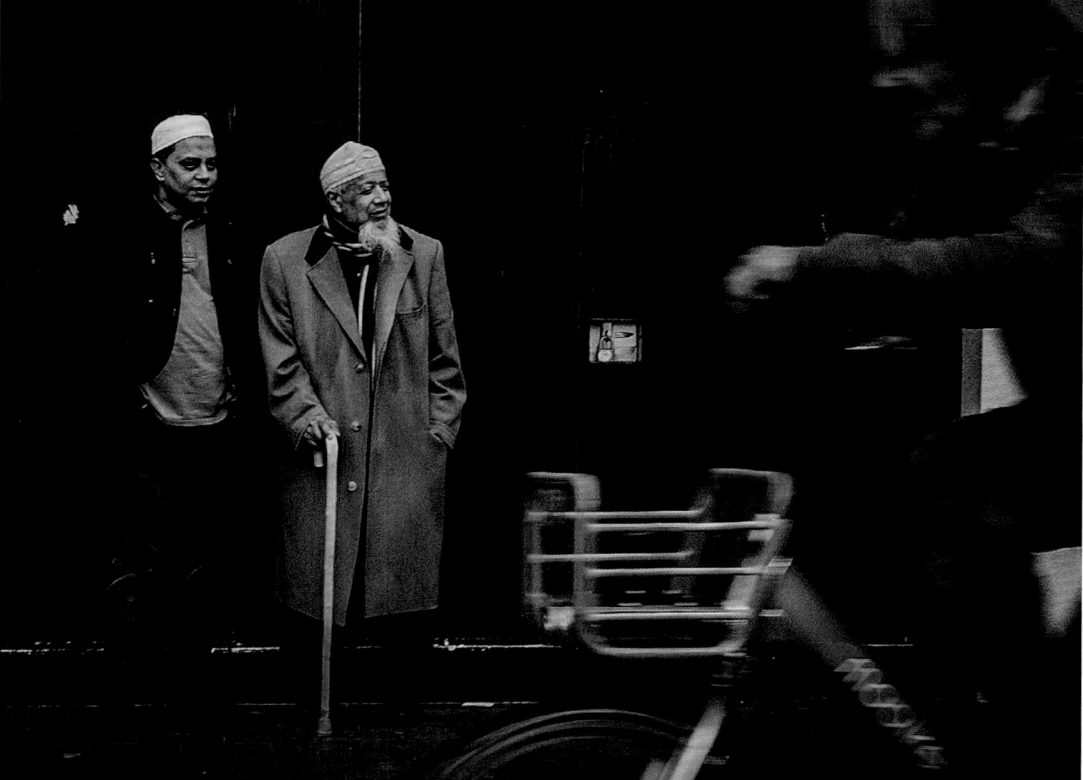

Right: Street photography can be used to draw attention to social issues, such as this image which was taken from a project that explores cultural diversity in East London.

Focal length: 28mm

Aperture: f/8

Shutter speed: 1/60 sec.

ISO: 1000

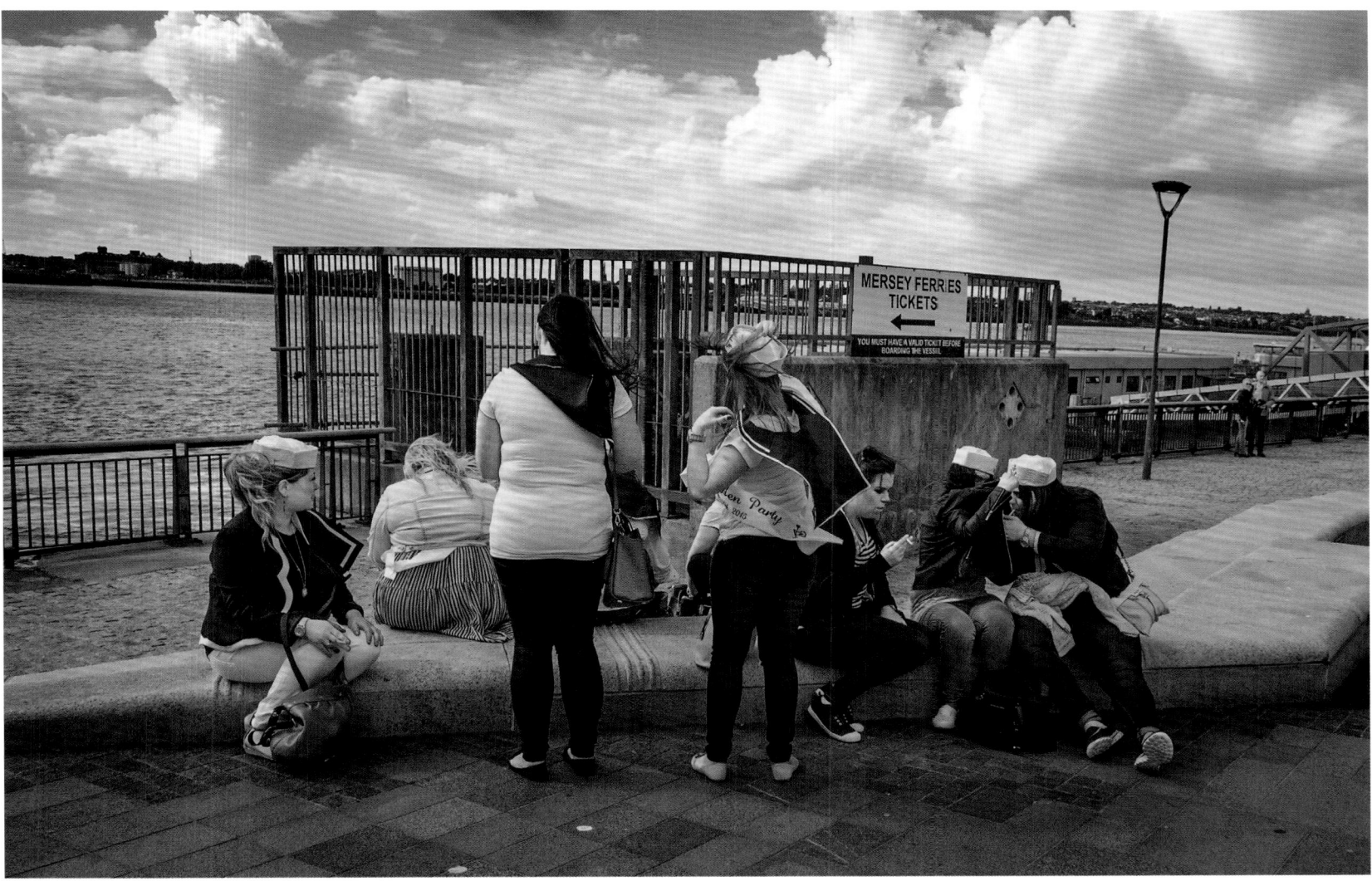

Tip

A good starting point for a social documentary project is a subject close to your heart, such as homelessness or climate change. Spend time (months or even years) tracking the issue and developing a body of work that highlights it.

Above: These women, out on the town for a bachelorette party (hen night), help tell a story about 21st-century city life. The fact that we can't see their faces doesn't detract from that narrative.

Focal length: 28mm

Aperture: f/7.1

Shutter speed: 1/2500 sec.

ISO: 1600

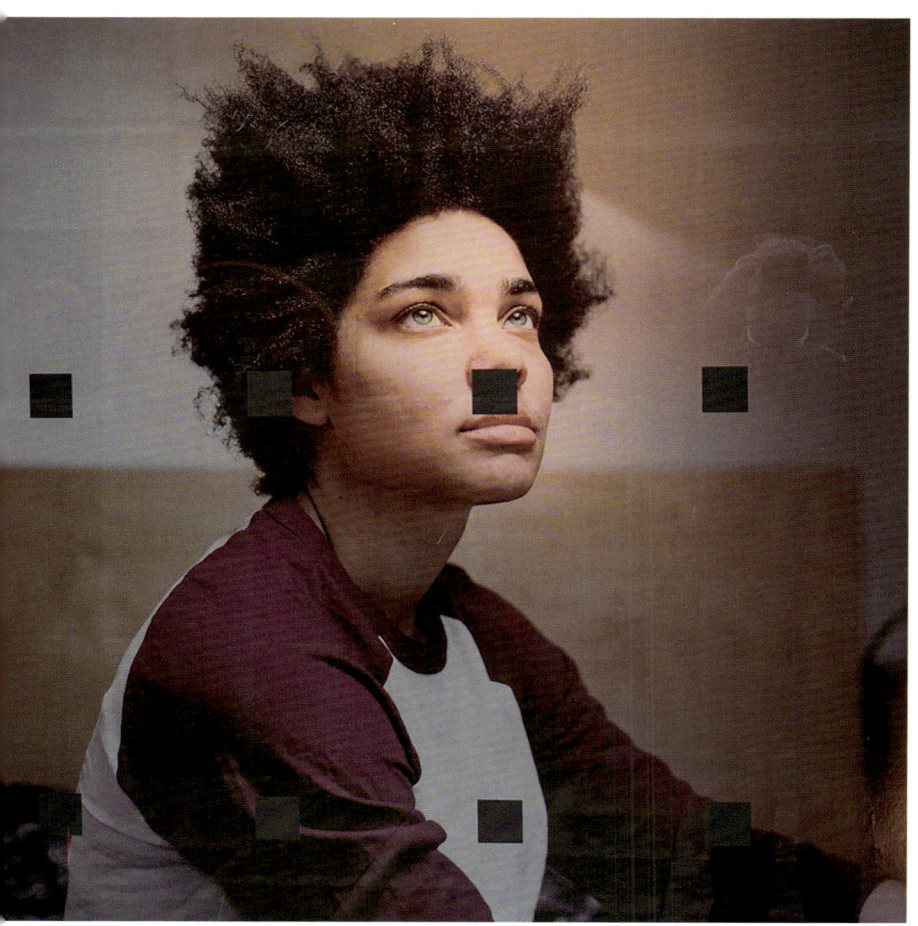

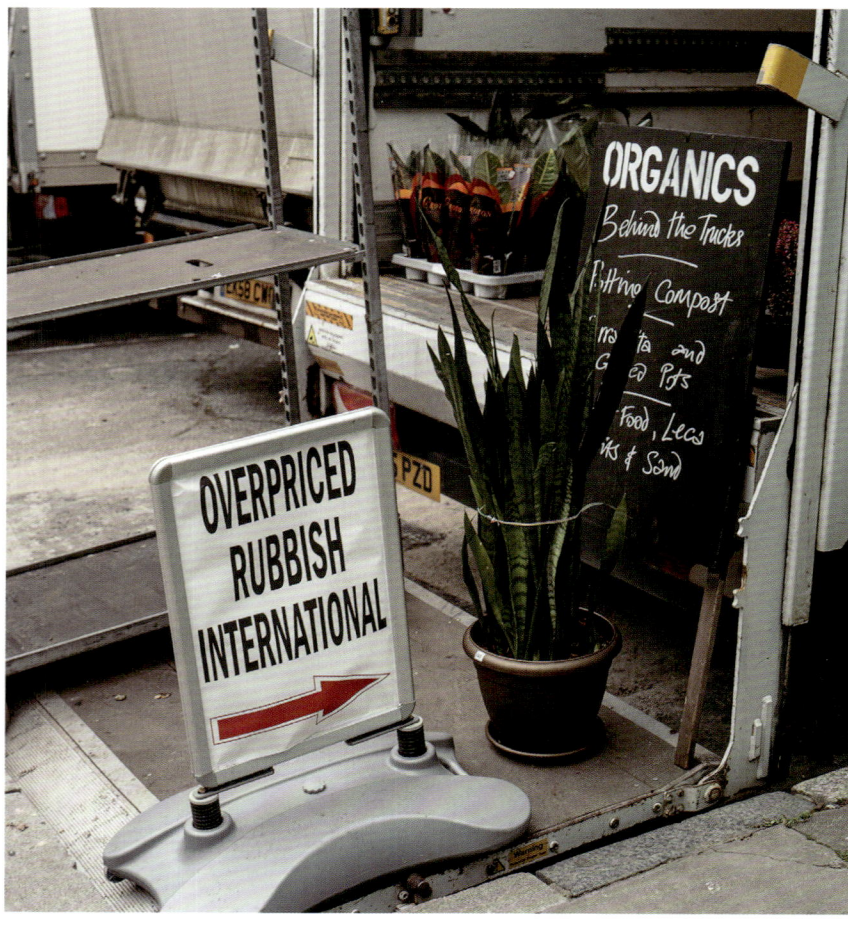

Juxtaposition

Juxtaposition is an important word in street photography and it can be used to great effect. Meaning "things being seen or placed close together with contrasting effect," the technique is often used to inject humor into a frame; we have all seen images that show deep contrasts between two or more elements in the frame—new/old, thin/ fat, safe/dangerous, left/right, and so on—and they usually make us smile. It is often based on the chance appearances of two or more elements, although it could potentially be manipulated. Each element must have the same visual weight, causing the viewer to look at each simultaneously and draw their own conclusions.

Another way of looking at juxtaposition is to include two or more objects that create an obvious comparison or contradiction and which add

contrast. Think, for example, of a scene in which you have a very old man walking past a lingerie store, appearing to look in the window. A cliché? Well, perhaps, but it still makes a visual joke that will bring a smile to most people's faces.

The point about juxtaposition is that it can turn an otherwise boring scene into an interesting and engaging one.

Tip

Spend a day looking for contrasts or contradictions and use them to produce a witty set of images. Look for people, signs, and graphic devices such as arrows.

Above left: It's easy to let potential juxtapositions pass us by and it's essential to be aware of any interesting detail which could be used to good effect.

Focal length: 35mm

Aperture: f/8

Shutter speed: 1/80 sec.

ISO: 1250

Above: Signs can be a useful juxtapositional device—and they are everywhere we look. Try to find a sign that conveys a message, then wait for the right element to come into the frame—perhaps a person who reinforces or contradicts the message.

Focal length: 43mm

Aperture: f/4

Shutter speed: 1/30 sec.

ISO: 100

Silhouettes

The silhouette has played an important role in street photography since the early days and today is a visual device much used by street photographers with an aesthetic bent. Silhouettes must have clear, simple shapes with black figures and light backgrounds. A good starting point is to find a strong light source facing you and wait for a figure to walk into the scene. It's important to get the black point on the figure just right (completely black) and don't worry too much if the highlights in the background are a little blown out.

Below: Minimalistic scenes work best with silhouettes; try to avoid overlapping figures and keep backgrounds as simple as possible.

Focal length: 35mm

Aperture: f/11

Shutter speed: 1/125 sec.

ISO: 3200

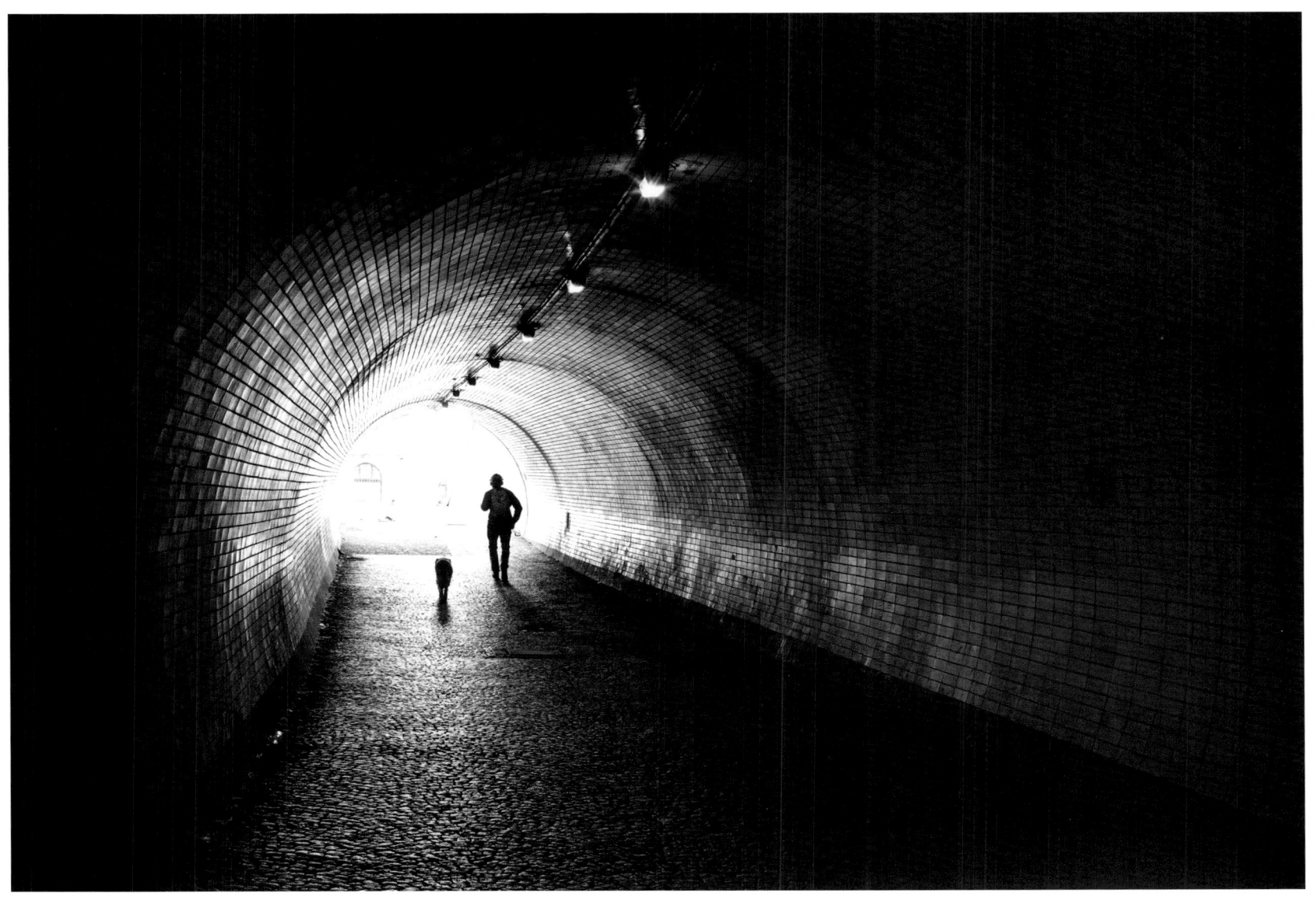

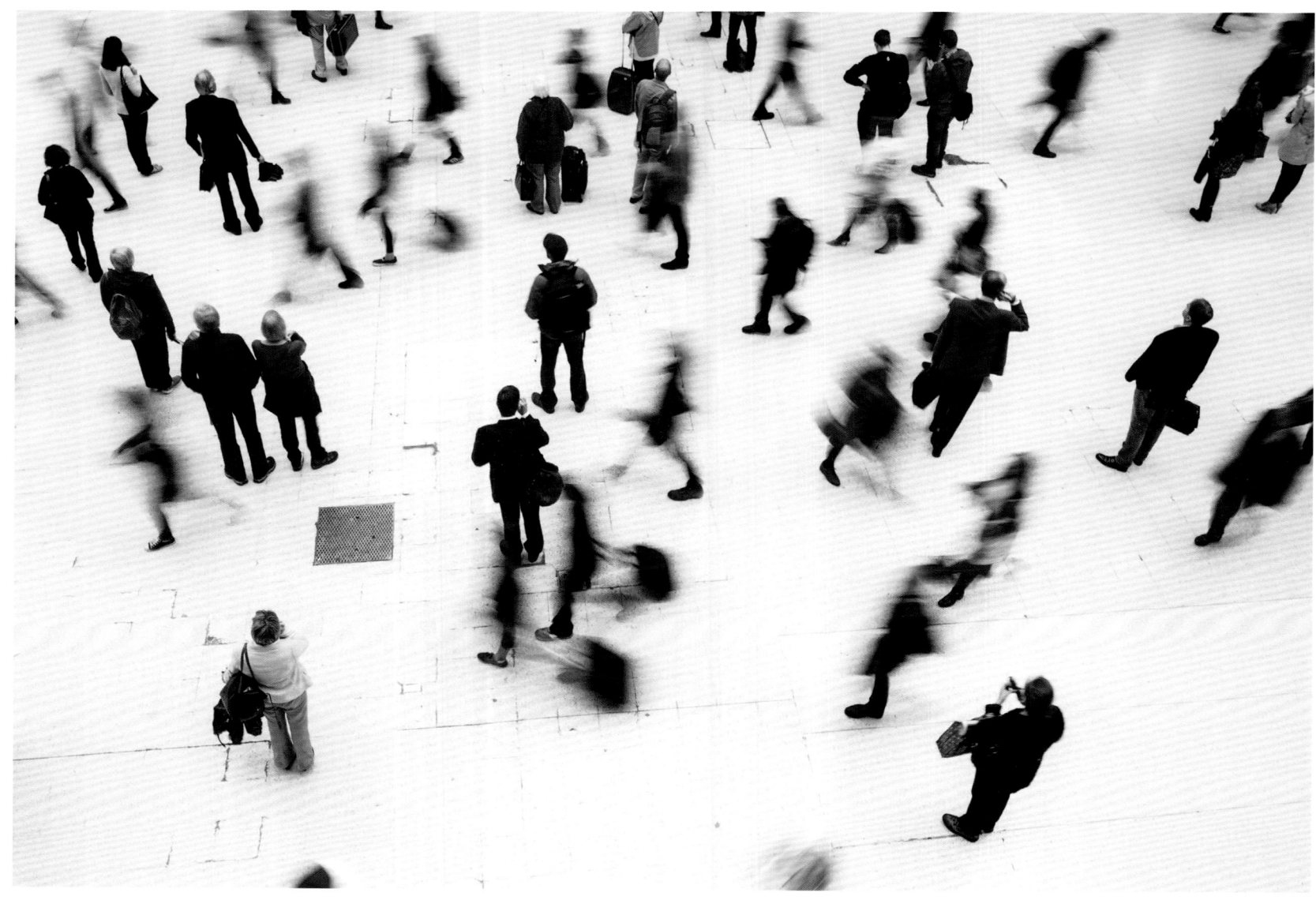

Intentional Blur

Blur is a great technique used by street photographers to emphasize or isolate something that is stationary while movement is going on around it. By selecting a slow shutter speed—say 1/4–1/8 sec.—the stationary object will appear sharp, while anything moving in the frame will be blurred. This technique works best if the subject is moving across the frame, rather than away from you or toward you.

The choice of shutter speed will depend on the speed and direction of the moving objects and you will need to experiment. You will probably need to reduce your ISO and use a smaller aperture to accommodate all the extra light being allowed into the camera.

Above: A slow shutter speed can be used to introduce deliberate blur, as was the case here. You will need to experiment with different shutter speeds, depending on the speed and angle of movement of your subjects—for this shot, 1/4 sec. was just about right.

Focal length: 28mm

Aperture: f/8

Shutter speed: 1/4 sec.

ISO: 200

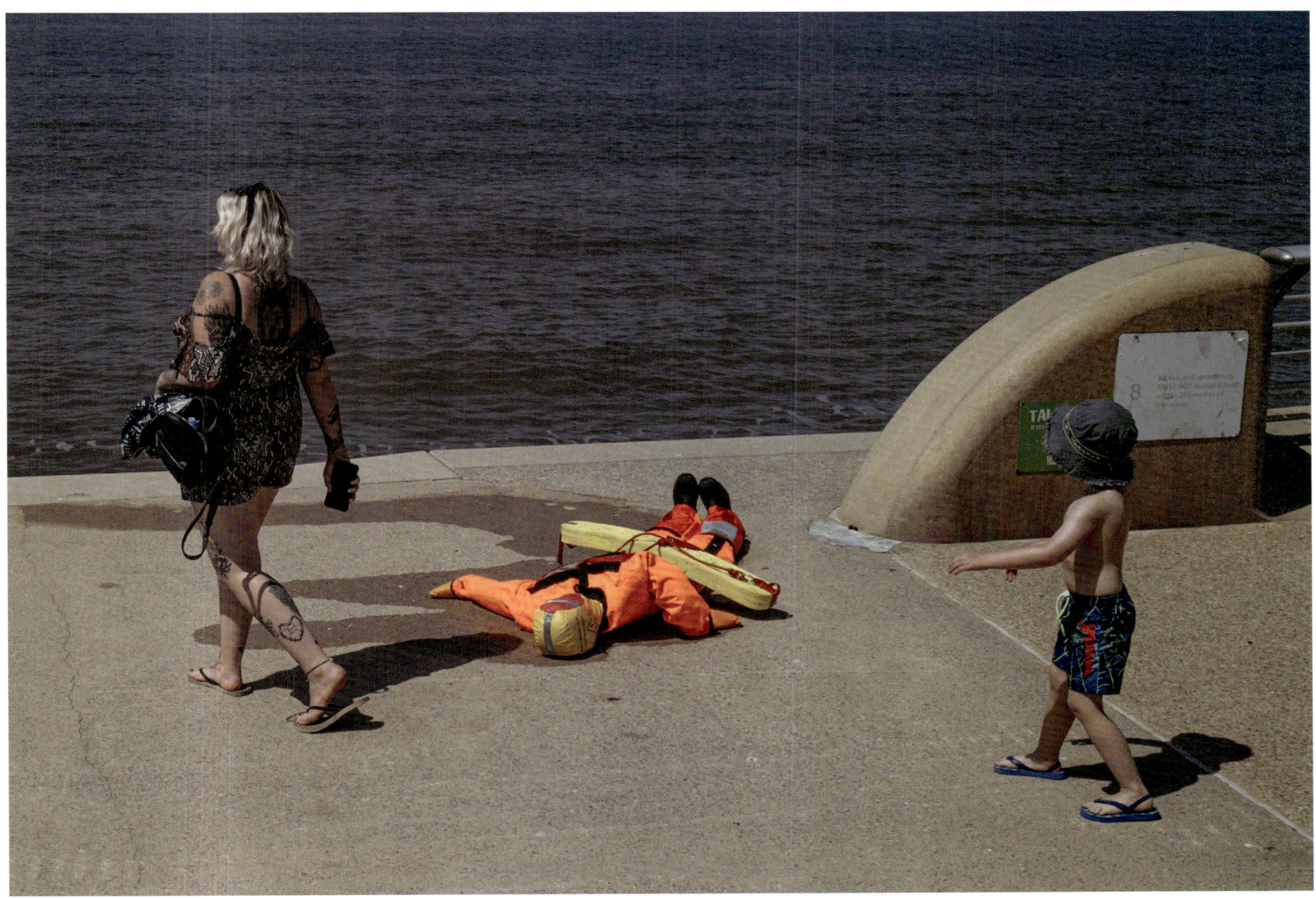

Children

Although children can make great subjects, it is a good idea to be cautious about photographing them on the streets, however worthy or innocent your intentions are. While the legal position is usually no different to that which applies to shooting adults, many societies have become paranoid about cameras around children (although in some regions, such as the Far East, the attitude is more relaxed).

If you do take photographs of children, try to be fairly open in your behavior, as covert shooting could appear to be "creepy" and people could easily misconstrue your intentions.

Above: It's generally OK if children are in the scene but not a close focus of attention—i.e., if they are incidental to the image.

Focal length: 35mm

Aperture: f/11

Shutter speed: 1/900 sec.

ISO: 400

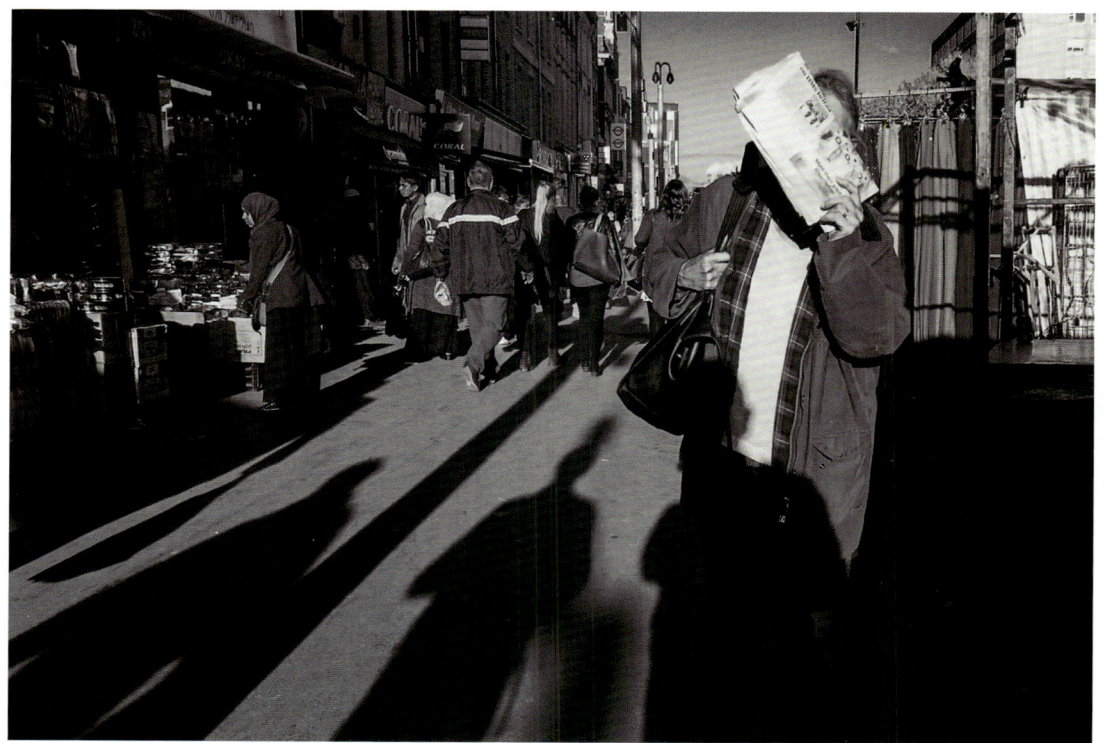

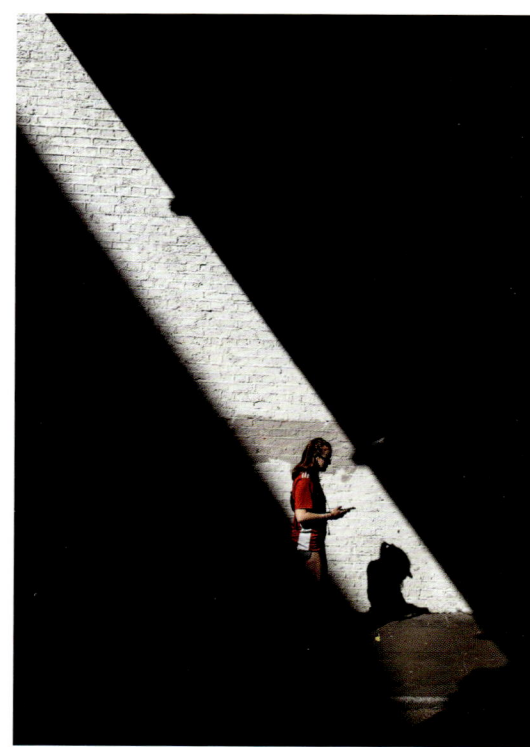

Shadows

While portrait photographers tend to avoid shadows, street photographers are drawn to them! In some images the shadow is incidental, whereas in others it is the primary focus of the composition. With the sun behind, in front, or to the side of the camera, the resulting shadows can produce a striking effect, particularly if they are dark, strong, and well defined.

Shadows can be used playfully—a shadow on a face could look like a silly mustache or a black eye, or it could make someone's head or another key part of a scene invisible. When people are in the shot, think about the shadows falling on them and also the shadows created by them. With the latter in mind, try experimenting with shadows at different times of the day; a midday shadow will have very different qualities to one cast early in the morning or late in the afternoon. Watch people as they move and observe how the shadows change, constantly creating new patterns.

Also consider the surface on which the shadow falls. A surface with an interesting texture, such as a cobbled road, can add another dimension to your shot, but a completely smooth surface can be equally pleasing.

Shadows work particularly well in the springtime (mid-morning during late May or early June is just about perfect), when they are deep and provide a lovely tonal range between them and the super-bright highlights.

As you become more practiced as a street photographer and your powers of observation develop, you should become more tuned in to the presence of shadows and the opportunities they can offer.

Above left: Long shadows can add a strong dimension to a street shot and tend to be at their most effective at the beginning or end of the day.

Focal length: 28mm

Aperture: f/8

Shutter speed: 1/480 sec.

ISO: 1600

Above: Try using a shadow as a strong graphical element which becomes the subject itself; this works best when the sun is low in the sky and the shadows are long.

Focal length: 35mm

Aperture: f/6.8

Shutter speed: 1/640 sec.

ISO: 160

Right: This embracing couple casts a shadow onto the church wall. Although it's not the main focus of the shot, it adds a pleasing compositional element.

Focal length: 28mm

Aperture: f/2

Shutter speed: 1/30 sec.

ISO: 6400

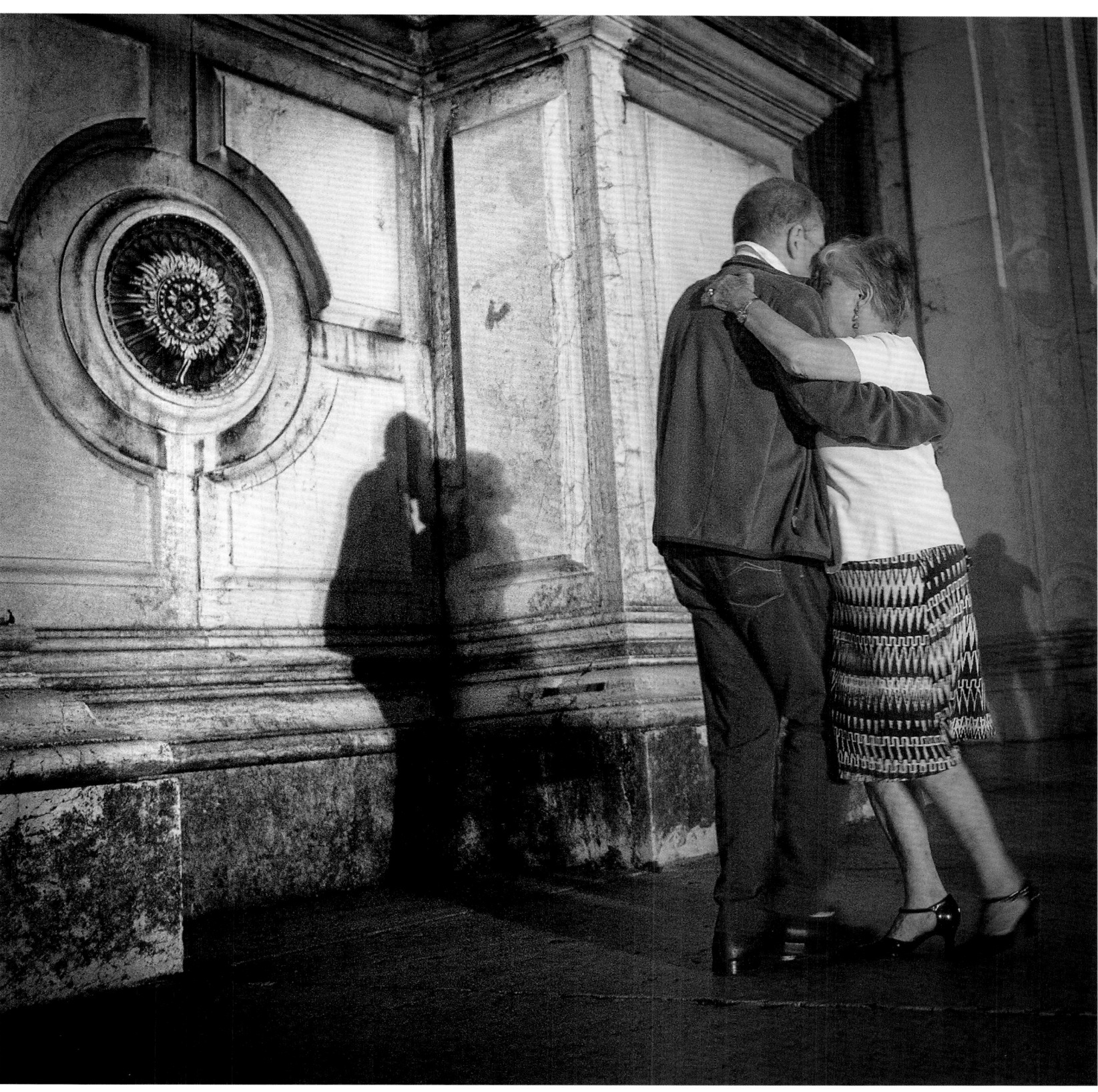

Shafts Of Light

Strong shafts of light, whether they are caused by the sun or by artificial light, can bring an image to life and make the subject in the frame pop. Keep your eyes open for situations in which beams or shafts of light fall onto dark areas, but be wary of letting the camera select the exposure—this situation requires spot metering from the smaller, brighter part of the frame that contains the principal subject.

Early morning is a great time to capture shafts of light, particularly just after the sun has risen during the winter and the air is crisp and moist. Dappled light, which filters through a screen such as the leaves of trees, can give an interesting result, although the contrast can be difficult to control. It can also pay to look for things that pollute the shaft of light, such as cigarette smoke or mist.

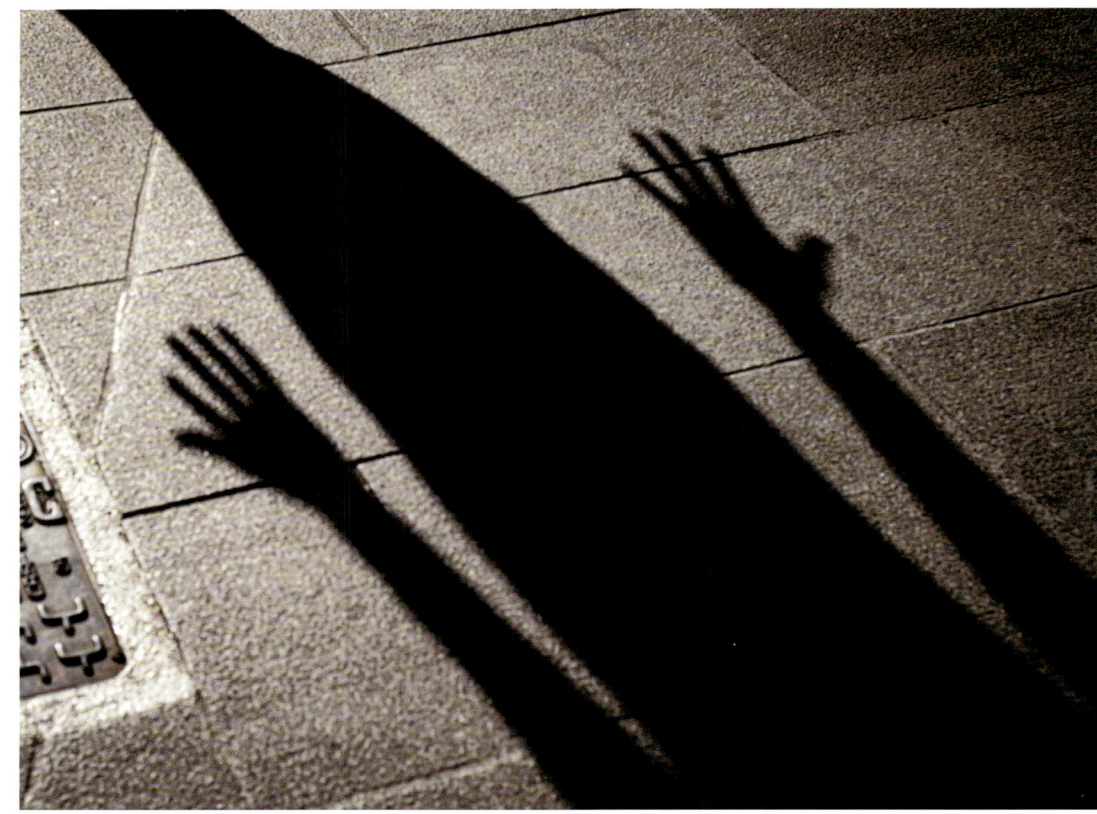

Above right: On sunny days, shafts of light are all around us. As this angular composition demonstrates, a shaft of sunlight in itself can be used to draw attention to a person or object.

Focal length: 35mm

Aperture: f/8

Shutter speed: 1/300 sec.

ISO: 100

Right: In situations like this, in which the main subject is much brighter than the background, use spot metering to get an accurate exposure.

Focal length: 35mm

Aperture: f/8

Shutter speed: 1/1700 sec.

ISO: 1600

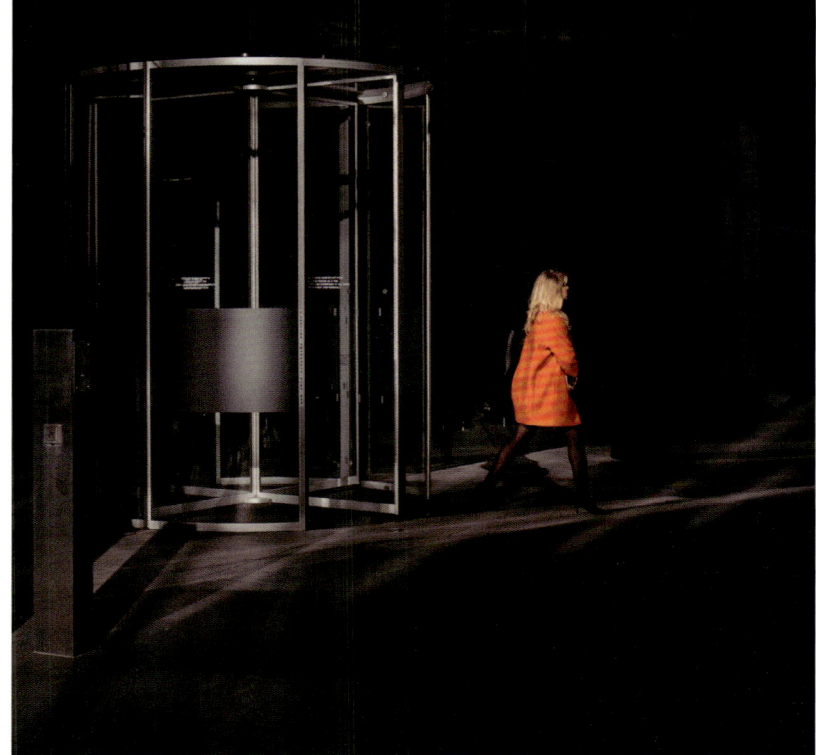

Street Still Life

Who says street photography needs people? Objects are all around us, from street signs to bicycles to litter in the street. Don't just walk past; see every object in the context of its environment. Does it have interesting form or texture? Is there something striking about the color or shape? Is there something witty about the position of the object in relation to other things or people around it? Shooting this kind of "street still life" is fun and you should find no shortage of photogenic material.

For inspiration, look no further than the imagery of Lee Friedlander, who produced an outstanding body of work based on signs and letters. Explore shop windows and doorways; look at signs, animals, hairstyles, tattoos, drinks, street furniture, neon lights, and puddles. Inspiration is all around you, and as your sense of observation develops, you will start to spot opportunities to make arresting images out of everyday objects.

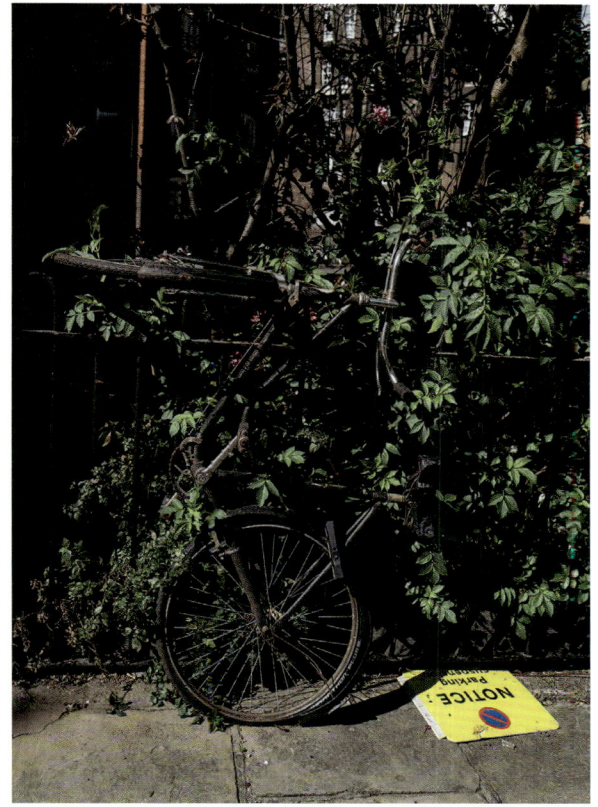

Above right: A bicycle growing out of a hedge: why not? It's still street photography, even though it's not about people.

Focal length: 35mm

Aperture: f/8

Shutter speed: 1/200 sec.

ISO: 320

Right: Red light districts are full of opportunities for off-beat shots. Photographing people can be tricky, so look for some of the quirky objects and paraphernalia that make these areas visually interesting.

Focal length: 70mm

Aperture: f/4

Shutter speed: 1/125 sec.

ISO: 1000

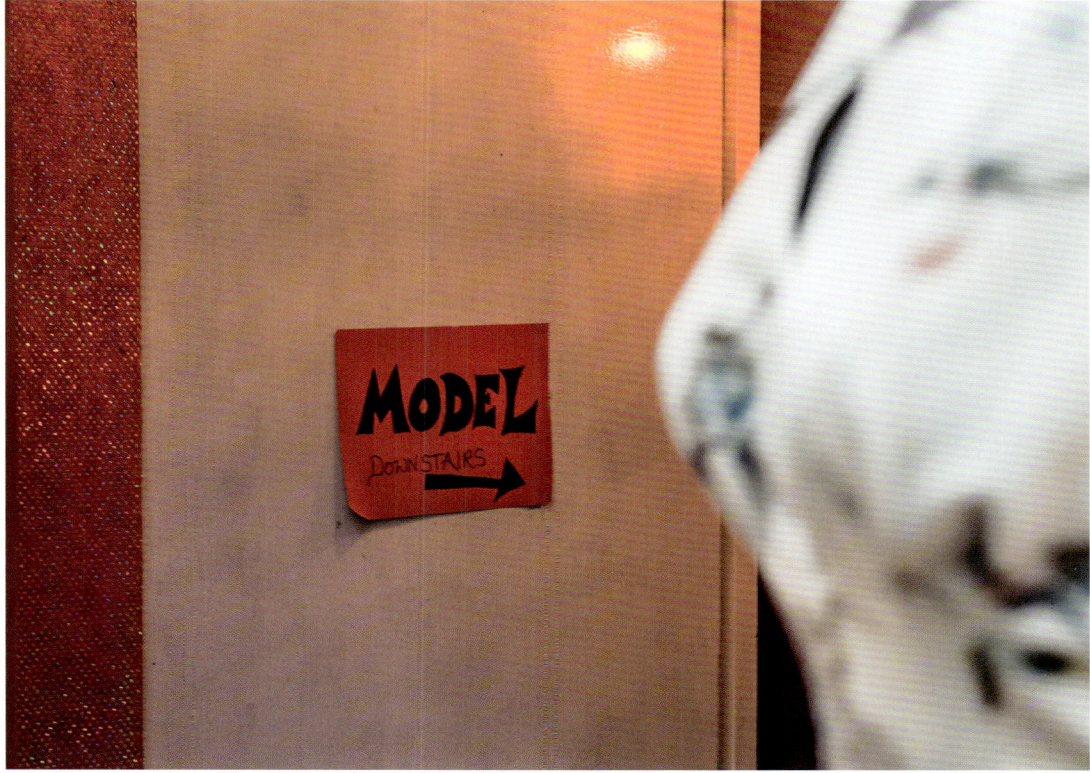

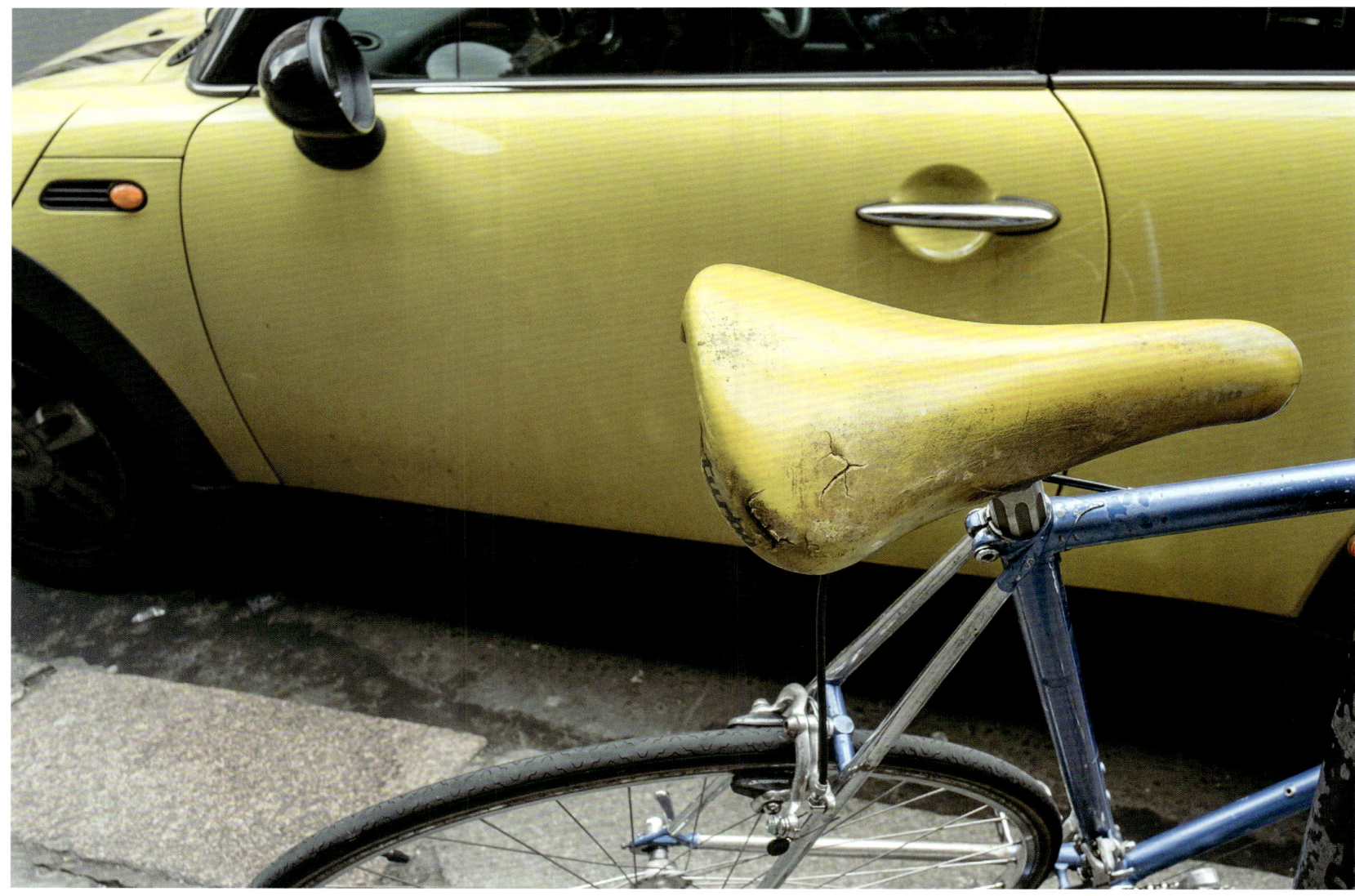

Above: Sometimes, strong colors will provide all the content an image needs. Always be on the lookout for coincidences like this, where the colors are a near-perfect match.

Focal length: 28mm

Aperture: f/8

Shutter speed: 1/100 sec.

ISO: 1250

Colors

There is no reason why a street photograph can't be based on color alone; contrasting or matching colors can sometimes offer enough content to provide a striking image. Remember to be prepared to wait for an opportunity to develop, though. Suppose, for example, you see a bright blue wall—all you perhaps need is someone in a yellow coat to walk through the frame and you'll have a vibrant image with a near-abstract quality.

Abstracts

Shooting people—candidly or otherwise—is not for everybody, and some photographers are so uncomfortable photographing strangers that they just can't bring themselves to do it. Thankfully, as photographic genres go, street photography is a fairly broad church, and there are plenty of non-human options available.

Abstracts, in whatever form they take, can make engaging street photography. Everywhere we go, there are lines, shapes, curves, reflections, shadows, colors, and textures, all providing potential for an engaging piece of abstract art.

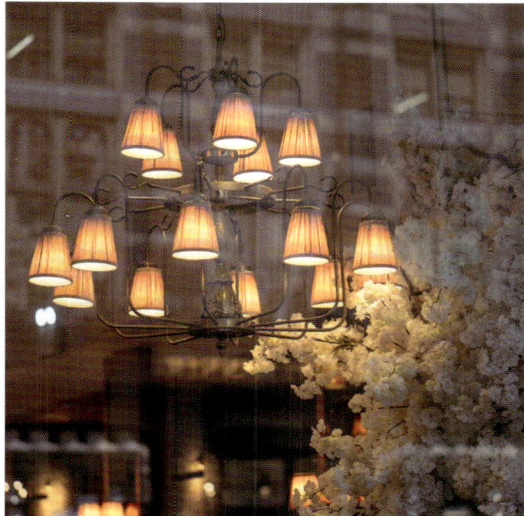

Above: This scene, based on reflections in a store window, has an abstract, almost ethereal feel to it.

Focal length: 85mm

Aperture f/1.4

Shutter speed: 1/125 sec.

ISO: 160

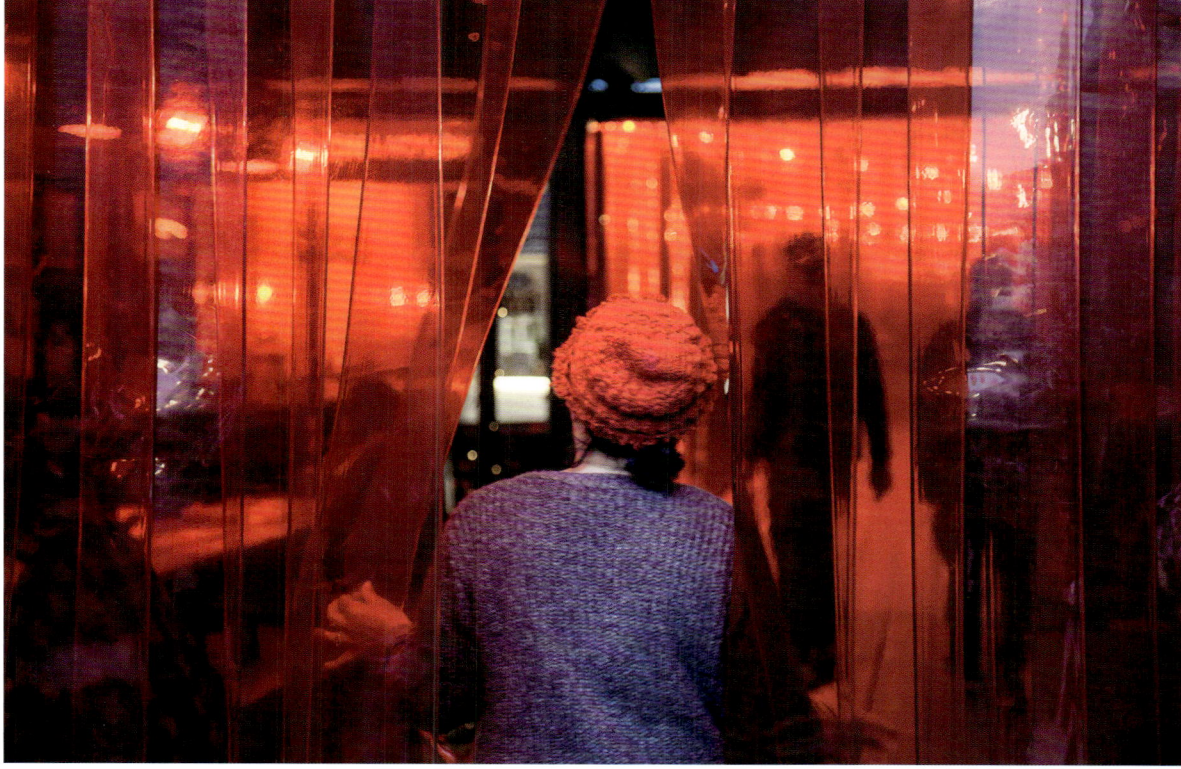

Above right: This image could only work in color. The woman's red hat complements the color of the curtain.

Focal length: 75mm

Aperture: f/4

Shutter speed: 1/80 sec.

ISO: 1600

Right: Something as simple as markings on the road can make a pleasing abstract. Look for strong lines, colors, or textures (or, in this case, all three).

Focal length: 45mm

Aperture: f/7.1

Shutter speed: 1/950 sec.

ISO: 1600

Where To Shoot

One of the great things about street photography is that it can be practiced just about anywhere—it's not necessarily confined to the streets! Don't feel constrained by the need to be in a densely populated city in order to take great shots: villages, the seaside, parks, and even the countryside all offer possibilities. Anywhere where there are people, or even simply "things" can produce results if you go with an open mind, a keen sense of observation, and lots of patience.

City Centers

From dawn until after dusk, city centers are a rich hunting ground for street photographers. The pace of life is usually fast, and people are wrapped up in their own worlds and are less likely to be concerned about you taking their picture—in fact they probably won't even notice you.

Walk slowly around a city center and spend time observing; see where people go, watch how they move, how they behave, and how they interact with each other and their environment. Seek out good vantage points, always looking for good light and interesting compositional devices such as leading lines (the modern architecture in most cities can provide us with strong vertical, horizontal, and diagonal lines, as well as swooping curves that are all great to use as leading lines or as a means to frame your subject). Try shooting from above or below your subjects to give a different and perhaps more dynamic perspective on city life.

The possibilities are almost endless, so if you're looking for some ideas or inspiration, try looking out for the following:

- **Commuters**. Commuters are often lost in their own worlds; for obvious reasons they are best photographed at rush hour in the early morning or late afternoon.

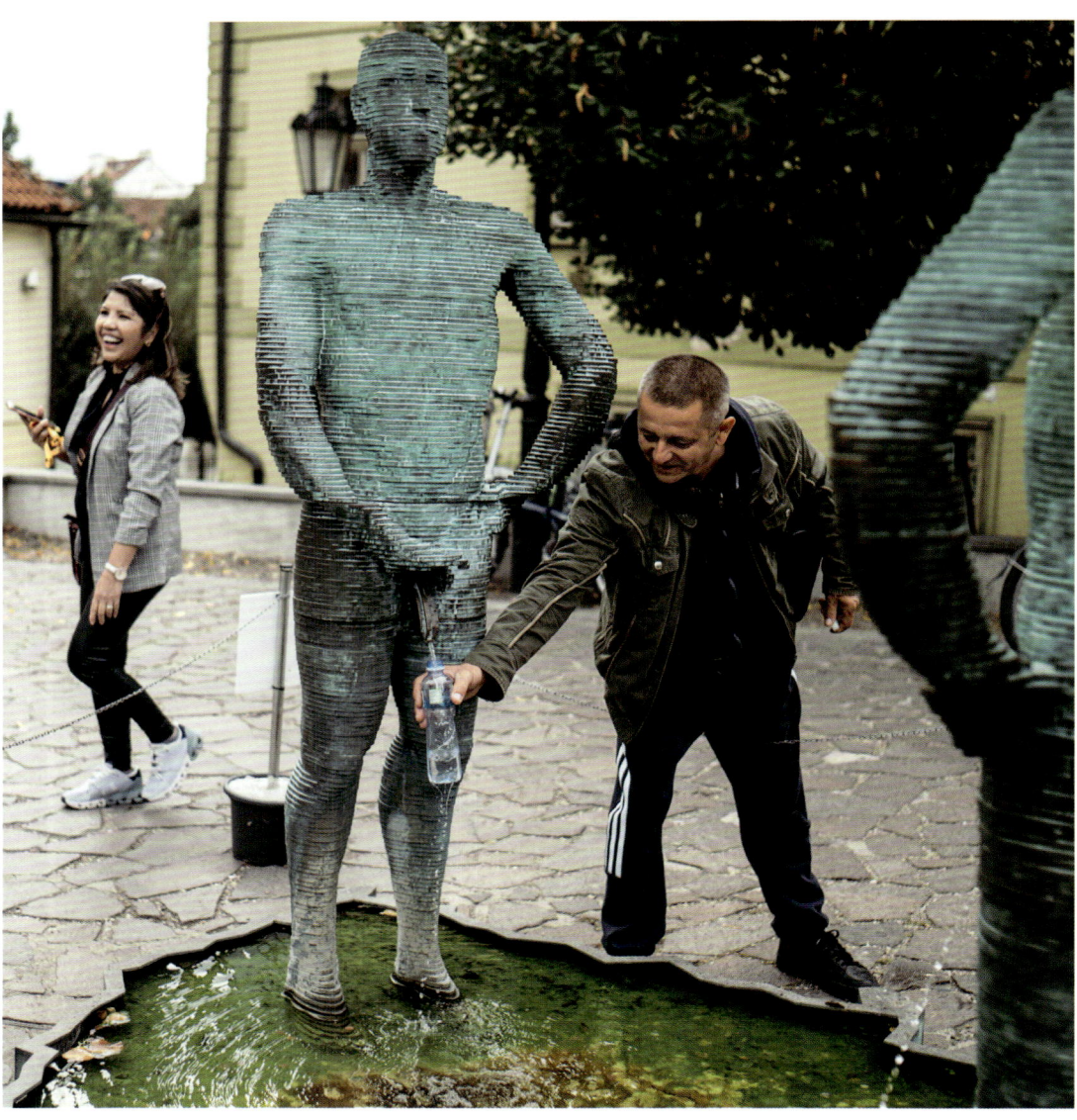

Tip

Always have a notebook with you and jot down the street photography "hot spots" you come across. Maybe you need more time, or to visit at a different time of day, or for there to be no traffic in the frame. Use these notes to build a running list of your favorite vantage points.

Above: Tourists do the strangest things! When you see a statue like this, just hang around for a while and you'll eventually get the shot.

Focal length: 35mm

Aperture: f/2

Shutter speed: 1/1000 sec.

ISO: 200

- **Café culture**. Watch people relaxing inside or outside cafés, bars, and restaurants. Alternatively, find yourself a good vantage point at a table outside a café, watch the world go by, relax, and shoot away!

- **Tourists**. People on vacation can make great subjects: watch how they get into peculiar positions to take selfies, for example.

- **Leading lines**. Seek out strong lines, diagonals, arrows, angles, squares, circles, or curves that lead the eye to a point of interest.

- **Reflections**. Windows, puddles, metallic surfaces, or mirrors will all provide good opportunities for abstracts, especially during or after heavy rain.

- **Shadows**. At the beginning or end of the day, long shadows can lead to striking compositions, particularly against the starkness of concrete or wet surfaces.

- **Signs**. The written word is all around us, and signs of all types can produce some interesting and witty juxtapositions. Sometimes you'll need to wait until another element comes along to "complete" the scene.

- **Nightlife**. Neon signs, twinkling lights, car lights, buses, and store windows—there are plenty of opportunities for the street photographer, although you will need a higher-than-usual ISO setting and you will need to open up your lens to a wider aperture. Try experimenting with a very wide aperture, taking a picture of, say, someone stepping out of a taxi with lots of lights in the background; with an aperture of f/2.8 or wider, the lights will produce lovely specular highlights to make an attractive composition.

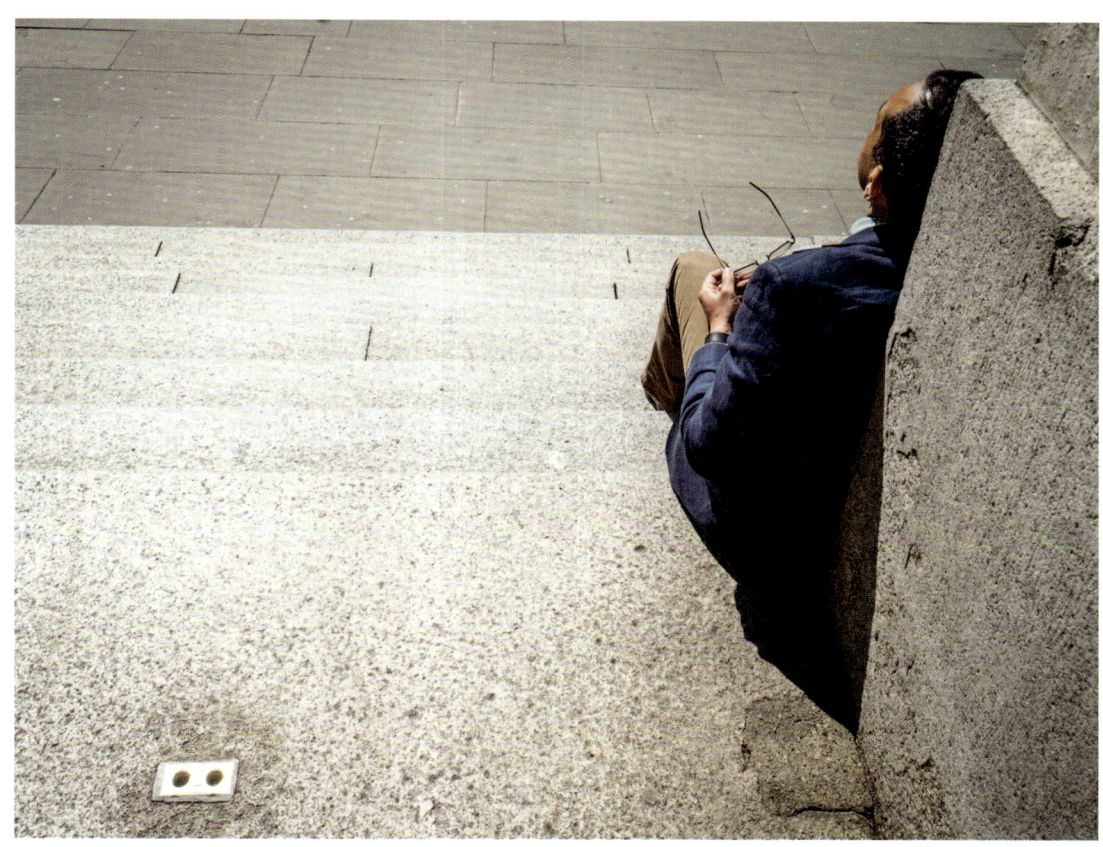

Above: Look for city workers relaxing during lunch breaks; you'll find them outside bars, cafés, in parks, sitting on steps, or on benches. This minimalist composition relies on having plenty of room around the subject to create a sense of relaxation and space.

Focal length: 35mm

Aperture: f/5

Shutter speed: 1/1000 sec.

ISO: 1250

Tip

Try using a slow shutter speed (1/8 sec. would be a good starting point) to capture blurred movement against a sharp background; this is a great way of illustrating the hustle and bustle of city life.

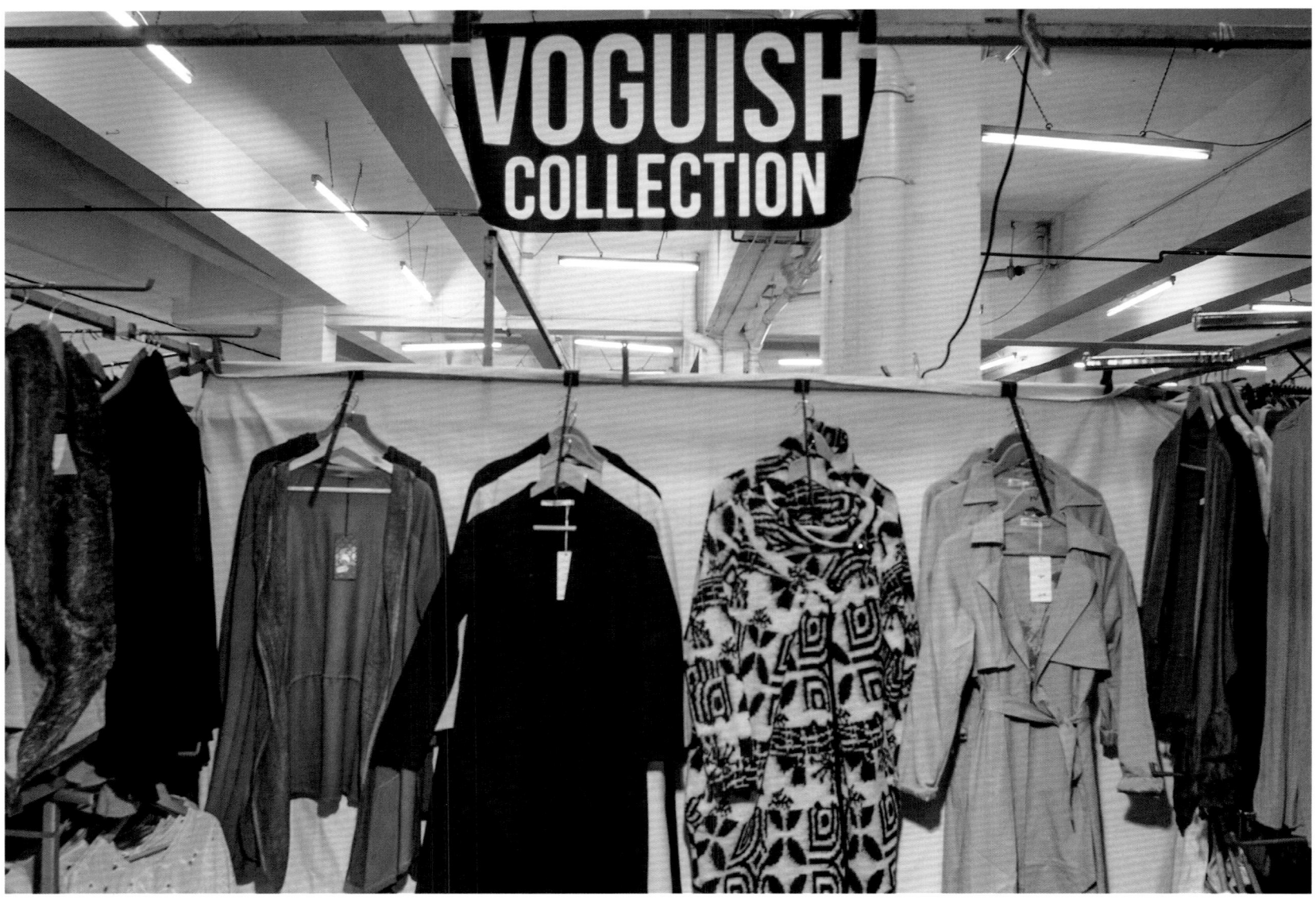

Markets

While indoor and outdoor markets can be full of color and character, they can also represent something of a cliché in street photography. Avoid the obvious shots such as the market traders and instead look for inspiration in the customers and their behavior, in objects, signs, and even piles of trash. There is plenty of potential material—just try something a little different.

Above: This market stallholder had a sense of humor, with a sign saying "voguish." With a rack full of tatty vintage-style coats and dresses on display, the stall was anything but "vogue," and the "–ish" suffix added a touch of irony.

Focal length: 28mm

Aperture: f/5.6

Shutter speed: 1/60 sec.

ISO: 1600

Public Transportation

There are lots of good shooting opportunities on public transportation, whether it's the bus, a train, or even a ferry. You could consider photographing your fellow passengers during the journey or on platforms, at stations, or anywhere else they may be waiting.

Be wary, however, of taking pictures that are meaningless; an image of a man on a train without any other interesting element or context is likely to be boring and have little visual appeal. Instead, look for people doing unusual things—standing or sitting in strange poses, or carrying peculiar objects, for example—or for scenes that somehow capture a rare moment in time.

If you are traveling on a bus, look outside for interesting happenings, as well as snapping the other passengers. If the window is wet or steamed up, consider making an abstract, shooting through the layer immediately before you.

If you commute regularly on the subway, always have your camera with you, possibly on your lap, ready to photograph people who are sitting opposite you: if you sit at the end of a row, you will also be able to photograph people stepping on or off the train.

Above right: Buses, trams, and trains provide plenty of opportunities for street photographers, particularly in dramatic light.
Focal length: 43mm
Aperture: f/2
Shutter speed: 1/500 sec.
ISO: 125

Right: Remember that sometimes an image of, rather than on, public transport can make an interesting street photo. Using a slow shutter speed, this tram in the Czech Republic makes a colorful urban landscape.
Focal length: 45mm
Aperture: f/3.2
Shutter speed: 1/5 sec.
ISO: 200

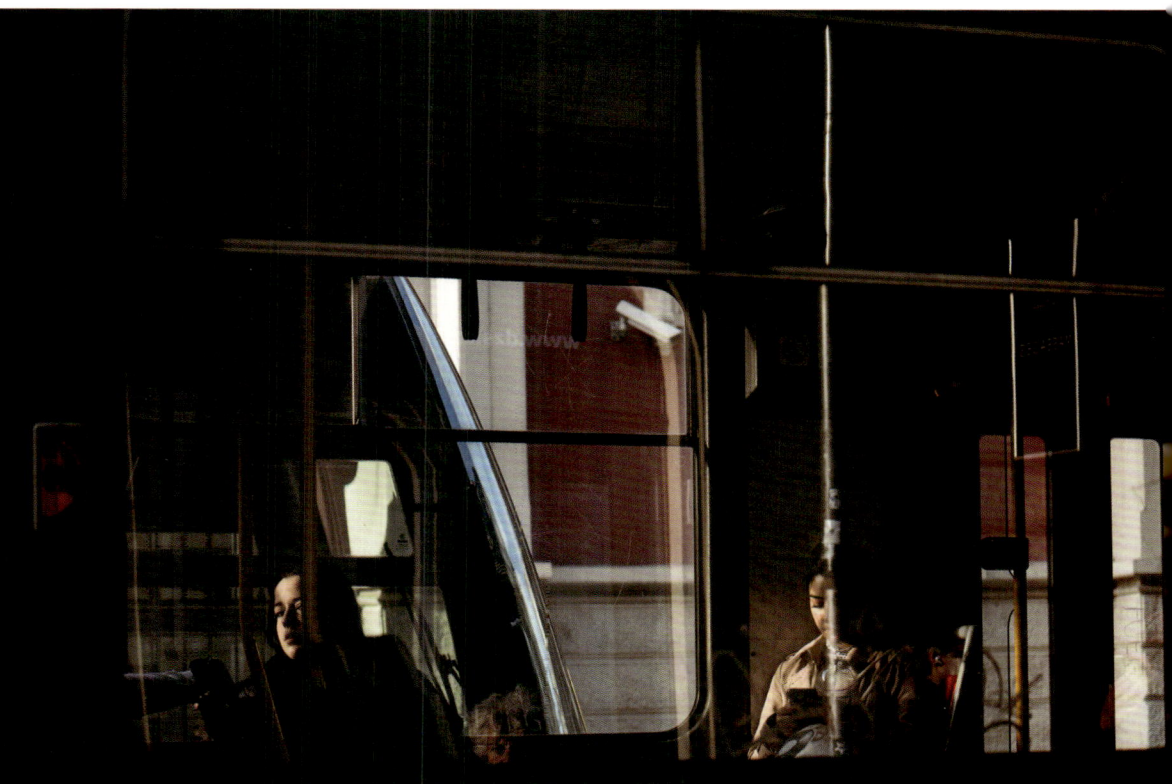

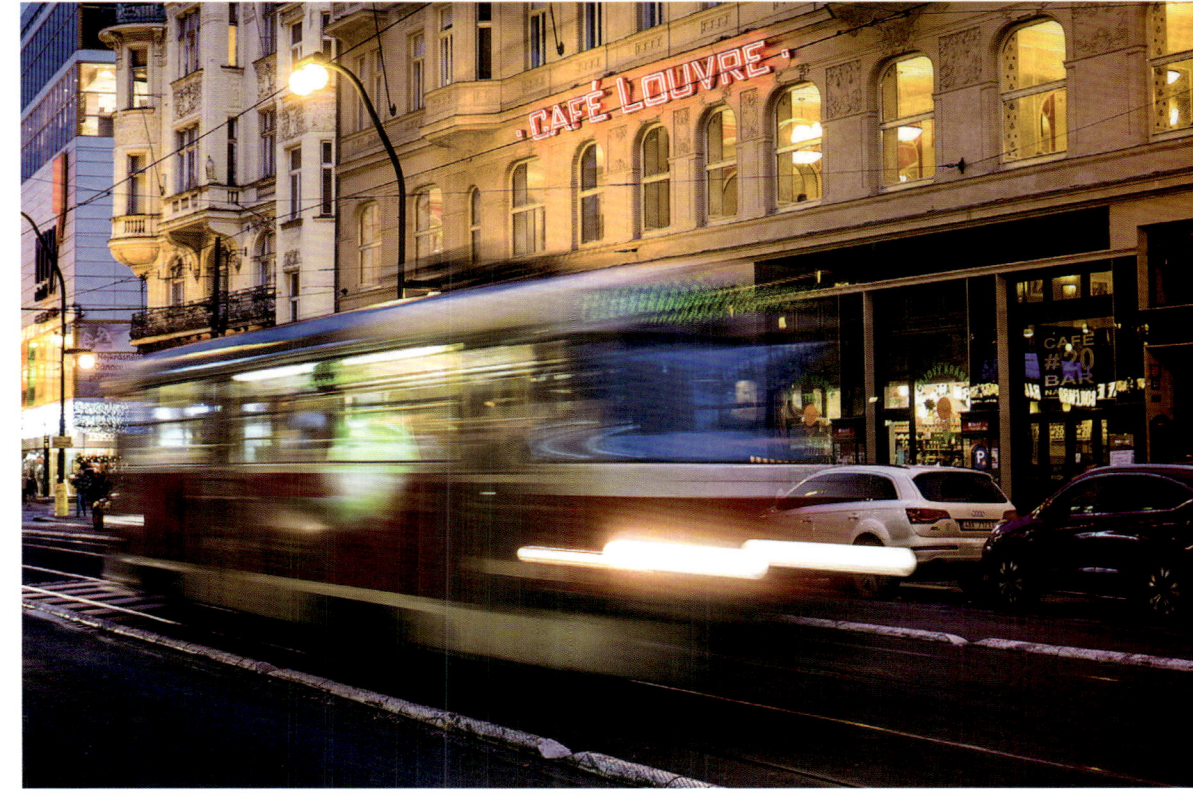

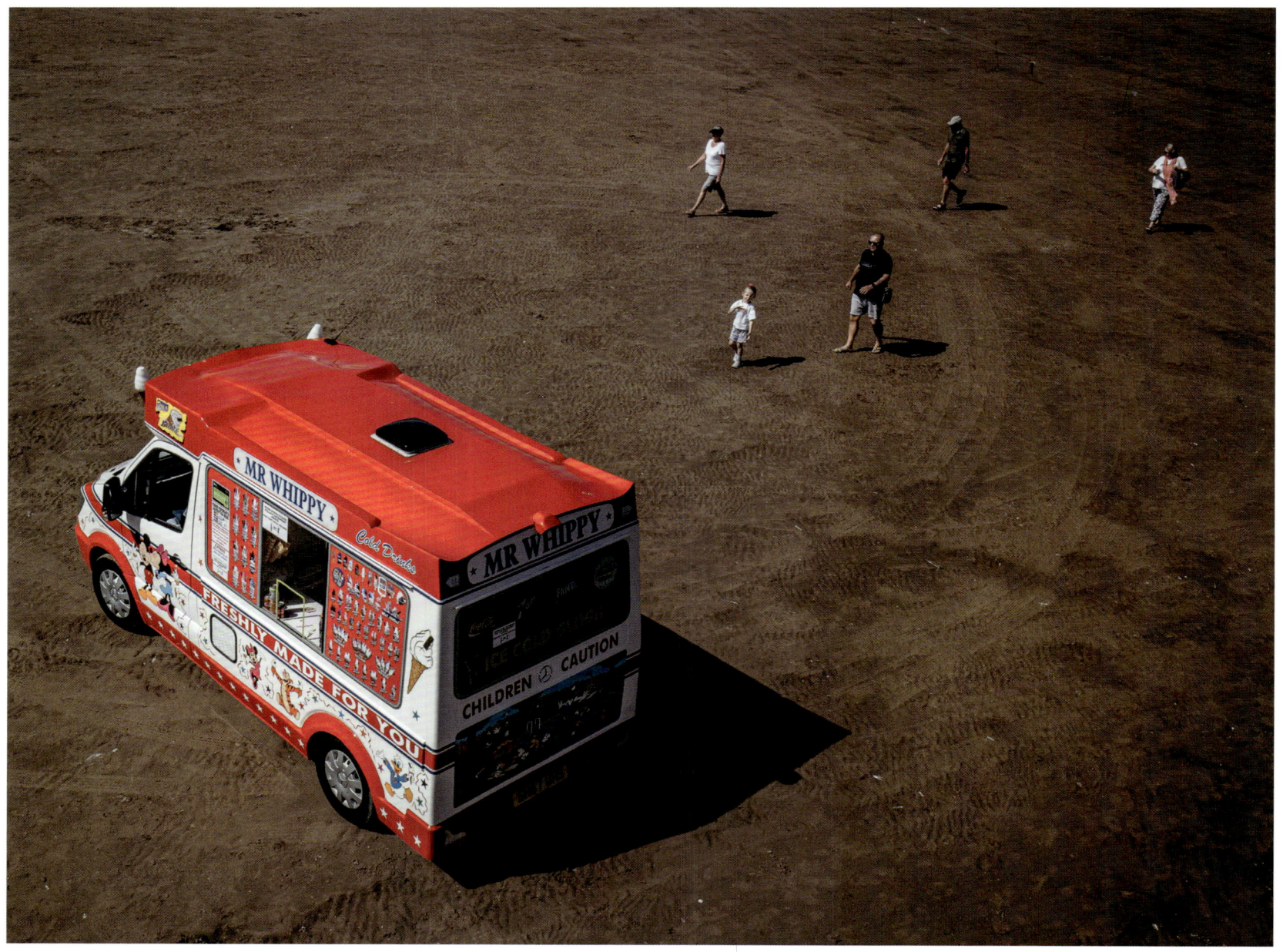

The Seaside

The seaside presents a world of opportunity for great street photography—to see great examples of what can be achieved, take a look at Martin Parr's 1985 book, *The Last Resort*.

Look at the beach for a "beauty and the beast" juxtaposition; people getting sunburned, paddling, picnicking, or fishing. Cafés and bars often have a lively life of their own, either in the bright sunlight or as darkness falls, while fairgrounds and funfairs have bright colors and fast-moving rides—try lowering your shutter speed to 1/8 sec. and shooting some blurred abstracts.

The seaside can also be interesting out of season, as once-vibrant resorts can appear more dilapidated and miserable. This works particularly well in black and white.

Above: As well as having fun with the humorous style of seaside street photography, don't ignore more reflective scenes such as this, which are as much about the composition as they are about the subject matter.

Focal length: 28mm

Aperture: f/9

Shutter speed: 1/2200 sec.

ISO: 200

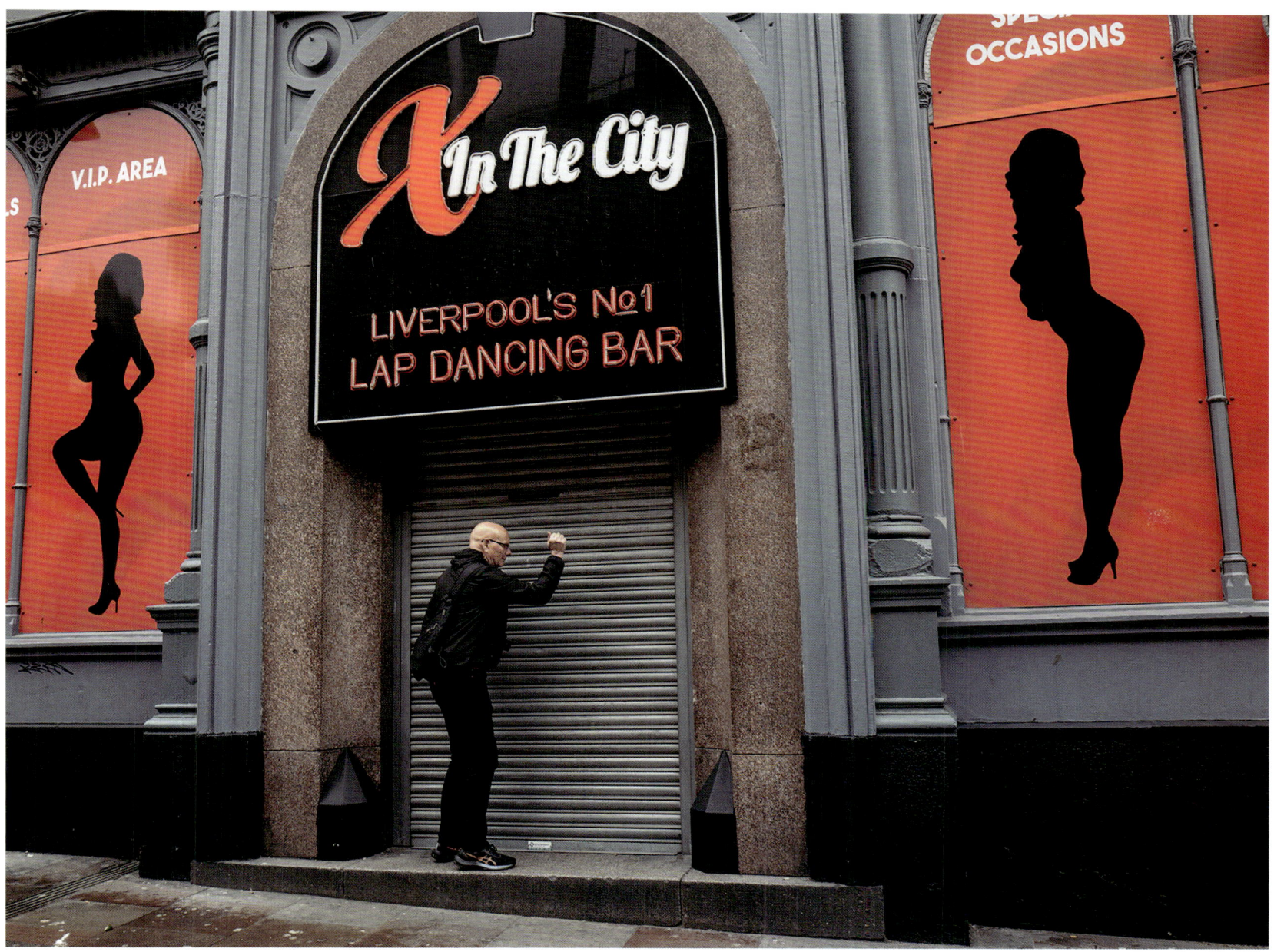

Shopping Areas

Retail areas are a good hunting ground for street photographers. While it can be difficult to shoot in large corporate malls (due to vigilant security systems), the streets provide us with ample opportunity to get some great shots. People tend to be concentrating on storefronts and are less likely to spot photographers, so you can shoot with relative ease.

In many countries, if you are shooting on the street and standing on public property, you are allowed to photograph just about anything you like; don't be harassed or bullied by over-zealous security guards who say "No cameras." However, be aware that the rules are not the same globally, so it's always best to check the local legalities before you go out on a shoot.

Above: There's usually lots of activity in retail districts and you need to keep alert for opportunities—sometimes you have only a brief second to react. And don't worry about copyright issues—as long as your image isn't being used commercially, you are allowed to take it for your own personal use.

Focal length: 125mm

Aperture: f/8

Shutter speed: 1/125 sec.

ISO: 1000

Protests & Demonstrations

Some would call this extreme street photography, as it can be both dangerous and exhilarating at the same time. Protests in the 21st century can escalate into public disorder in no time at all, so your priority should be to stay safe at all costs.

Emotion can run high at such events, so try to capture this in your photographs. Watch out for faces showing anger or rage; signs and other props will be everywhere and they are often humorous. Follow these general tips to help ensure you get a good crop of usable pictures from your efforts:

- Avoid general views of crowds; get as close as you safely can so that people's faces feature prominently in your shots.

- Watch the side roads, alleyways, and storefronts for fringe action away from the main event.

- Work quickly and unobtrusively. Use a prime (fixed focal length) lens so you don't waste valuable seconds zooming.

- Set your camera to a high ISO (around 1200) so you can use a fast shutter speed to freeze the action and avoid blur.

- Be discreet if you're shooting people's faces. Going in too close or "monstering" your subject could provoke an angry reaction.

- To help you focus on producing a meaningful body of work, treat the day as a project.

SAFETY TIPS

- Travel light. Take the minimum amount of gear possible. Don't flash your latest expensive gear around—instead, take an old compact that you're not afraid of losing.

- Blend in. Don't dress or behave like a photographer or look out of place in any way. Ideally, wear dark clothing and don't carry a photographer's bag. Avoid any clothing or behavior that may draw attention to yourself.

- Leave expensive watches, jewelry, and other valuables at home. Don't take anything you can't afford to lose!

- Know the geography. With planned events it's a good idea beforehand to familiarize yourself with routes in and out of the area, escape routes, and good vantage points. Be aware that public transport may not be operational, so be prepared for a long walk to a bus, train, or taxi point. Print off a map of the area.

- With a huge influx of people into a confined area you may find it difficult to get phone coverage. If you're with other people, ensure you have a set meeting place and time, in case you get separated from each other.

- If you're challenged when taking someone's photo, smile, say "Thank you," and walk away. Most of the time this will diffuse the situation.

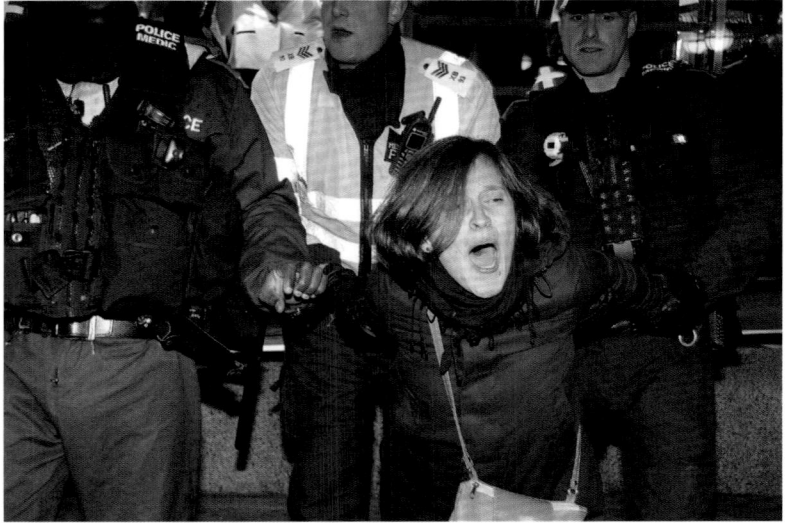

Above: In some (not all) countries you're allowed to photograph police officers doing their job. Wherever you can, inject some raw emotion into your shots by looking for situations like this, which can happen in places away from the main event.

Focal length: 50mm

Aperture: f/4.5

Shutter speed: 1/50 sec.

ISO: 800

Right: Smoke bombs are often used at demonstrations and can add atmosphere and drama to a shot.

Focal length: 35mm

Aperture: f/10

Shutter speed: 1/500 sec.

ISO: 1000

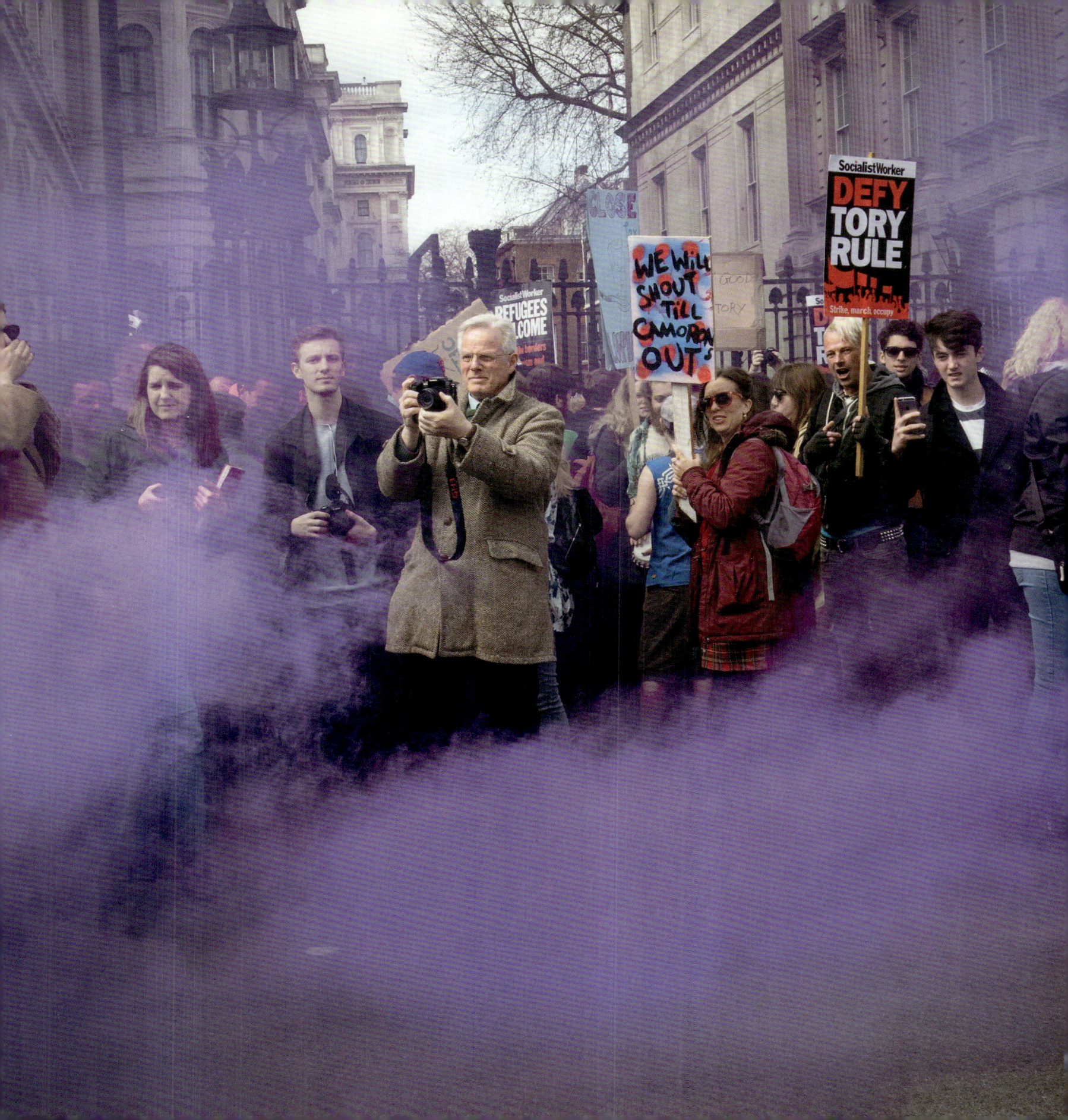

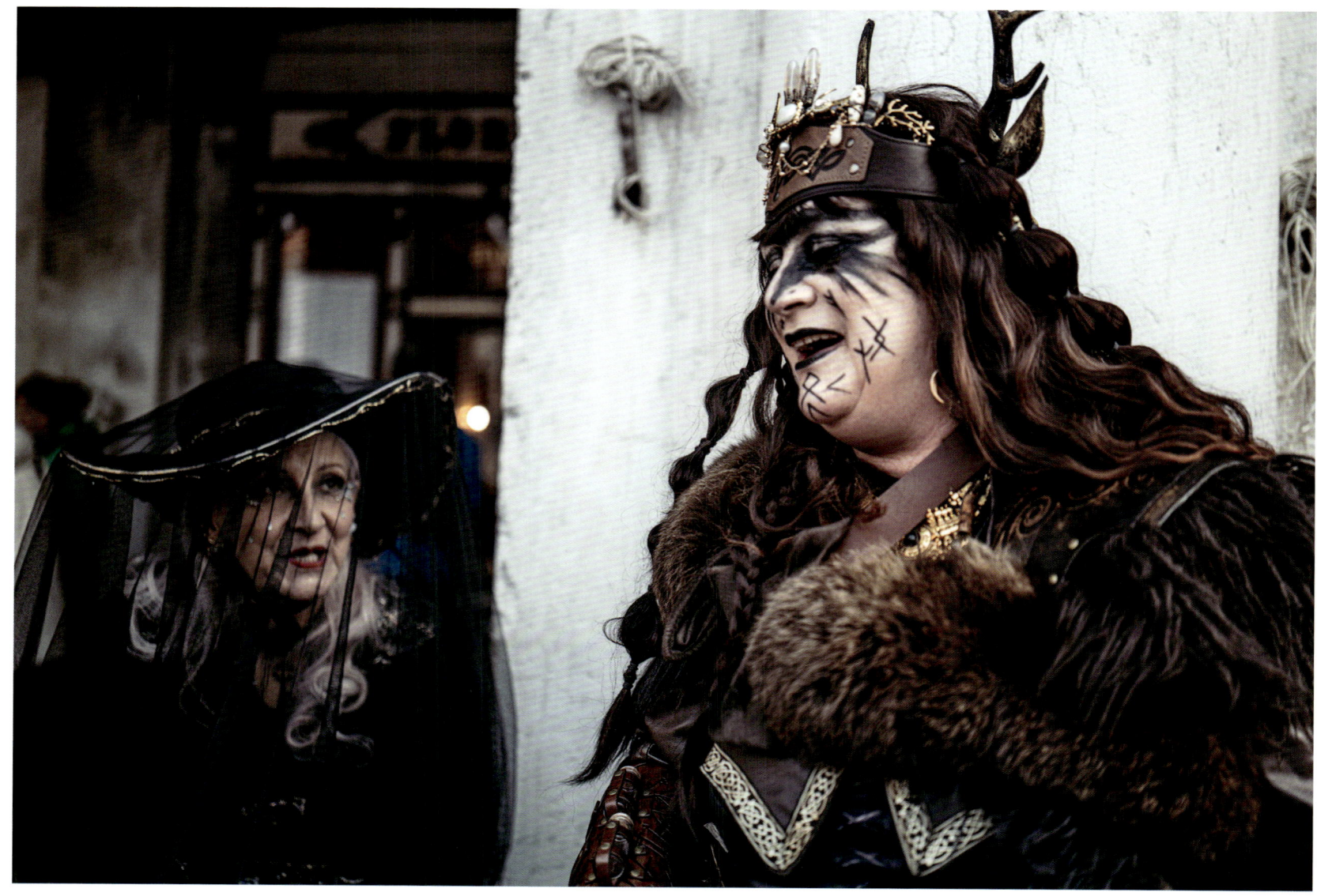

Festivals, Carnivals & Events

Most towns in most countries hold public events, ranging from large gatherings with tens of thousands of visitors to small village events. There is usually enough color, interest, and eccentricity to keep most street photographers happy.

Music festivals—especially major ones—can also provide us with great shooting opportunities, but rather than focusing on what's on the stage, look at what the people around you are doing— check out the audience, the bars, and around barbecues. As the sun goes down, look for campfires and lanterns, and don't be afraid to open up your aperture and set a high ISO.

Sporting events also take place around us, all year round. Look for events at which people dress or behave eccentrically; these could be race meetings, rowing festivals, or even small local competitions.

Above: Large events such as the Venice Carnival can be visually confusing with masses of people and clutter. Look for offbeat behind-the-scenes moments to help tell the story of the event.

Focal length: 43mm

Aperture: f/2

Shutter speed: 1/320 sec.

ISO: 200

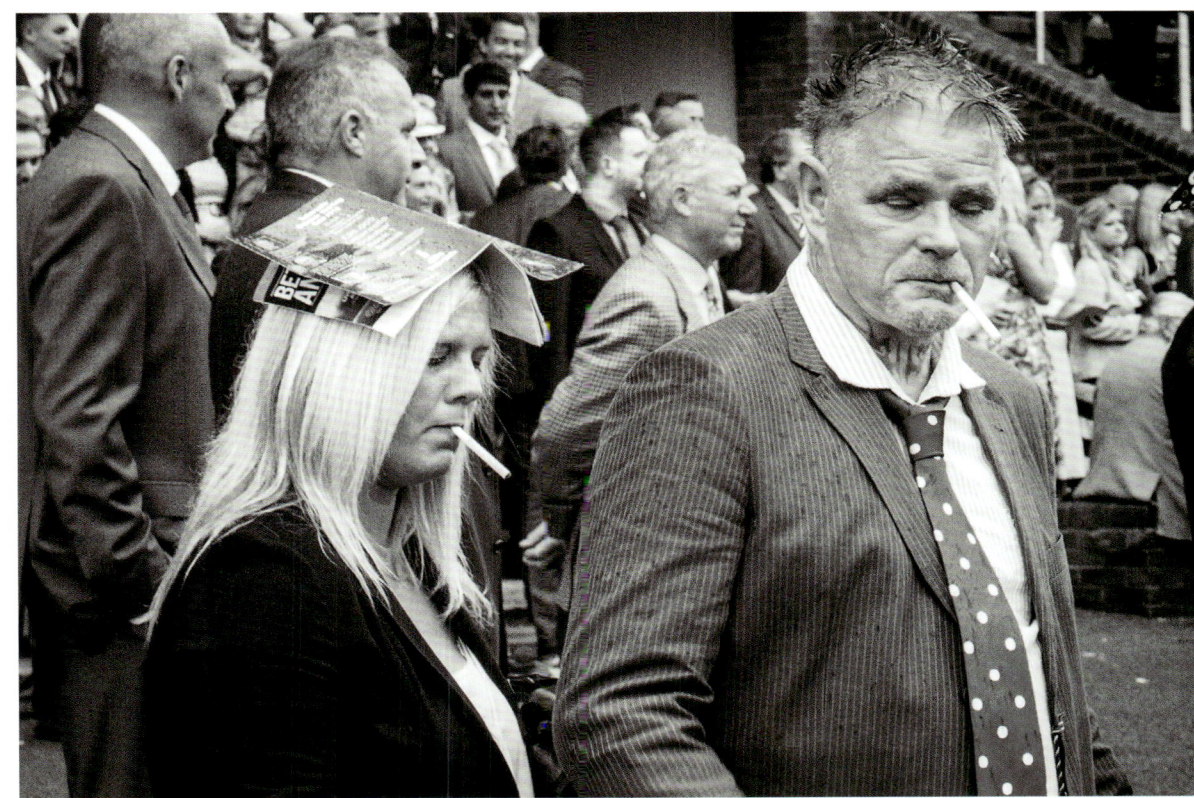

Right: This couple at the races seemed to be having a good day out! When you see someone who looks interesting, it's fine to stalk them (or at least keep an eye on them) until the time is right to snatch a frame or two.

Focal length: 30mm

Aperture: f/10

Shutter speed: 1/100 sec.

ISO: 3200

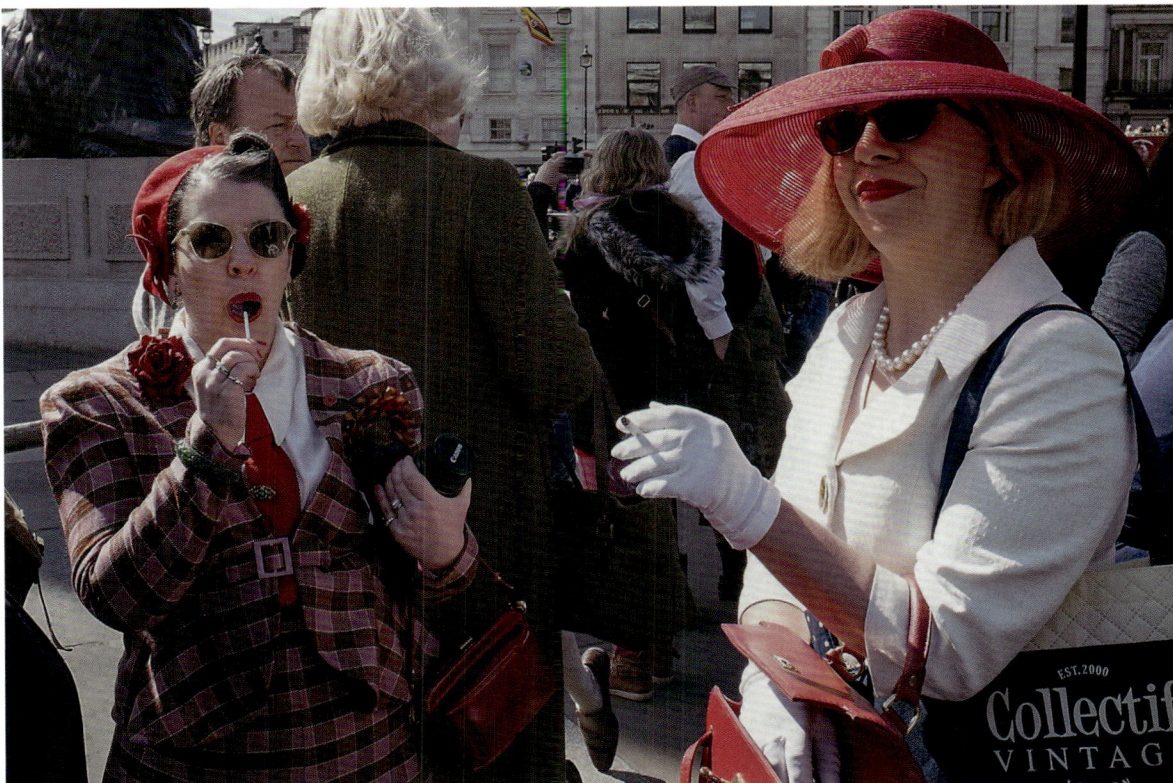

Right: If you can find an event with an element of eccentricity, so much the better.

Focal length: 35mm

Aperture: f/11

Shutter speed: 1/240 sec.

ISO: 800

Assignment 3: Juxtaposition

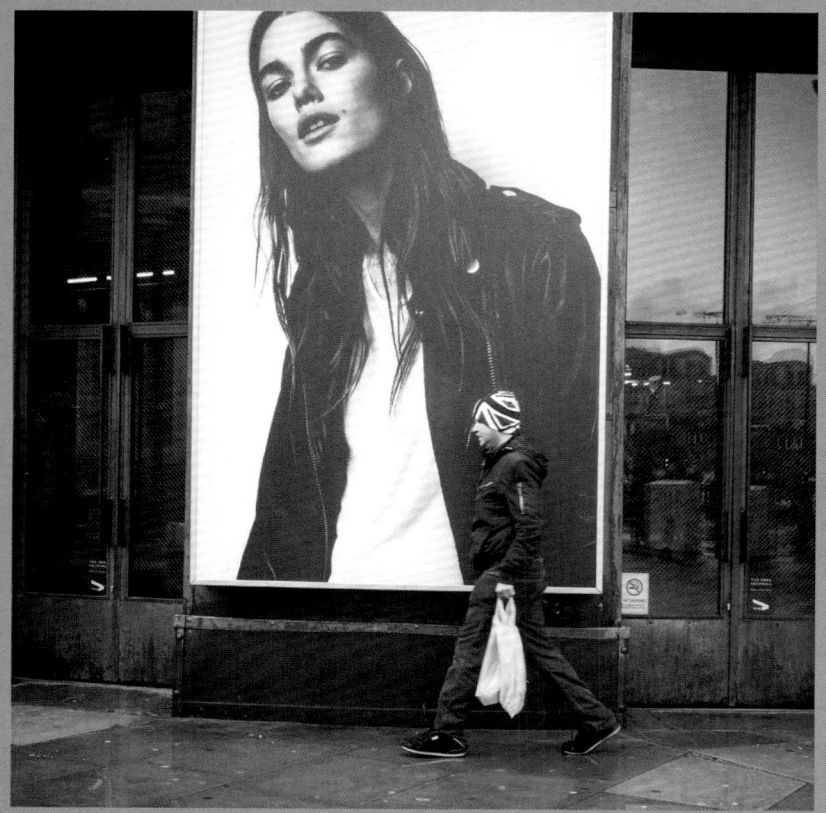

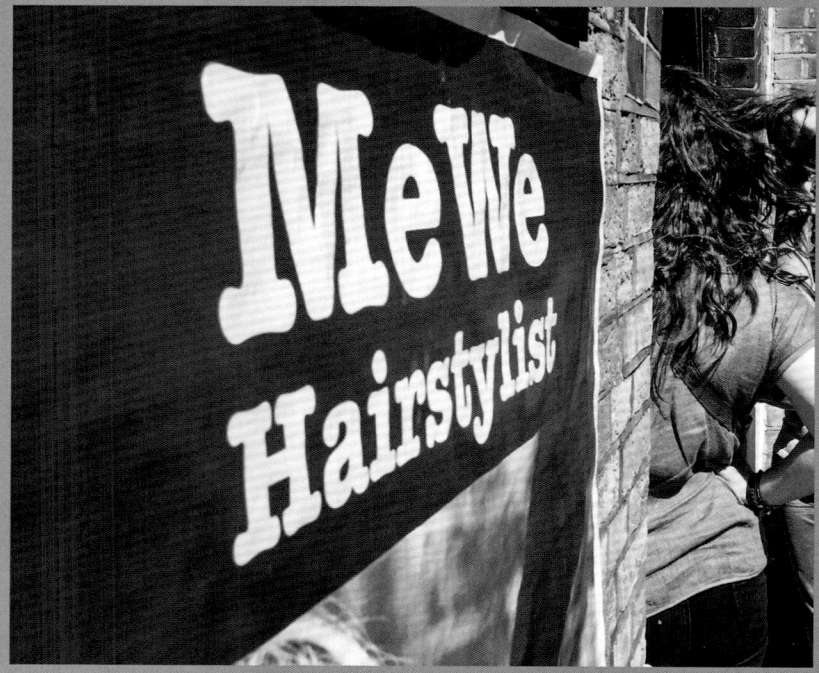

Above left:
Focal length: 35mm
Aperture: f/8
Shutter speed: 1/60 sec.
ISO: 1000

Above:
Focal length: 28mm
Aperture: f/8
Shutter speed: 1/300 sec.
ISO: 200

The Challenge

Contrasts, contradictions, or juxtapositions have always played a part in street photography and it is important that you are able to recognize and take advantage of them. Whether you live in a small town or a major city, retail areas will offer plenty of contrasts; it's where you're going to see a large person eating an enormous burger outside a health food store, or a less-than-beautiful person stood alongside a stunning model on a poster.

Juxtaposition happens when you place two or more contrasting objects, images, or ideas together, so that the differences between them are emphasized. Juxtapositions can involve a person and a sign or inanimate object, two or more people, or two or more inanimate objects.

You may find juxtapositions that happen naturally, or you may have to think carefully about how you compose your shot: sometimes waiting for one or more elements to come into the scene. The effect may be obvious from the outset or the viewer may have to think their way around the picture, not getting it immediately.

Your challenge with this assignment is to produce a set of images that has a lighthearted, playful feel to them, ideally bringing a smile to the viewer's face.

LOCATION

A busy retail area in your local town or city.

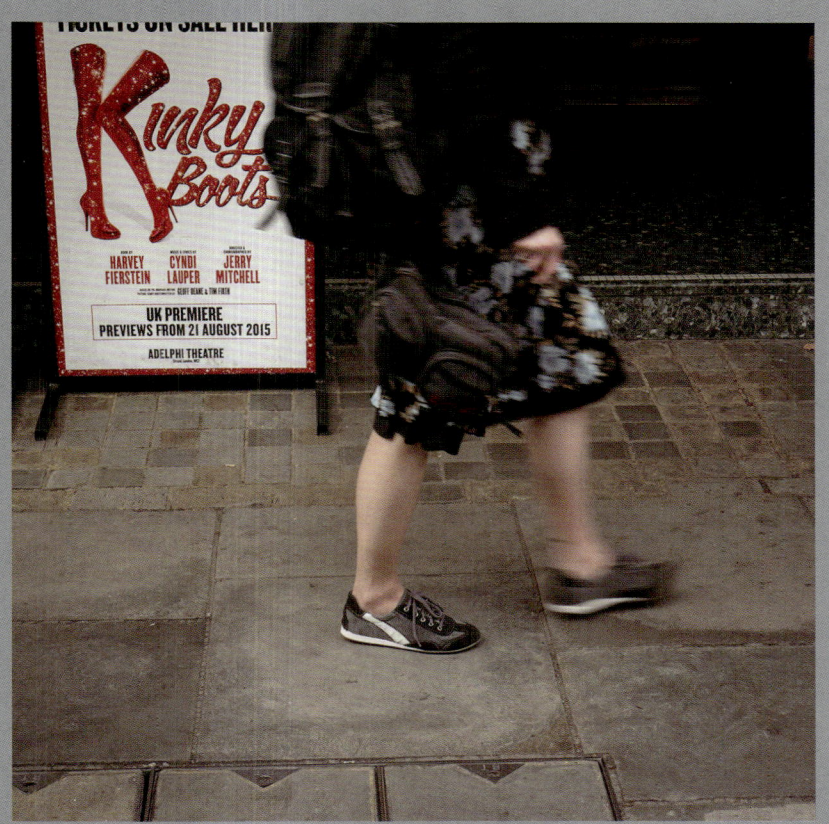

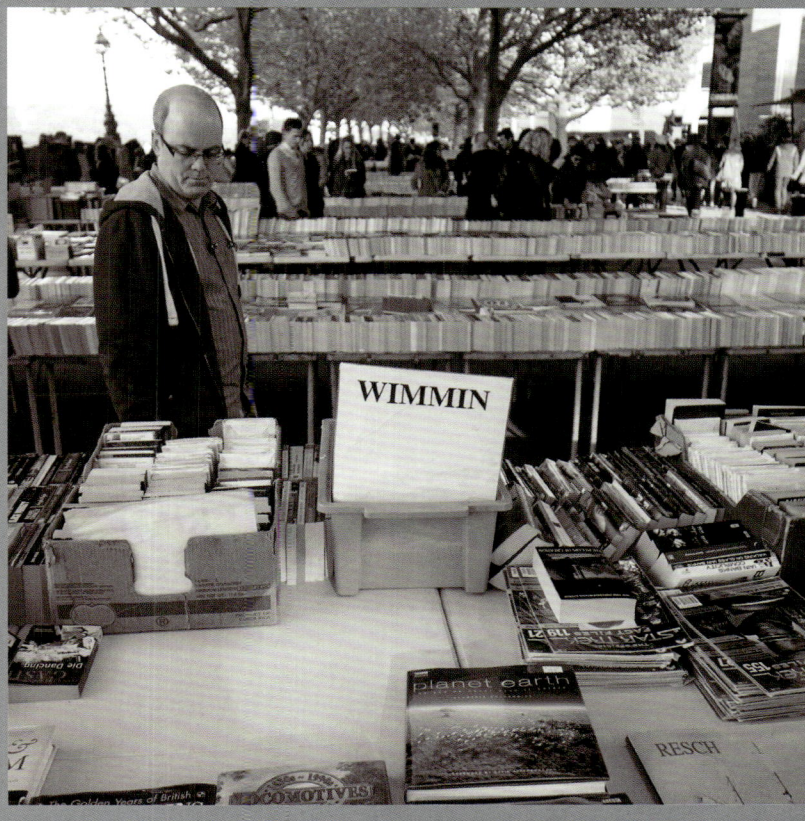

TECHNIQUES

- Shoot this assignment in color: retail areas tend to be full of vibrant, contrasting colors.

- Be patient. You may need to wait for the right elements to come together to complete the composition, so pick a good spot and wait!

- Blend in to your environment and try not to be outed as a photographer.

TOP TIPS

- Be inquisitive. Look ahead, behind you, and all around you (the best opportunities are not always directly in front of you).

- Be ready and in a position to shoot quickly.

- Look carefully at all the signs you see and ask yourself if they have the potential for a good shot.

- Don't forget abstracts: contrasting colors, shapes, and textures can work.

Above left:
Focal length: 50mm
Aperture: f/8
Shutter speed: 1/100 sec.
ISO: 250

Above:
Focal length: 24mm
Aperture: f/1.7
Shutter speed: 1/1000 sec.
ISO: 200

Assignment 4: Objects

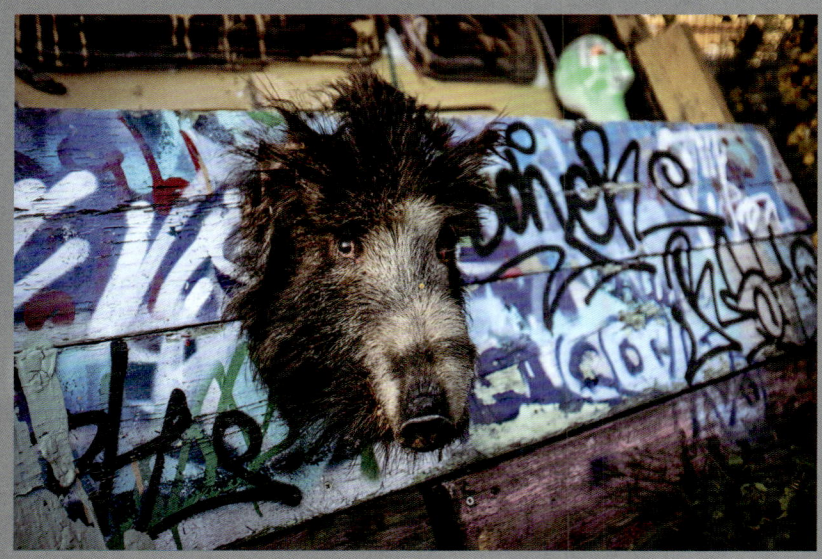 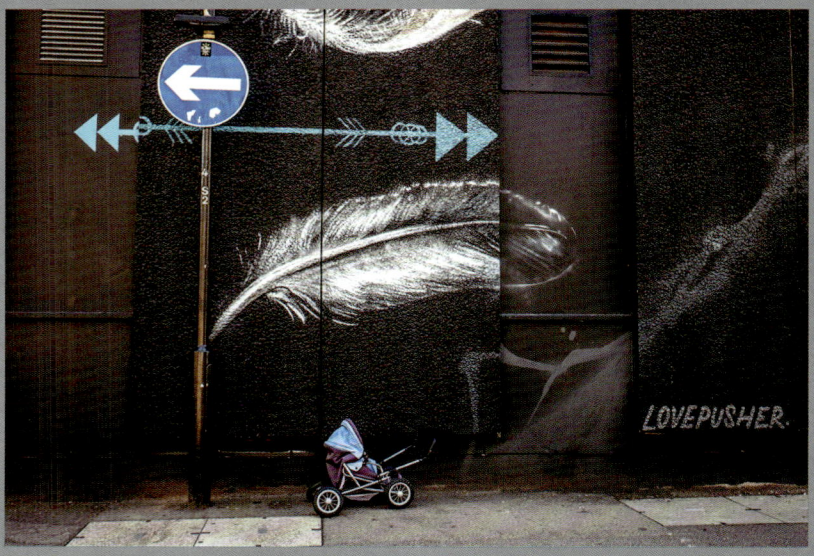

The Challenge

Objects surround you wherever you are on the streets: signs, boxes, arrows, street furniture, dogs, strollers, litter—if you keep your eyes open you'll see just about everything imaginable. In terms of their physical presence on the streets and in our lives, these objects are valid subjects for street photographers. Whether they are things that move or they're inanimate, they can provide us with interesting material.

Try to focus your attention on a particular type of object: it could be bottles, litter, pigeons, balloons, cardboard boxes, discarded furniture—whatever takes your fancy. Spend perhaps a month looking for and photographing these objects and develop your work into a mini project.

LOCATION

Streets, the local market, the train station, or the beach would make a good starting point, although you can find objects to photograph just about anywhere.

Above left:
Focal length: 35mm
Aperture: f/2
Shutter speed: 1/700 sec.
ISO: 1000

Above:
Focal length: 28mm
Aperture: f/8
Shutter speed: 1/60 sec.
ISO: 500

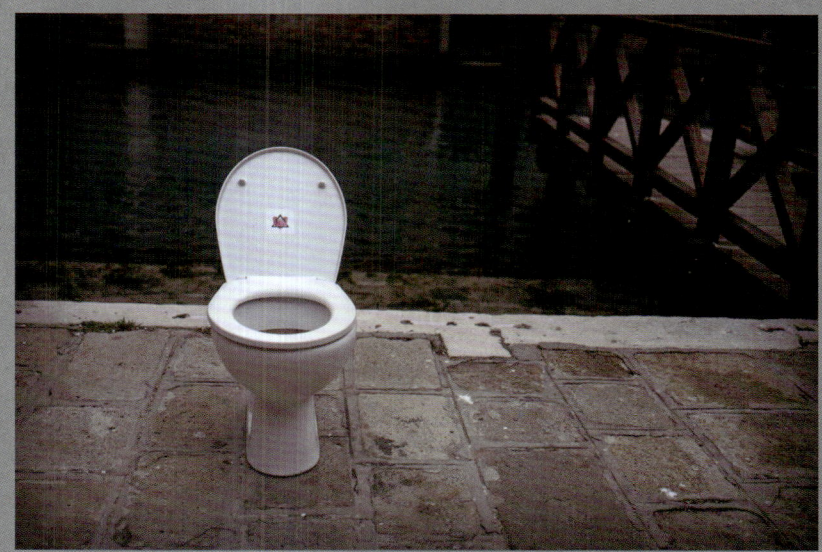

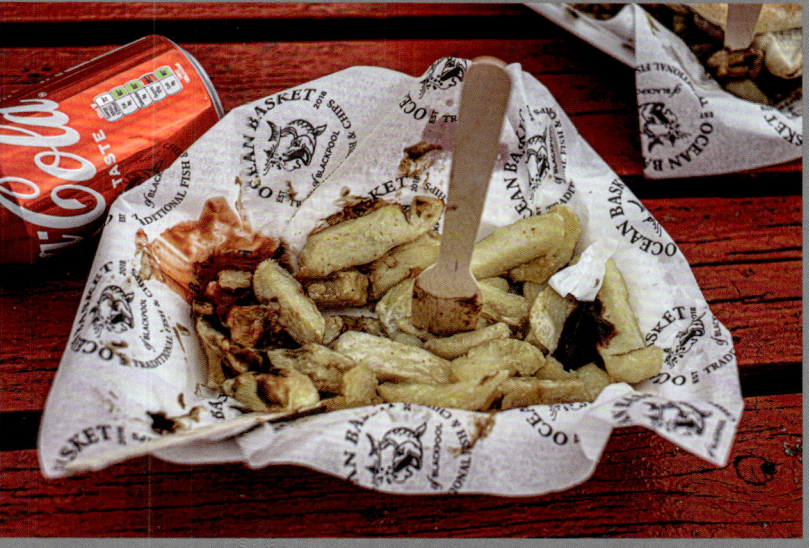

TECHNIQUES

- Observational skills and a strong sense of curiosity.

- Composition. Think about the positioning of your object in relation to its environment; will the rule of thirds help you frame the object? Are there any other compositional techniques you can use?

- The ability to persist with a project and see it through to conclusion.

TOP TIPS

- Look at how objects fit in (or don't) with their environment.

- Abandoned items can make good subjects, so maybe consider decaying fruit, discarded flowers, or old mattresses.

Above left:
Focal length: 35mm
Aperture: f/1.5
Shutter speed: 1/1500 sec.
ISO: 200

Above:
Focal length: 50mm
Aperture: f/2.8
Shutter speed: 1/800 sec.
ISO: 200

Chapter 4
On Location

There are some tried and trusted ways of working the streets as a photographer; spies would call this tradecraft. Unlike most other genres of photography, street photography has its own set of distinct working practices or, in some respects, rules. If you were to search the Internet for "the rules of street photography," you would come across many, many words of wisdom about what you can and can't do. Don't let any of this put you off; street photography is a fluid, free-flowing art form and the only rule that really matters is to do what works for you.

This chapter is all about working in the field and the essential techniques that street photographers need to deploy. You will explore key topics such as planning a shoot, developing projects, using techniques to remain unobserved, and looking at how to overcome fears of photographing strangers in public places. You will also look at developing observational skills, blending in, and techniques that can speed up your shooting.

Right: When working on the streets, you need to become part of the fabric of street life—to the point where you go unnoticed because you just fit in.

Focal length: 28mm
Aperture: f/5.6
Shutter speed: 1/1100 sec.
ISO: 200

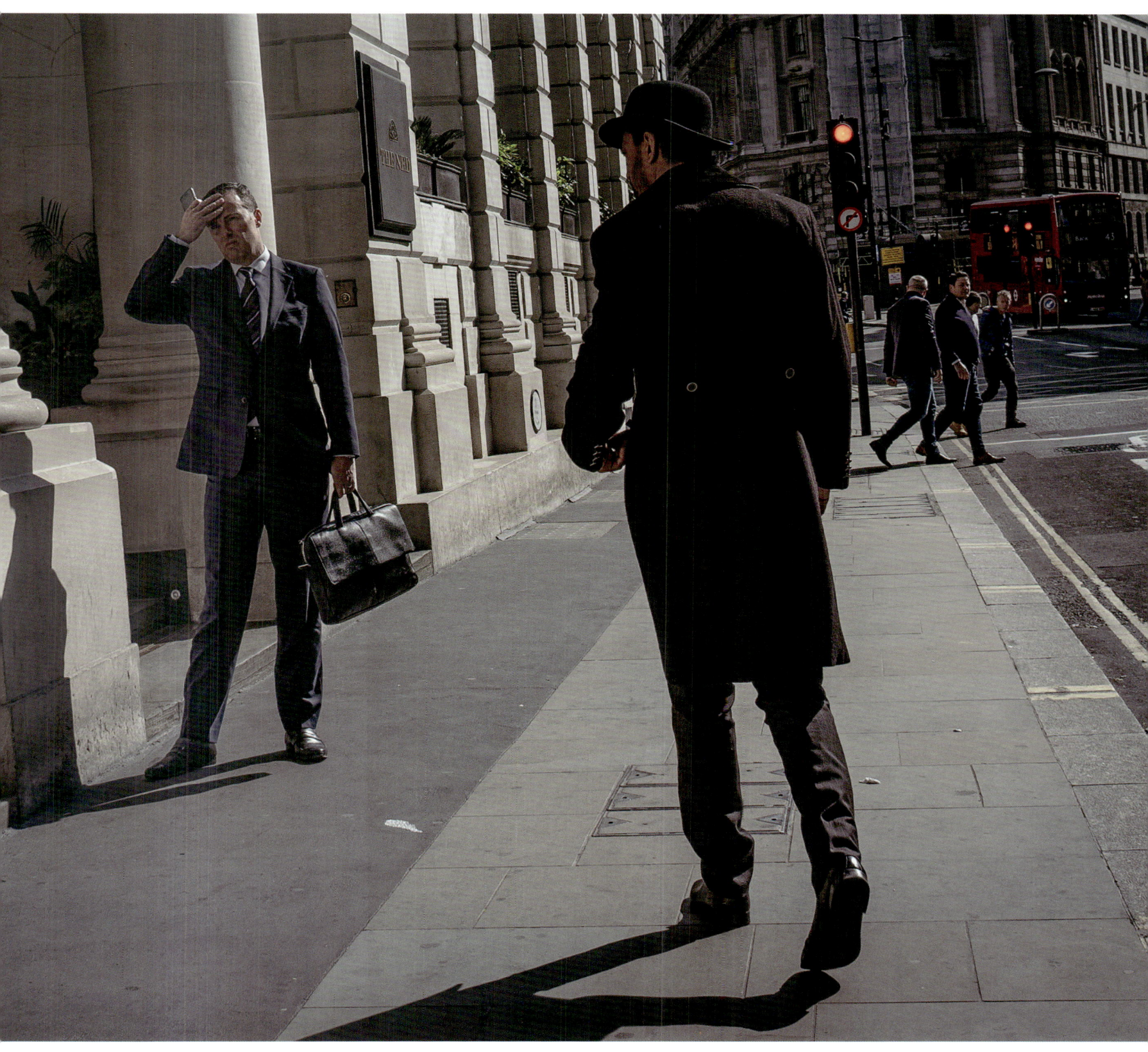

Planning A Shoot

Can you identify with the following scenario? You leave home in the morning, embarking on a street photography expedition, fired with enthusiasm and expectation, but by lunchtime you're wondering what it's all about. Where are all those photo opportunities? Why is nothing happening? By this time your feet are tired, your memory card's empty, and heading home seems the best option. We call this "street fatigue," and it's something that's happened to all of us. However, the good news is that it's totally avoidable.

To start with, don't leave home without a real sense of purpose. Have at least a rough idea of the sort of subjects you want to shoot and where you might find them. If you're visiting an area which is new to you, do some simple image research on the Internet to get a feel for where the street photography hot spots might be; look at what other photographers have done there, not with the intention of replicating their work, but to get a feel for what might work.

Think about where you are going, how you plan to get there, and what you will pass on the way. Consider packing a guide book, a map, and, ideally, some of your own notes about where you plan to go and what you hope to shoot there. Don't let this planning get in the way of making the most of spontaneous opportunities, though. From the minute you leave home you should be in shooting mode; tuned in to possible opportunities, with your camera switched on.

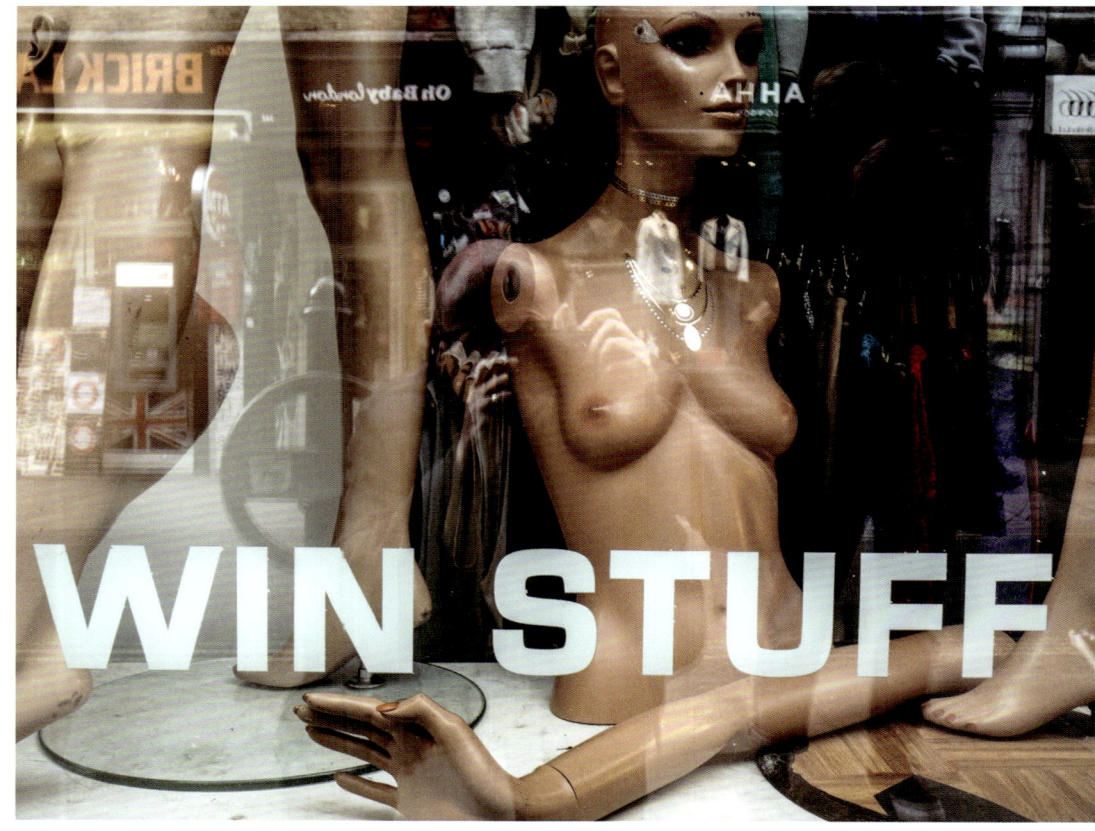

Above: You don't have to look far to find potential for a shot—and you don't necessarily need people. These disembodied mannequins, along with the unlikely phrase "win stuff," caught the eye.

Focal length: 35mm

Aperture: f/8

Shutter speed: 1/100 sec.

ISO: 1000

"One doesn't stop seeing. One doesn't stop framing. It doesn't turn off and turn on. It's on all the time."

—Annie Leibovitz

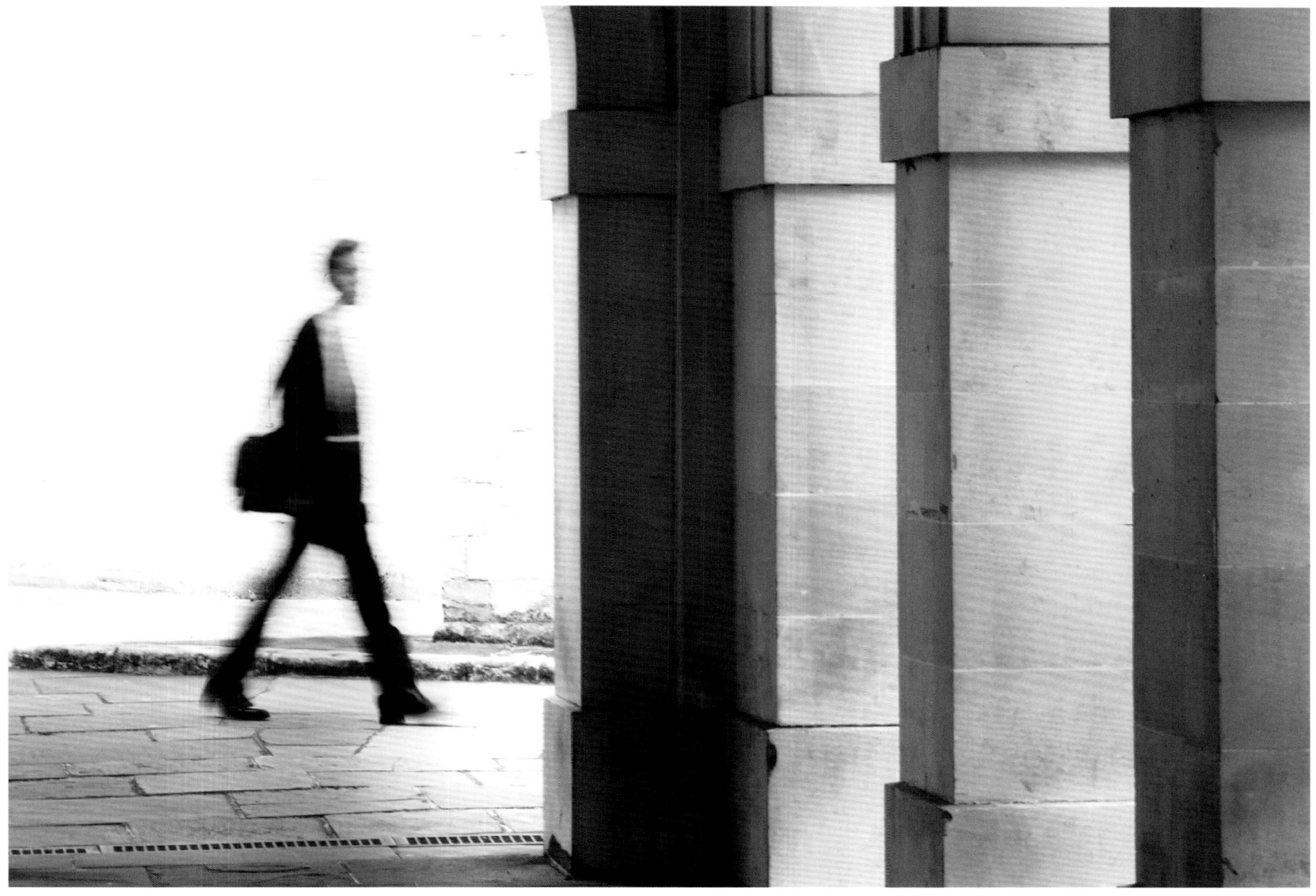

Managing Your Expectations

The ability to manage your expectations is essential to help maintain your confidence and your motivation. A lot of us are guilty of having hard drives containing many thousands of images that will never see the light of day.

Part of the problem is that digital photography makes it easy for us to overshoot to start with, while street photography—with its relatively large margins for error—also means that overshooting is, in some ways, preferable. It may take a dozen or so frames to get that perfect shot, but out of

that dozen, how many frames do you really need to keep?

So, to start with don't set your expectations too high! Two or three strong images from a day of shooting is pretty good going—some of the leading names in this field are happy to produce between six and ten outstanding images per year, which is a clear indication that quality, not quantity is the order of the day.

Above: This image looked dull in its original color form, but it came to life with a monochrome conversion, so don't be too quick to delete your images!

Focal length: 80mm

Aperture: f/16

Shutter speed: 1/10 sec.

ISO: 100

The Weather

Don't be put off by the thought of bad weather! In the art of street photography, there is no such thing as bad weather and you need to make the most of whatever the elements throw at you.

Rain is possibly the element most likely to convince you to stay at home, but don't let it! Rain presents some very good opportunities, such as reflections, puddles, umbrellas, people running for cover, miserable faces, people huddled in doorways, spray caused by traffic, and raindrops on glass—you will probably have seen some very good examples of street photography taken in the wettest of conditions.

Furthermore, when it's raining, people tend to be focused on getting from A to B as quickly as they can, and are less likely to notice (or be interested) in someone taking their picture. The same principle applies to snow, ice, and fog; any extreme weather conditions can make the perfect environment for street photography.

You should also be happy to venture out on brighter, sunnier days as well. Think about long shadows, screwed-up faces looking into the sun, vibrant colors, contrast, people sitting outside cafés and bars, and a general air of high spirits and positivity.

When it comes to lighting, it pays to be aware of the "golden hour"—the hour just after sunrise and the hour before sunset—when the light is at its most photogenic. Also called the "magic hour," this is the time of day when the sun is at its most diffuse and shooting at this time can produce some very atmospheric results. There are online calculators that will tell you the golden hour for your specific location on a particular day.

So, whatever the weather, there's no reason not to get out there—just make sure you have protection for yourself and your equipment and your tenacity will be rewarded.

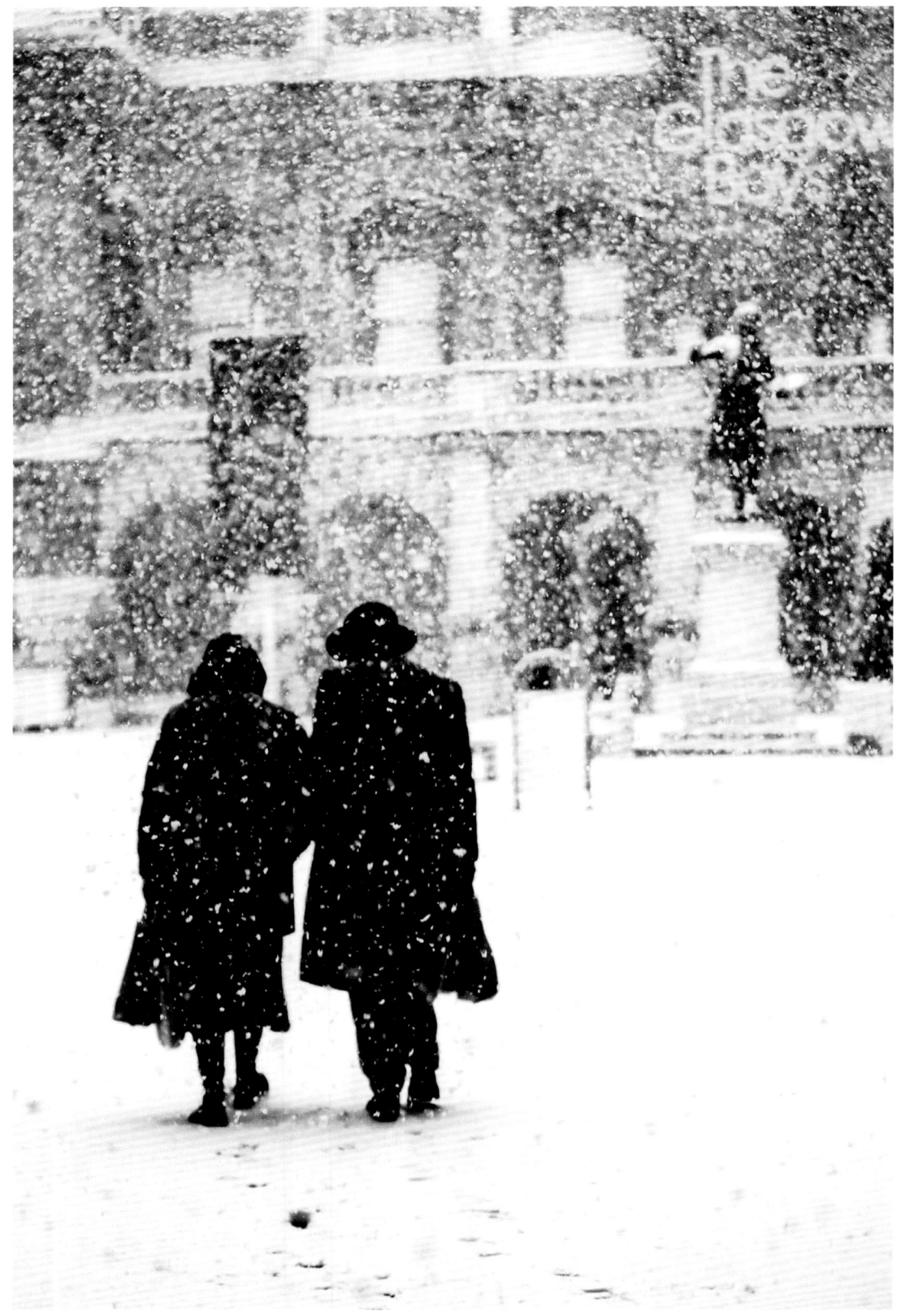

Left: When photographing in the snow, take care not to underexpose your shots: most cameras will be fooled into thinking the scene is brighter than it actually is, so you may need to apply a touch of exposure compensation.

Focal length: 105mm

Aperture: f/2.8

Shutter speed: 1/250 sec.

ISO: 200

Below: Umbrellas, wet sidewalks, reflections, miserable faces—they all provide street photographers with good raw material. Just remember to keep the rain off your lens!

Focal length: 35mm

Aperture: f/7.1

Shutter speed: 1/100 sec.

ISO: 1250

"Twelve significant photographs in any one year is a good crop."

—Ansel Adams

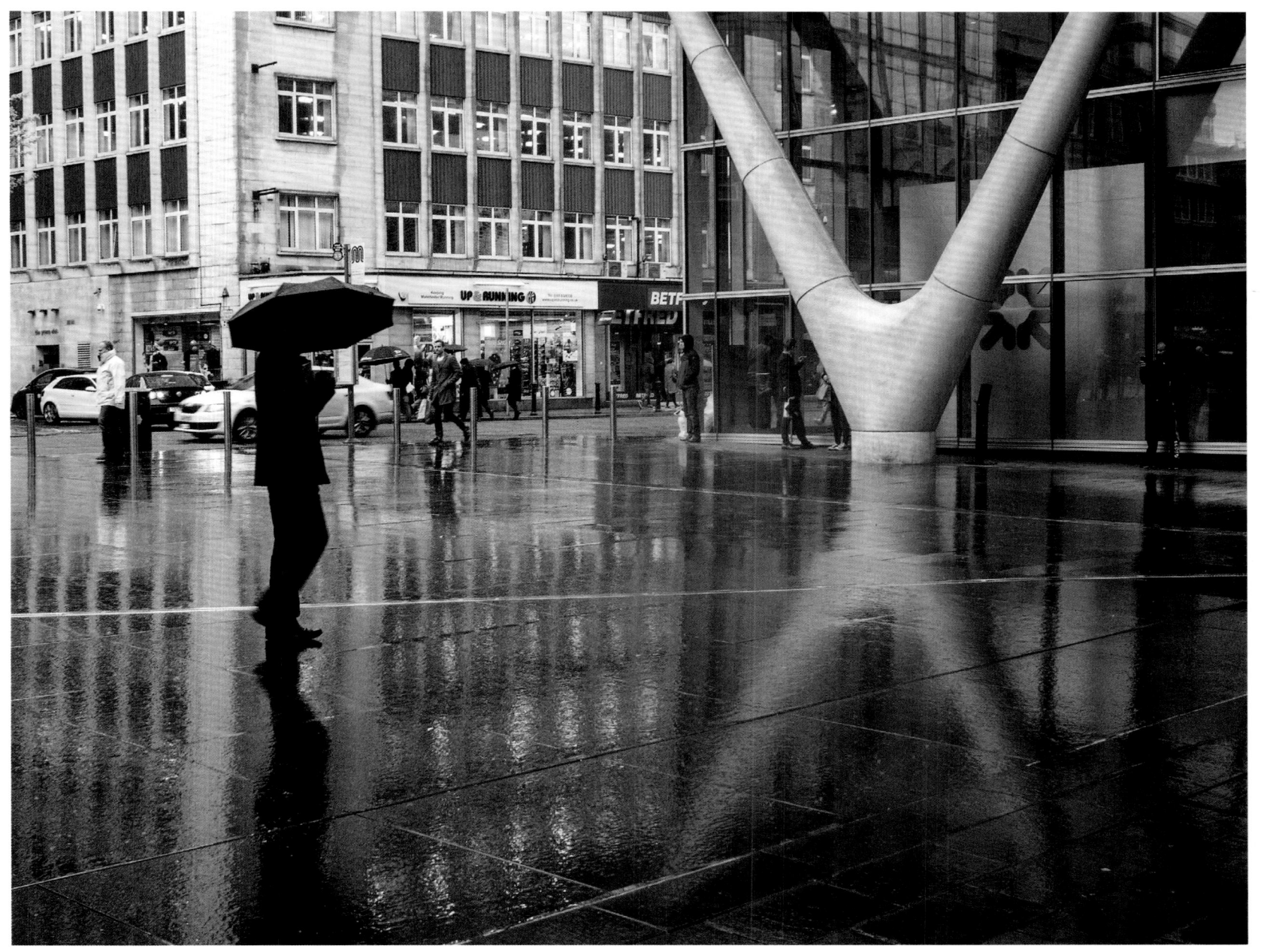

Working Safely

The streets are not always as safe as you would like them to be, but your personal safety is of paramount importance. Although street photographers rarely encounter serious problems, you must do all you can to minimize the dangers to yourself and your equipment. Keep yourself as safe as possible by following these simple guidelines:

- Try not to look like a photographer. Avoid clothing such as photographers' vests and large bags carrying photographic brand names; never walk around with more than one camera slung over your shoulder.

- Travel with the minimum of kit, ideally with a small shoulder bag rather than a big backpack. Whatever kit is not in use should be stored in a bag or pockets.

- If you have an expensive camera, think about how you can "uglify" it—maybe by putting black tape over the logo? Also, ditch the bright, branded strap that came with the camera and get something more anonymous.

- Look where you're going. When you're concentrating on getting the picture, it is easy to step into the path of traffic or to trip over a step. If you need to walk while looking through the viewfinder, have your other eye on what is ahead of you.

- Be aware of people who may be watching you or behaving suspiciously, particularly when nobody else is about.

- Know what you can and can't (or shouldn't) do. Find out the laws and the cultural sensitivities of where you are shooting.

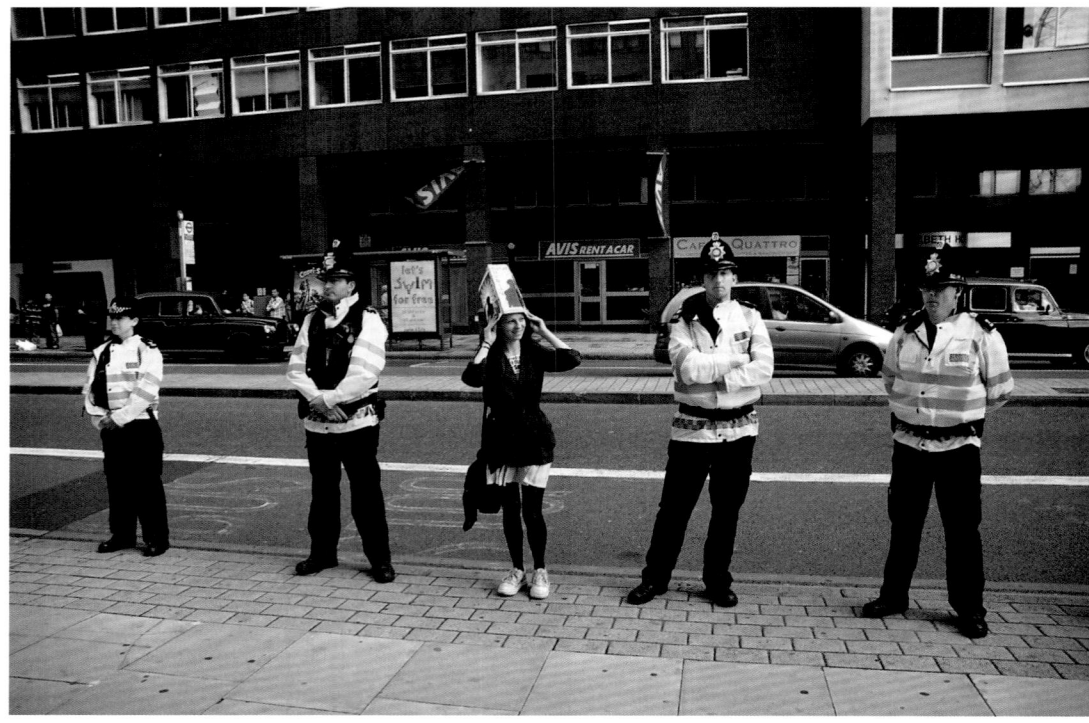

- Don't draw attention to yourself. Walk slowly, with your elbows in, and avoid making eye contact with anyone. If you can manage to look miserable, so much the better.

- Try to gauge a person's mood before photographing them (or taking pictures near them). If in doubt, don't shoot.

- If you're going to a potentially "bad" area, consider going with a friend. People in pairs are less likely to be challenged.

- Carry a good supply of memory cards with you and keep them in a different place to the rest of your gear; change them frequently and don't keep the whole day's shoot on one card.

Above: If you become concerned for your safety, look for police officers and stay close to them. And don't forget to get a picture of them while they work!

Focal length: 28mm

Aperture: f/4

Shutter speed: 1/320 sec.

ISO: 400

Developing Observational Skills

The best street photographers are great observers of life; they absorb the human spirit like a sponge absorbs water. Some people are naturally observant, while for others it's a skill that needs to be acquired. Don't lose heart if you think your skills in this area are lacking—people who study and practice the art of street photography tend to become more observant as their work progresses.

However, well-developed observation skills are a must. You need to know what is going on around you and be able to anticipate and predict the actions of others so you are in a state of readiness to capture a moment.

Here are a few tips to help boost your powers of observation:

- Listen to your instinct. It's usually right! If you can sense something going on around you, tune in and follow the scent.

- Be curious. Always ask yourself what is around that corner, who is inside that store, or what is behind that door. Be nosy and it will pay dividends.

- Be outwardly focused. Pay more attention to others than to yourself. Many street photographers are overly interested in how they look or behave; nobody is interested in you, so focus your attention on others.

- Don't be easily distracted. In order to really concentrate on the here and now, switch off your phone, open up all your senses, and tune in to where you are and what you are doing at that precise moment.

- Pay attention to body language; it can be a strong indicator of what a person is likely to do next.

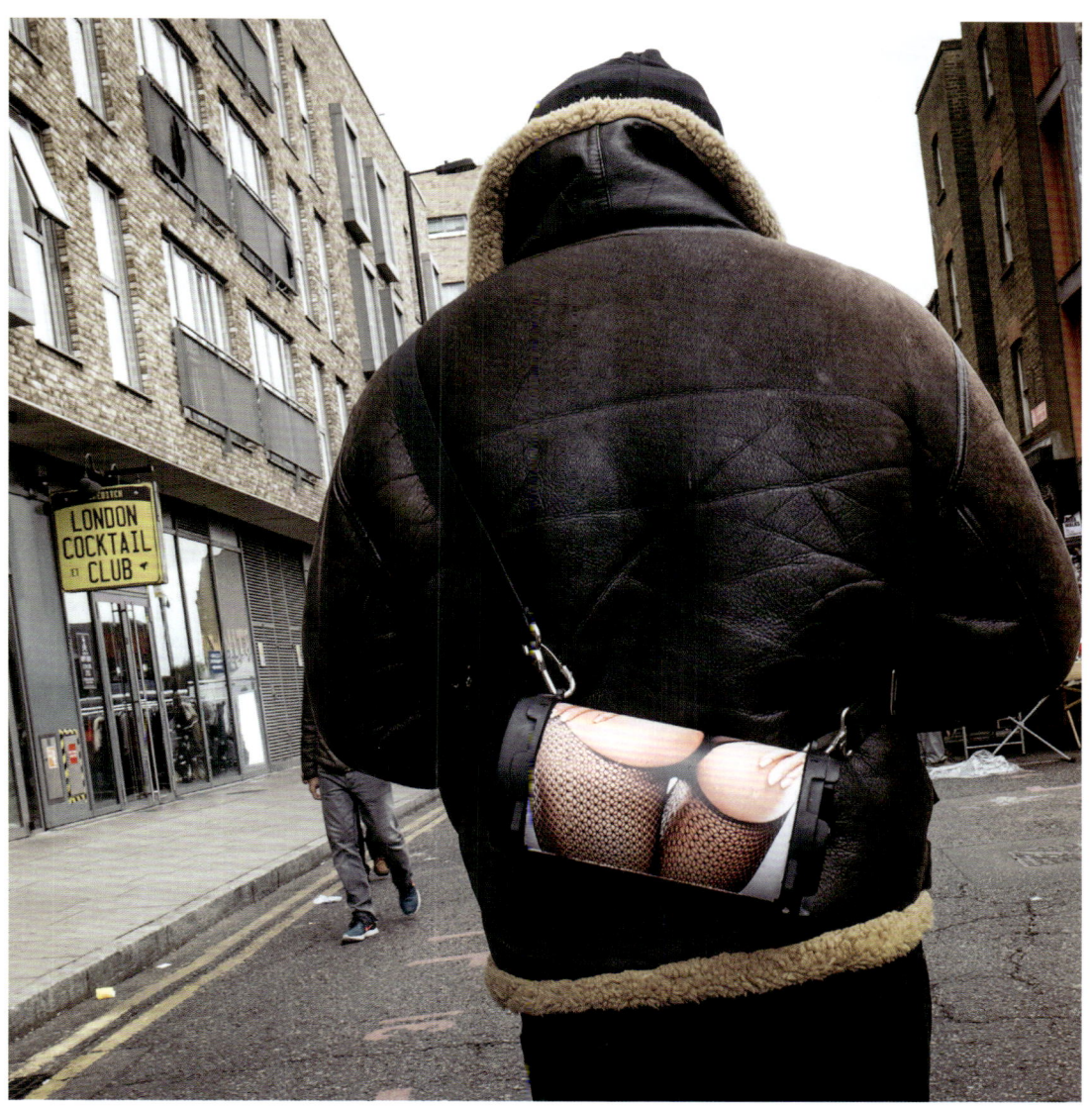

Above: Interesting possibilities are happening all around you and often it's down to sheer luck—and being observant.
Focal length: 28mm
Aperture: f/8
Shutter speed: 1/180 sec.
ISO: 1250

How To Be Invisible

Street photographers generally prefer to be unobserved and not outed. There are two principal reasons for this. Firstly, you need to preserve the integrity of the scene. Once you have been spotted, something in the scene will change; people will modify their behavior and what you saw originally will not be what the camera records; Joel Meyerowitz called this "bruising the scene."

Secondly, it's in our nature to want to avoid confrontation. If you can work without being seen, so much the better, although any challenges are unlikely to have serious consequences.

MAKE YOURSELF UNAPPROACHABLE

If you wear a series of barriers you are less likely to be noticed and far less likely to be approached or challenged. Such barriers are an effective psychological technique and the more barriers there are, the more invisible you will become. Barriers can include:

- Sunglasses, which make eye contact impossible.

- Wearing earphones; people are less likely to challenge you if you appear to be lost in your own world.

- Wear a hat, particularly one with a peak pulled down low.

- Don't look too happy. Smiley, happy people tend to draw attention to themselves; people are less likely to want to engage with you if you look miserable.

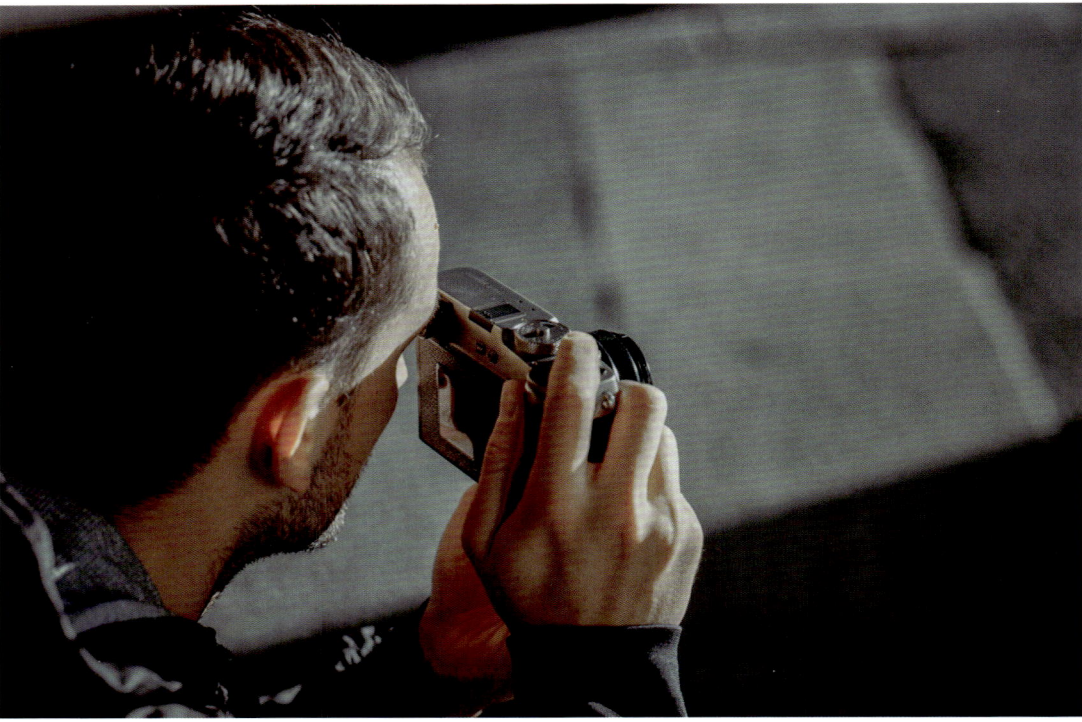

Above: If you move quietly, slowly, and avoid jerky movements, you are less likely to draw attention to yourself. The same principle applies if you're shooting in a position like this when you are below eye level and out of people's normal line of sight.

Focal length: 35mm

Aperture: f/4.5

Shutter speed: 1/550 sec.

ISO: 160

Blend In

Think about your environment and the people around you. Do you look as though you belong there? Do you blend in? People are less likely to notice you if you look like everyone else; it is important not to stand out in any way—and even more important not to look like a photographer. You will blend in more easily if you walk slowly and avoid sudden, jerky movements.

Shoot From The Hip

Bringing your camera up to eye level will always draw attention to you. With a bit of practice (and lots of wasted frames along the way), you will get to know your camera and lens combination really well and you will know exactly what shooting angle is required to compose the shot. If your camera has an articulated (hinged) rear viewing screen, shooting from the hip becomes considerably easier. While some street photographers shun this as an easy option, it is a useful technique that can work well with a wide-angle lens.

However, beware of becoming overly reliant on this technique and using it as a crutch; you should get into the habit of using the viewfinder in the normal way, only shooting from the hip when you really need to do so.

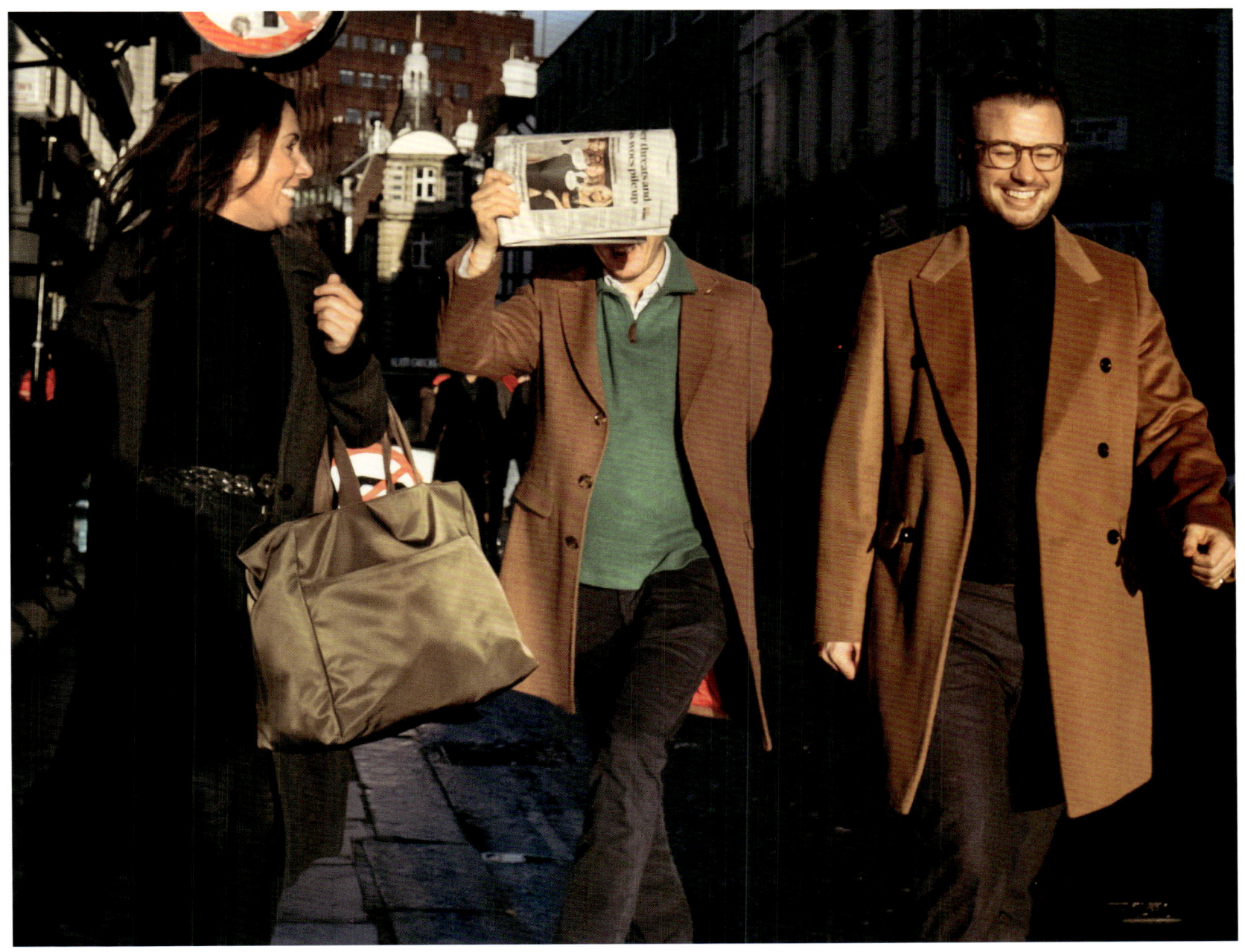

"A good photograph is knowing where to stand."

—Ansel Adams

Above: You can often go unnoticed if you shoot from the hip. It's a technique that requires practice, but it works—the people in this shot were oblivious to the photographer.

Focal length: 24mm

Aperture: f/10

Shutter speed: 1/250 sec.

ISO: 1250

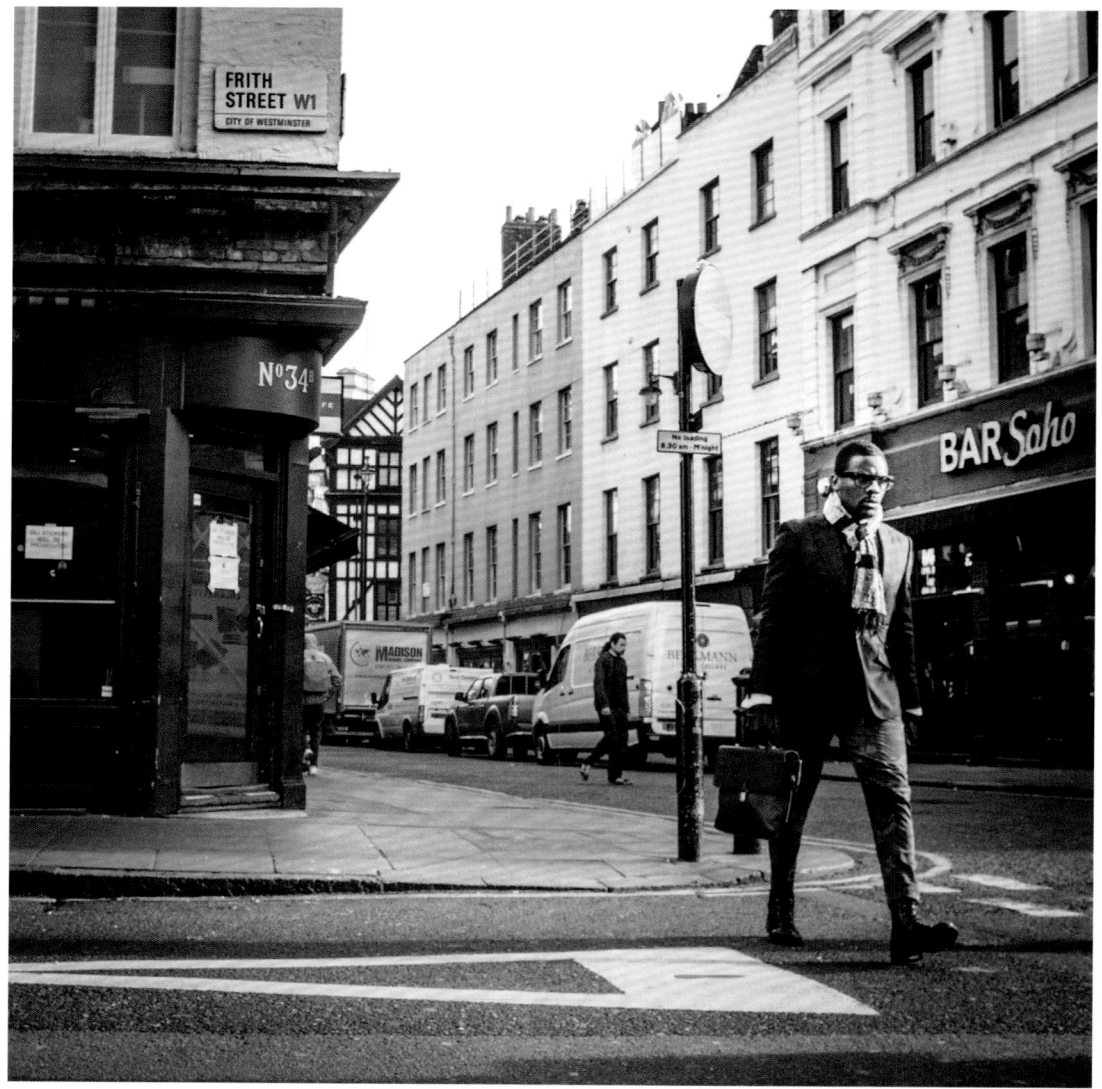

Above: This was shot with the camera placed on a table outside a café. The shot had been set up to include context (such as the street sign and bar sign), so it was then just a case of waiting until the right person walked into the frame.

Focal length: 28mm

Aperture: f/8

Shutter speed: 1/210 sec.

ISO: 800

Use Your Articulated Screen

If your camera has an articulated viewing screen you can use it to look down, rather than up, when taking a picture, so people will think you are messing with your camera. On the subject of viewing screens, avoid "chimping," which is when you look at the picture you have just taken on your camera's viewing screen. Many photographers are serial "chimpers" and not only will this draw attention to you, it can interrupt your creative flow and deplete your camera's battery more quickly.

Shoot Past People

This technique works particularly well when people are walking toward you and you are using a wide-angle lens. You simply bring your camera up to eye level, ignoring the people directly in front of you, and pretend to be shooting something in the distance. Don't look at them and focus your attention on the space behind them. Then, when they are in your frame, take the picture. Keep the camera at eye level until they have passed and they will be none the wiser.

Avoid Eye Contact

If you make eye contact with someone you are about to photograph and they spot your camera at the same time, your intentions will be clear and your cover will be blown. While this doesn't always mean you'll lose the opportunity, it inevitably leads to a change in behavior, so the scene you originally envisaged will no longer be the same.

This also applies after the picture has been taken. Eye contact could lead to a conversation you would probably want to avoid, or even a confrontation. Once the picture has been taken, look away and give the impression that your attention has been elsewhere.

Be A Lamppost

Find a good shooting position—perhaps a busy street corner—and find something to lean against or sit on. Stay there, with your camera constantly at eye level and shoot people as they come into the frame. Keep it there after you have taken a picture and most people will assume you have been shooting something behind them. The same principle works well when sitting outside a café or on a park bench, with your camera on a table or in your lap.

Work Quickly & Quietly

If you are to go unobserved, you need to work quickly and quietly. Shoot without fuss or drama, and then move on to the next subject.

You could try not raising the camera until you have mentally composed the shot, then bring the viewfinder up to your eye at the very last moment. When you have taken your picture, lower the camera as smoothly and as naturally as possible and avoid any jerky or unnatural movements.

If you use a wrist strap to carry your camera, you should be able to work more quickly than if it were around your neck—or in your bag. Make sure the camera is constantly on and ready for action; if it is programmed to go into sleep mode every five minutes or so, keep tapping the shutter-release button lightly to keep it awake.

If your camera has sounds that can be turned off, turn them all off! This includes all bleeps and pings. If you have a silent shutter mode, make sure it is enabled.

Finally, a messenger-type shoulder bag will allow you to access your gear more quickly than a backpack will. A smaller bag is always better than a big one; it will not only look less obtrusive, but it will also overcome the natural tendency to fill a bigger bag with loads of gear you shouldn't need.

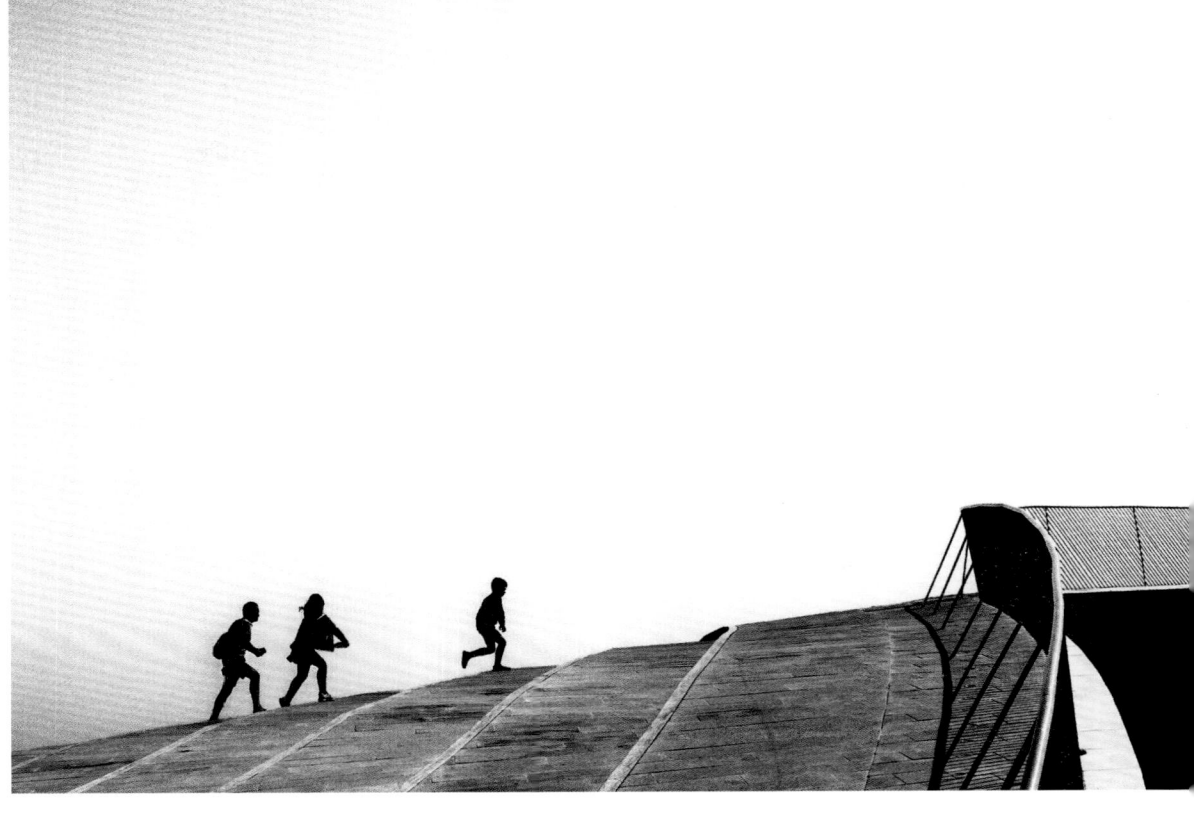

Above: Here's an example of a shot taken using the "fishing" technique: find a good position, lean against a lamppost, and wait for the right subject to come into your frame. In this case, the combination of light and the background was always going to make a strong silhouette shot.

Focal length: 35mm

Aperture: f/16

Shutter speed: 1/850 sec.

ISO: 320

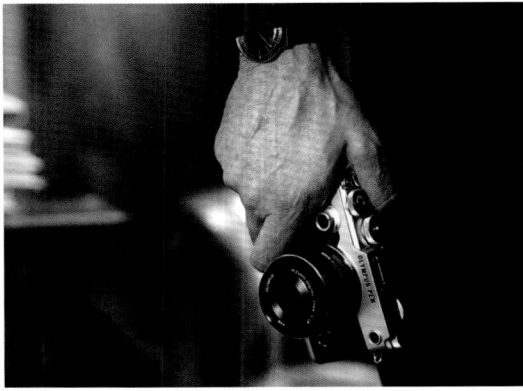

Above: Keeping your camera at arm's length, down near your waist, makes it less conspicuous, while maintaining a good "ready" position.

Conquer Your Fear

Ask anyone who runs a street photography workshop and they will tell you that the most frequently asked question is: "How do I overcome my fear of shooting strangers on the street?" It's an emotion that most of us go through—or have been through—and feelings can range from mild apprehension to uncontrollable terror.

In terms of our psychological make-up, fear is a defense mechanism; a warning system that aims to keep us out of danger. In fact, a small element of fear is no bad thing! It keeps us sharp and can provide a quick dose of adrenalin that will motivate us to get the picture. On the other hand, fear can be debilitating; it can prevent us from getting the picture—or any picture at all—and make us retreat to the nearest café for refuge.

To help deal with this fear you need to get a couple of things firmly fixed in your mind. First, you're doing this for fun, not for pain, so relax and enjoy it! The more you relax and enjoy yourself, the less fearful you will be. Second, people generally won't notice you and are not in the least bit interested in you; this is particularly true if you are shooting in a busy town or city.

More importantly, you should have belief in the notion that you are not *taking* photographs, but are *making* them. Street photographers are often thought to be prowling the streets, stalking their prey and then sneakily grabbing a shot without the subject being aware. In other words, it feels naughty; it feels like stealing and we eventually start to feel we're up to no good. If we banish thoughts such as these and believe, instead, that we are creating something artistic—even doing some good—our outlook changes and we adopt a more confident psychological (and probably physical) posture.

Remember, in most countries you are perfectly within your rights to take photographs of strangers in public places. If you have the firm belief that you are doing nothing wrong, your life as a street photographer will become easier.

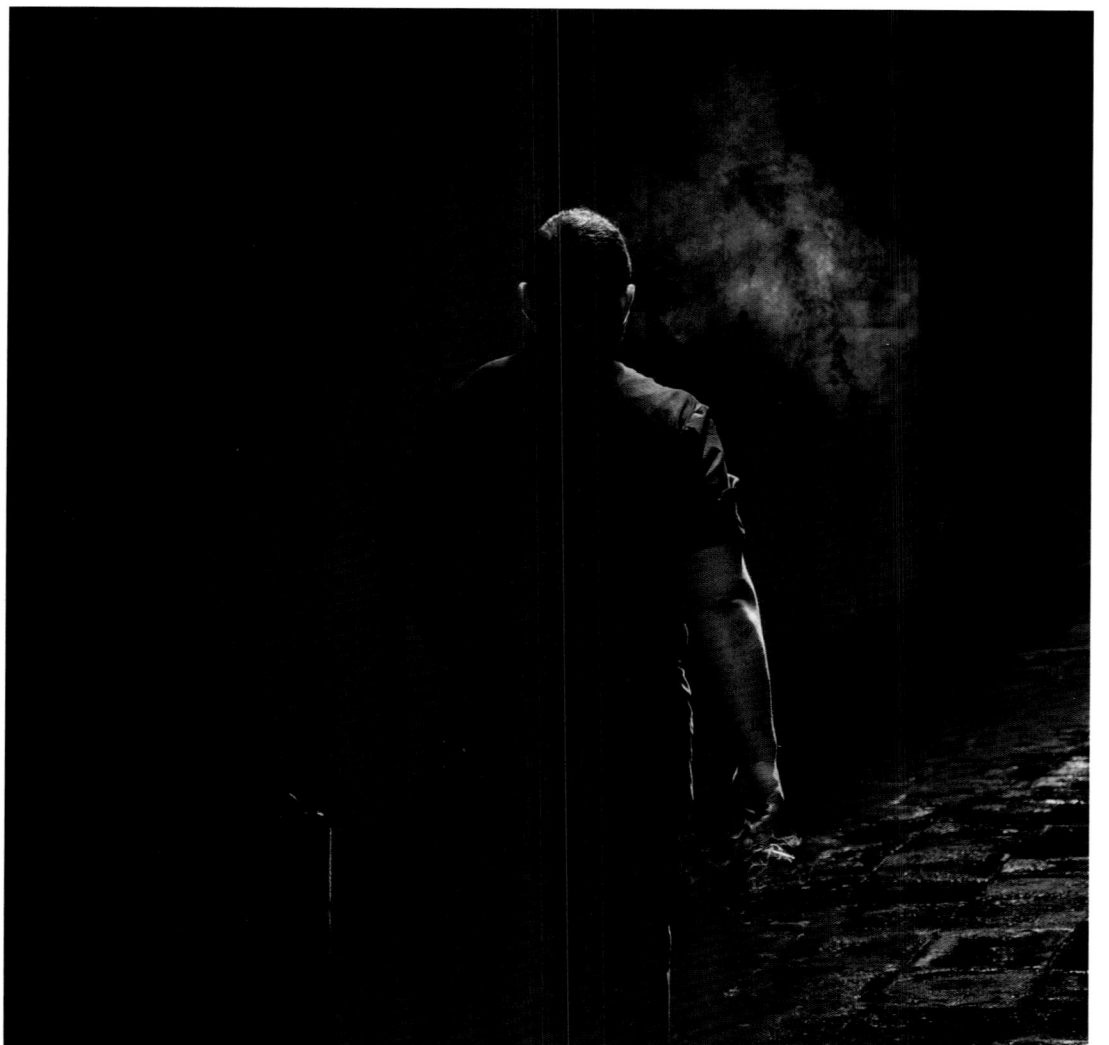

Left: Sometimes, photographing a person from behind can create an air of mystery or intrigue. Who are they? What are they thinking? It can also be a useful starting point if you are worried about photographing strangers' faces; get comfortable with taking pictures like this and work your way around to capturing their faces.

Focal length: 85mm

Aperture: f/4

Shutter speed: 1/200 sec

ISO: 800

Fear Of Being Challenged

If people notice you taking their picture and blow your cover, it is not usually bad news. They are probably curious, sometimes bemused, and often flattered; they are rarely offended. However, many of us are still worried about being challenged and this is one aspect of street photography that we all need to deal with at some point—some of us more than others. We don't want to be asked why we are taking someone's photo, or get asked to delete an image, or—even worse—be threatened with physical violence. Naturally, the best course of action is to avoid being challenged in the first place, and your chances of this are increased if you work quickly and quietly, and follow some of the previous invisibility tips.

Most challenges arise out of your subject's curiosity; they simply want to know why you are taking their picture. Of course, you're under no obligation to explain yourself, and some street photographers refuse to engage in any way with their subjects (although this can seem a little rude). People's curiosity is often satisfied with a simple stock explanation, which you should work out in anticipation of these situations: you might say you're working on a project, that you're doing a photography course, or simply that you are documenting street life in that particular area. Just remember to smile, be non-confrontational, and confident of your reason for taking the picture.

In most circumstances, if you are spotted taking someone's photo, your best reaction is to smile, say "Thank you," and turn and walk away. Most people will simply smile back and that will be the end of it. Ideally, you want to avoid getting into conversation, as this will probably lead to you showing the person the image you have just taken of them, which in turn may lead to you being asked to delete it.

Should you ever delete an image if asked to do so? Much depends on the circumstances and how confident you feel about refusing. Did you photograph someone in a compromising or embarrassing situation? Were they doing something illegal? If a refusal may lead to physical violence, you should probably consider deleting the image and retreating from the situation, but you are under no obligation to do so.

"I like photographing the backs of people. It lets me imagine their stories."

—*Garry Winogrand*

Right: If you're worried about being outed as a photographer, start with an easy target such as street performers, who are used to being photographed. While photographing performers is something of a street photography cliché, you will often catch an unguarded moment, as with this picture.

Focal length: 35mm
Aperture: f/5.6
Shutter speed: 1/900 sec.
ISO: 800

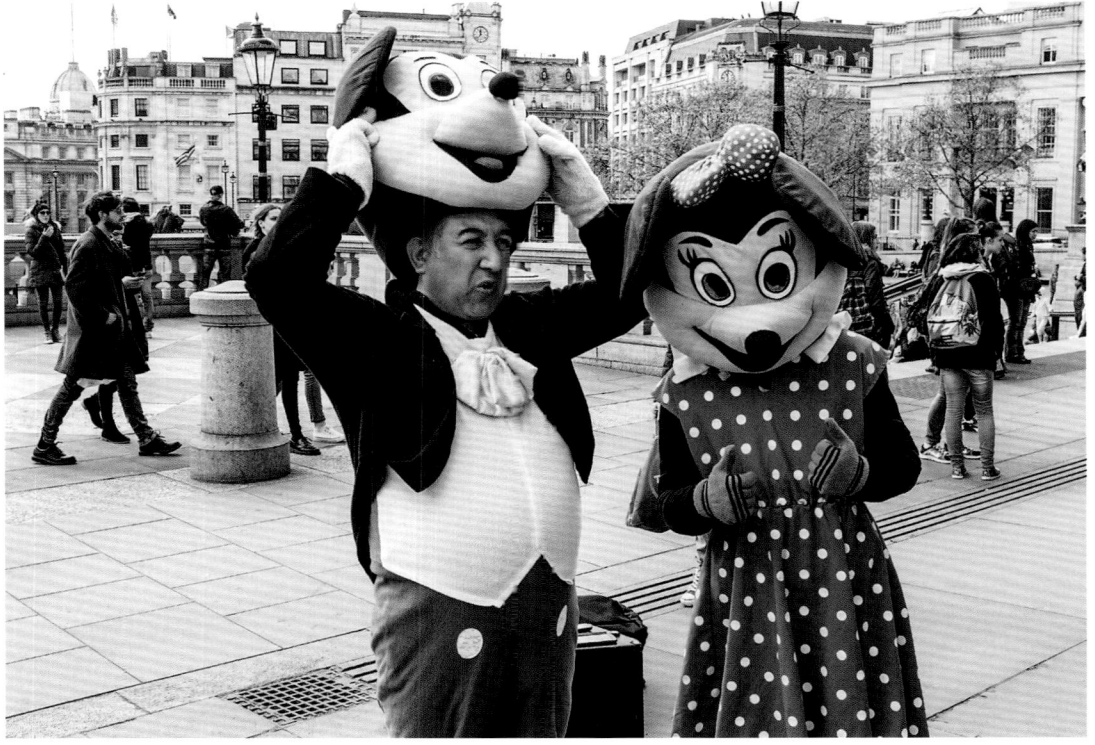

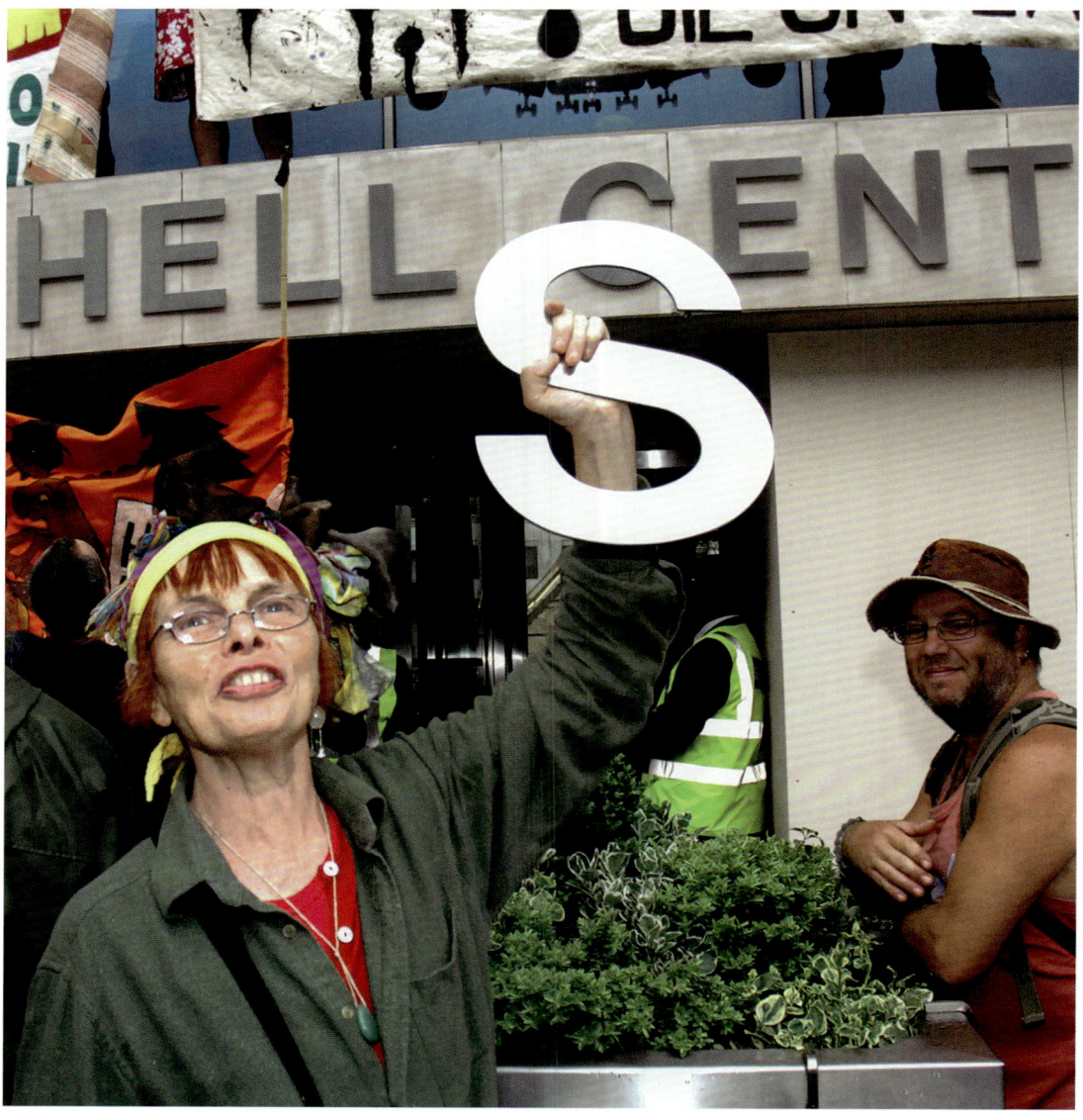

The "Get In Close" Myth

You'll hear a lot about the need to get really close to your subjects in order to produce great street photographs, and some photographers insist that close-quarters shooting is the only way. But is it?

Legendary photojournalist Robert Capa advocated getting in close, but he probably meant fairly close—in other words, close enough to get the right composition. A fair amount of today's street shooting involves poking the camera right in the subject's face—maybe from one or two feet away—but is that really what you want to do? It may be edgy and provocative, and it may be fashionable for a while, but it can have a claustrophobic feel to it that possibly lacks longevity as a style.

The opposite approach—and perhaps the easiest option—is to keep your distance, and this is a trap we all fall into from time to time. Shooting from across the road on a long 300mm lens might give you a nice crisp headshot with an out-of-focus background, but little else. This voyeuristic style of shooting removes the element of context, which is essential in street photography: What's going on around him? Why is she smiling? Who is he shaking his fist at? Without context, the picture tells us little.

The truth is, in order to capture the emotion, feeling, or drama in a scene, you need to be reasonably close to your subjects, but not too close. Many street photographers believe the ideal focal length to be 35mm (on a full-frame camera), or around 24mm with a cropped-sensor camera. On the busy streets of today's towns and cities, this gives you enough space to compose with some degree of freedom, while leaving a good margin for error.

Alternatively, you can look at it in a slightly different way and say that street photography is all about recording everyday life. In our daily lives, our eyes see the world in roughly the same perspective as a standard 40–50mm lens; it follows that using a standard lens like this will give your photographs a realistic feel.

Above: It's usually a good thing to get close to your subject, but don't become obsessed by it! However, if you can get into the habit of shooting at close range you will reap the rewards.

Focal length: 28mm

Aperture: f/4

Shutter speed: 1/250 sec

ISO: 400

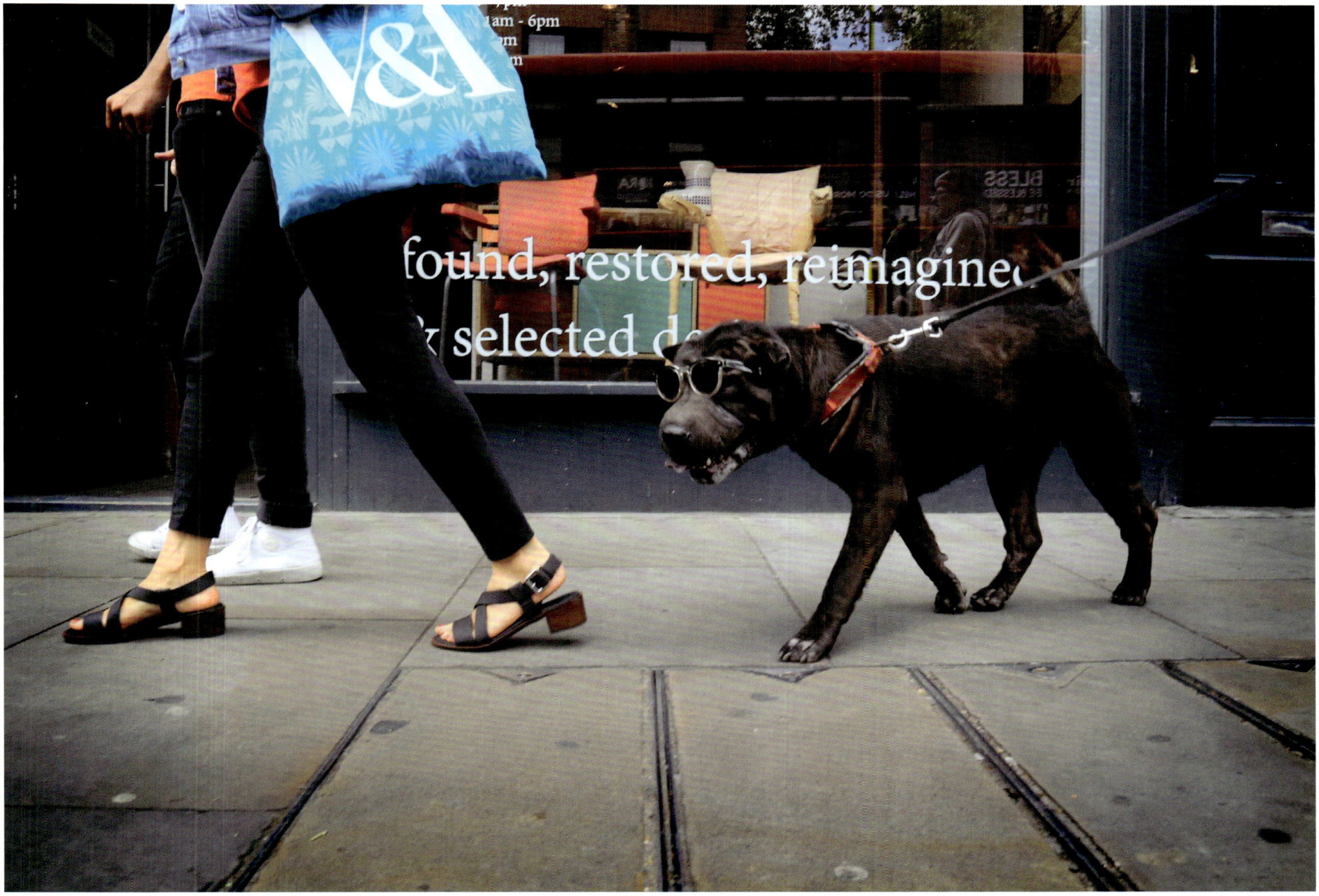

> "If your photographs aren't good enough, you're not close enough."

—*Robert Capa*

Above: Shooting at close range doesn't mean you have to focus on people exclusively; look at objects, abstract patterns, and animals. This cool dog was hardly likely to object to having his picture taken!

Focal length: 24mm

Aperture: f/10

Shutter speed: 1/320 sec.

ISO: 1250

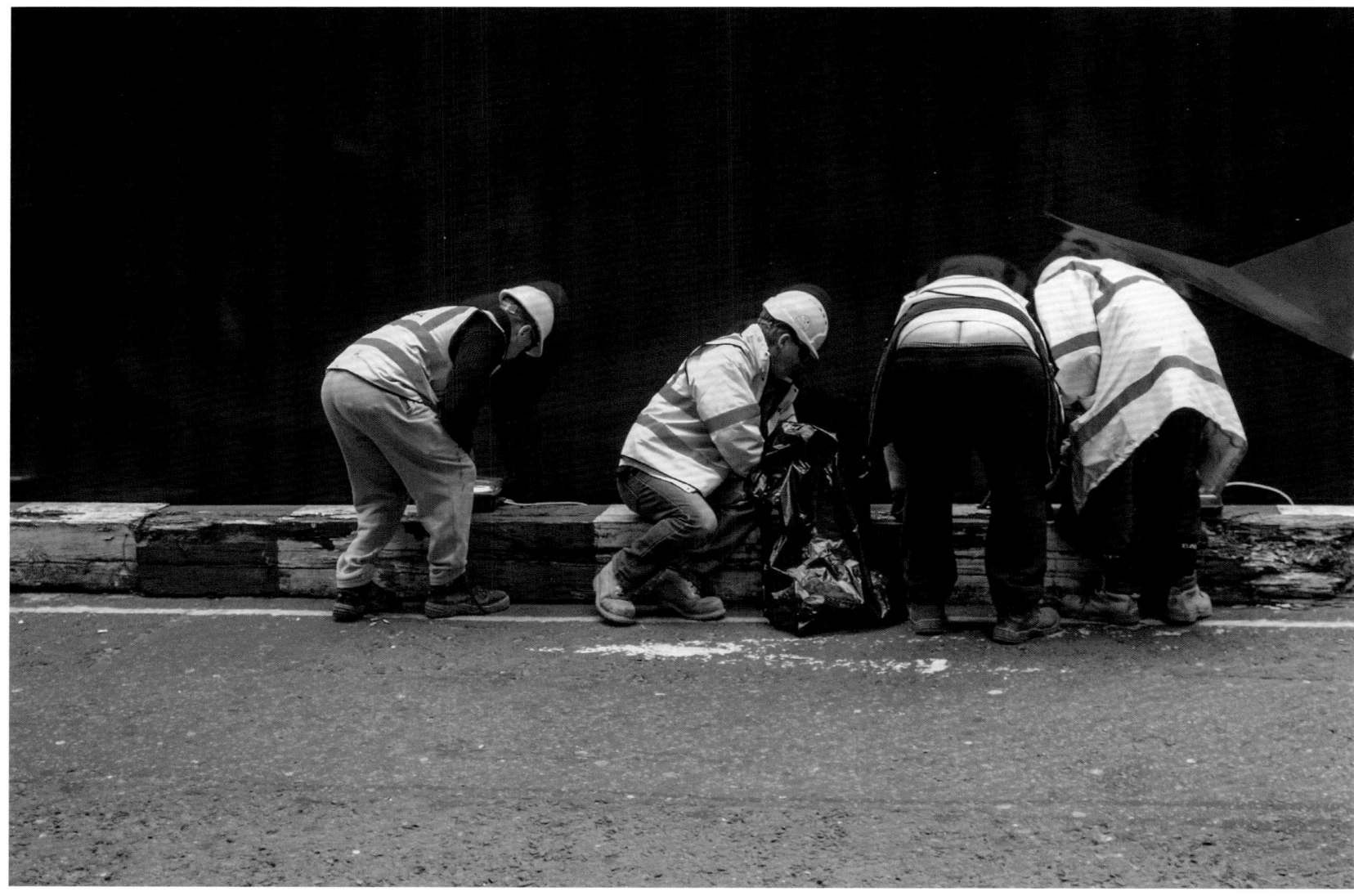

Desensitization

In psychology, desensitization is a method by which we can aim to reduce or eliminate a negative reaction to a stimulus. If, for example, you are terrified of going to the dentist, your first appointment would involve nothing more than visiting the surgery, meeting the dentist, and having a look around. Your second (and maybe your third) appointment would involve nothing more than a check-up, and any treatment would come much later.

In other words, you are exposed to small, but gradually increasing doses of the stimulus, building up to a level of eventual comfort with (or acceptance of) that stimulus.

You can apply the same principle to your fear of photographing people on the streets. Start shooting from a distance with a long focal length and, over a period of weeks, move closer to your subjects using a wider lens. Gradually you would be desensitizing your fear to the point where it is either eliminated or becomes unimportant. How long it takes to reach this stage will depend on your level of fear to start with and your own psychological make-up, but do try it—it works!

Above: If you really struggle to find the courage to shoot people, perhaps start by shooting them from behind. It won't always make a great composition, but there are plenty of occasions when it can.

Focal length: 28mm

Aperture: f/9

Shutter speed: 1/60 sec.

ISO: 1000

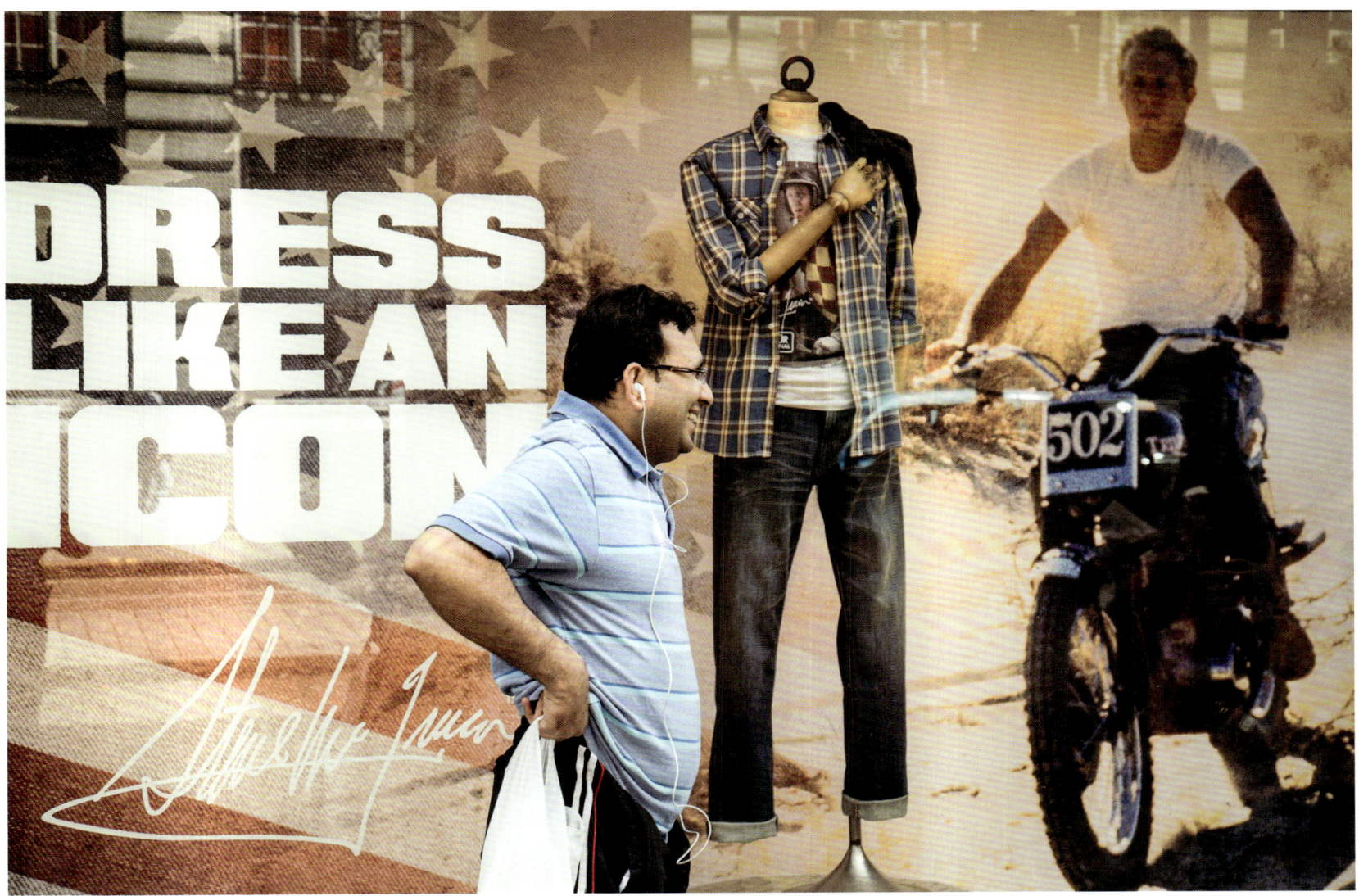

Above: No matter how close you are, some subjects will never notice you. This is especially true if you are shooting side-on, like this, and in larger towns and cities, where people are often self-absorbed.

Focal length: 65mm

Aperture: f/8

Shutter speed: 1/800 sec.

ISO: 400

BANISH YOUR FEAR: SIX THINGS TO TRY TODAY

1 Shoot from the hip. With a little practice, a wide-angle lens, and zone focusing, you'll soon be shooting with confidence.

2 Plant yourself. Find a good vantage point, set up your camera, and wait for people to come into the frame.

3 Consider who you photograph. Avoid subjects who look angry or menacing. Don't make life too difficult for yourself!

4 Imagine you're a tourist, not a photographer. Pretend to be shooting all that's around you, not just your intended target.

5 Shoot with a buddy. You'll be surprised how much more confident you feel when you're with someone else.

6 Know the law. With a good basic understanding of what you can and can't do, you'll approach the streets with more confidence.

Timing

Subject matter falls into two camps: spontaneous shots and those pictures you plan for. In each instance, timing is important in different ways.

Taking that one in a million picture, in which all the elements come together and lead to a perfectly lit, composed, and focused street image, is 99 percent luck and 1 percent planning. Henri Cartier-Bresson's decisive moment is well documented, but there is more to his way of working than meets the eye. If you were to look at Cartier-Bresson's contact sheets you would rarely see one single image that captures the decisive moment. Instead, many of the brilliant pictures he took would probably be part of a series of images of the same subject, each taken from a slightly different viewpoint, angle, or perspective. In other words, he wasn't as lucky as you perhaps think. Instead, he was a master at working the scene, taking multiple pictures in order to get one winning shot.

Part of the ability to take spontaneous photographs that record the elusive decisive moment comes from being in a state of mental alertness and physical readiness. Your mind needs to be focused and tuned in to any possible opportunities and your camera needs to be switched on, set up, and quickly accessible. The rest is down to pure good luck.

Move Slowly

If you amble around, you are more likely to be invisible and see much more of what is around you. So stop every few minutes, lean against a wall, and take stock of your surroundings.

When you get into position to take a picture, make your actions as smooth and as quiet as possible. Most importantly, stop completely when you need to take a picture, however tempting it may be to take it while you're on the move: it is rare to get a sharply focused, well-composed picture while walking.

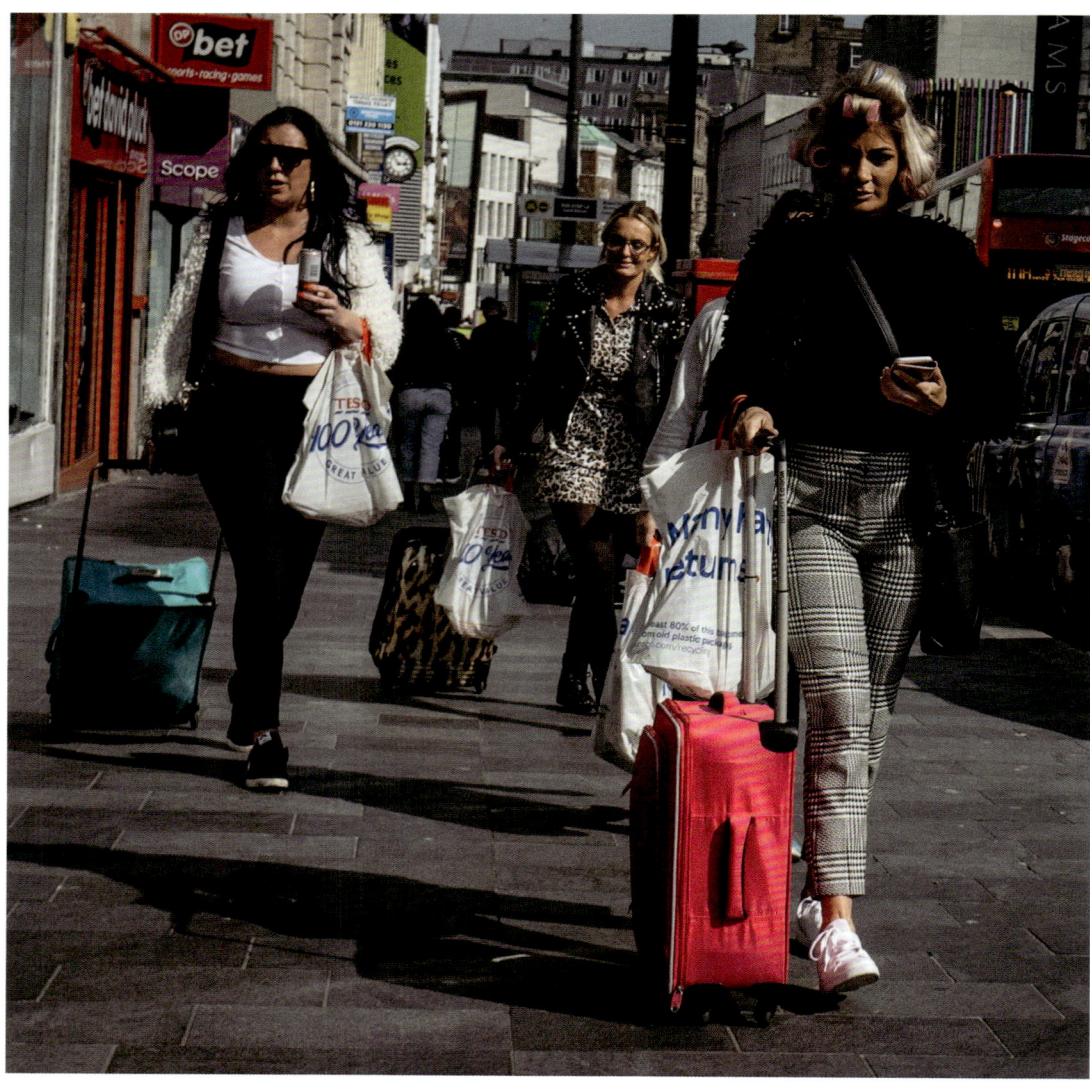

Above: One of the great things about street photography is that you often encounter unusual or off-beat scenes, such this woman walking down the street wearing hair curlers. If you are tuned in to what's going on around you, and your camera is switched on and awake, you'll be well placed to capture opportunities like this.

Focal length: 28mm

Aperture: f/8

Shutter speed: 1/2500 sec.

ISO: 640

Anticipation

Good street photographers are able to absorb the world around them and will anticipate events as they evolve. Always look ahead of you, into the middle distance. What's happening there? Who is coming toward you? Where do you need to position yourself to get a good picture? What shooting position will you adopt? Do any camera settings need to be altered? By anticipating what may be about to happen, you will become more effective when it does happen.

When you are among people, observe their body language and watch their eyes; with a little practice, you'll soon be able to predict their behavior and second-guess what's going to happen next.

Patience

As you walk around, camera at the ready, you will occasionally stumble across a unique photo opportunity—a chance to capture that elusive decisive moment you keep hearing so much about. Most of the time, such spontaneous opportunities will not simply fall at your feet, so you will need to be patient.

Imagine, for example, that you spot a potential photo opportunity in a giant billboard that has "Healthy Eating" written on it in large red letters. In itself, the billboard will not make an interesting picture, so you will need another element to make it work. Let's say you have decided that you need a large person munching on a burger to make a strong contrast. You would be extremely lucky if such a person turned up instantly, so find a good position, make yourself comfortable, and wait. It is not unreasonable to wait for an hour or more for all the elements in a shot to come together!

Many street photographers rush about, trying to cram as many locations as possible into a session, and, in the process, miss much of what is going on around them. Instead, take your time, walk slowly, and quietly contemplate your surroundings. You will find that this relaxed style of shooting is far more productive.

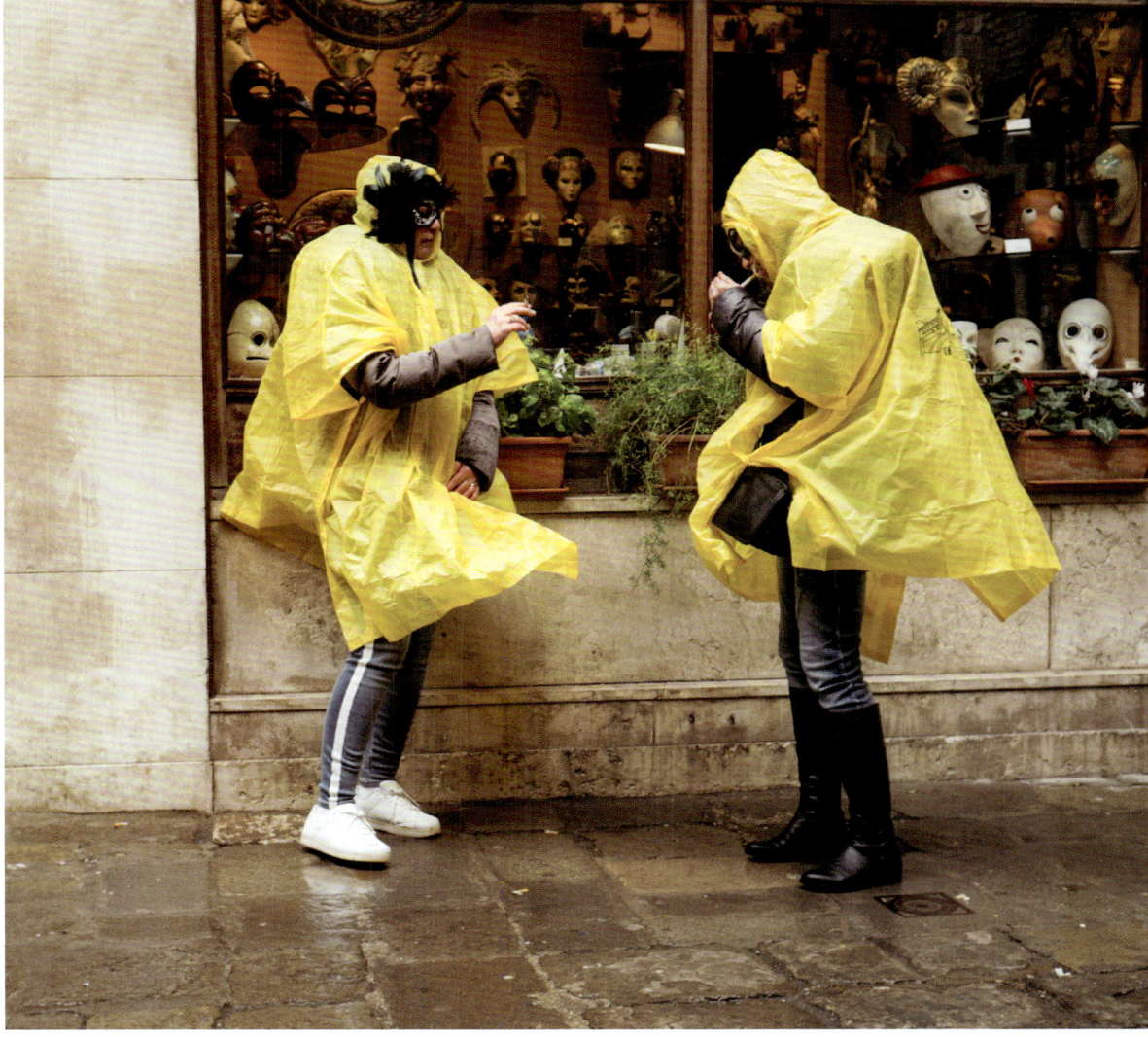

Above: When you spot the potential in a scene, it often pays to wait until the subjects are in just the right pose and position.

Focal length: 40mm
Aperture: f/8
Shutter speed: 1/180 sec.
ISO: 2000

Don't Hesitate!

One final point about timing: just do it! How many great street shots have you missed because of hesitation? Once you have seen an opportunity don't hesitate for one second—take it.

It's something we all experience: that "shall I/shan't I?" moment in which you have a split second to compose the frame and fire the shutter. However, by the time you've thought about it, the moment will be gone forever. Fishermen are well known for having regrets about the one that got away, and it's just the same for street photographers. Any slight hesitation could make the difference between going home with a very poor catch or getting a terrific picture.

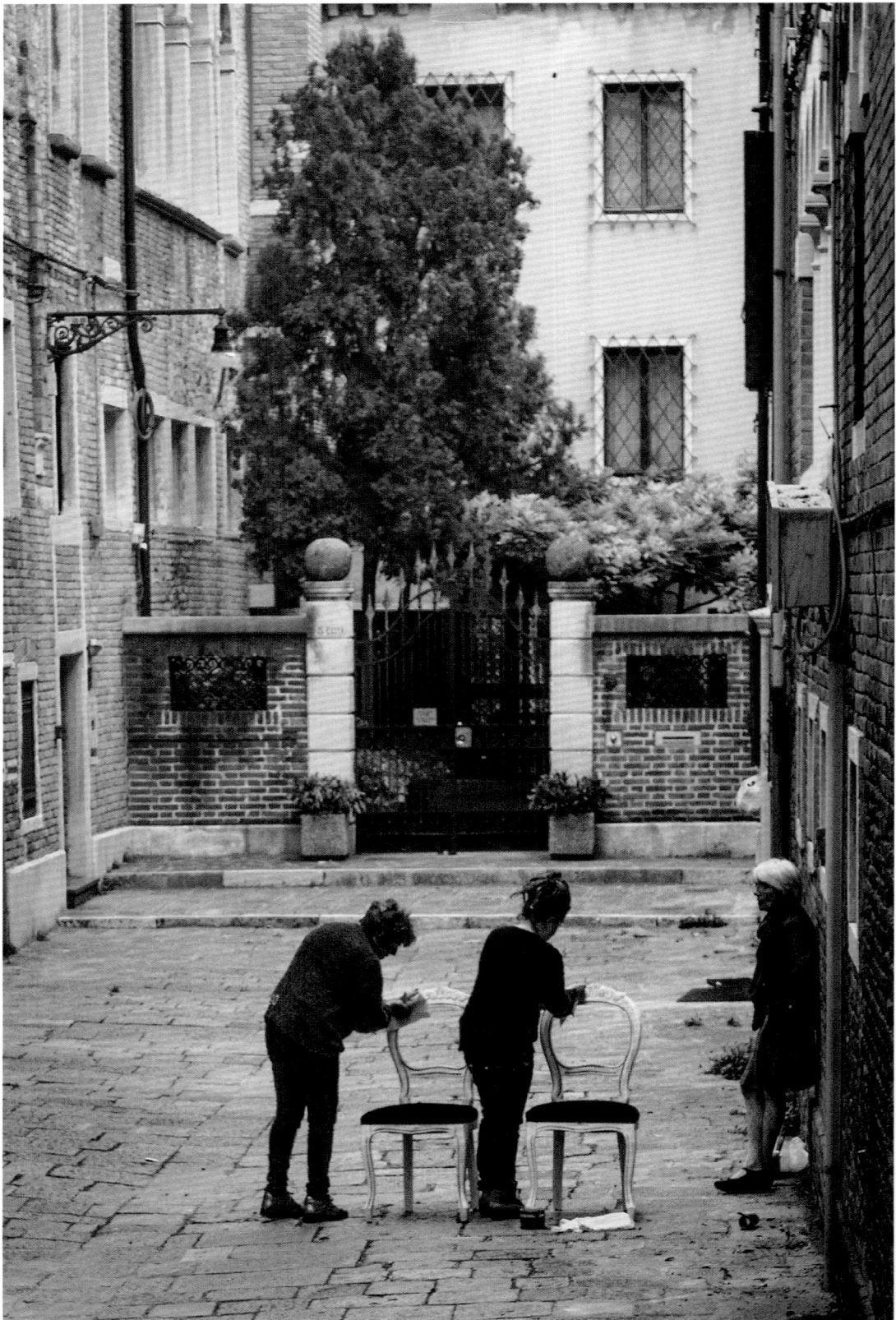

Right: The decisive moment is hard to define and even harder to find! In this example, the decisive moment was that briefest of windows when both women were standing in the same position.

Focal length: 75mm

Aperture: f/5.6

Shutter speed: 1/125 sec.

ISO: 800

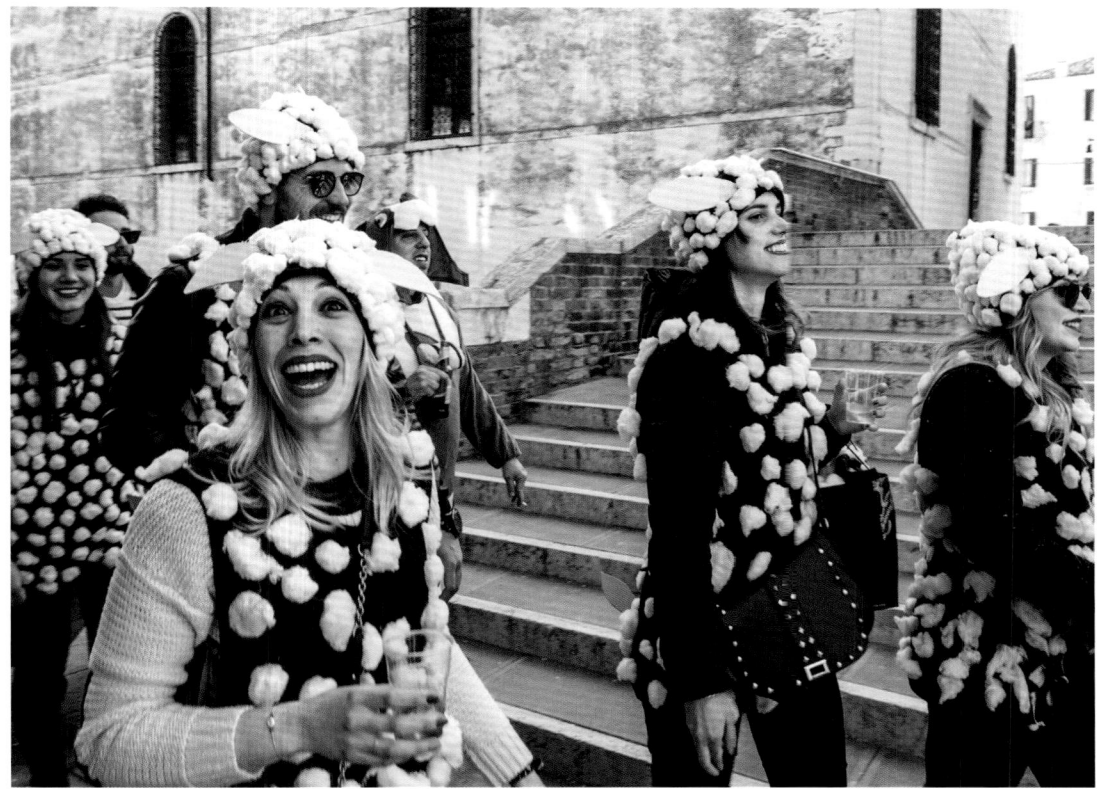

Left: People are quite easy to photograph when they're having fun. This group was moving fairly quickly and were gone in a second; even a tiny bit of hesitation would have meant a missed frame.

Focal length: 24mm

Aperture: f/9

Shutter speed: 1/125 sec.

ISO: 500

Bottom left: Contemporary art galleries can be a good hunting ground; watch people as they study the exhibits and try to second-guess their next move. In this picture, a fast reaction was needed to grab the shot before the woman stood up again.

Focal length: 35mm

Aperture: f/8

Shutter speed: 1/80 sec.

ISO: 1250

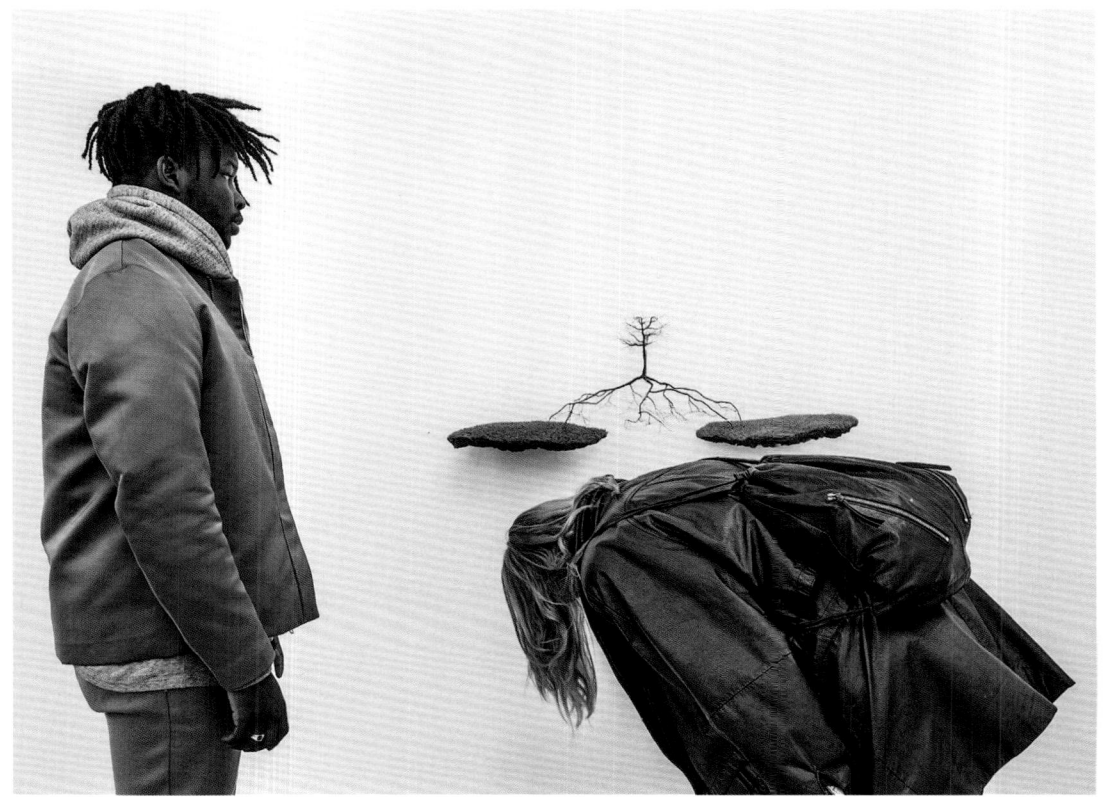

TOP 10 CHARACTERISTICS OF A SUCCESSFUL STREET PHOTOGRAPHER:

1. Well-developed observational skills
2. Patience
3. Realistic expectations
4. Curiosity
5. Confidence and a thick skin
6. Ability to blend in and look anonymous
7. Anticipation
8. Fast reactions
9. A liking of people
10. Stamina

Assignment 5: Up Close & Personal

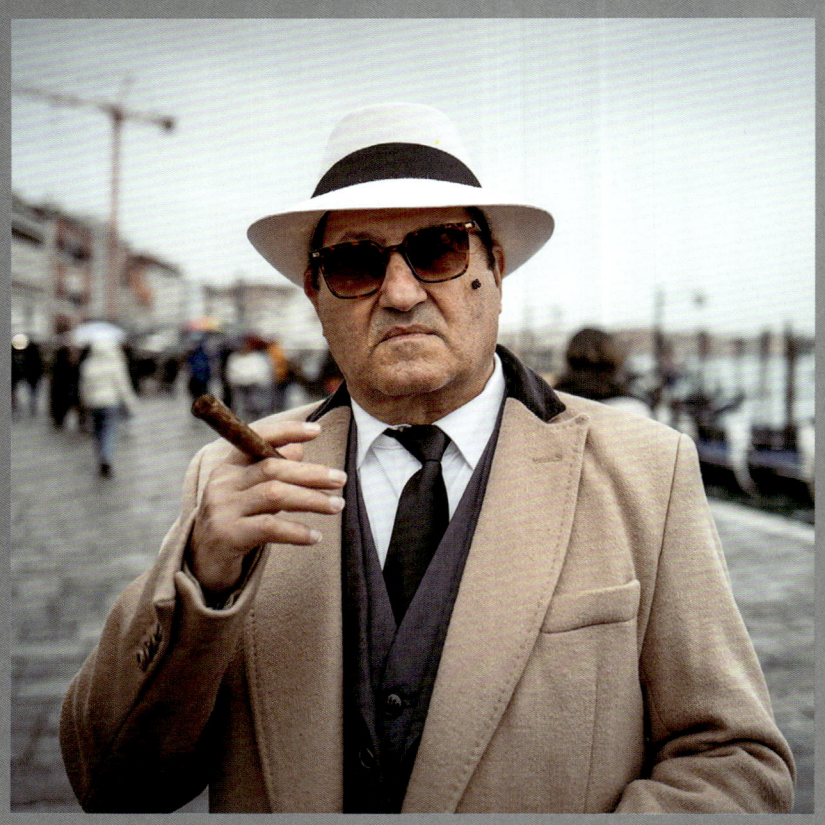

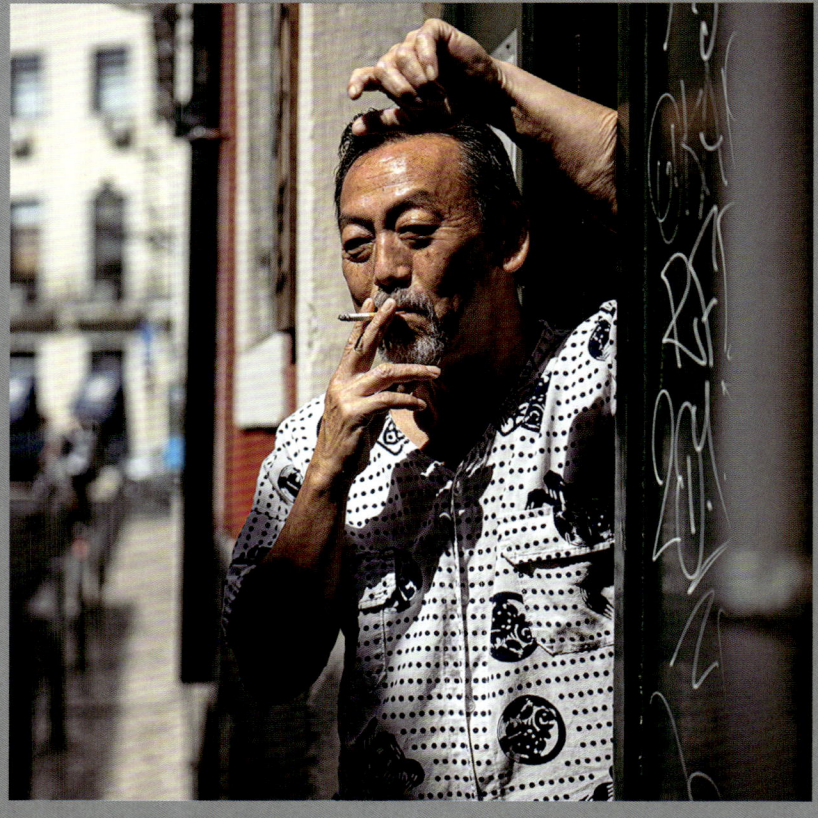

The Challenge

Getting in close is something all street photographers should/must/need/want to do at some stage, but many of us find the whole thing difficult. The purpose of this assignment is to help build your confidence and make you more comfortable photographing strangers on the street.

This isn't about emulating Bruce Gilden's machine-gun style of extreme close-ups, nor is it about shooting with a long lens from across the street. Instead, it's about getting reasonably close to your subjects, using a wide-angle lens (ideally 28mm or 35mm), and taking candid portraits without being spotted.

Think about how your images will work together as a series—you may even find you can turn this assignment into a worthwhile long-term project.

LOCATION

Try shooting in retail areas when they're fairly quiet, so you can isolate your subject from their background clutter.

Above left:
Focal length: 28mm
Aperture: f/1.7
Shutter speed: 1/250 sec.
ISO: 250

Above:
Focal length: 43mm
Aperture: f/4.5
Shutter speed: 1/50 sec.
ISO: 100

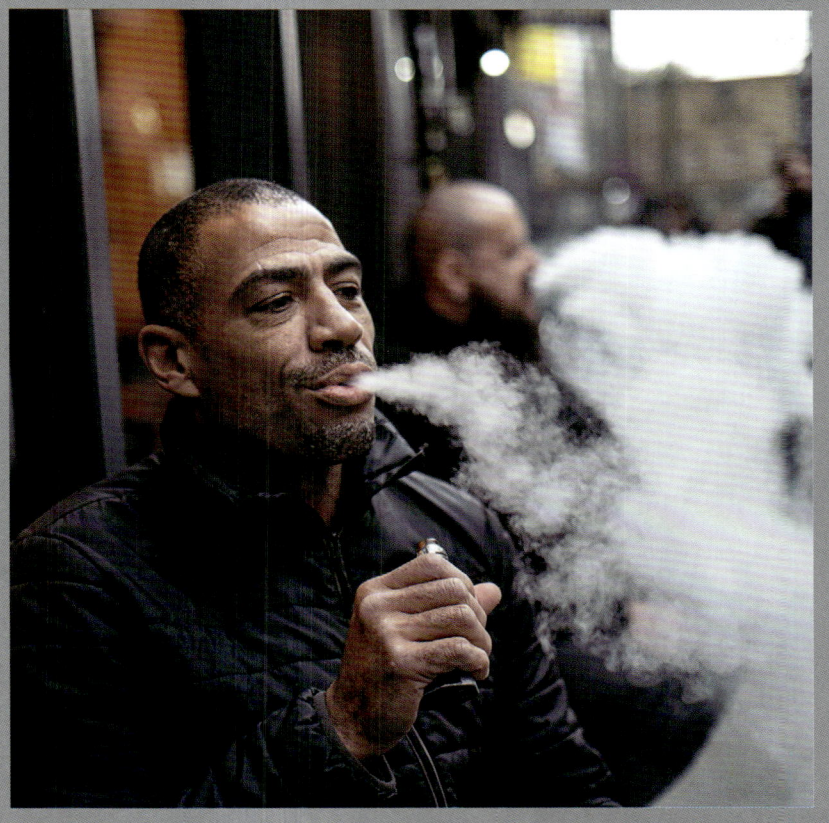

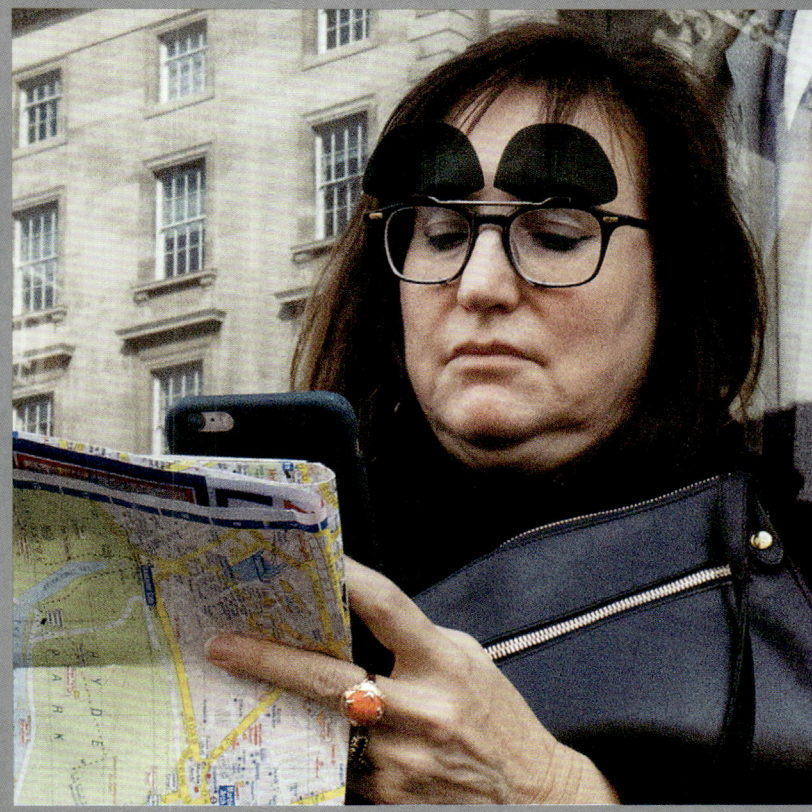

TECHNIQUES

- This is a good opportunity to practice your covert shooting techniques, especially shooting from the hip.

- Use zone focusing, as outlined on page 37.

TOP TIPS

- Always be in the ready position for these shots: camera in your hand, switched on (and awake), and with the lens cap off.

- Practice with one lens and familiarize yourself with its field of view. This will make it easier to shoot without having to look through the viewfinder.

- Try to stand still when you're taking pictures (if both you and the subject are moving, there's a high chance of camera shake, even with a fast shutter speed).

Above left:
Focal length: 50mm
Aperture: f/1.4
Shutter speed: 1/280 sec.
ISO: 400

Above:
Focal length: 12mm
Aperture: f/8
Shutter speed: 1/1000 sec.
ISO: 4000

Assignment 6: Where I Live

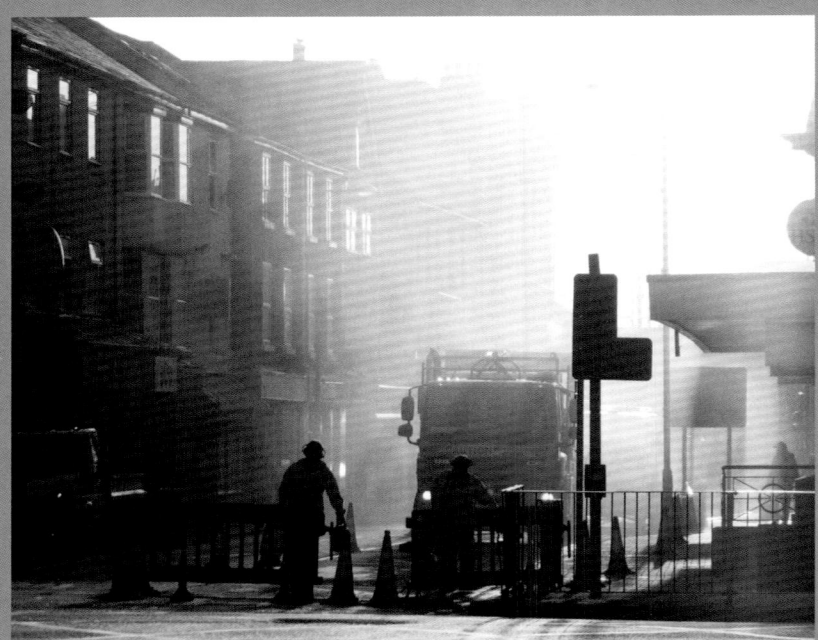

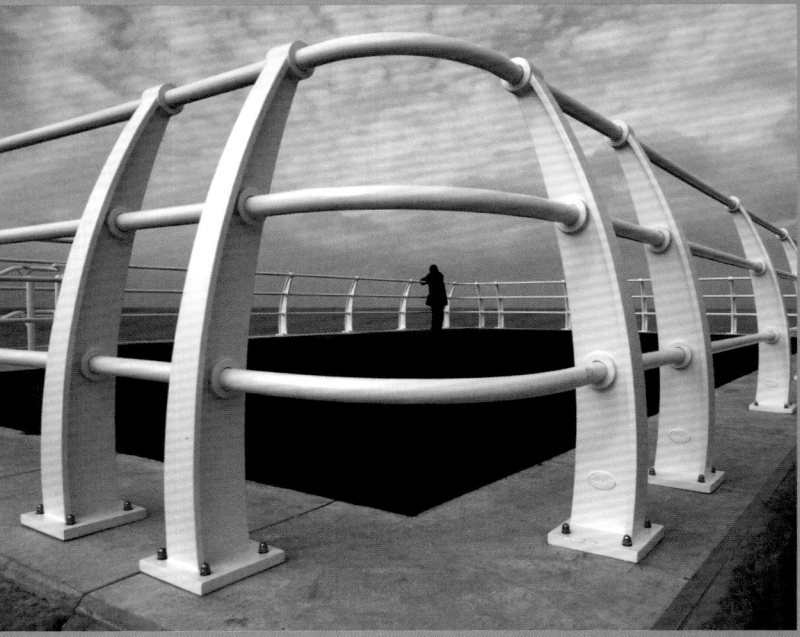

The Challenge

No matter where you live there is a story to be told. This assignment is all about storytelling—using a set of images to build a narrative about a specific location. Your images should convey a real sense of place, demonstrating the unique character of the area. You can show the people, the buildings, the objects—everything that tells the story of life as it happens.

LOCATION

This assignment is all about locality and should be focused on where you live, whether that's a village, a town, or a large city.

Above left:
Focal length: 40mm
Aperture: f/5.9
Shutter speed: 1/340 sec.
ISO: 100

Above:
Focal length: 24mm
Aperture: f/8
Shutter speed: 1/400 sec.
ISO: 200

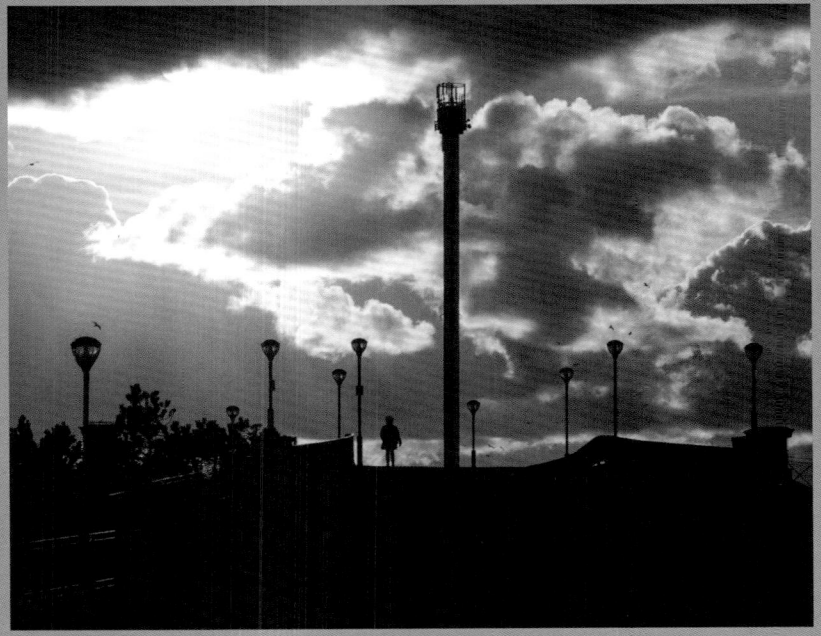

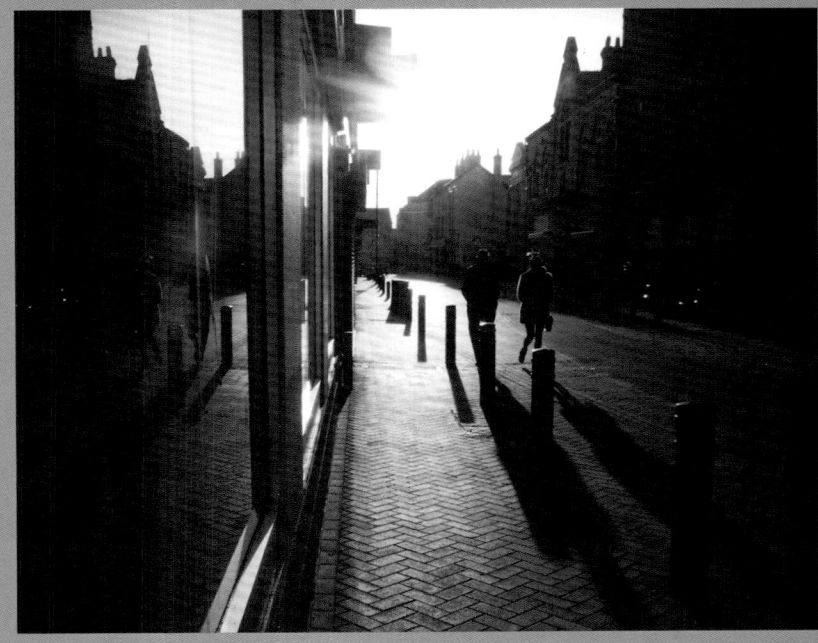

TECHNIQUES

- Blend in. If you go unnoticed you'll be able to record a more realistic picture of local life.

- Produce your story in either black and white or color, but adopt a consistent approach and do not mix the two.

- Take a mix of landscape and portrait shots.

- Walk slowly and absorb your surroundings; keep your eyes open and be ready for the unusual or the unexpected.

- Practice shooting from the hip to capture candid shots of some of the local characters.

TOP TIPS

- Think beyond the obvious and explore the back streets where nothing normally happens; check out the bus station, the local art gallery, and so on.

- Take care of yourself and your gear if you're shooting in more edgy areas.

Above left:
Focal length: 35mm
Aperture: f/9
Shutter speed: 1/1600 sec.
ISO: 200

Above:
Focal length: 14mm
Aperture: f/9
Shutter speed: 1/950 sec.
ISO: 400

Chapter 5
Legal & Ethical Issues

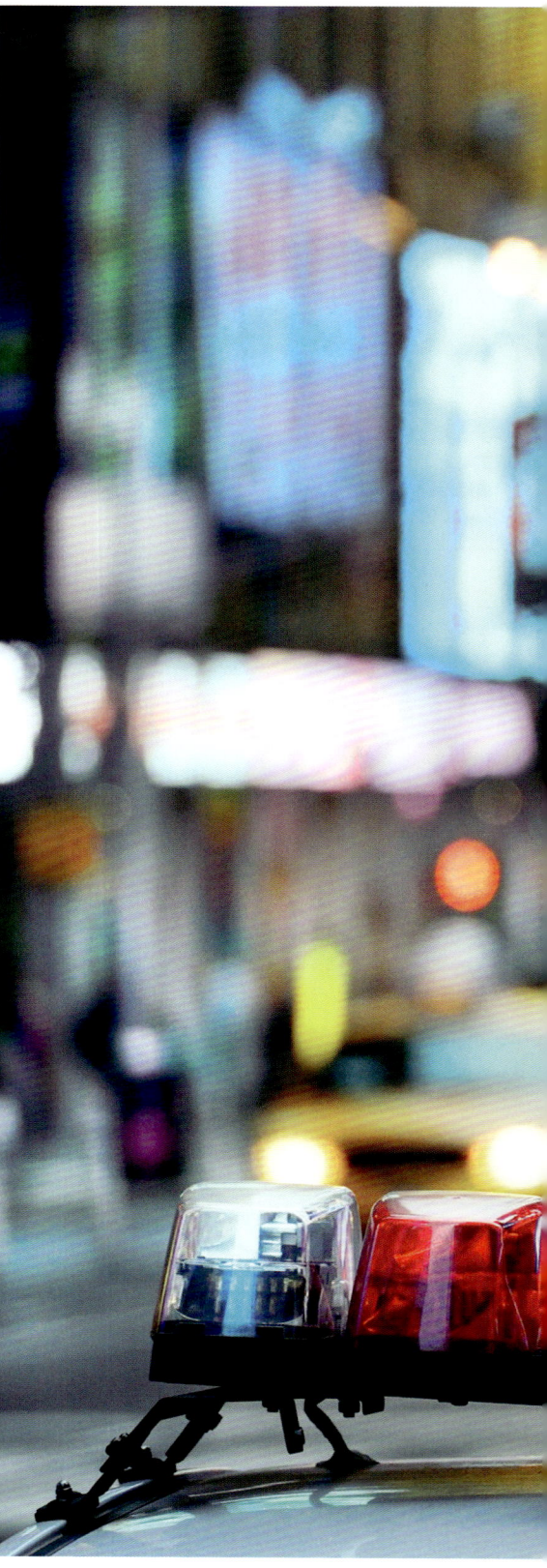

If you're shooting in a public place, you need to have a clear understanding of your rights as a photographer: you should know whether or not you can take photographs and what you can do with them later. While the laws and regulations will vary according to which country you are in, most of the underlying principles are similar and will apply wherever you are. However, if you are visiting a country you are unfamiliar with (or simply don't know the rules in your own country), it's always worth checking the local laws before you head out with your camera.

Right: Where and what you are legally allowed to photograph will vary depending where you are on the planet. In general, photographing anything in or from a public space is usually acceptable, but it pays to know your rights in case you are challenged.

Focal length: 200mm

Aperture: f/5.6

Shutter speed: 1/320 sec.

ISO: 800

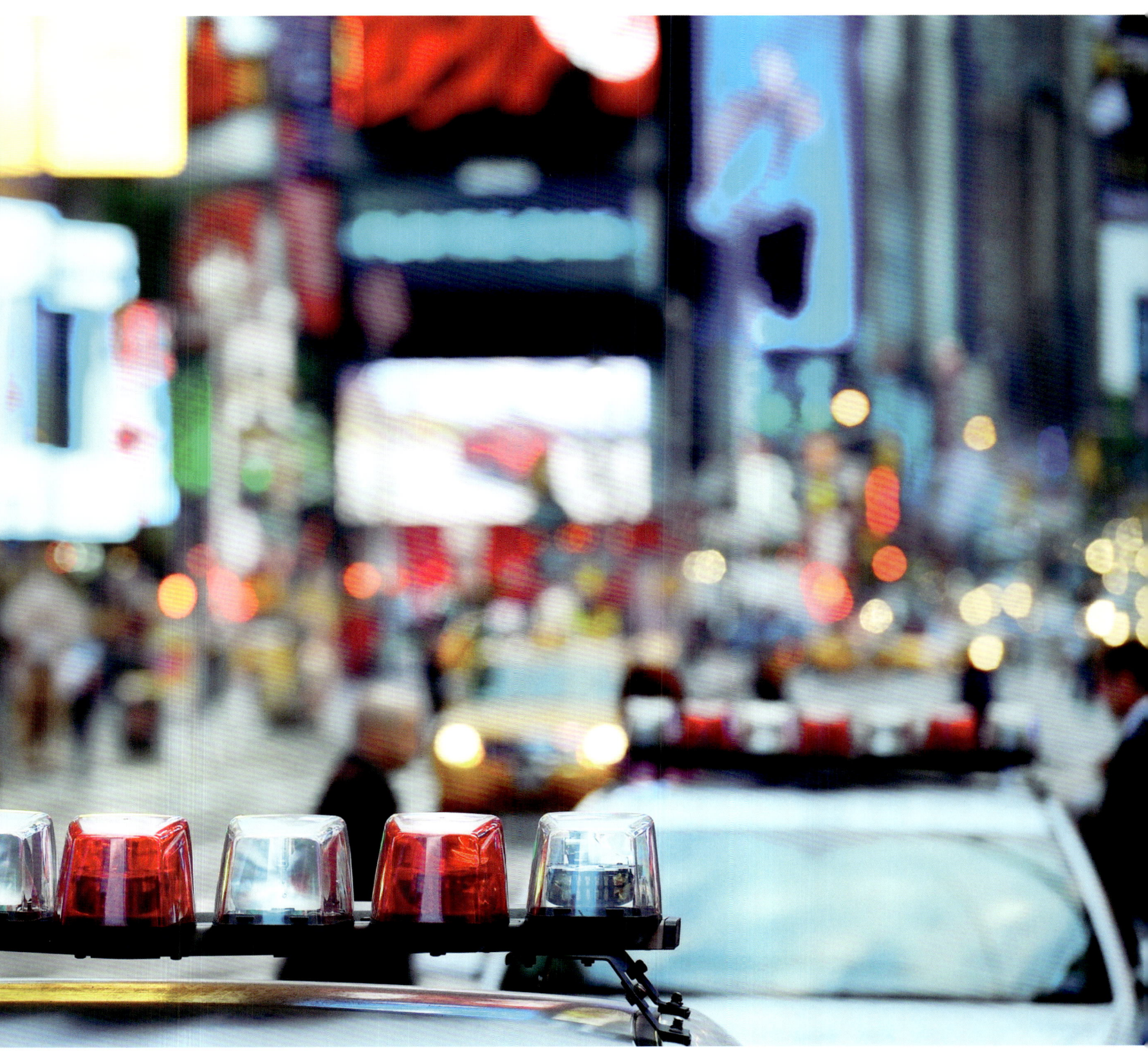

Shooting On The Streets

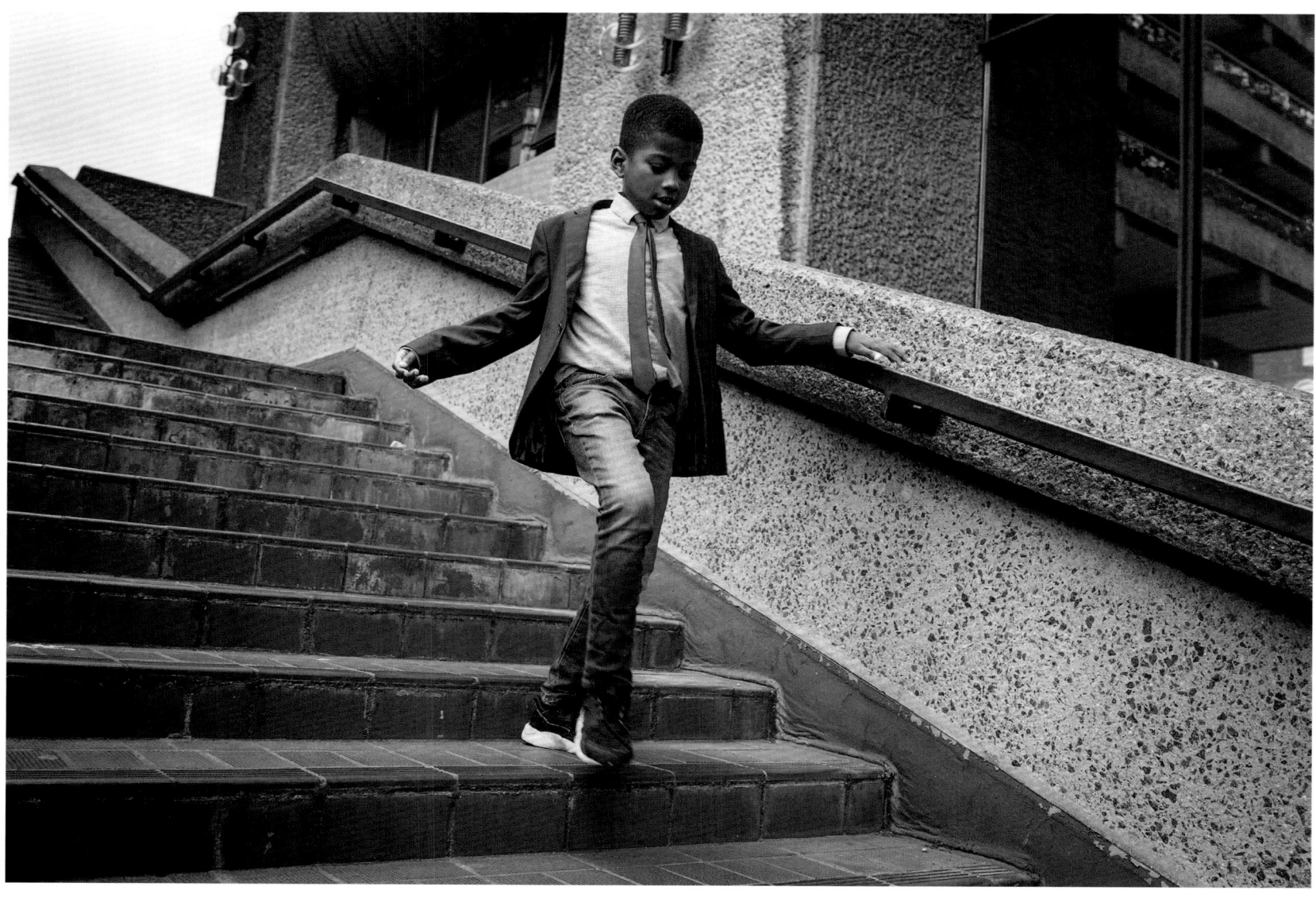

There is much misunderstanding—and many urban myths—about what street photographers can and cannot do. Therefore, to begin to understand your rights, you need to understand the concept of shooting in a public space.

Above: Despite urban myths to the contrary, in almost all countries it's fine to shoot strangers—including children —in a public place. Unless the image is destined for third party commercial use (which usually refers to advertising), you are within your rights to photograph anyone, anywhere, doing anything.

Focal length: 28mm

Aperture: f/4

Shutter speed: 1/250 sec.

ISO: 1250

Above right: Places which would seem to be public spaces are often private—and it can be difficult for photographers to know the difference between the two. Sometimes signs will make the position clear, other times there may be some other means of showing the public/private boundary.

Focal length: 28mm

Aperture: f/8

Shutter speed: 1/200 sec.

ISO: 640

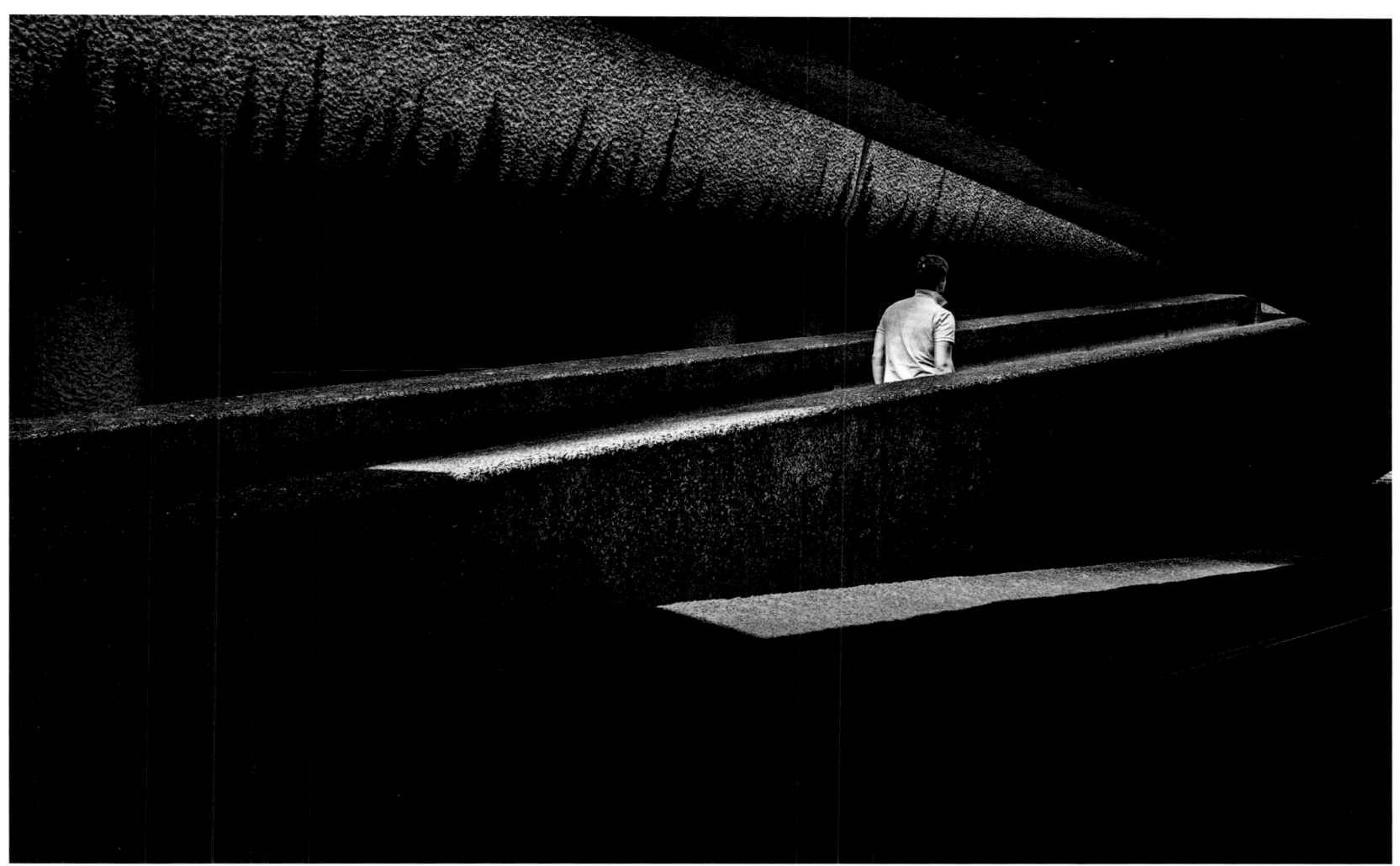

Public Or Private Property?

Where you are standing when you take a picture has a crucial bearing on your legal position. In most countries there is no law to prevent you from taking a picture in a public place. This includes photographing people, buildings, (most) government buildings, police officers, and so-called VIPs. There are some sensible exclusions to this rule, which include, for example, certain properties belonging to the Ministry of Defence (in the UK), and similarly sensitive locations; in these situations, a photography prohibition order may be in place and there are usually clear signs to that effect.

If you are on public property you can photograph anything or anyone you wish, even if you are told not to do so by a security guard. In the UK you can even photograph subjects who are on private property, unless you harass or target them persistently or aggressively.

However, if you want to shoot on private property—which could include areas such as shopping malls—you usually need the owner's express consent to do so. The biggest difficulty arises when it comes to making the distinction between public and private land. The increasing "corporatization" of public space in towns and cities has blurred the boundaries. Swathes of land have been bought by developers and turned into gigantic shopping areas, which are nearly always private property.

So how do you know whether you are on public or private property? Well, it is often difficult to be sure, so you may have to make an assumption. If you are in doubt about the ownership of the land, it is often worth shooting anyway. Do this on the basis that if photography is not allowed, you will soon be told—security guards usually pounce quickly and tell you to stop shooting or leave. Bear in mind, though, that they are not allowed to touch you and cannot—under any circumstances—demand to see your pictures or order you to delete them.

Counterterrorism Legislation

When photographers are stopped by security guards or by the police, anti-terrorism is often cited as the reason for the challenge. While this is understandable, a certain type of paranoia seems to be on the increase, whereby anyone with a camera is deemed to be up to no good.

In the UK, Section 47a of the Terrorism Act 2000 allows the police to stop someone if they have reasonable suspicion that you are involved in terrorist activities; the logic behind this is clearly designed to catch people with cameras who are undertaking hostile reconnaissance. If you are stopped under S47a of this Act, you could be arrested (under Section 43 of the Act) and your memory cards or film seized. However, without an actual arrest the police do not have a right to see or to seize your material—and may not delete it under any circumstances.

The regulations in the USA can change according to the state you are in. In California, for example, police officers can now report photography and other seemingly innocent activities to their counterterrorism division.

It is important to remember that without reasonable suspicion none of this may take place, so exercise common sense when out shooting on the streets and try to avoid any suspicious behavior. If you are stopped by the police (or military) be polite and cooperative and you will (hopefully) find that you are treated with equal common sense and respect.

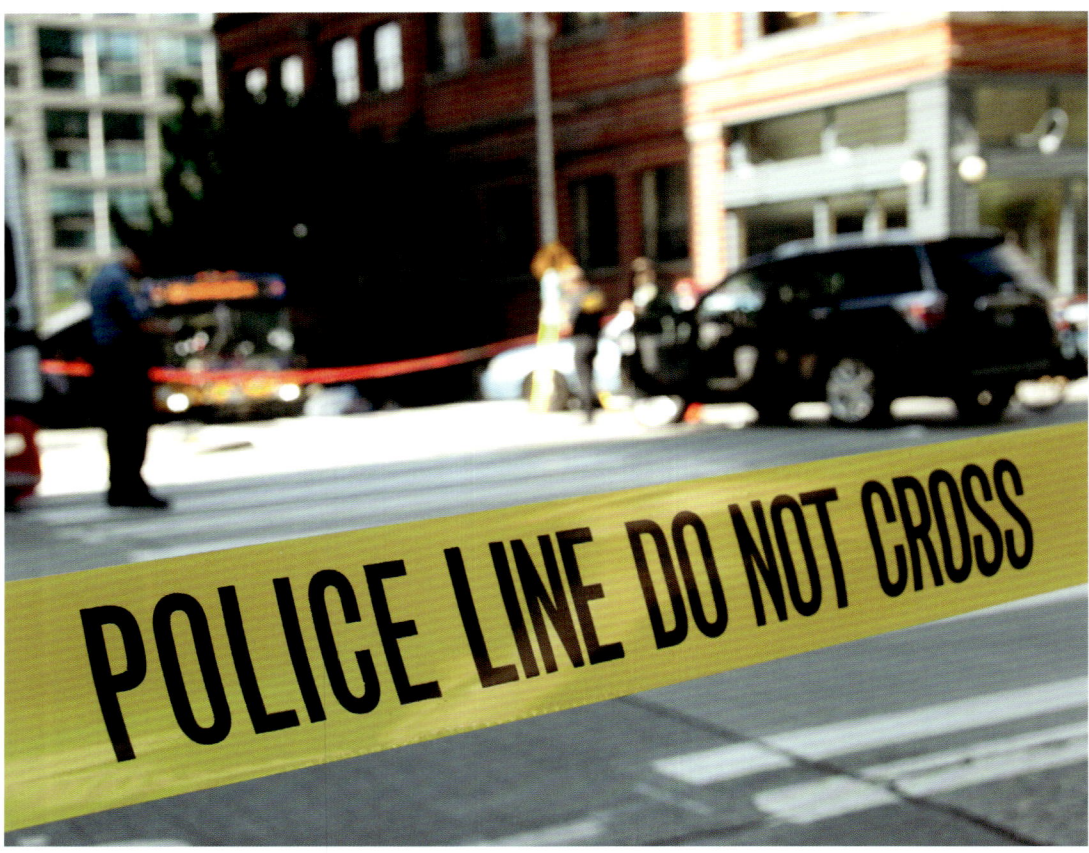

Above: With the world in a state of heightened security following numerous terrorist acts it is even more important to familiarize yourself with local regulations before photographing on the streets.

Focal length: 34mm

Aperture: f/9

Shutter speed: 1/200 sec.

ISO: 200

Right: Most police forces are well briefed in how to handle photographers. Whether you are a professional press photographer or an amateur hobbyist, you should be afforded the same rights and left alone to photograph what you wish—as long as you don't prevent the police from carrying out their duties.

Focal length: 28mm

Aperture: f/10

Shutter speed: 1/6 sec.

ISO: 800

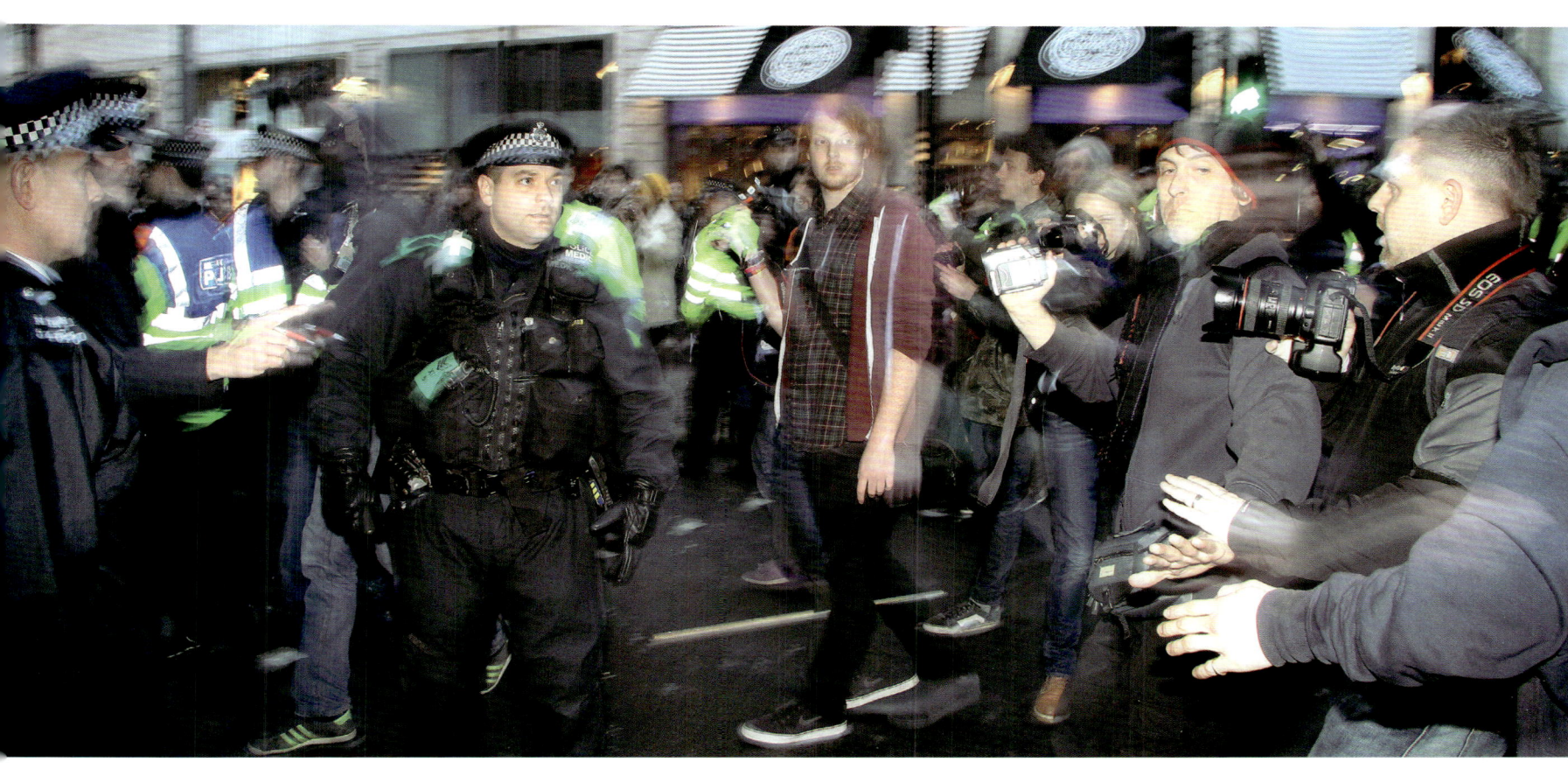

KNOW YOUR RIGHTS

	CAN YOU TAKE PICTURES OF PEOPLE IN PUBLIC PLACES?	CAN YOU PHOTOGRAPH THE POLICE AND OTHER OFFICIALS?	CAN YOU BE ORDERED TO DELETE A PHOTOGRAPH?	CAN YOU PHOTOGRAPH BUILDINGS?	CAN YOU TAKE PICTURES INSIDE SHOPPING MALLS OR MARKETS?	CAN YOU PHOTOGRAPH LOGOS AND BRAND NAMES?
UK	*Yes, without restriction, but make sure you know what's public and what's private.*	*Yes. You can photograph any public (or private) official going about their normal duties.*	*No.*	*Yes, without restriction, as long as you are standing on public property when you take the picture.*	*These are usually private spaces and usually prohibit photography.*	*Usually, but beware of the context. Some may be registered trademarks and any reproduction could constitute an infringement.*
USA	*Yes, although the definition of a public place is narrower than in the UK.*	*Yes, although you should tread with caution in less cosmopolitan areas as the police may be unfamiliar with dealing with photographers.*	*No.*	*Yes, but check the rules of the state you are in.*	*As above.*	*As above.*

Who Are You Allowed To Photograph?

The short answer is just about anyone! Whether your subjects are the general public, police officers, storekeepers, or royalty, you are allowed to photograph them if you are in a public place.

In the UK, privacy laws are fairly unrestrictive, the key point being that everyone has the right to his private and family life. It is really a matter of common sense: if you think that what you are doing may be infringing someone's privacy, stop doing it. On the other hand, don't be bullied by someone who tells you not to take their picture: unless they are doing something that compromises their right to privacy you can photograph them freely.

You should always check out the local laws if you are visiting a different country, though. In France, for example, privacy is a completely different ball game and the creation and/or publication of images of a person without their consent is illegal (perhaps this is why we see relatively little street photography in such a photogenic city as Paris). In Germany, there is a "right to one's own image" principle, which aims to strike a balance between personal privacy and freedom of speech.

Some countries take a more harsh approach. In Hungary, for example, you are technically breaking the law if you take a picture on the streets and someone wanders into shot—a new civil code outlaws taking pictures without the permission of every single person in the photograph!

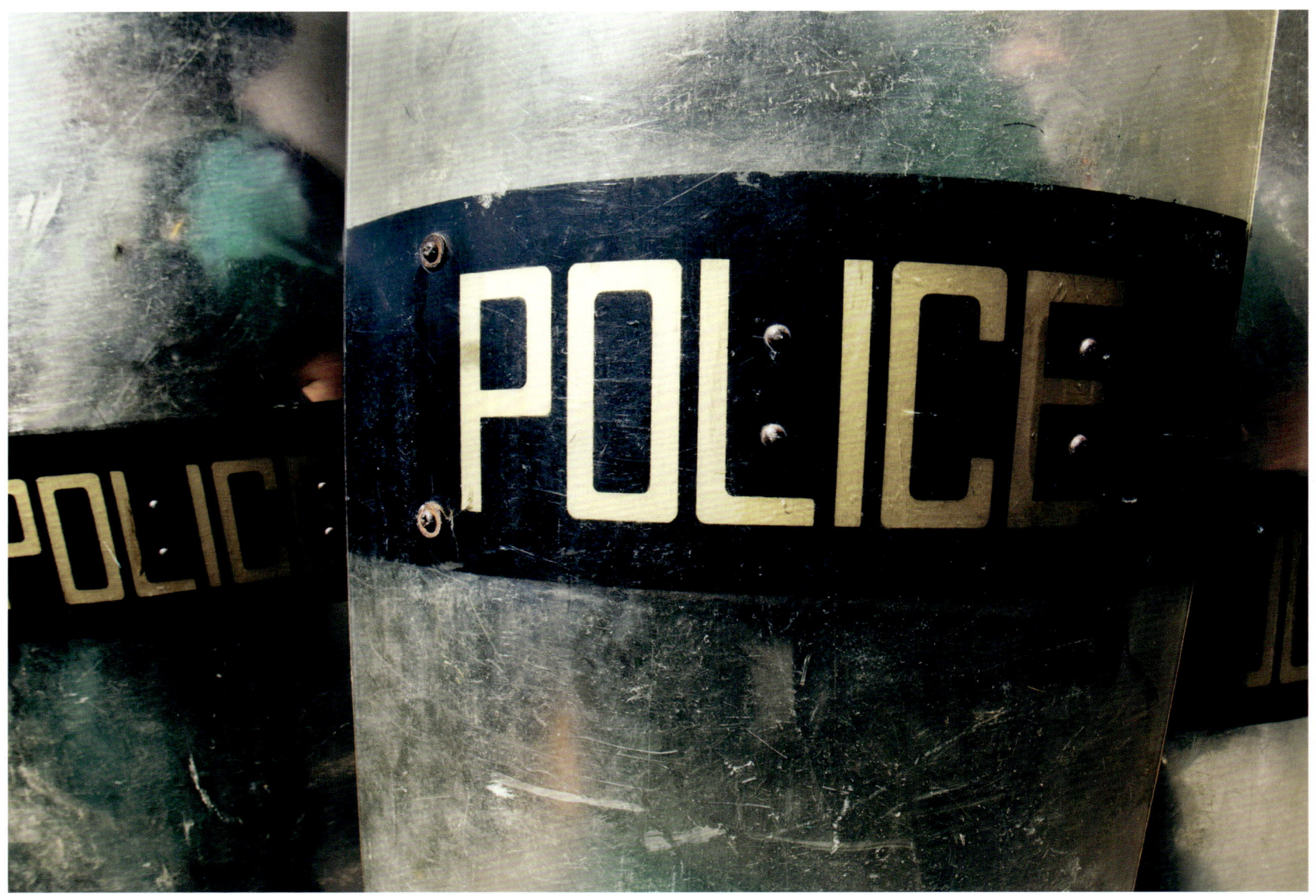

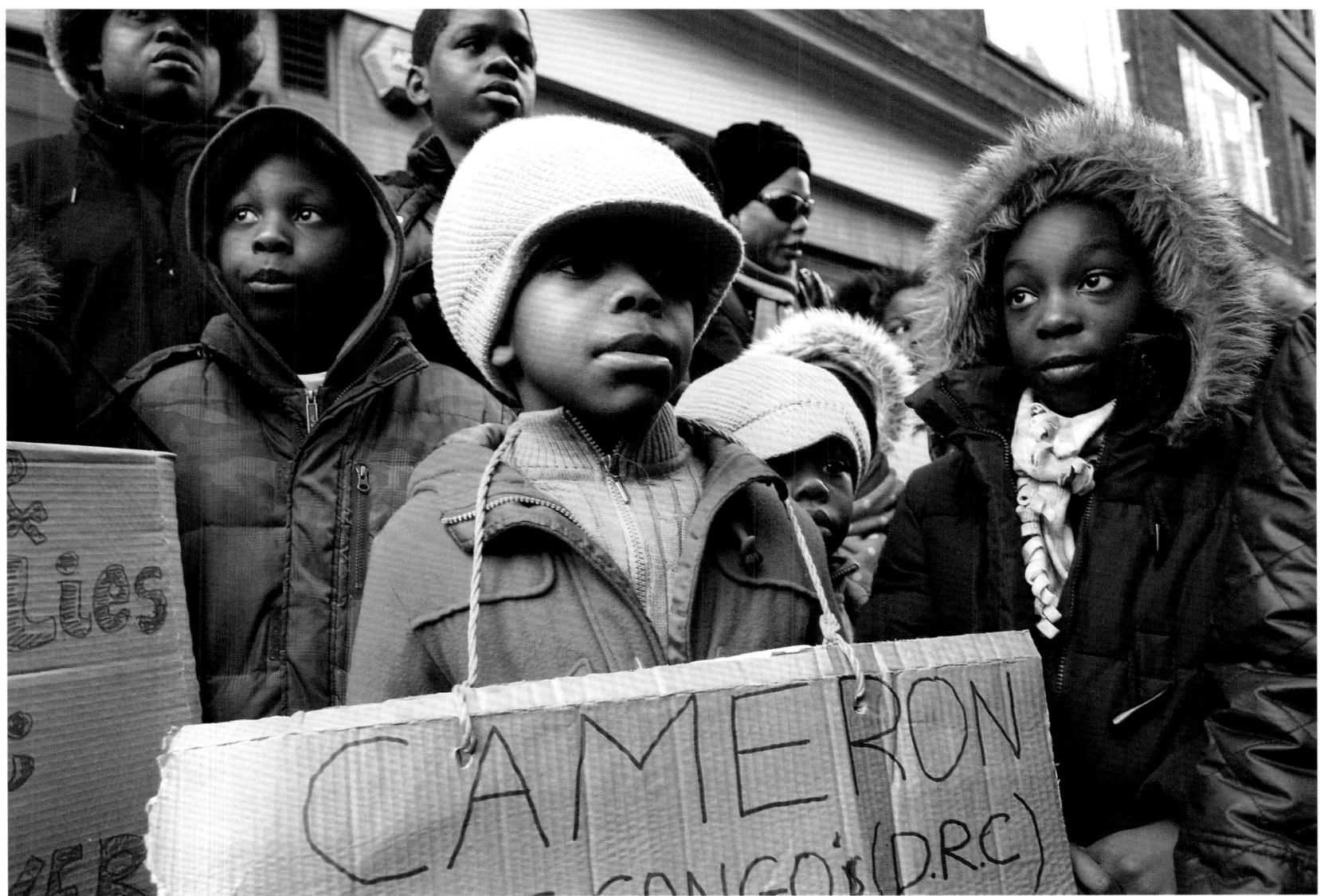

Left: In many countries police officers are NOT entitled to see the pictures you have taken (or to ask you to delete them) unless they reasonably suspect you to be a terrorist. However, this may not stop them asking.

Focal length: 16mm

Aperture: f/11

Shutter speed: 1/200 sec.

ISO: 250

Above: In most countries (the UK and USA included), you are allowed to photograph pretty much anything or anyone—including children—provided you are in a public place.

Focal length: 24mm

Aperture: f/4

Shutter speed: 1/60 sec.

ISO: 640

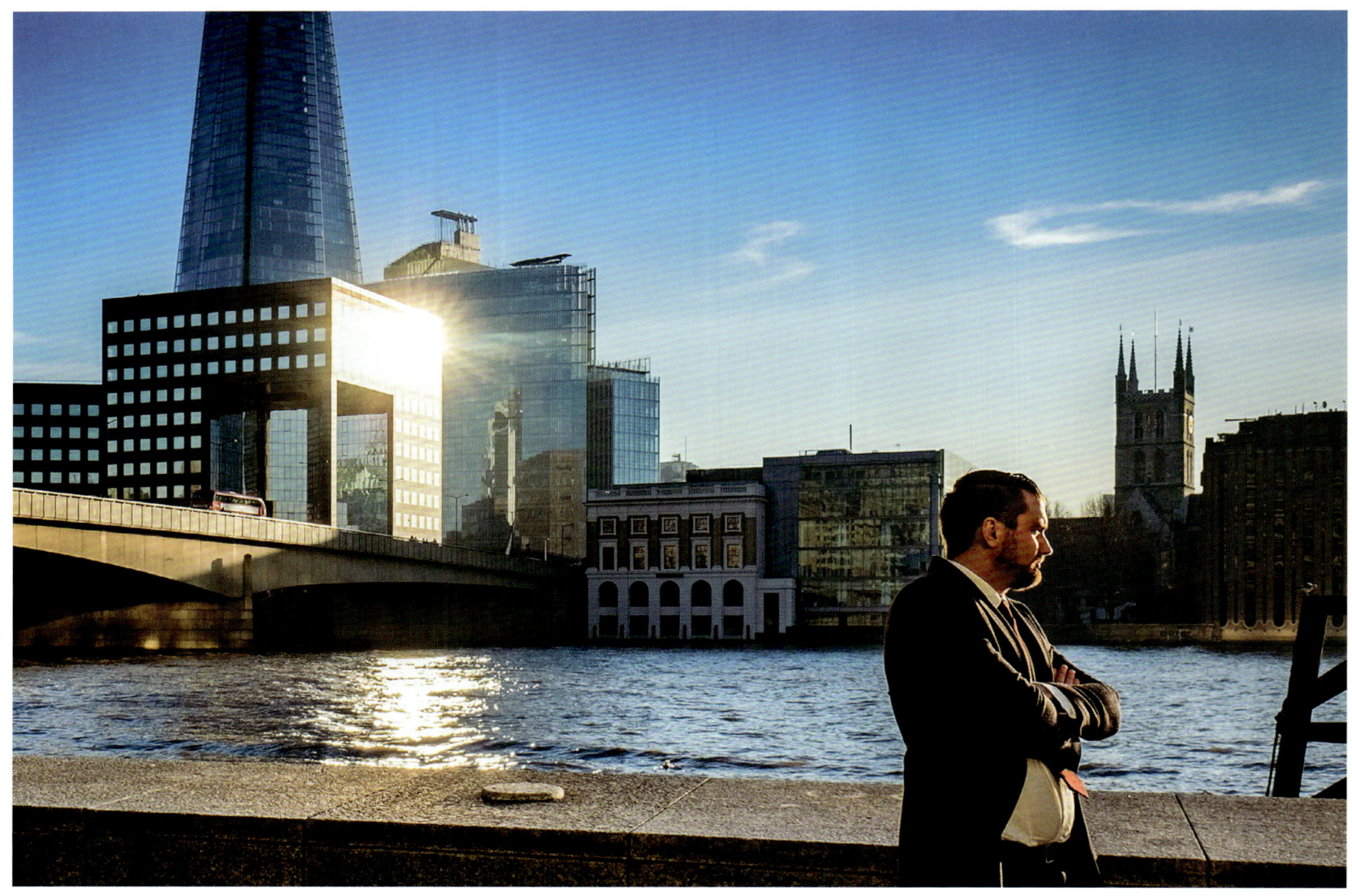

Photographing Buildings

As long as you are standing on public property, you can photograph any building without restriction, despite what a security guard may tell you. In the UK and USA, buildings themselves are not subject to copyright law as far as photography is concerned: you can photograph what you like and then sell your images.

In some countries, such as France, the issue is more complex. You can, for example, photograph the Eiffel Tower, but not at night as the tower's lighting design is protected by copyright law. Again, a common-sense approach is needed; if you look like a tourist and not a professional photographer, you are not likely to be troubled by officials (although difficulties may come later if you try to publish your pictures).

In the USA, however, buildings created after December 1, 1990, are protected by copyright regulations. Fortunately, this doesn't preclude you from taking and distributing photos of a building if the building is located in a public place or is visible from a public place. So, you don't need permission to stand on a public street and photograph a building, no matter if it's public or private.

Certain places such as art galleries, museums, concert venues, and sports arenas make it a condition of entry that photography is not allowed; the same applies to many other private places that allow public access, such as offices and stores. However, it's important to appreciate that this applies when you *enter* the private property, and not if you're outside in a publicly accessible space.

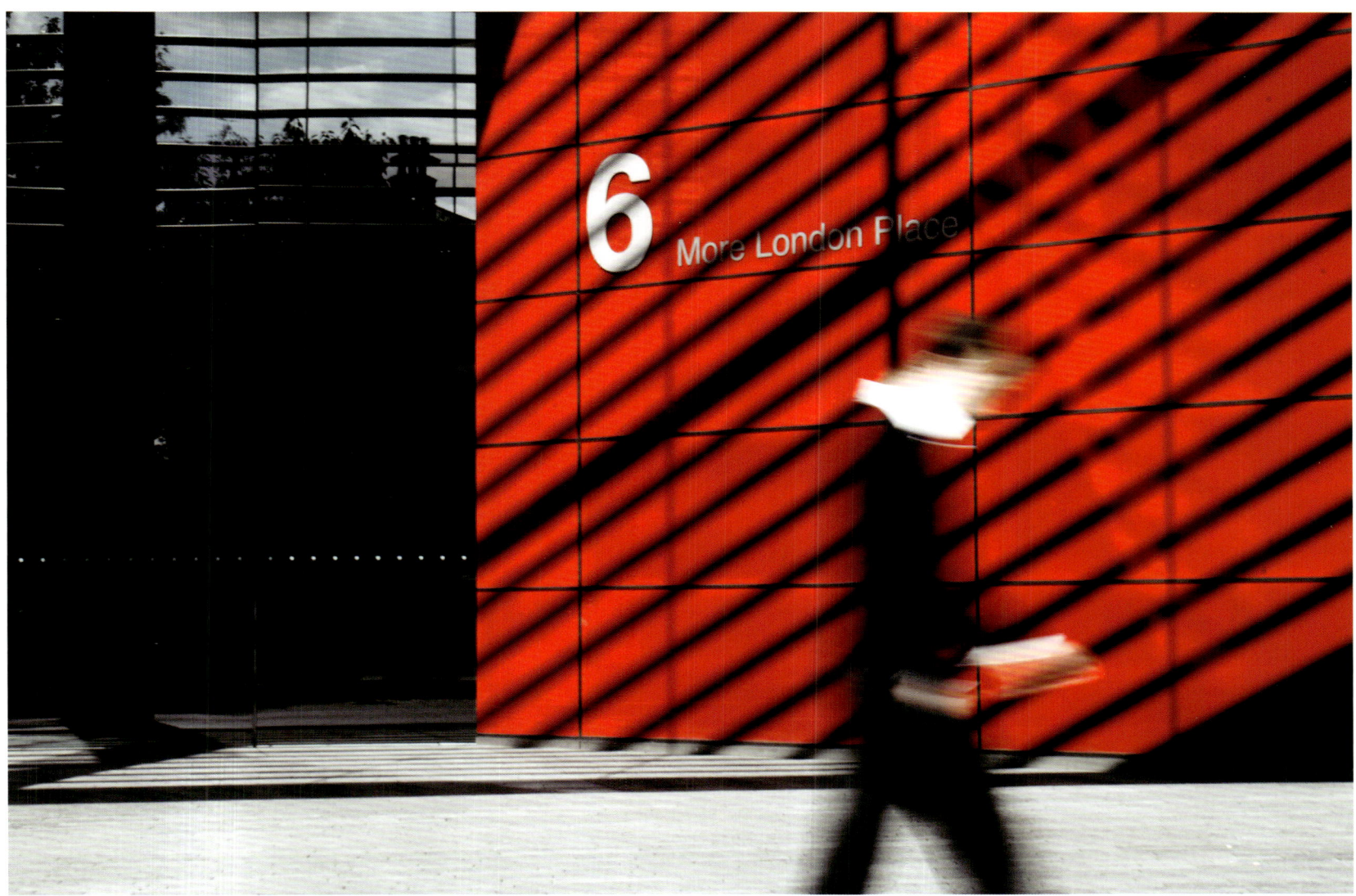

Above left: If you are standing in a public space you can photograph any aspect of any building, regardless of who owns it.

Focal length: 38mm

Aperture: f/8

Shutter speed: 1/1000 sec.

ISO: 400

Above: You can photograph any building without permission, as long as you are standing on public property. A slow shutter speed was used here for a dramatic effect.

Focal length: 60mm

Aperture: f/25

Shutter speed: 1/10 sec.

ISO: 100

Photographing Children

Taking photographs of other people's children is a difficult issue. While it is perfectly legal to do so, there is a certain—perhaps understandable—paranoia about photographing children, so you are advised to proceed with caution.

If children are part of a much wider scene, you won't necessarily have a problem, but if they form the main subject of your shot it is a good idea to speak to their parents, assuming they are nearby, and explain what you are doing before you start shooting. More often than not you will come up against a firm "No," but it's always worth a try. Whatever you do, avoid shooting covertly—particularly with a long lens—and be cautious about taking pictures near schools or in parks (and certainly not in swimming pools).

The situation differs throughout the world, though: in some countries, such as India, it is perfectly natural to photograph children, but in certain parts of the Middle East it is a taboo.

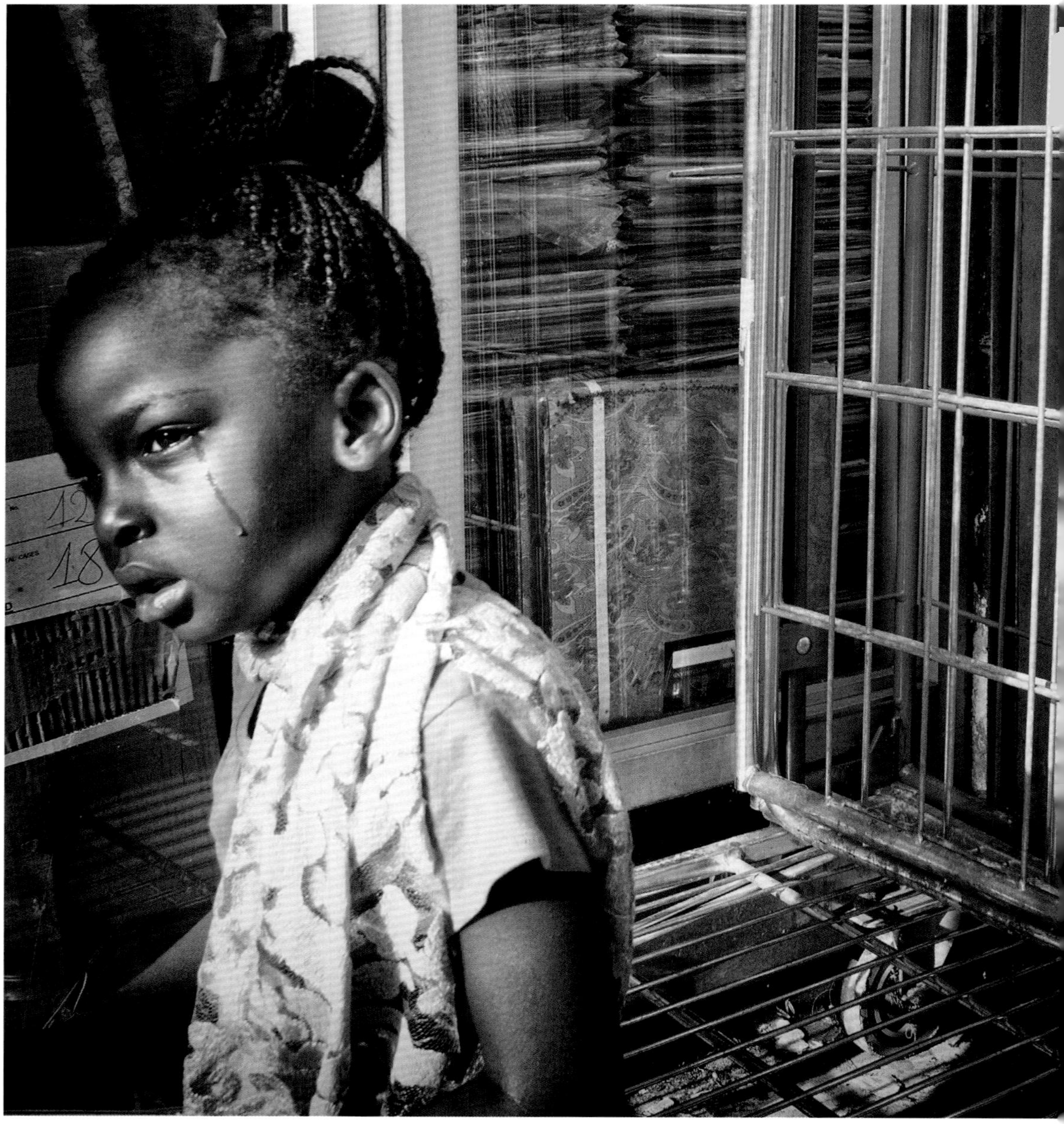

Right: Despite this being a perfectly innocent and legitimate image of a little girl crying, the photographer's intention could have easily been misconstrued. It's often best to avoid photographing small children, but if you do so, try to speak to their parents first and explain what you are doing: an angry or outraged parent can cause you a whole world of problems.

Focal length: 35mm

Aperture: f/8

Shutter speed: 1/640 sec.

ISO: 1600

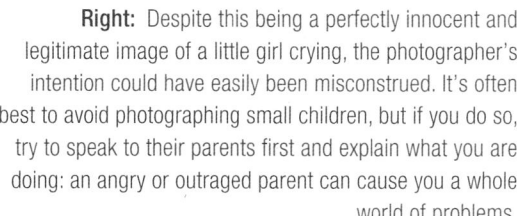

Cultural Issues

When you're in or around a different culture, it's a good idea to be aware of your surroundings and to behave accordingly. Weigh up the benefits of getting a great shot against the downside of really offending someone.

The old maxim "When in Rome, do as the Romans do" is a good principle to apply in street photography. Do your research before arriving at a new destination, watch what others are doing and remember the importance of blending in. In some cities, such as London, people like their personal space and expect a degree of privacy; the opposite could be said for a city like Mumbai, where people's attitude to being photographed is far more relaxed.

You may consider, particularly when overseas, offering money to locals who have been a subject for you—either before or after the event. There is no right or wrong approach—this is a judgment call you have to make in the circumstances.

Some countries are particularly sensitive about photography of—and around—military installations and even police stations. If you are in any doubt, put your camera away and don't shoot. It isn't worth a night (or longer) in a police cell!

Exercise common sense, be tuned in to what is going on around you, and be respectful at all times—and you won't go far wrong.

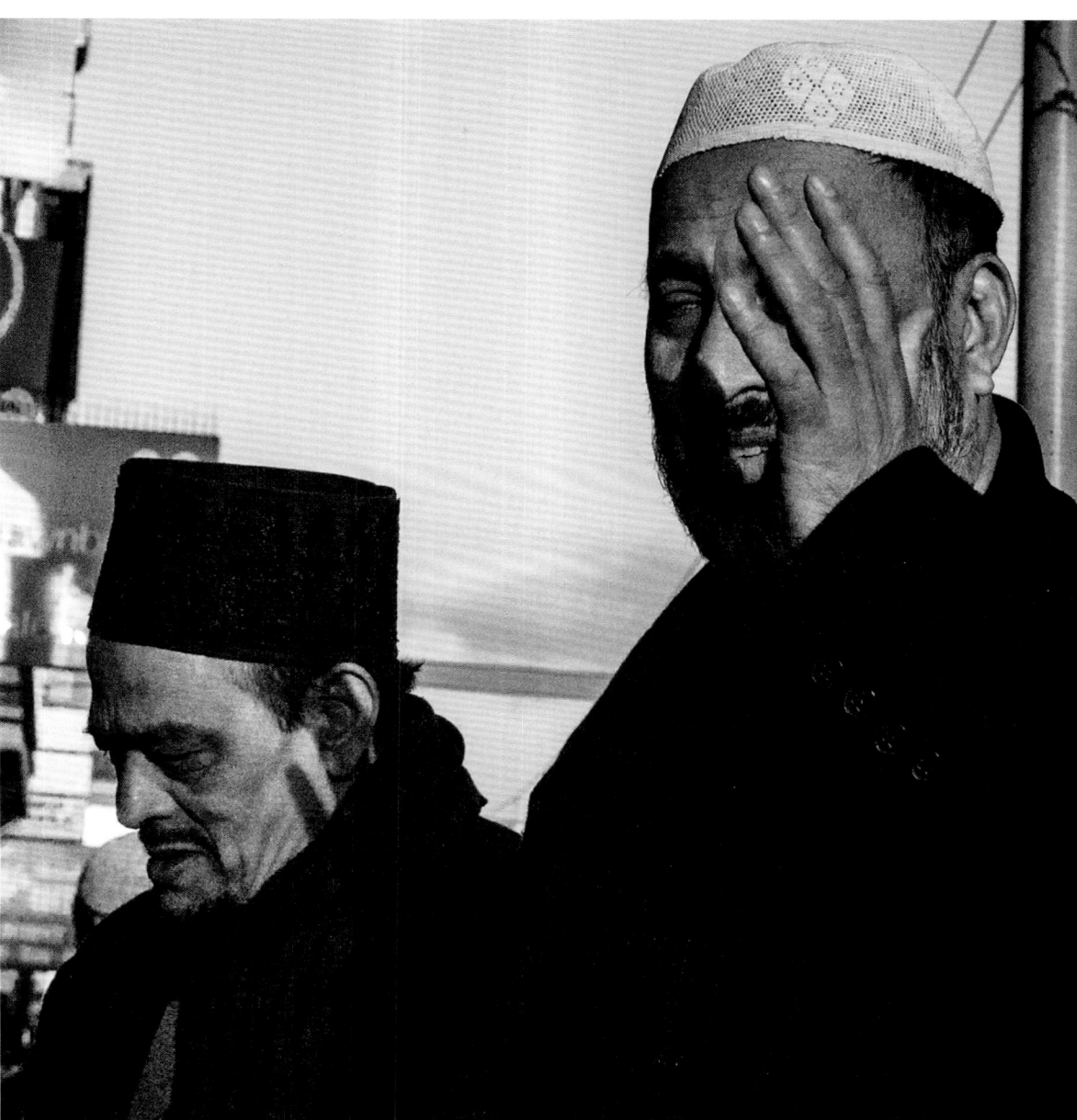

Right: For religious or cultural reasons some people just don't want to have their photograph taken. Be sensitive when photographing people from different cultures; if you get a negative vibe, sometimes it's best to just stop.

Focal length: 50mm
Aperture: f/9.5
Shutter speed: 1/4000 sec.
ISO: 1600

Red Lines

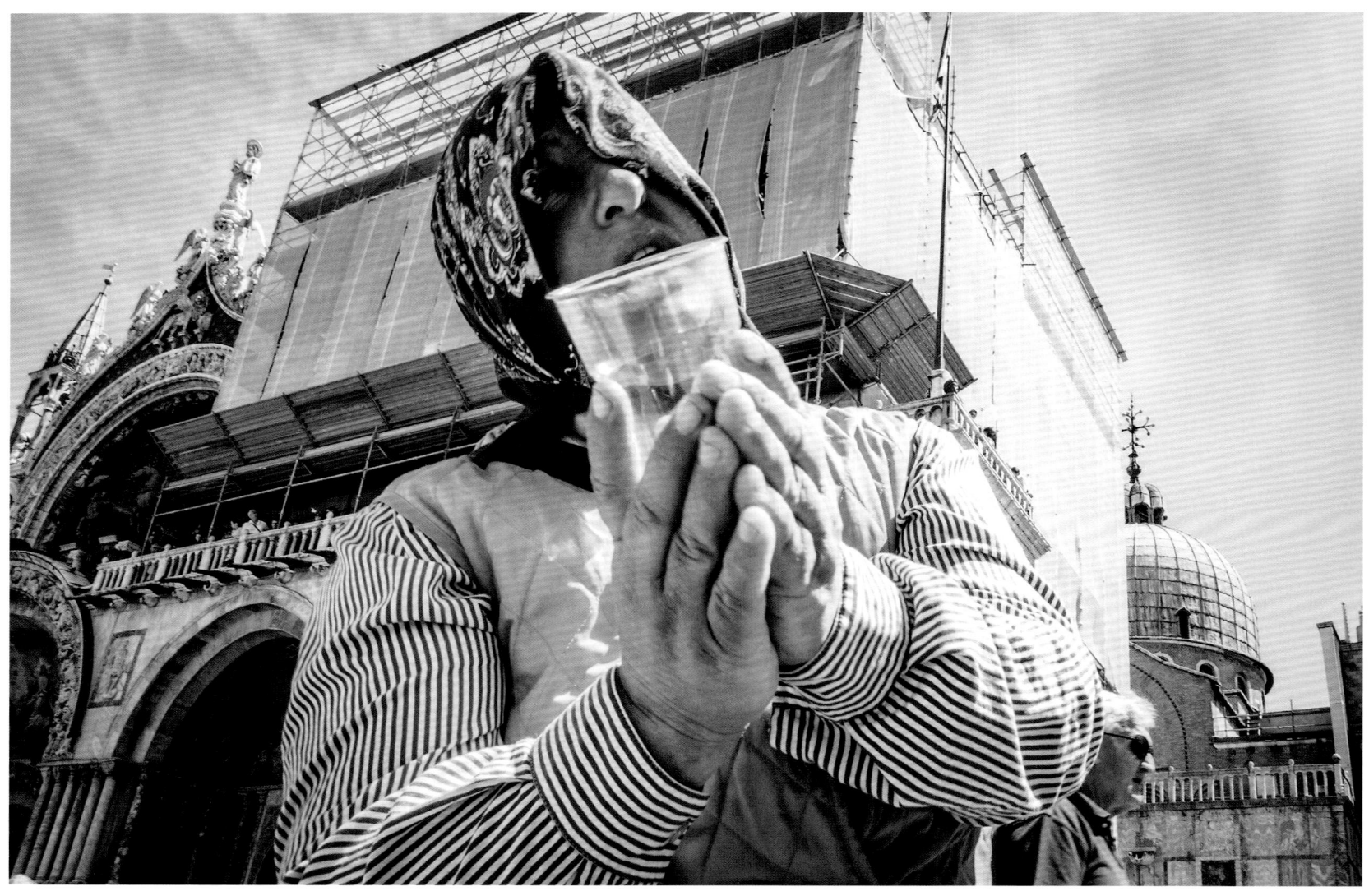

We all have our own boundaries when it comes to deciding what is and isn't acceptable in terms of subject matter. For example, you may feel that photographing homeless people is voyeuristic or exploitative, and simply prefer not to do it. You might also draw the line at photographing disabled people, or children, or those who are having a tough time for whatever reason. It is entirely up to you—and your moral compass—where you draw the line.

Above: Although you can get some interesting shots of homeless people, it's a red line that many photographers won't cross. However, as this particular woman fell into the category of "professional beggar," taking her picture didn't feel exploitative.

Focal length: 28mm

Aperture: f/16

Shutter speed: 1/75 sec.

ISO: 200

Copyright

Copyright is a legal concept that applies in a similar manner in most countries. This gives creators of works of art (just like you) the exclusive right to publish, adapt, and license their work for financial benefit. In the USA and in the UK, copyright in a photograph lasts for 70 years from the end of the year in which the photographer dies; after the 70-year period the rights will transfer to someone else, usually through a will or by inheritance.

Who Owns A Photograph?

In the USA, the UK, and most other countries, the default position is that the copyright owner of a photograph is the photographer who created it. While you will hear the word "author" used in relation to copyright, this simply means the creator of the work in question (in this case the photographer) and not necessarily a writer.

Copyright is granted automatically, as soon as the photograph has been taken, and you don't need to register a photograph to have copyright (in the UK there is no official body with which to register images). However, although it is not essential in the USA to register an image for it to be protected by copyright, it is advisable to do so in order to avoid difficulties later on. You can register images with the US Copyright Office.

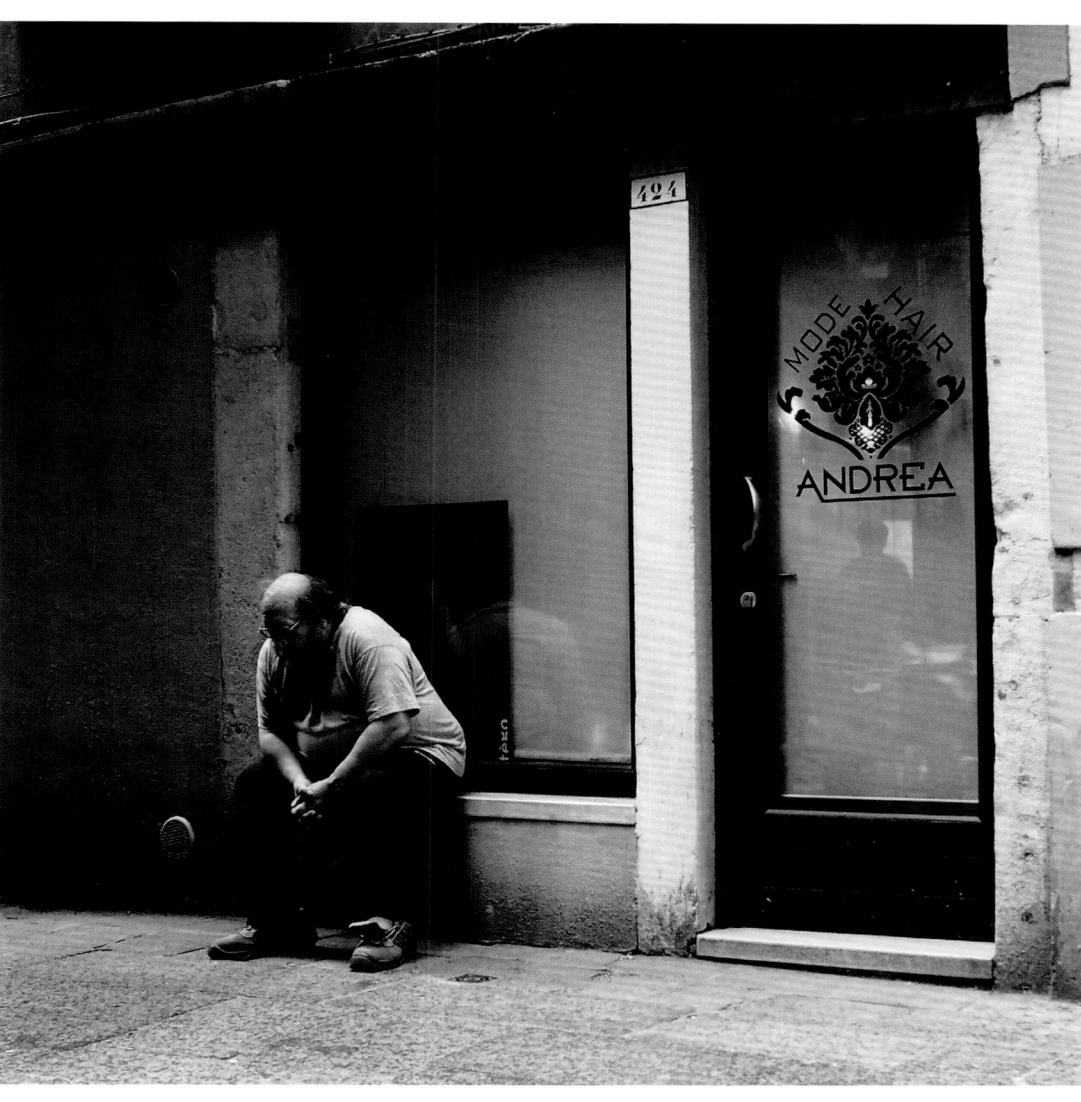

Copyright On The Streets

You will probably come across situations on the streets where you take someone's picture and they insist they own the copyright to it. They don't, and never will. Even if they believe they have a moral right to the image, there is nothing they can do to force you to part with it or to sign it over to them.

The same goes for buildings. It is certainly not an infringement of copyright to photograph buildings that are situated in a public place or to shoot in premises that are open to the public.

Above: Who do you think owns the copyright in this picture? Is it the seated man? Is it Andrea, the hairdresser? It's actually the photographer, as it is in nearly all cases. There is often much confusion around the issue of copyright, but almost without exception, copyright remains with the photographer unless he or she re-assigns it.

Focal length: 28mm

Aperture: f/5

Shutter speed: 1/50 sec.

ISO: 1600

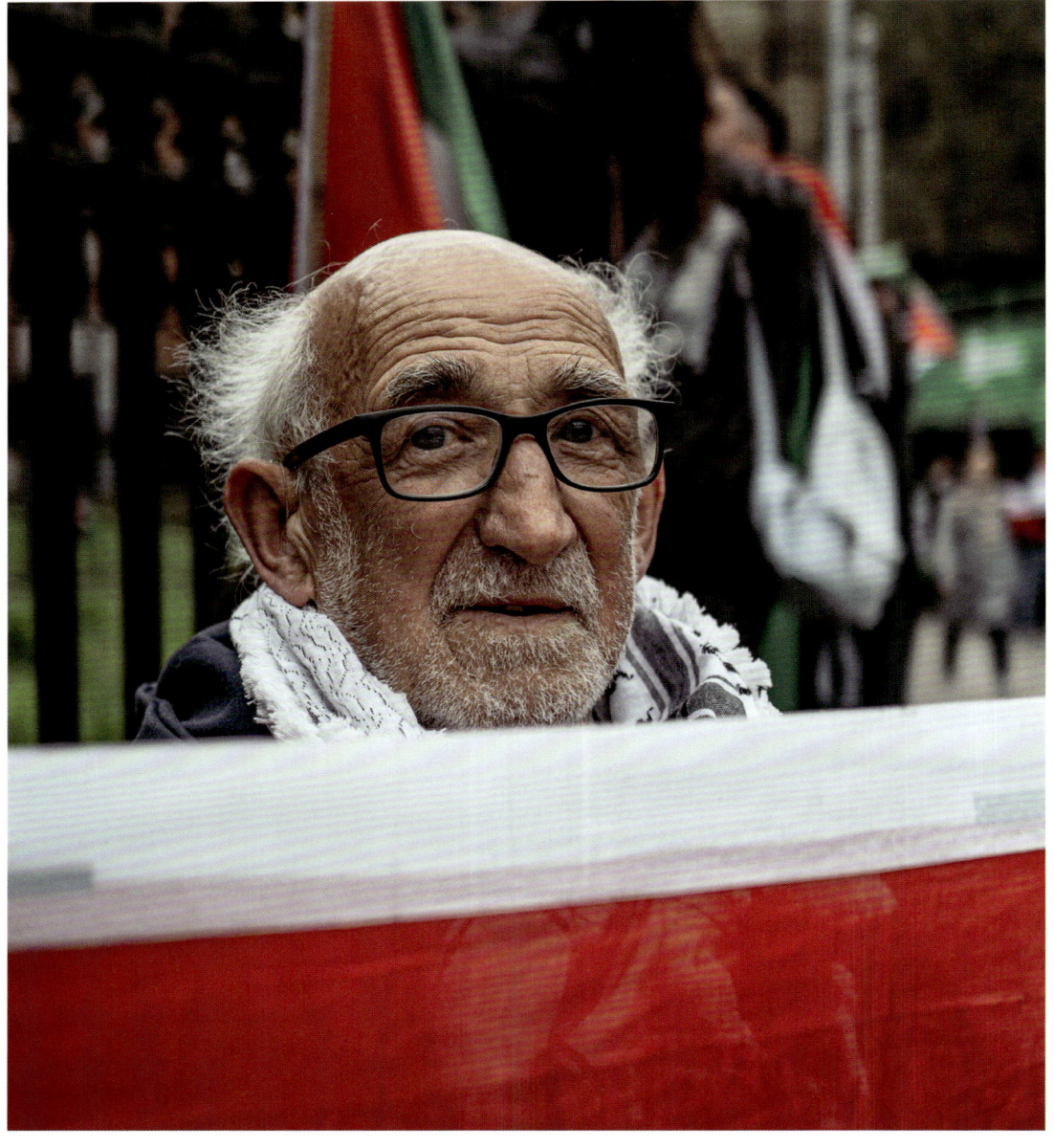

Model Releases

If you intend to use the pictures you take of people for commercial purposes you will need them to sign a model release form. So, how do we define commercial purposes? This simply means using the image of a person to promote or advertise another person, product, or enterprise (even if you, as the photographer, are not getting paid for the work). Commercial use includes advertising, but excludes editorial use (newspapers, magazines, and online media), publication in books, and work in exhibitions or on websites.

If you want to sell your images through an image library, any that contain recognizable faces will require a model release form. This is a widely available document that is signed by your subject and gives you permission to use the image for commercial purposes.

Because you can never guarantee what or whom you will be photographing, it's worth keeping a few model release forms in your bag; they are also available as apps for your cellphone. However, be aware that there is no standard form, and each agency or publisher will have its own preferred version.

Defamatory Pictures

Let's say you take a picture of a teenager and sell it via an image library to an advertising company that uses it in the context of drug abuse. This could reasonably be expected to cause your subject embarrassment, so if they have not given you (written) permission to use their picture in this way, you could end up in court. Of course, if you were in possession of a signed model release you would be free to use the picture as you wished.

TIP

Most professional photographic bodies will have their own accepted model release forms, as will most image libraries. You can find a host of release forms online by searching "Photography Model Release Form," but it's a good idea to pick a source that you trust.

Above: You don't need someone's permission to take their photograph, although you should have written permission if you want to sell the image for commercial gain. Most street photographers, however, take pictures for personal—and perhaps editorial—use, for which no permission is required (this includes publication in books and zines).

Focal length: 28mm

Aperture: f/1.7

Shutter speed: 1/2000 sec.

ISO: 100

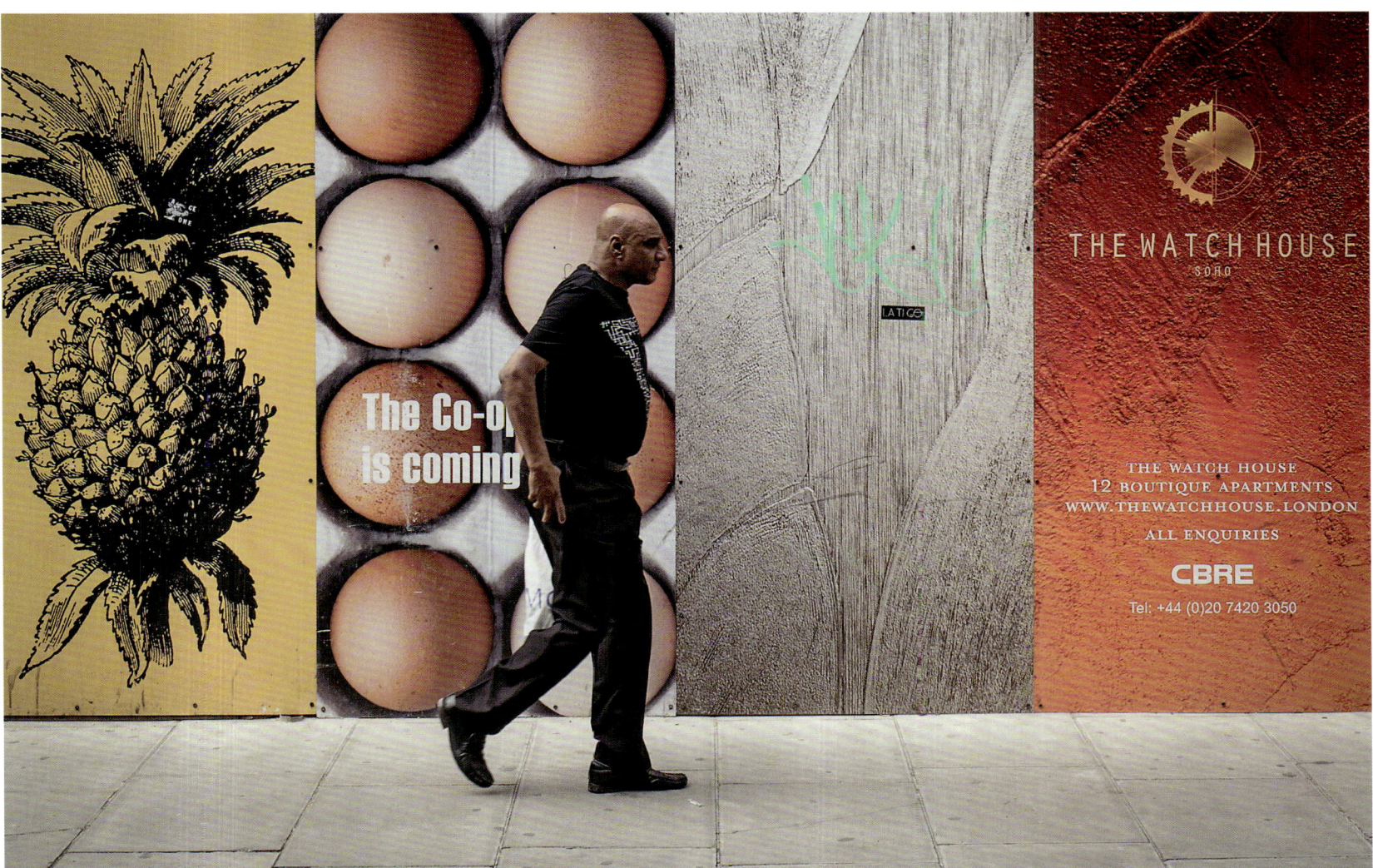

Licensing Work

As the copyright holder of an image, you (and only you) can decide what can and can't be done with it. This includes:

- Allowing someone else to reproduce the photograph.

- Allowing someone else to distribute copies of the photograph to the public.

- Renting or lending the work to the public.

- Broadcasting the work to the public.

You may come under pressure to surrender these rights—essentially "signing over" copyright—but it is nearly always a mistake to do so. If you want to allow someone else to use your images (note that it is use and not own), you can provide them with a license to do so. This is usually for a pre-determined period of time (say three years), for a defined use (perhaps in a brochure or magazine), and in a specific geographic area (such as Europe). Granting a license in this way would generate a fee for you, the photographer. Licenses are granted in this way when images are sold through online stock libraries.

Above: What would happen if this picture appeared in a newspaper and the man objected to it because it was unflattering? What if he thought the subtext suggested he was an "egg-head?" Although the image may be unflattering, it is not defamatory, and as it was taken in a public place he would have no grounds for complaint. Merely "embarrassing" rarely provides a sound enough reason for legal redress.

Focal length: 28mm

Aperture: f/5.6

Shutter speed: 1/250 sec.

ISO: 100

Protecting Copyright

Due largely to the rise in the online use of imagery, copyright has become a big issue for photographers. Whenever you post a photo online, it is a potential target for image theft, which is rife across the world. Whether you watermark your images (which detracts from their impact) or you place tough copyright warnings in the metadata, you run the risk of someone, somewhere, stealing them.

Sharing your images on social media such as Facebook, X, Instagram, and other platforms can be great fun, but you should always assume that people will somehow manage to copy and use them without your permission; if you're not prepared to accept this, don't share them! Furthermore, you should always read the terms and conditions relating to social media outlets; by accepting the T&Cs, which you will almost certainly do, you will automatically waive some of your legal rights to your images. Always check!

Unfortunately, there is little you can do to prevent image theft. It helps if you enter your copyright information into the image's metadata, but this won't deter a determined thief. Some of the latest website technology aimed at photographers has clever security features, such as SmartFrame technology, while others make theft as easy as right-clicking with your mouse.

Right: Remember that by adding social media "share" buttons you could be giving your work away. Right clicking is still possible on many social media sites and if you're not careful, your images could go viral within a few seconds of being posted.

Protecting Images Online

Unfortunately, your images will never be 100 percent safe on the Internet, but there are several steps you can take to help minimize the risk of image theft:

- **Watermarking**: This serves as a form of guaranteed attribution (if the watermark is your name); you can also add your telephone number or email address as part of the watermark to encourage easy contact from interested parties.

- **Metadata**: This can be a useful way of embedding your data inside the image in text format. However, metadata alone is not sufficient to protect your copyright. It isn't always readily and easily seen, and is readable only if you know how to read it and have the software required to do so. Another drawback is that images uploaded to pretty much any social network will have the metadata removed instantly, so in this respect it is useless. Having said that, it is still advisable to embed as much metadata as you can into your images.

The simple alternative to all of this is just don't put your images on the Internet to start with. While this is an option that a few people choose to employ, it has very obvious drawbacks. Most of us want to share and sometimes even sell our work, and at the very least we want to be able to show it off to a wider audience. The Internet is the perfect place to facilitate this.

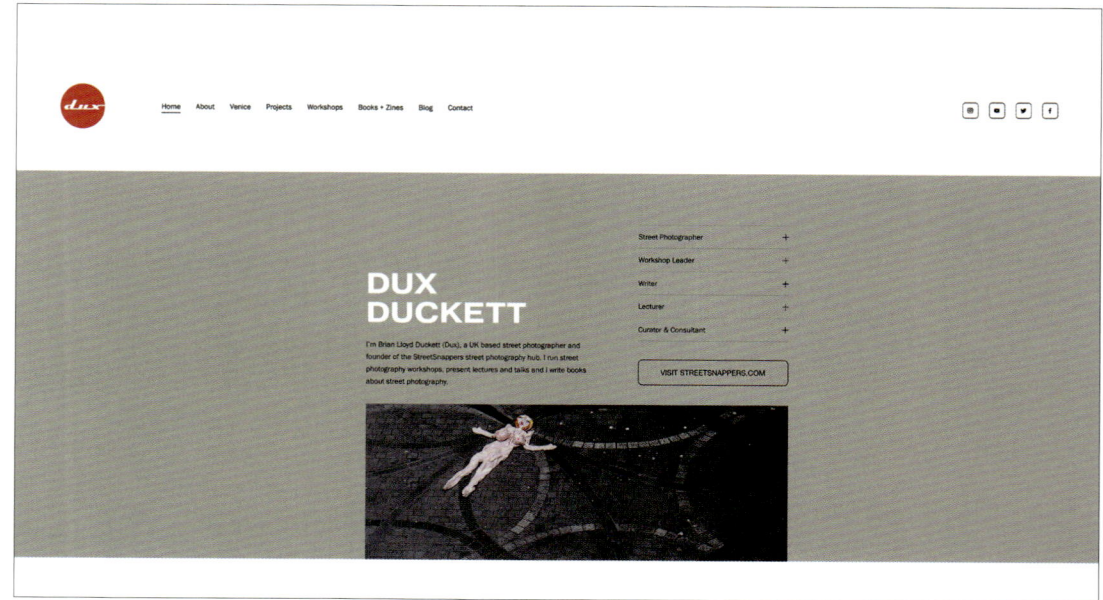

A Fair Price

At some stage, most of us will have an image (and ideally lots of them!) that a commercial organization wants to buy. But how do you know what to charge? The correct market price will normally be determined by usage—in other words what media the image will appear in, over what time period, and in which geographic location. There are some online calculators that will help you arrive at a price using this formula, the most popular being that run by the Alamy stock library.

Tip

If you watermark your images, make sure the watermark is complex enough to prevent cloning out, but not so complex that it ruins the visual impact of the image.

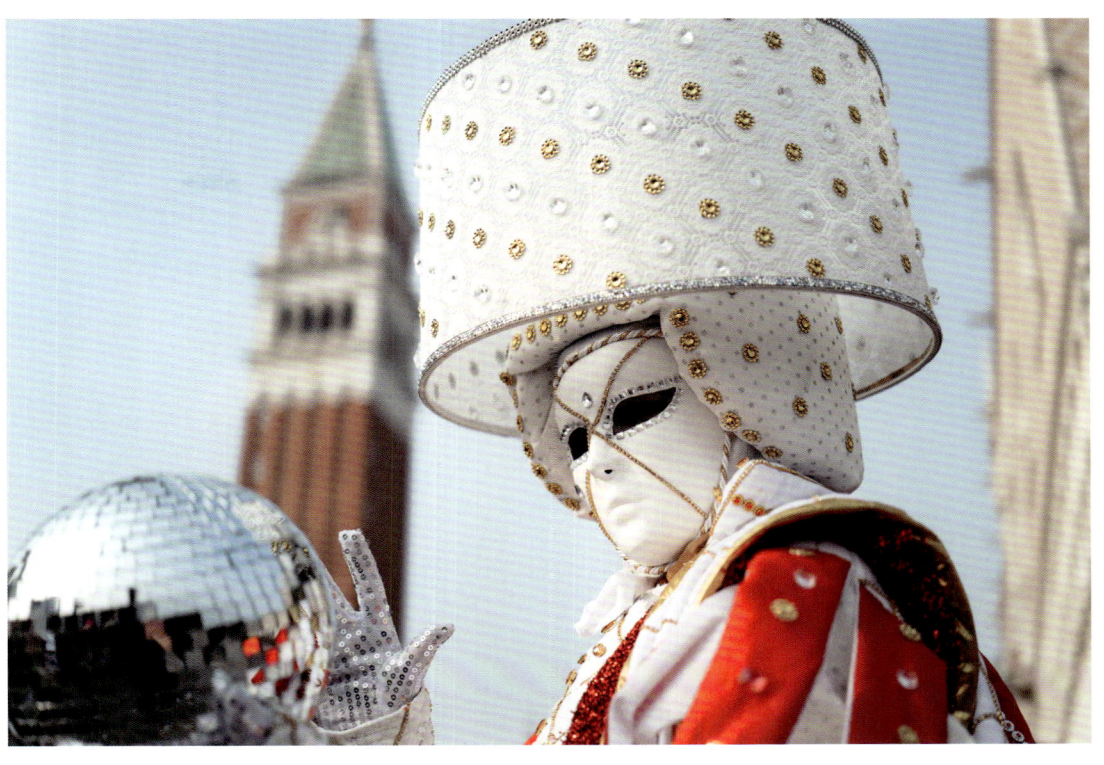

Above: It's often possible to sell this type of image to a tourist board, particularly to help with the promotion of an event—in this case, the Venice Carnival. Always make sure you get a fair market price for your images—many organizations will expect them for free.

Focal length: 43mm

Aperture: f/2

Shutter speed: 1/2000 sec.

ISO: 100

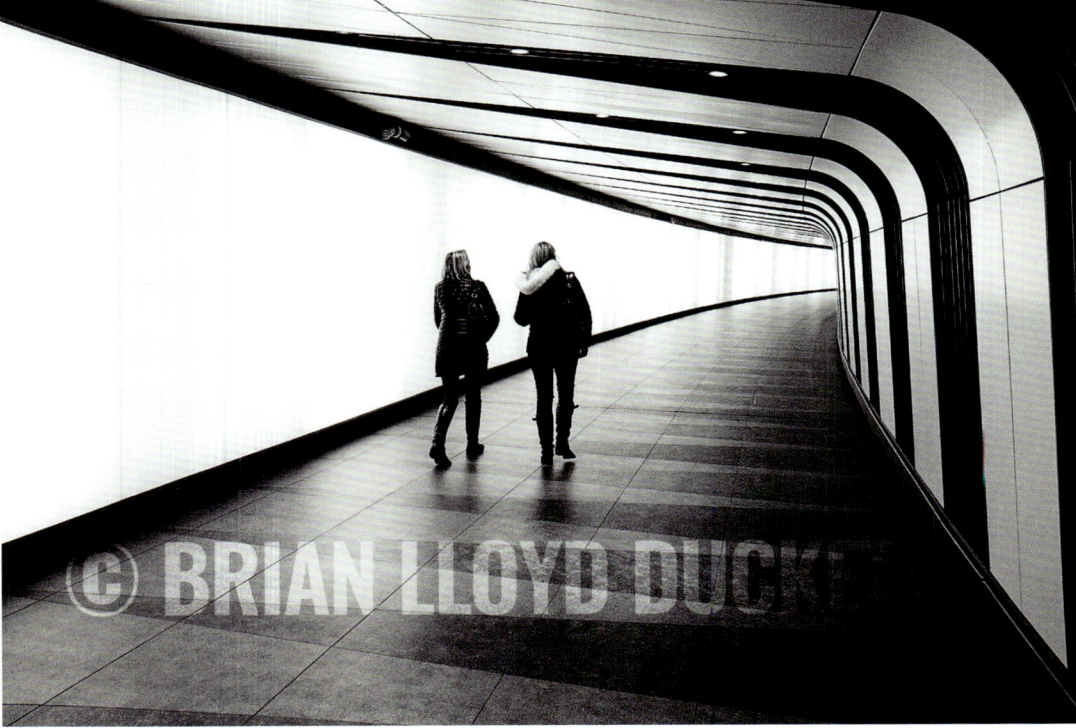

Left: A subtle (or not so subtle, depending on your preference) watermark can help prevent unauthorized use of your images.

Chapter 6
Postproduction

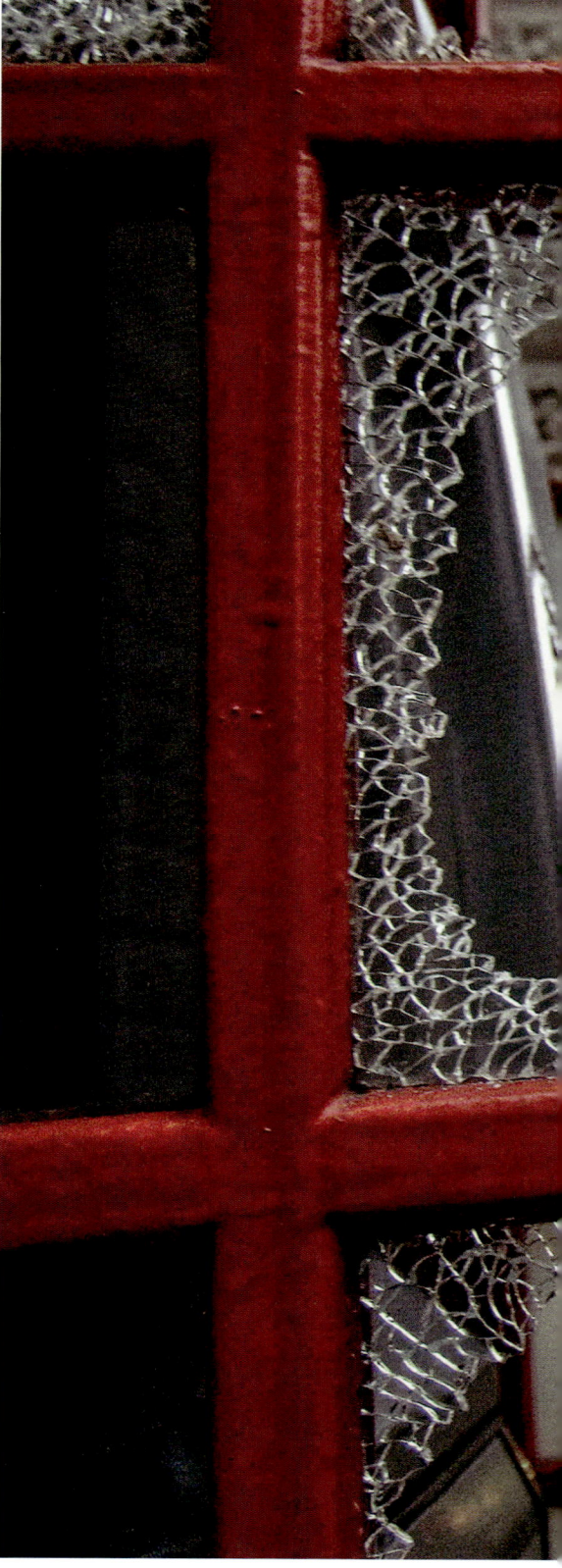

Now, you're perhaps thinking: "Some of the world's greatest street photographs had no image-editing techniques applied to them, so why should I bother?" While this is a fair question, the basis for it is arguable. A great many iconic street images that were taken in the film era were subjected to similar postproduction techniques to those we would apply today, such as cropping, adding contrast, dodging, and burning. The difference is that nowadays we do the work on a computer rather than in the darkroom.

Right: This image was used to help tell the story of "Broken Britain"—a popular and recurring news theme. When shooting for editorial use, a minimal amount of postproduction is considered acceptable: some cropping, corrections to levels, contrast, and color balance, and a little sharpening. However, anything else is considered to be "off-limits."

Focal length: 28mm
Aperture: f/8
Shutter speed: 1/25 sec.
ISO: 1250

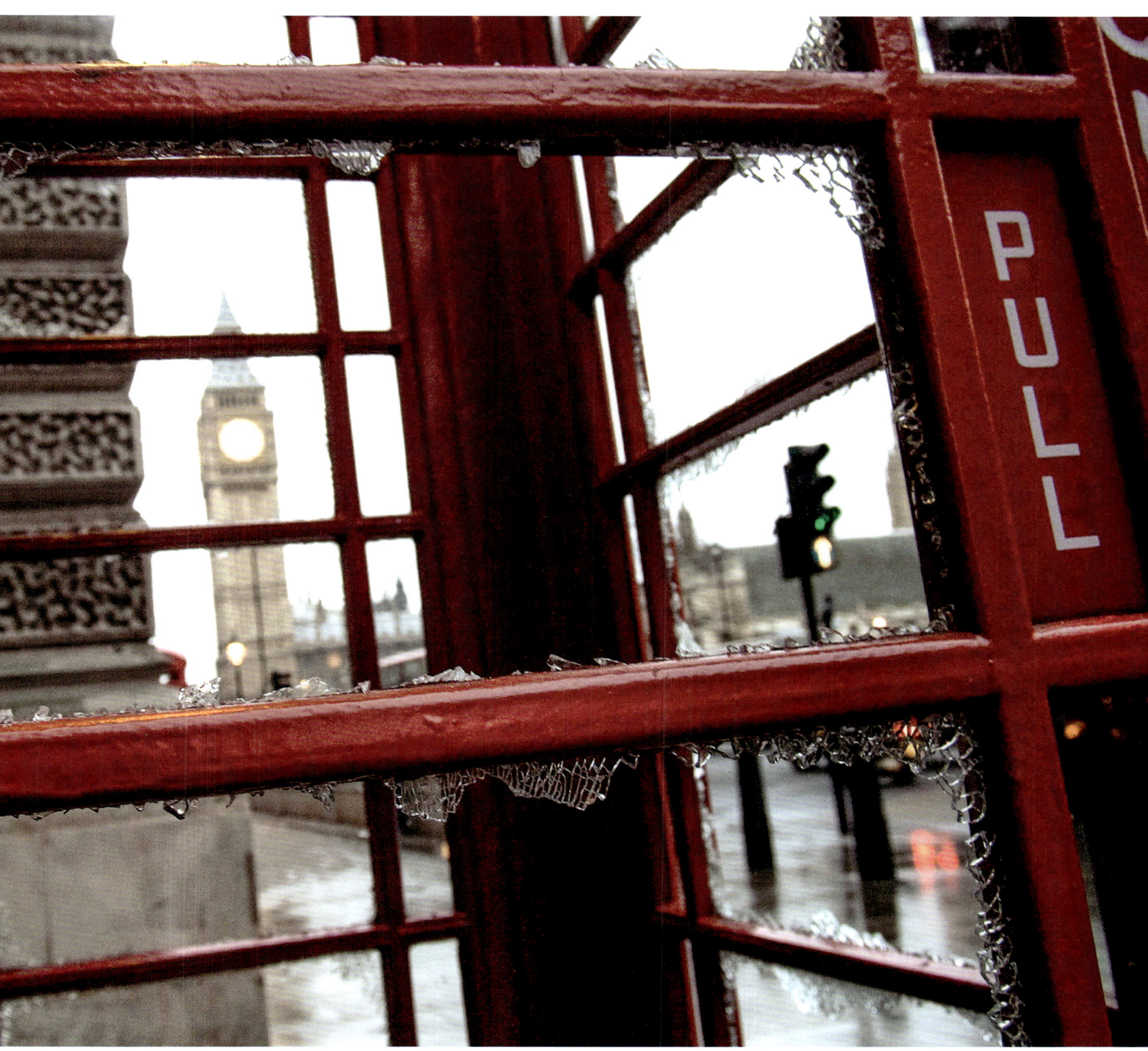

The Integrity Of The Image

Most street photography is about capturing real life—a snapshot in time—and you may hear people say that postproduction takes away the integrity of that moment; some purists still maintain that no postproduction should be necessary. Sometimes it isn't, but if you have the opportunity to significantly improve an image, why not take it?

As digital cameras become more sophisticated, postproduction can easily become "pre-production," in that effects that were typically applied on the computer can now be applied in-camera, before the picture is taken. But let's leave that concept aside for the moment and concentrate on what happens once your image files have been downloaded onto your computer.

When we talk about computers, your choice of machine is largely irrelevant; an Apple Mac and a Windows PC will do the same job and will use similar software. The crucial factor is the machine's speed and processing power. Older, slower computers can take an age to process digital files of the size produced by modern cameras, so invest in the most powerful model you can afford, whichever platform you choose.

As with any other form of photography, it is important to get it right in-camera in the first place—there is no point spending hours in front of a computer unnecessarily! More importantly, each step in the image-editing process has a detrimental effect on the quality of the final image. As one well-known street photographer said: "If your camera can't get it right, neither can your computer."

Most of us want to capture exactly what we see: nothing more, nothing less. With this in mind, image manipulation—or postproduction—is usually kept to a minimum, with little need for software that can remove unwanted elements, add missing ones, or otherwise compromise the "documentary" nature of the image. Compared to, say, landscape photography, street photography is fairly unsophisticated in this respect!

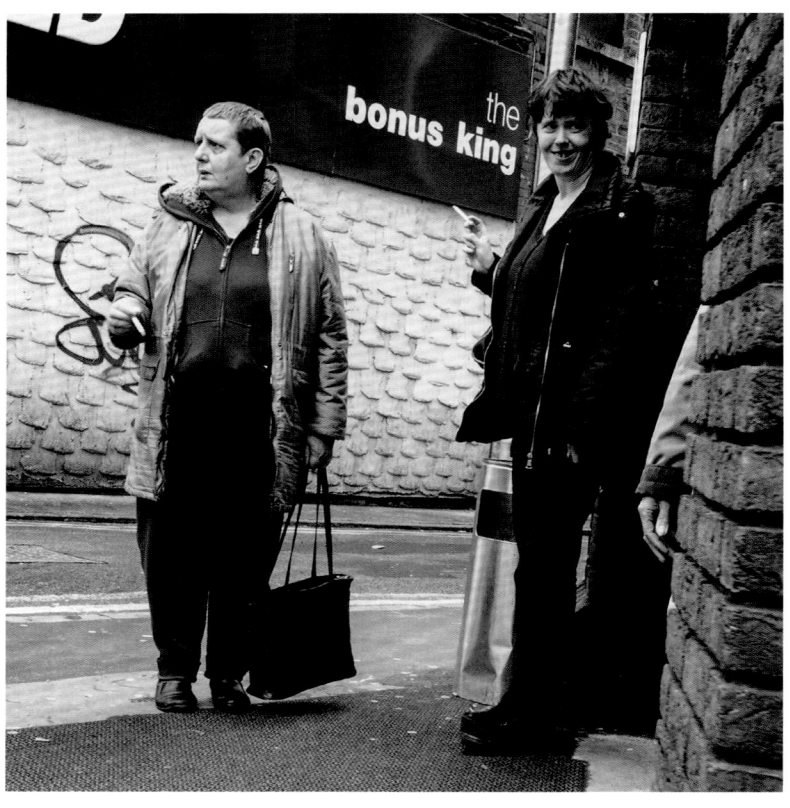

YOUR POSTPRODUCTION COOKBOOK: SEVEN ESSENTIAL INGREDIENTS

1 Cropping
2 Exposure
3 Contrast
4 Clarity
5 Noise reduction
6 Vignette
7 Sharpening

Above: After converting this image to black and white and cropping to a square format, all that was required was a small increase to the Clarity setting to increase midtone contrast and add a gritty feel (resist the temptation to go overboard with the clarity slider— it can easily ruin an image).

Focal length: 35mm

Aperture: f/7.1

Shutter speed: 1/250 sec.

ISO: 1250

Right: A little cropping is fine. The sign in the background says "The Avenue," but a tight crop reduced it to "Heaven." Cropping can change the entire nature of an image, but it's often better used judiciously to balance a composition.

Focal length: 35mm

Aperture: f/4

Shutter speed: 1/40 sec.

ISO: 200

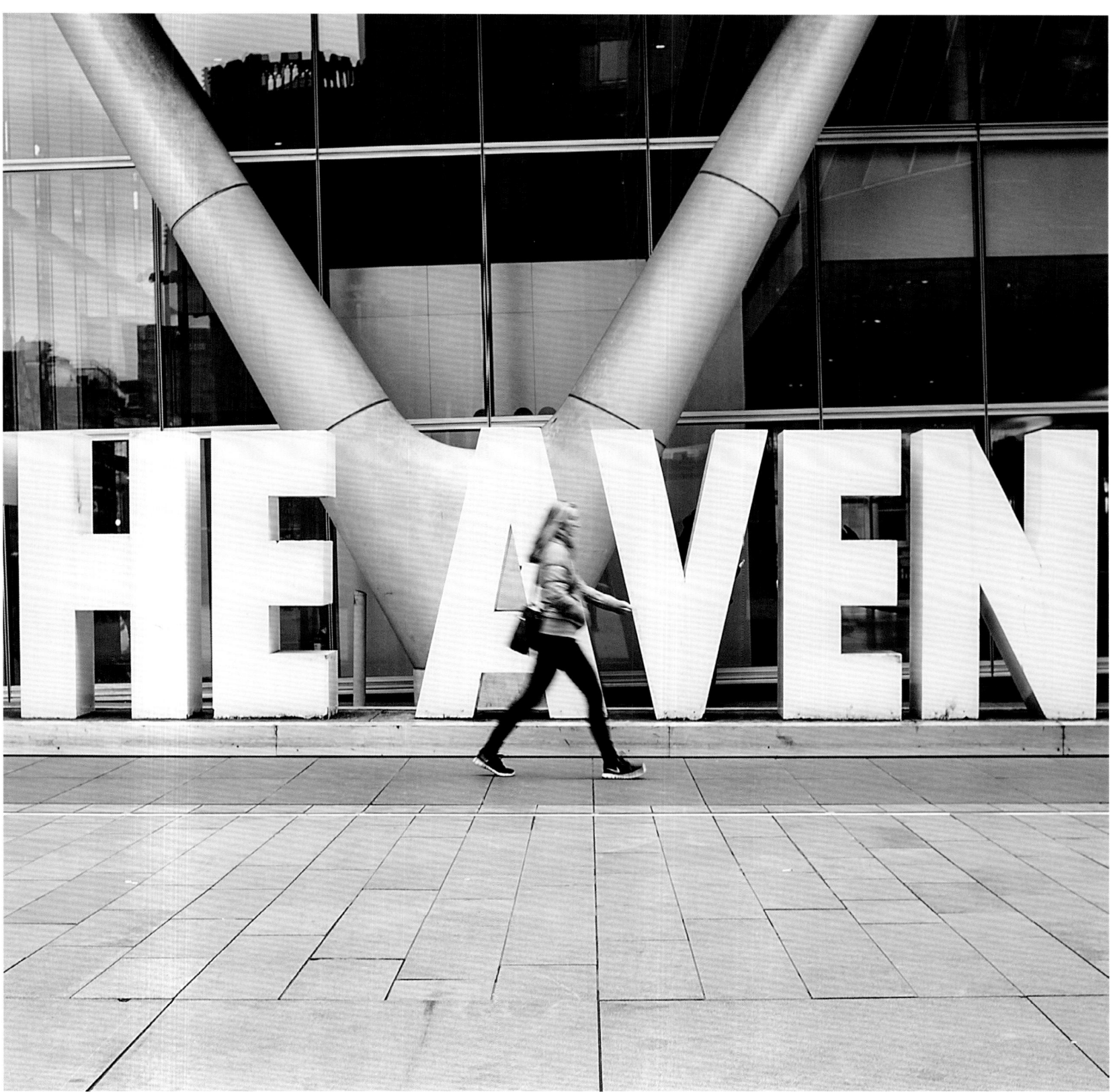

Image-Editing Software

There are three types of image-editing software to consider: those that offer extensive editing tools (such as Adobe Photoshop); those that provide image management capability and offer some editing tools (such as Adobe Lightroom or Capture One); and plug-ins that can be bolted-on to a program to increase its functionality (such as Silver Efex Pro).

Adobe Photoshop

Although there are cheaper (and even free) alternatives available, the industry standard in image editing is Adobe Photoshop. This can be purchased as a full version or as a much cheaper light version in the form of Photoshop Elements; the full version can be paid for on a monthly subscription basis.

Photoshop gives you the most control over how an image will look, from simple cropping to extensive retouching. The built-in Adobe Camera Raw converter will also give you a huge amount of control over your Raw files.

Is there a downside to using Photoshop? Bought outright, it can be very expensive, and there is a lot to learn. However, it will probably be a worthwhile investment for most serious street photographers and there is a plethora of online tutorials, books, and magazines that make learning the program straightforward.

Above right: Adobe Photoshop is the industry standard image-editing program. However, if you're unlikely to use all of its functionality (and many of us don't), a scaled-down (and much less expensive) version called Photoshop Elements is available.

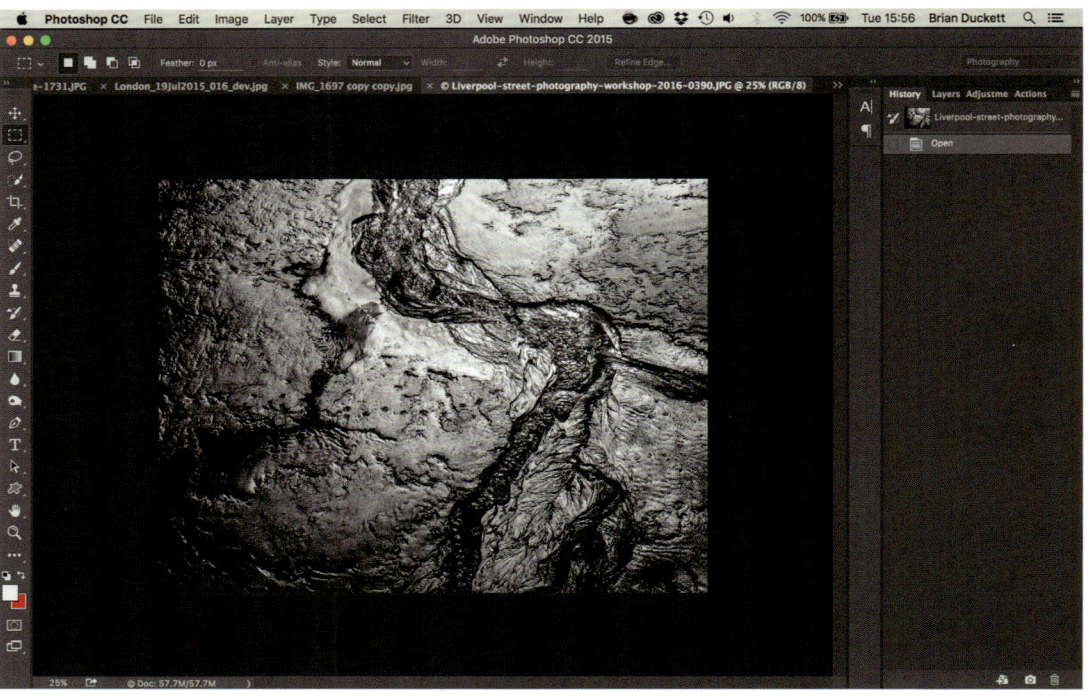

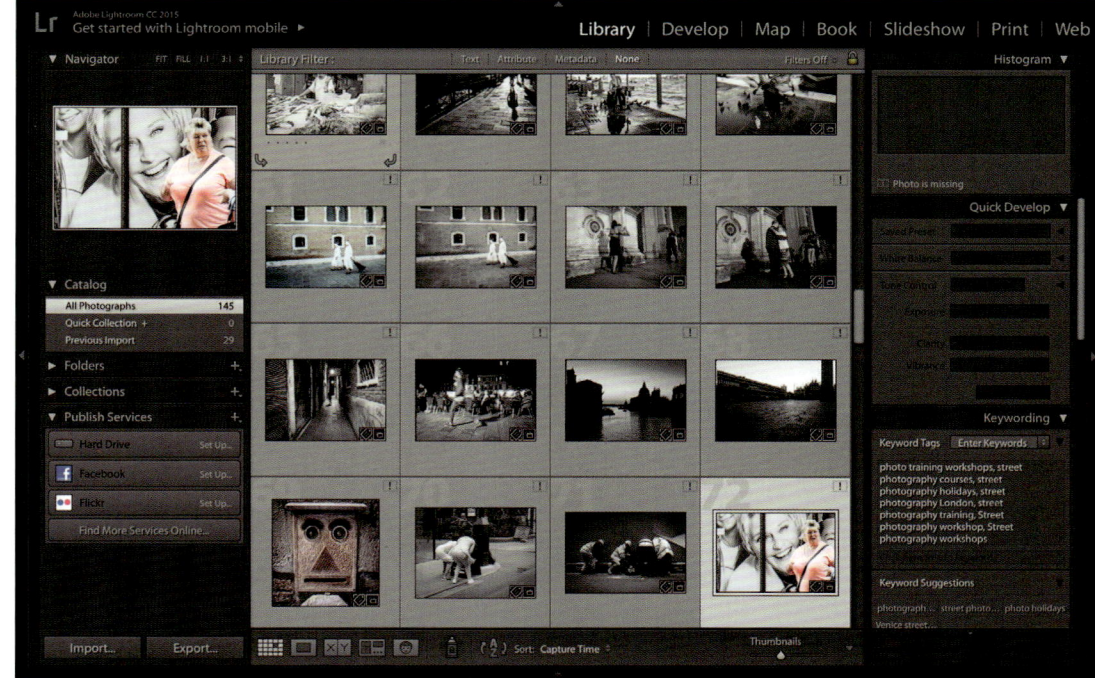

Adobe Lightroom

Adobe Lightroom (or an equivalent, such as Capture One Pro), offers a comprehensive solution: it provides Raw conversion, a fairly extensive range of image-editing options, and—making it different to Photoshop—the ability to manage and archive your image collection. Keywords and other metadata can be added at a stroke and you can file your images in a logical and searchable order. Lightroom does most (but not all) of the things that Photoshop can do, and many photographers find it does everything they need. However, others wouldn't be without the full processing power of Photoshop; it's a very personal choice.

Capture One

Capture One (also known as Capture One Pro or C1Pro) is an image-editing program and Raw processor that does a very similar job to Lightroom. It seems to have been designed with the professional commercial photographer in mind and is particularly favored by those who need to work tethered in the studio.

The Capture One interface may at first seem alien to those who are used to Lightroom (or who still use Apple's now defunct Aperture software), but it's easy to live with once you get over the relatively steep learning curve.

TIP

Before committing to either Lightroom or Capture One (or any other piece of image-editing software), it's worth downloading a free trial version to see which feels best. While they all do a broadly similar job, you will probably find that one instinctively works better for you than the other.

Below: Capture One is an alternative to Lightroom, but while it offers broadly similar features, the interface is very different and can take some getting used to. Those who do use it are usually evangelical about how it manages their workflow and the quality of its Raw image processor.

Left: Adobe Lightroom combines Raw processing with image manipulation and file management, making it a good all-round tool.

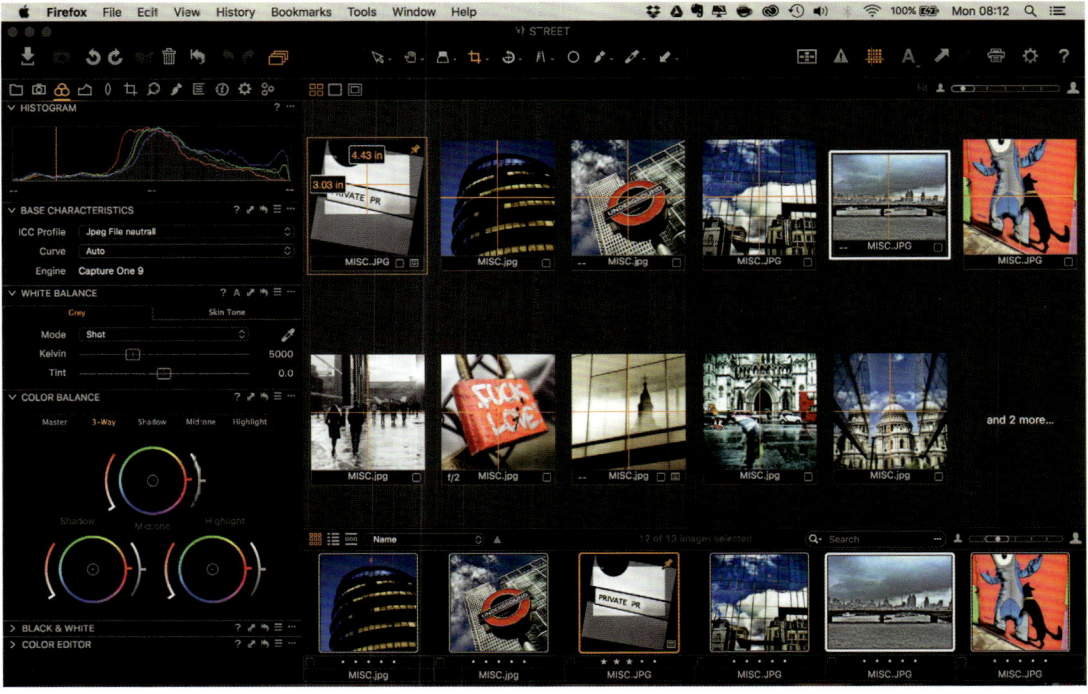

Plug-Ins

Plug-ins that add functionality to programs such as Photoshop and Lightroom are widely available. You can buy plug-ins to help you convert to monochrome, to sharpen images, to apply color filters, to add special effects—the list is extensive. Monochrome conversion plug-ins such as Topaz and Silver Efex Pro are probably of most use to street photographers.

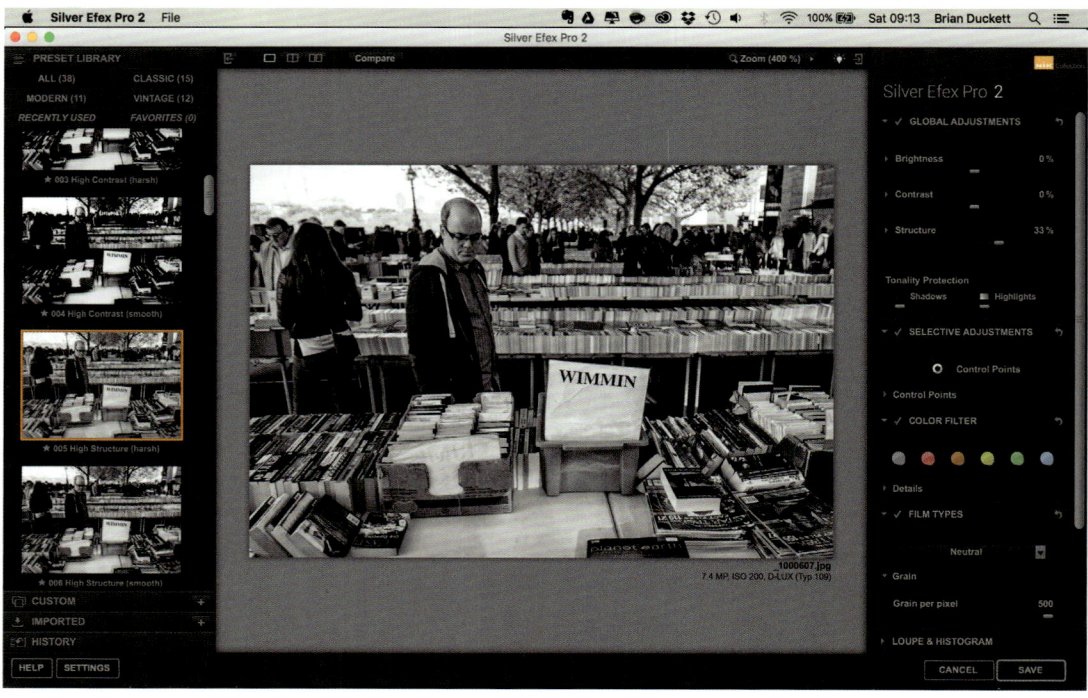

Right: Silver Efex Pro is a very useful plug-in for fine tuning and applying creative effects to monochrome images.

TIP

Don't get too carried away with plug-ins. While they can offer some interesting creative enhancements, street photography is generally not the place for wacky effects! So choose your plug-ins with care and use them judiciously.

Image Browsers

Provided you can make them fit into your workflow, image browsers such as Adobe Bridge or Photo Mechanic can speed up certain processes such as transferring files from camera to computer, adding metadata, and batch processing your images. Photo Mechanic is used by documentary photographers the world over and is an essential step in their workflow.

As your photographic journey develops, your body of work will increase in size and it is important to manage your library efficiently. You need to be able to organize, sort, label, find, and retrieve images quickly. To help you with this you should add as many keywords as you can.

Keywording not only helps you pinpoint specific images in a large collection, but vastly increases your chances of sales if you place your collection with an online image library such as Alamy. No matter how amazing your pictures are, if your keywords are inadequate or inaccurate, no-one will ever find them and they will sit on the shelf forever. Between 10 and 20 keywords is thought to be ideal—any less than that and you risk your images not being found; any more can dilute a search and your images could be pushed further down the page. Your keywords should:

- Illustrate what is in the image
- Tell the "Who? What? When? Where? Why?"
- Stick to the facts
- Be as descriptive as possible
- Contain no spelling errors
- Apply to that specific image (beware of batch keywording where too many generic keywords are applied)

A further benefit of using an image browser is the option to add copyright information. Image theft is rife, and for the sake of a few clicks of the mouse, your legal rights can be better protected and your work will be safer online. Whichever software you use, you should be able to set up a metadata template and enter your copyright notice details as required.

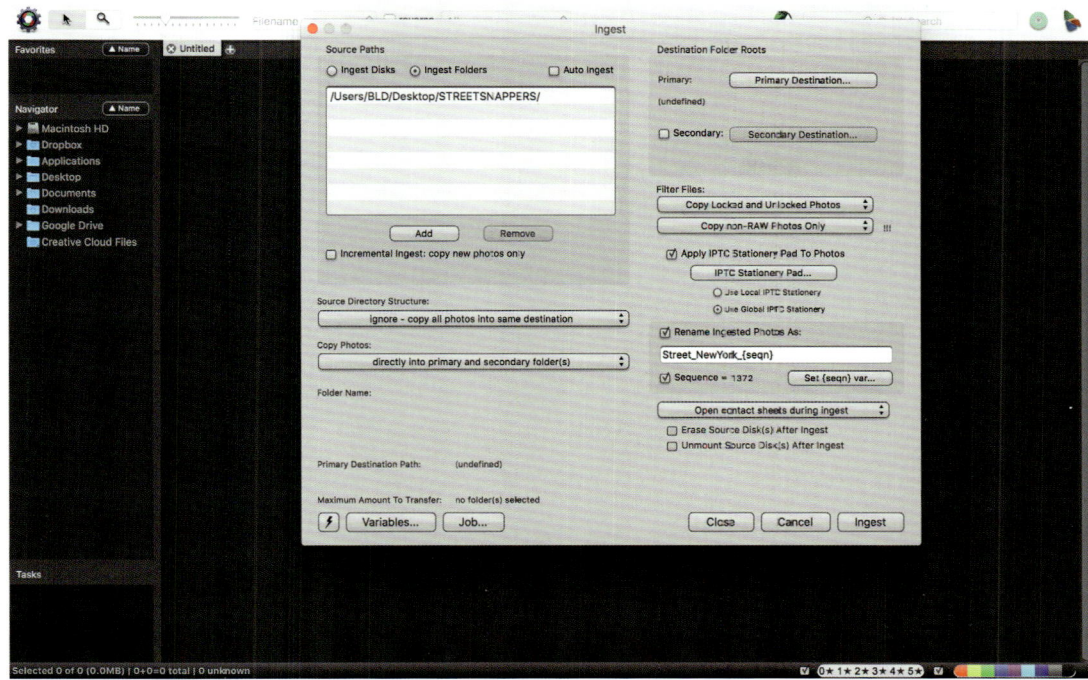

Left: Applications such as Photo Mechanic can speed up your workflow with powerful ingest, keywording, renaming, and batch-processing features.

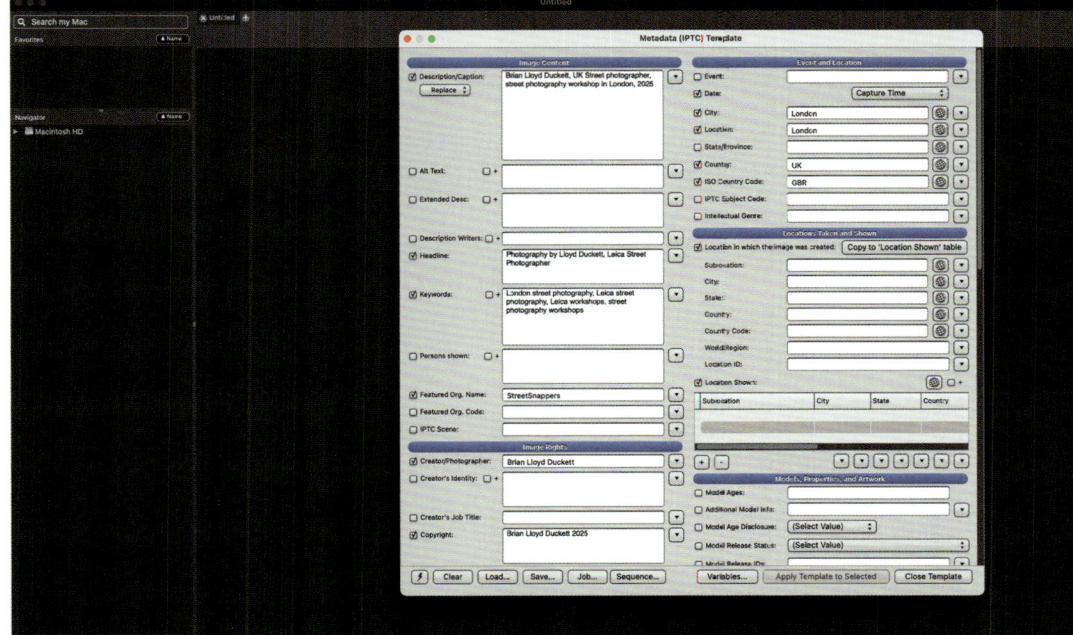

Left: Get into the habit of embedding metadata at the uploading stage in your workflow. Programs like Photo Mechanic simplify this task, allowing you to quickly add captions, keywords, and copyright information.

Cropping

To crop or not to crop? We will, for these purposes, ignore the "never crop" school of thought and consider how cropping can improve our images. Cropping can change the look of an image in a fairly insignificant way or it can radically change it, but you would usually consider cropping an image for one of three main reasons:

- **To straighten horizontal or vertical lines**: It can be frustrating to look at a picture with a sloping horizon or a building that leans like the Tower of Pisa when it shouldn't. Use the crop tool to straighten your key lines.

- **To remove unwanted elements**: Because street photographers often work quickly and compose on the fly, it's easy to find elements in the frame that ruin a composition—there's nothing wrong with cropping them out.

- **To focus on a smaller area of the frame**: Use this with caution and don't become overly reliant on it. Shooting much more of a scene than you need because "I can always crop it later" will make you a lazy photographer—don't fall into this trap.

Tip

If you crop an image, you may want to keep the aspect ratio consistent, to preserve the integrity of the photograph.

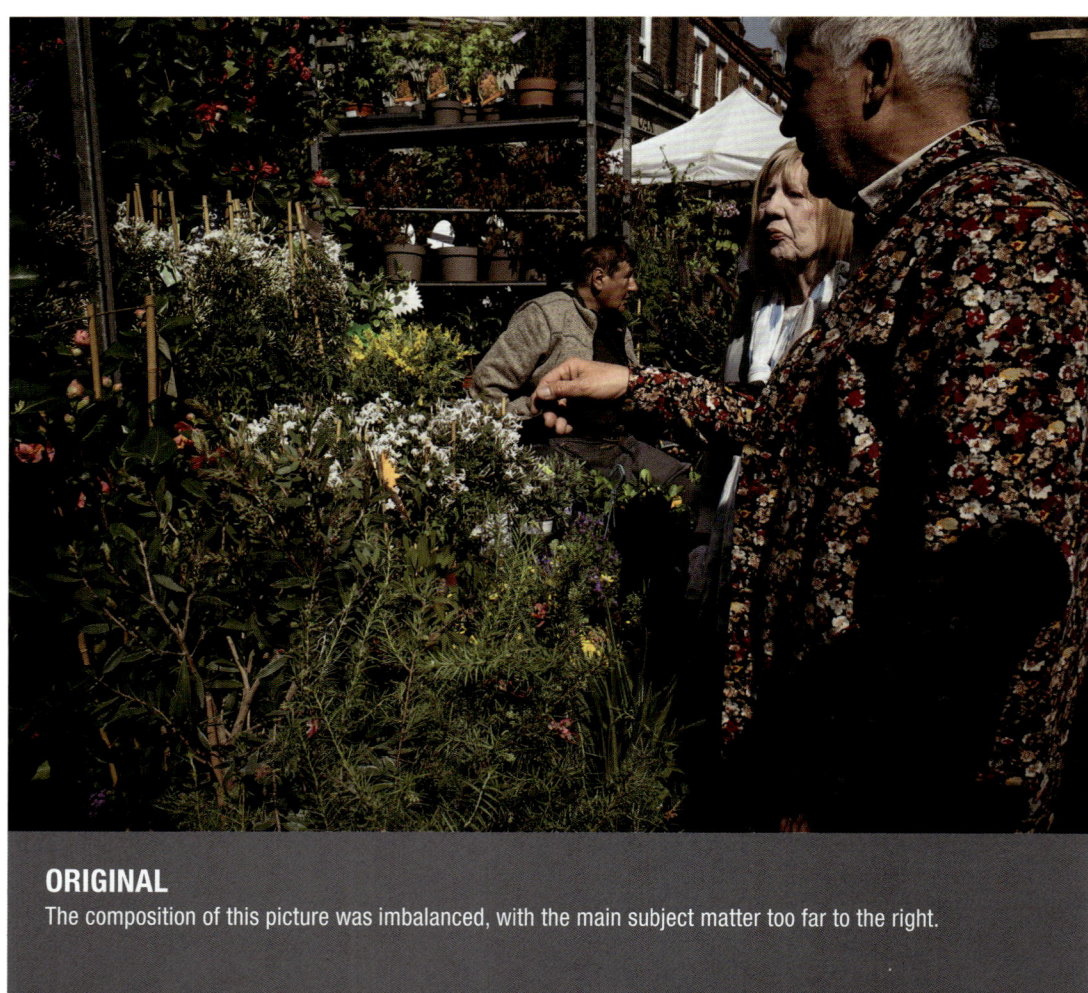

ORIGINAL
The composition of this picture was imbalanced, with the main subject matter too far to the right.

Above and right:
Focal length: 28mm
Aperture: f/8
Shutter speed: 1/400 sec.
ISO: 100

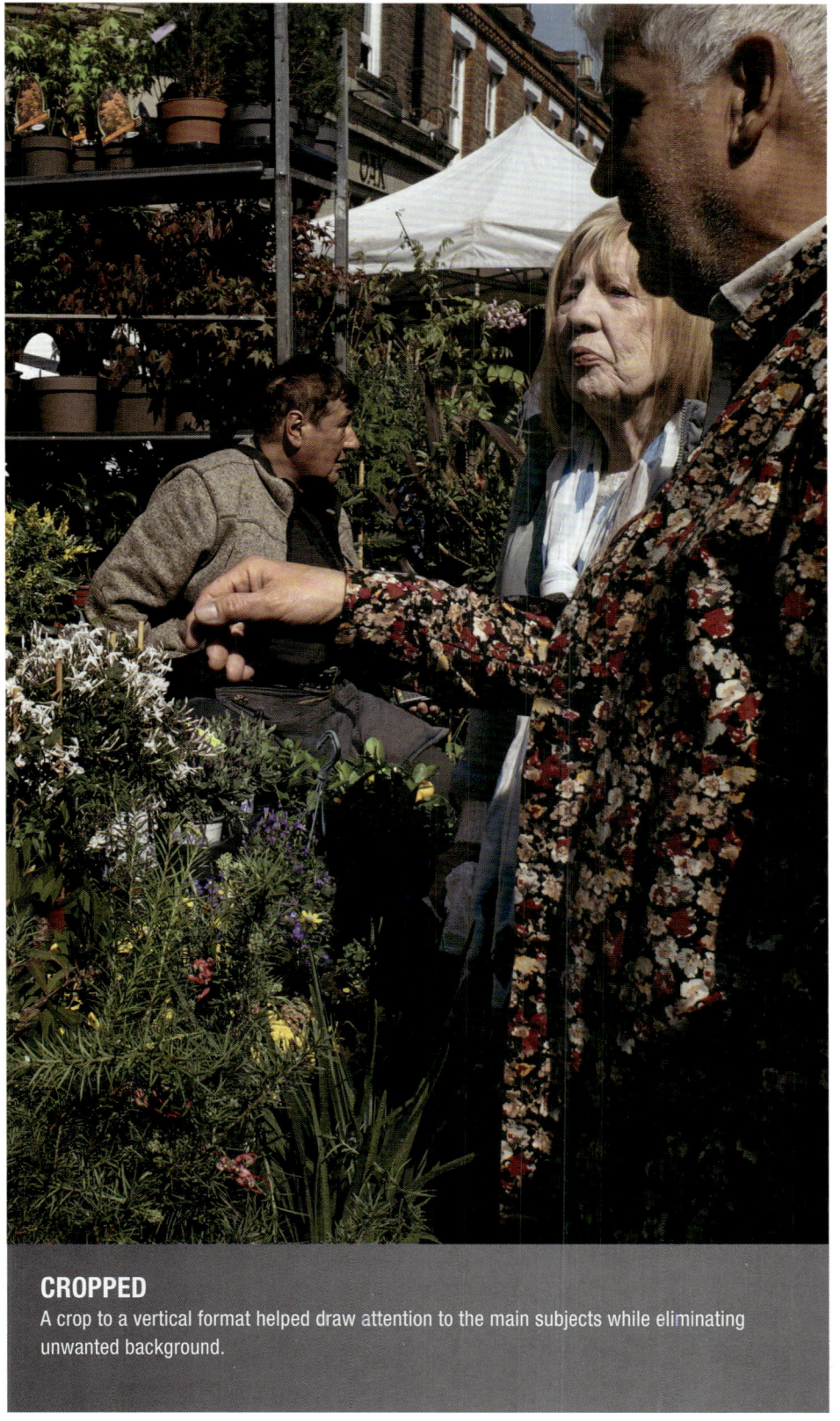

CROPPED

A crop to a vertical format helped draw attention to the main subjects while eliminating unwanted background.

Editing Raw Images

Let's look at some of the steps you might take to edit your images when working with Raw files. Once you have completed these basic Raw adjustments the rest of the fine tuning can be done on the JPEG. Try to make as many adjustments as possible at the Raw stage to help maintain the quality of the file (every time you make an adjustment to a JPEG there is a loss in quality—sometimes significantly so).

Basic Raw Adjustments

Try to keep any manipulation to an absolute minimum. Not all of the steps below will be necessary in every image, so tread carefully—it's easy to get carried away and go over the top. Of course, these are not the only controls available to you, but they are probably the most useful.

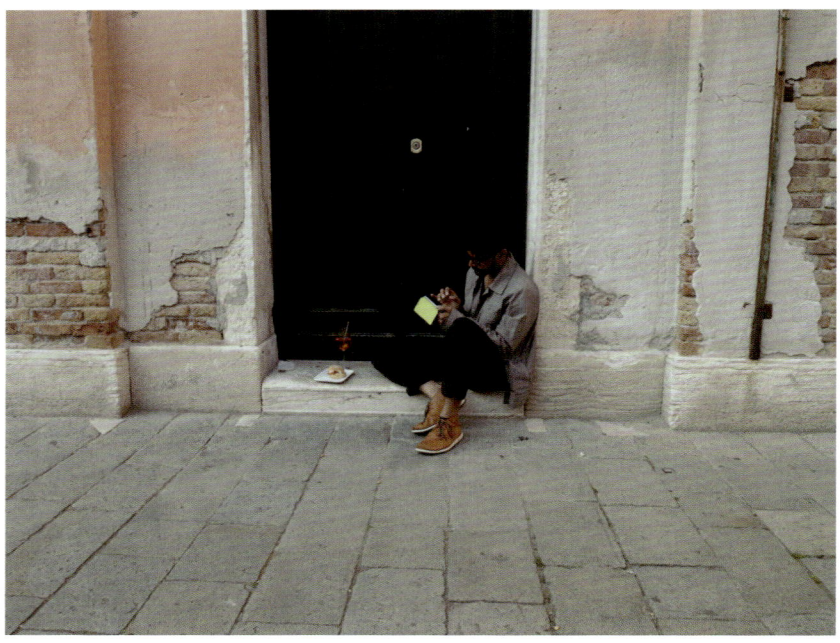

Above: The original Raw image with no adjustments.

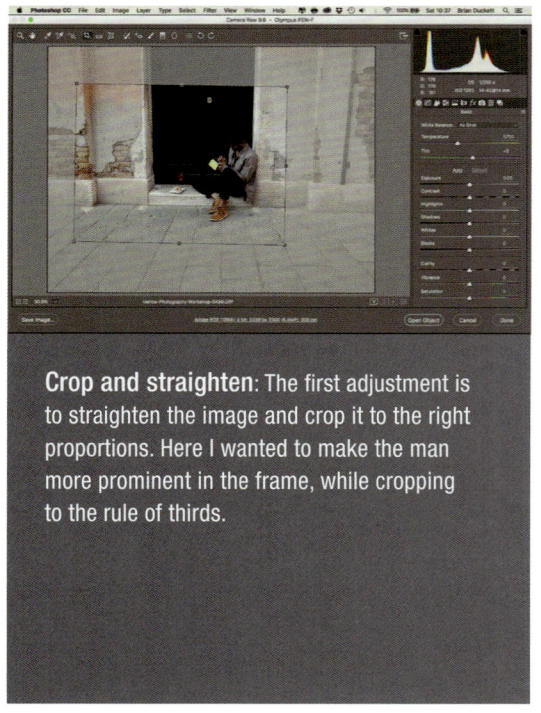

Crop and straighten: The first adjustment is to straighten the image and crop it to the right proportions. Here I wanted to make the man more prominent in the frame, while cropping to the rule of thirds.

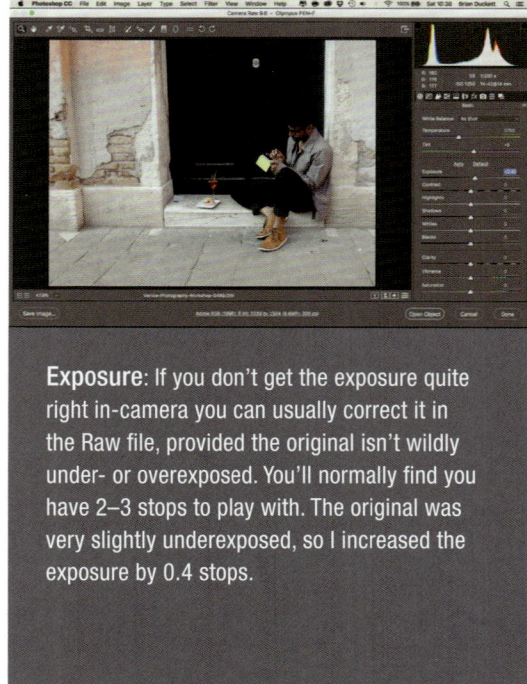

Exposure: If you don't get the exposure quite right in-camera you can usually correct it in the Raw file, provided the original isn't wildly under- or overexposed. You'll normally find you have 2–3 stops to play with. The original was very slightly underexposed, so I increased the exposure by 0.4 stops.

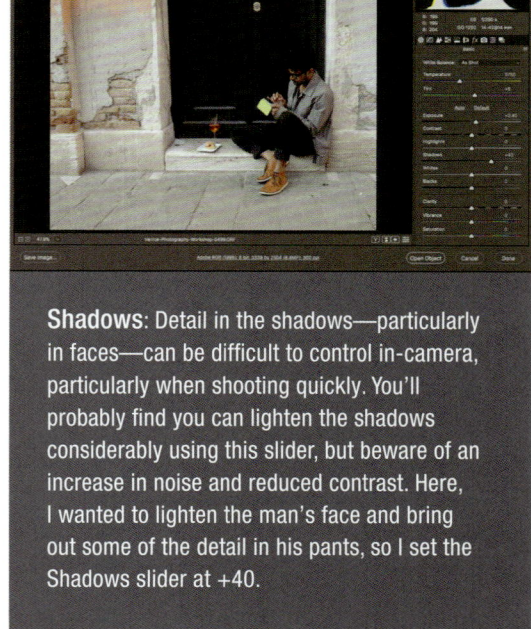

Shadows: Detail in the shadows—particularly in faces—can be difficult to control in-camera, particularly when shooting quickly. You'll probably find you can lighten the shadows considerably using this slider, but beware of an increase in noise and reduced contrast. Here, I wanted to lighten the man's face and bring out some of the detail in his pants, so I set the Shadows slider at +40.

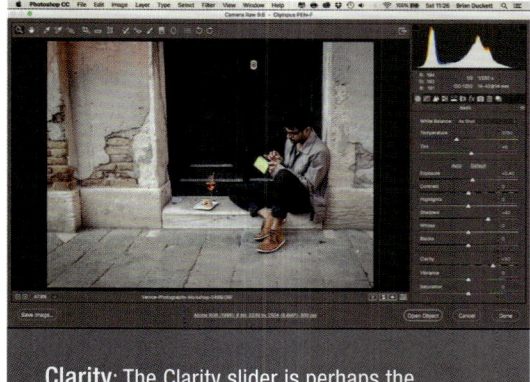

Clarity: The Clarity slider is perhaps the street photographer's most useful adjustment tool. It increases detail and contrast in the midtone areas and can produce a gritty, punchy effect. Increasing clarity often works better in monochrome than it does in color, where skin tones can become blotchy. In this instance the texture in the stone walls and sidewalk could be enhanced with a good whack of Clarity (+50).

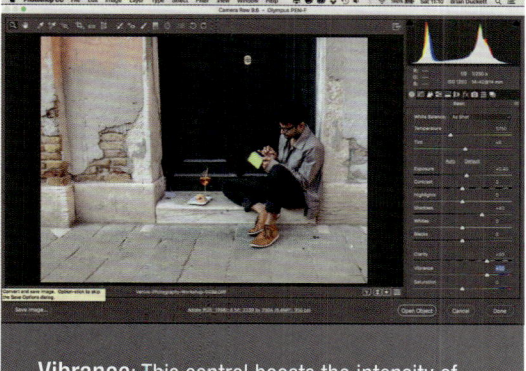

Vibrance: This control boosts the intensity of lower-saturated colors, while leaving skin tones (and already bold colors) largely unaffected. Here I needed to add a little extra color to the shoes, the drink, and some of the brickwork, so made a Vibrance adjustment of +50.

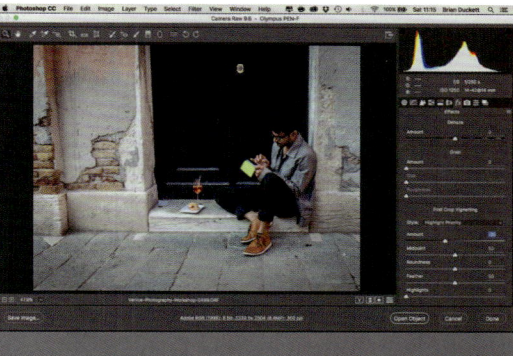

Vignette: Finally, in order to draw the eye into the man and his drink, I added a modest vignette, which also deepened the contrast in the stonework surrounding him.

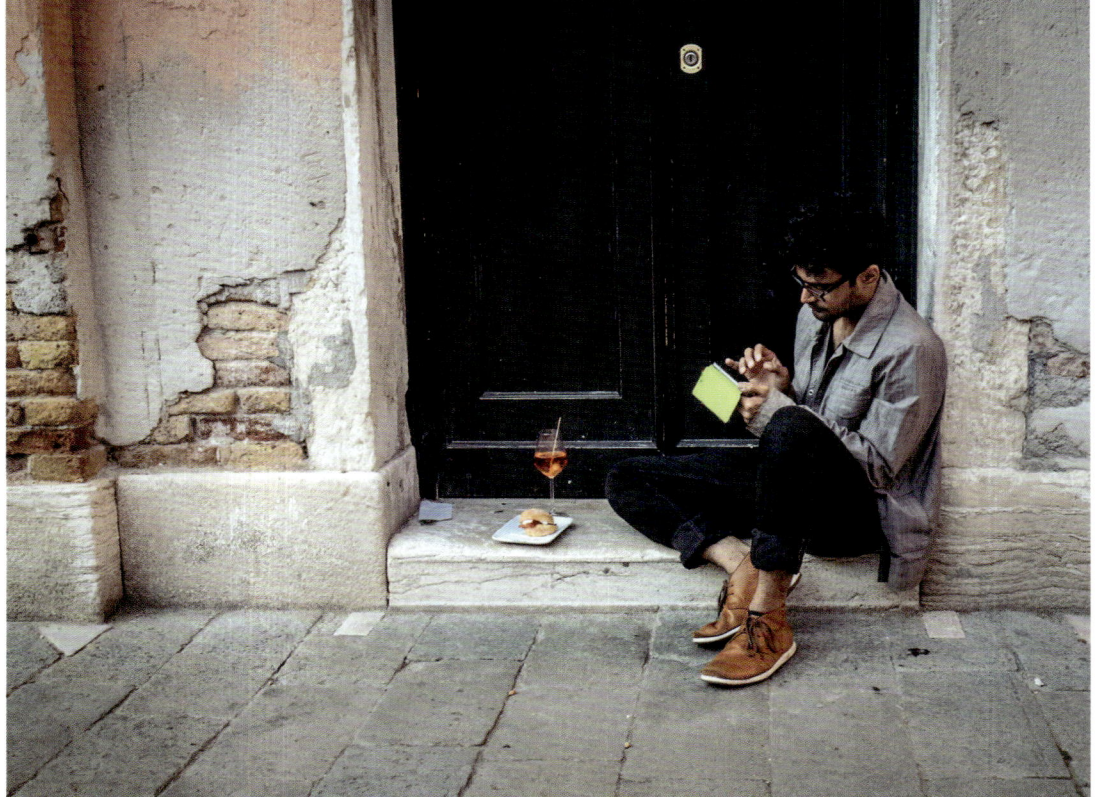

Left: The finished image.

OTHER USEFUL RAW TOOLS

Contrast: Kodak's Tri-X black-and-white film was a longstanding favorite with street photographers, and was typified by its contrasty, punchy style. A small boost in contrast can help give your images a similar kick, but be careful not to overdo the effect.

Highlights: Highlights can easily blow, particularly if you are shooting in bright sunlight. Conversely, if the light is low the highlights may need a boost to make them brighter.

Converting To Monochrome

There are many ways in which you can convert a color image to black and white. Perhaps the most effective method is at the Raw stage, and that is what we will concentrate on here. Follow these simple steps for a high-quality conversion that allows you to change the color mix:

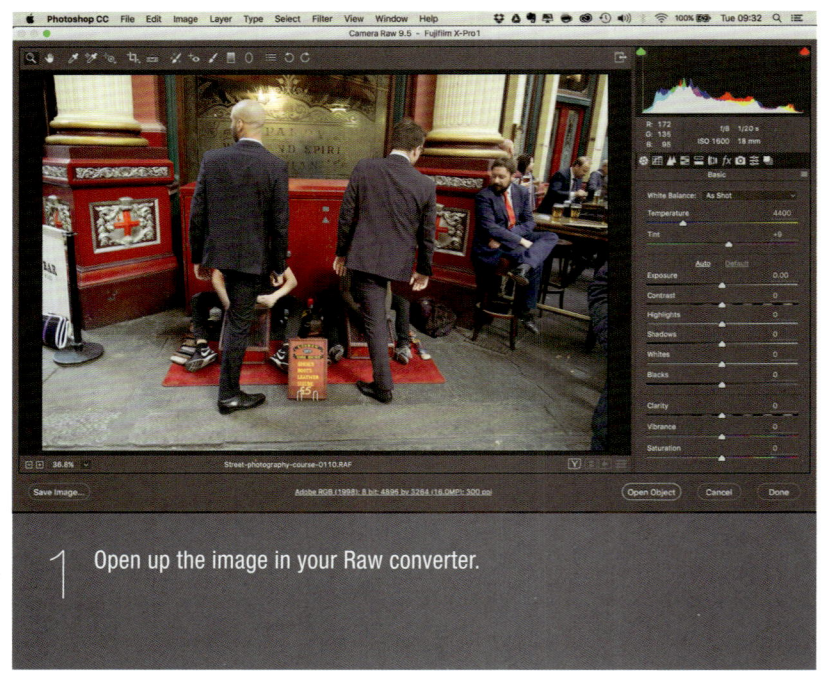

1 Open up the image in your Raw converter.

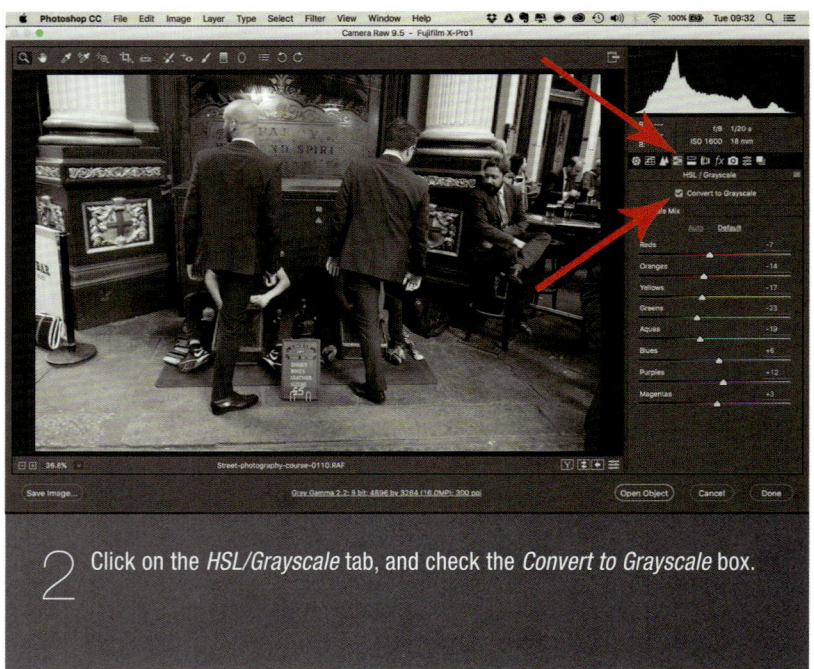

2 Click on the *HSL/Grayscale* tab, and check the *Convert to Grayscale* box.

Using A Plug-In

A popular plug-in for monochrome conversions is Nik Software's Silver Efex Pro, which works with a number of image-editing programs. To get the most out of it, make all your basic adjustments in Raw, exporting the image in color.

Then, open it up as a JPEG, and fire up the plug-in. You will then be able to choose from a large number of preset "looks," as well as being able to add color filters and make localized adjustments to parts of the image. You can even give your image the look of a particular film, such as Ilford HP5 or Kodak Tri-X.

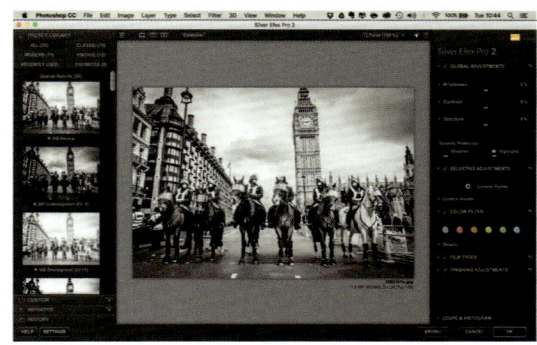

Right: A plug-in such as Silver Efex Pro gives you a flexible and versatile solution for monochrome conversions.

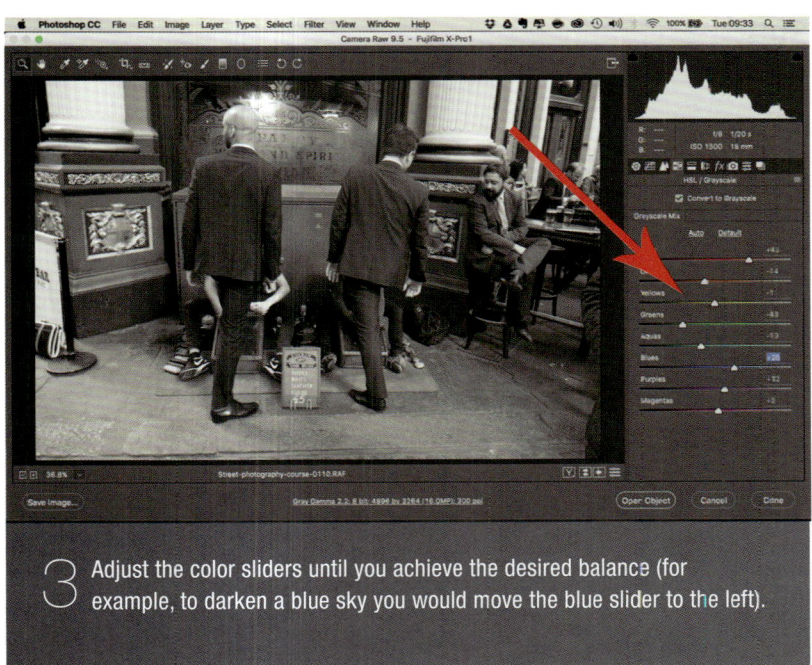

3 Adjust the color sliders until you achieve the desired balance (for example, to darken a blue sky you would move the blue slider to the left).

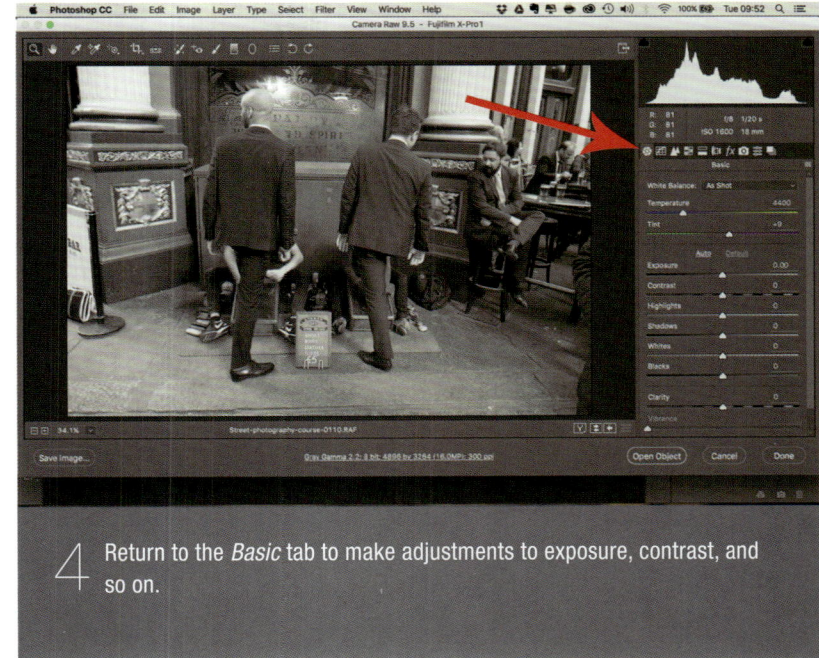

4 Return to the *Basic* tab to make adjustments to exposure, contrast, and so on.

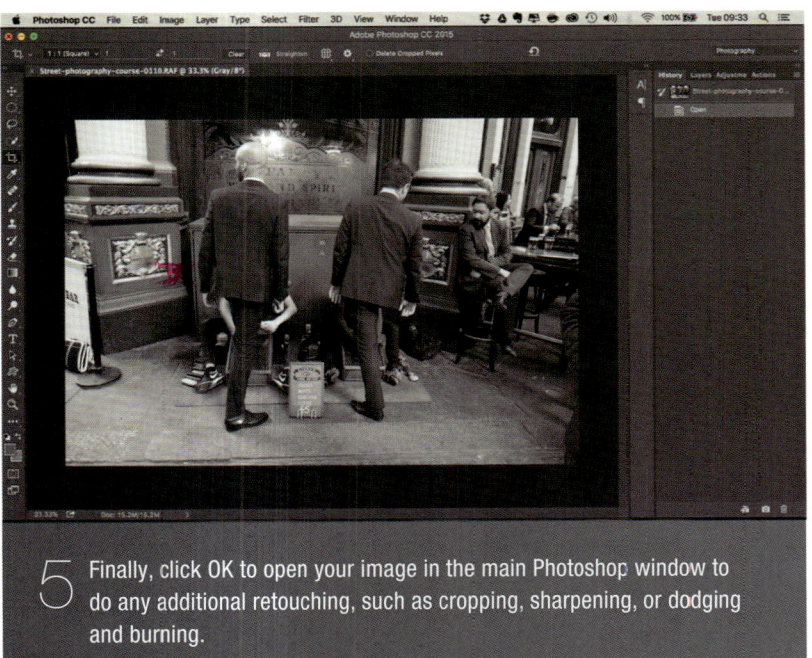

5 Finally, click OK to open your image in the main Photoshop window to do any additional retouching, such as cropping, sharpening, or dodging and burning.

CONVERTING A JPEG TO MONOCHROME

If you're starting with a JPEG image you can use Photoshop's *Black & White* tool (*Image>Adjustments>Black & White*) to make the conversion. As with Adobe Camera Raw's HSL/Grayscale tab you will be able to use color sliders to filter the image and control the tonal range.

There are simpler methods of conversion, but these give you less control over how the image will look. The most straightforward method is to select *Image>Mode>Grayscale* from the main menu (or its equivalent keyboard shortcut) and check the box to "Discard color information." The result will be a monochrome image—albeit one lacking in contrast and depth.

Fine Tuning In Photoshop

Once the basic adjustments (such as exposure and contrast) have been made to the Raw file, and you have a JPEG version of your image, you can set about making some final enhancements.

Sharpening

There are numerous ways of sharpening an image and most photographers have their favorites. One of the most reliable is Photoshop's Unsharp Mask filter (*Filter > Sharpen > Unsharp Mask*). This will not actually create additional detail, but it can greatly enhance the appearance of that detail by increasing small-scale acutance. There are plenty of other methods of sharpening, along with third-party plug-ins that do a similar job, so it pays to experiment and find a method that works for you.

However, regardless of the option you choose, beware of oversharpening; a heavily sharpened image might look fine on a laptop, but when viewed on a large screen or in print, the image quality may be seriously compromised.

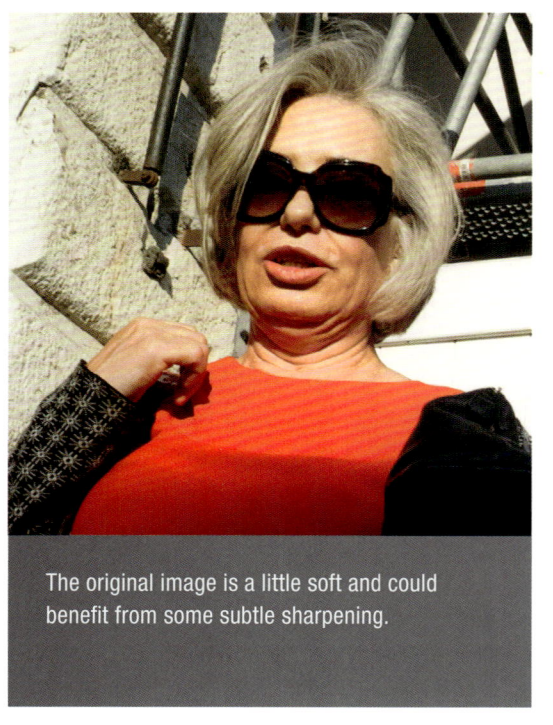

The original image is a little soft and could benefit from some subtle sharpening.

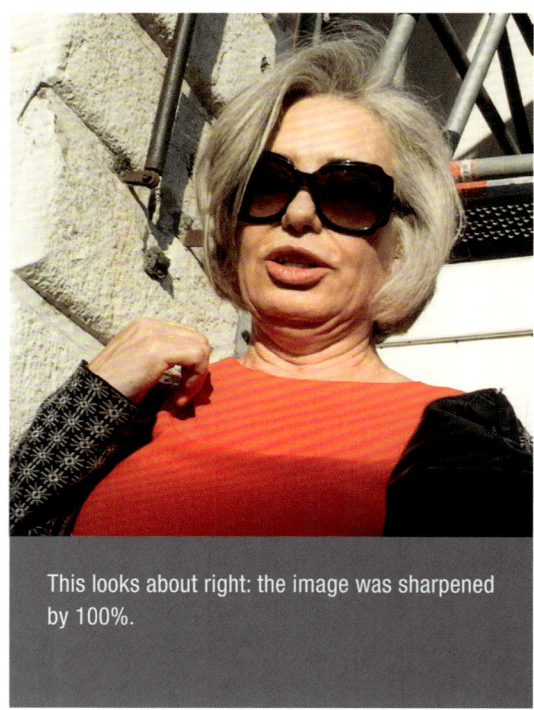

This looks about right: the image was sharpened by 100%.

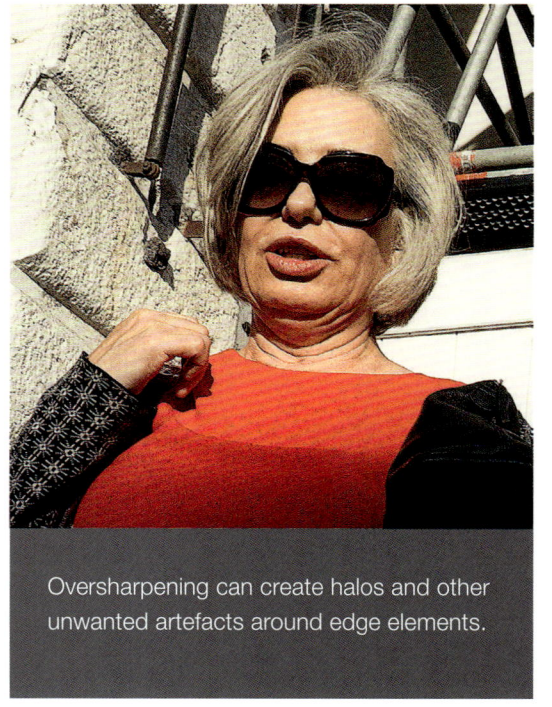

Oversharpening can create halos and other unwanted artefacts around edge elements.

The Unsharp Mask Filter

When you open the Unsharp Mask filter, you are faced with three sliders: Amount, Radius, and Threshold.

- **Amount**: Photoshop examines the edge between two colors and lightens the light pixels and darkens the dark pixels. The Amount determines how light the lighter pixels become, and how dark the darker pixels become; if you set this too high, you'll start to lose fine detail: a value of 80–100 is a good starting point.

- **Radius**: This defines the overall area to be sharpened. With a low value, only the pixels right next to the edge will be sharpened. A high value will allow a wider area to be sharpened. Start with a value of 1 or 2.

- **Threshold**: This determines how much contrast there needs to be between colors for them to be sharpened effectively. A higher value means high-contrast areas will be sharpened, but low-contrast areas will be left alone. Experiment with values of 0–4 and look closely at the results.

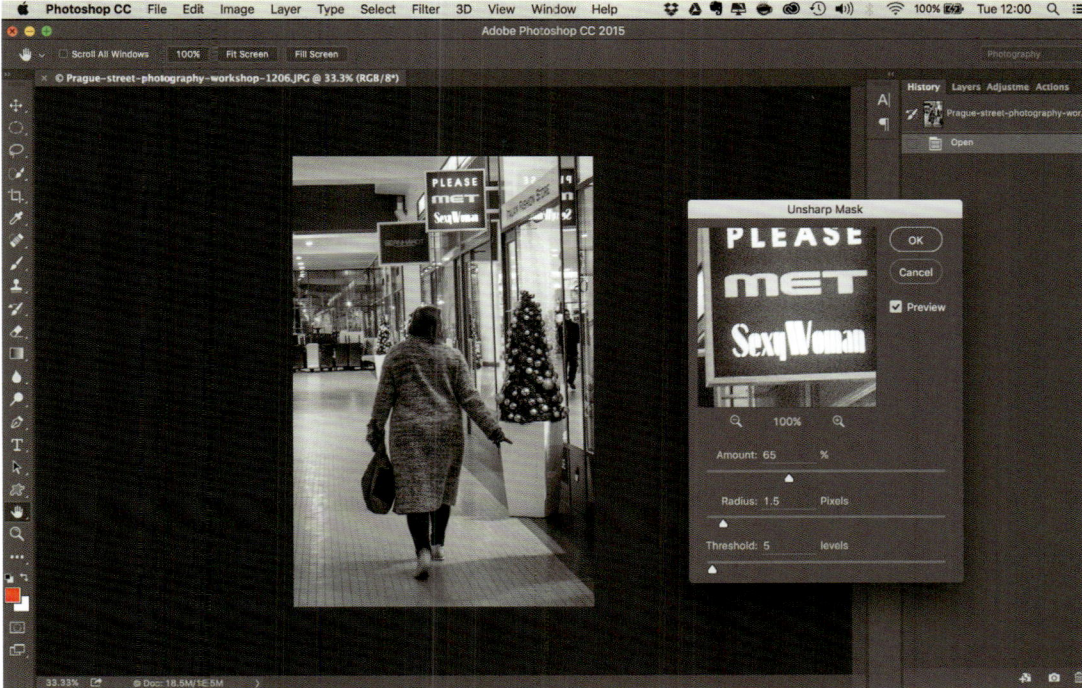

Above: Photoshop's Unsharp Mask filter offers a consistent and controllable sharpening method. Don't overdo it though!

Reducing Noise

When you shoot in low light, use a high ISO setting, or crop an image to a much smaller area, you increase the risk of inducing noise. We are sometimes happy to see an element of noise in our street images, especially in monochrome, because it gives a vintage look—rather like the crackle on a vinyl record gives it a vintage sound.

The development of noise reduction technology is moving at a fast pace and many photo-editing programs now offer an AI noise reduction facility—which generally does an excellent job. However, resorting to more traditional techniques, you can introduce noise reduction at the Raw processing stage or in-camera with a JPEG. As with sharpening, there are numerous techniques

and plug-ins available, so it's worth doing some research and experimenting to discover what works best for you. As a starting point, try Photoshop's *Reduce Noise* filter (*Filter > Noise > Reduce Noise*), which does a pretty good job of reducing noise without sacrificing image detail.

However, if you want to reduce noise in color images, there is a better way, which involves reducing the color rather than the underlying texture; it is this reduction in color that gives the illusion of less noise:

1 Duplicate the background layer by dragging the background layer onto the New Layer icon at the bottom of the Layers pane.

2 Change the duplicate layer's blending mode from Normal to Color.

3 Apply the Gaussian Blur filter (*Filter > Blur > Gaussian Blur*). The amount of blur will determine the amount of noise reduction. Clearly, you need to take care with this as over-blurring will take some of the color information away from the image.

Because the blending mode is set to Color, all that is being blurred is the color information. To increase the accuracy of the effect, you can add a layer mask to the new layer and choose where noise is removed, and where it is not.

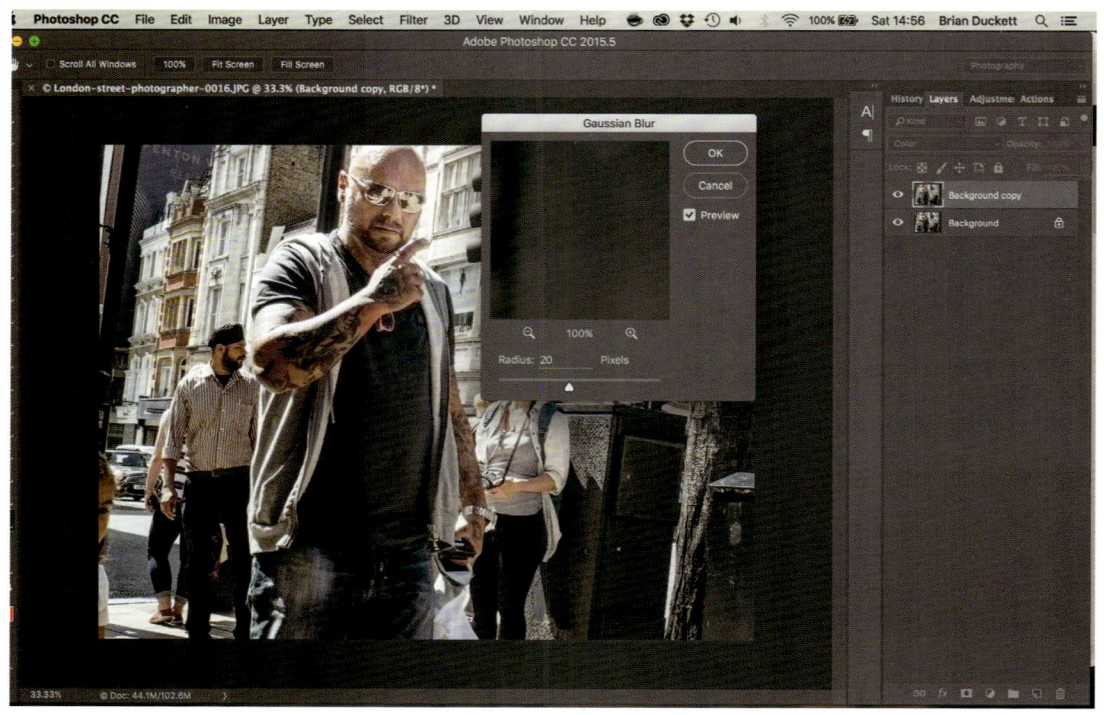

Above: The method of removing noise from a color image described here takes less than a minute and the results are usually perfectly acceptable.

Adding Noise

If you want to add noise to a picture (in the context of grain), you can do this just as easily by selecting *Filter > Noise > Add Noise* from Photoshop's main menu. This is sometimes used to give images a timeless, nostalgic feel. Take care with color images, though, as the addition of noise can introduce unwanted artifacts.

Adding A Vignette

A dark vignette around the edges of an image can draw the eye to the center of the frame and emphasize the main subject. As with sharpening, it's easy to overdo it and care is needed to create a subtle effect. If you want examples of how vignetting can be over-cooked, look no further than Instagram, where you will see millions. It's a case of "less is more!"

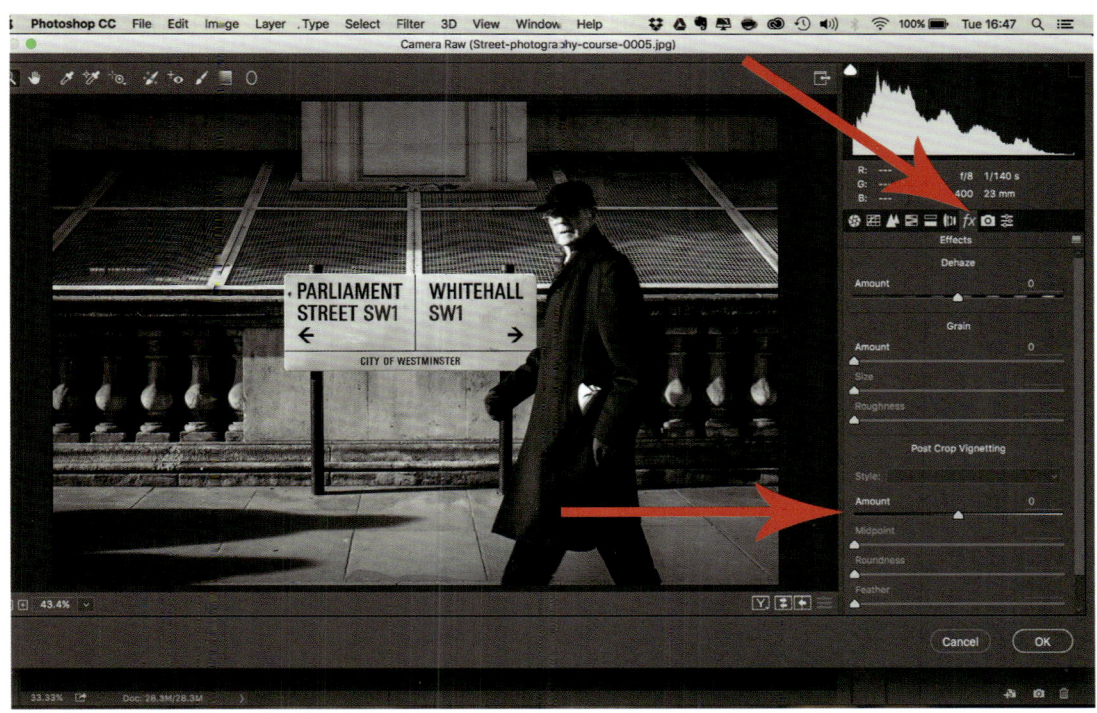

Below left & Below right: Without a vignette, this image is a little flat. However, with the corners darkened slightly the image appears to have more depth and the eye is drawn to the glass.

Focal length: 40mm

Aperture: f/3.4

Shutter speed: 1/350 sec.

ISO: 500

Above: The easiest way to add a vignette is at the Raw editing stage. First click on the Effects tab and then set the amount of vignetting you require.

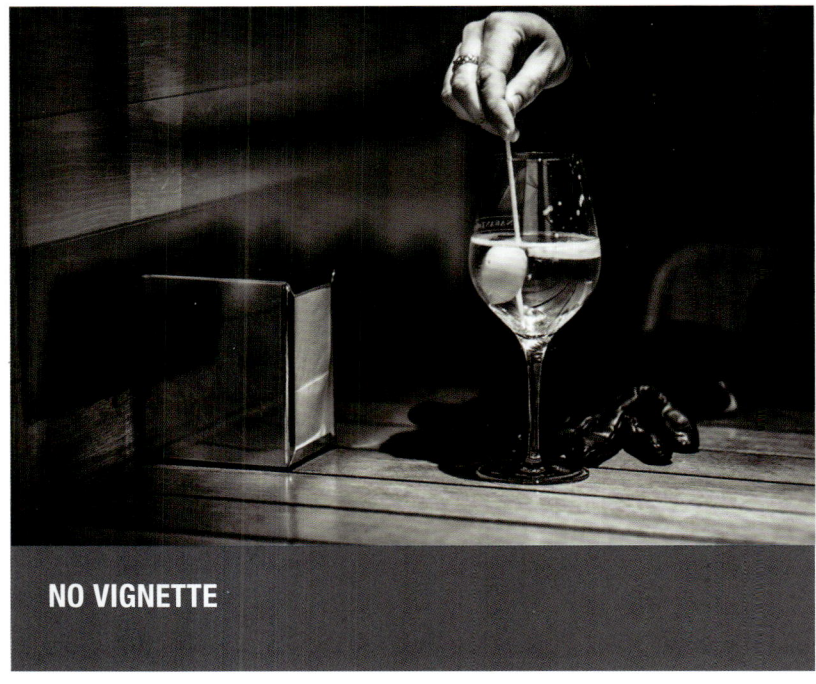

NO VIGNETTE

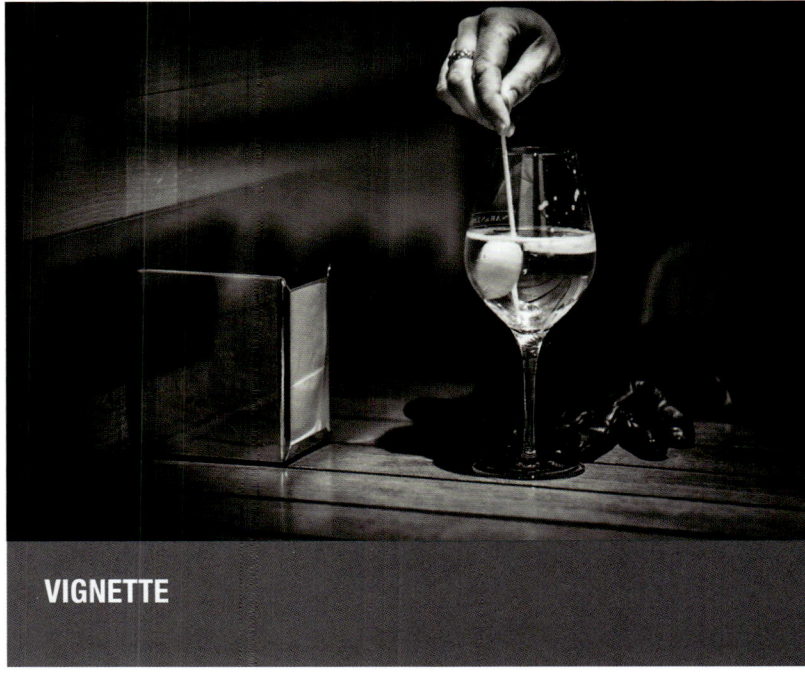

VIGNETTE

Glossary

Aberration An imperfection in a photograph, usually caused by the optics of a lens.

Angle of view The area of a scene that a lens takes in, measured in degrees.

Aperture The opening in a camera lens through which light passes to expose the sensor. The relative size of the aperture is denoted by f/stops.

Autofocus (AF) A reliable through-the-lens focusing system allowing accurate focus without the photographer manually turning the lens.

Bracketing Taking a series of identical pictures, changing only the exposure, usually in ⅓-, ½-, or 1-stop increments.

Buffer The in-camera memory of a digital camera.

Camera shake Image fault caused by camera movement during exposure.

Center-weighted metering A metering pattern that determines the exposure by placing importance on the light meter reading at the center of the frame.

Color temperature The color of a light source expressed in degrees Kelvin (K).

Compression The process by which digital files are reduced in size. Compression can retain all the information in the file (lossless compression), or lose data for greater levels of file-size reduction (lossy compression).

Contrast The range between the highlight and shadow areas of a photo, or a marked difference in illumination between colors or adjacent areas.

Depth of field (DOF) The amount of an image that appears acceptably sharp. This is controlled primarily by the aperture: the smaller the aperture, the greater the depth of field.

Digital sensor A microchip consisting of a grid of millions of light-sensitive cells. The more cells, the greater the number of pixels and the higher the resolution of the final image. The two most commonly used types of digital sensor are CCD (Charge-Coupled Device) and CMOS (Complementary Metal-Oxide Semi-conductor).

Distortion A lens fault that causes what should be straight lines in an image to bow outward from the center (referred to as barrel distortion) or inward (referred to as pincushion distortion).

dpi (dots per inch) Measure of the resolution of a printer or scanner. The more dots per inch, the higher the resolution.

Dynamic range The ability of the camera's sensor to capture a full range of shadows and highlights.

Evaluative metering A metering system where light reflected from multiple subject areas is calculated based on algorithms.

Exposure The amount of light allowed to hit the digital sensor, controlled by aperture, shutter speed, and ISO. Also, the act of taking a photograph, as in "making an exposure."

Exposure compensation A control that allows intentional over- or underexposure.

Fill-in flash Flash combined with daylight in an exposure. Used with naturally backlit or harshly side-lit or top-lit subjects to prevent silhouettes forming, or to add extra light to the shadow areas of a well-lit scene.

Focal length The distance, usually in millimeters, from the optical center of a lens to its focal point.

fps (frames per second) A measure of the time needed for a digital camera to process one photograph and be ready to shoot the next.

f/stop Number assigned to a particular lens aperture. Wide apertures are denoted by small numbers (such as f/1.8 and f/2.8), while small apertures are denoted by large numbers (such as f/16 and f/22).

Highlights The brightest part of an image.

Histogram A graph representing the distribution of tones in a photograph.

Hotshoe An accessory shoe with electrical contacts that allows synchronization between a camera and a flash.

Interpolation A way of increasing the file size of a digital image by adding pixels, thereby increasing its resolution.

ISO The sensitivity of the digital sensor measured in terms equivalent to the ISO rating of a film.

JPEG (Joint Photographic Experts Group) JPEG compression can reduce file sizes to about 5 percent of their original size, but uses a lossy compression system that degrades image quality.

LCD (Liquid crystal display) The flat screen on a digital camera that allows the user to compose and review digital images.

Megapixel One million pixels is equal to one megapixel.

Memory card A removable storage device for digital cameras.

Metering Act of measuring the amount of light falling on a scene to determine the required exposure.

Mirrorless Common name given to a camera that doesn't have a reflex mirror (*see* SLR). The photographer views a live image streamed from the digital sensor to an LCD.

Monochrome A synonym for black-and-white photography.

Noise Interference visible in a digital image caused by stray electrical signals during exposure.

Overexposure A result of allowing too much light to reach the digital sensor during exposure. Typically, the highlights in an overexposed image will be burnt out to pure white and the shadows will appear unnaturally bright.

Pixel Short for "picture element"—the smallest bit of information in a digital photograph.

Predictive autofocus An AF system that can continuously track a moving subject.

Private property Property owned by an individual or organization over which they have full and exclusive rights. This can extend to prohibiting photography on or in the property.

Public property Property that is not owned by a single individual or company, to which the public usually has full access. There are few restrictions on street photography in public places.

Raw The file format in which the raw data from the sensor is stored without permanent alteration being made.

Resolution The number of pixels used to capture or display a photo.

RGB (Red, Green, Blue) Computers and other digital devices understand color information as combinations of red, green, and blue.

Rule of Thirds A rule of composition that places the key elements of a picture at points along imagined lines that divide the frame into thirds, both vertically and horizontally.

Shadows The darkest part of an image.

Shutter The mechanism that controls the amount of light reaching the sensor, by opening and closing.

SLR (Single Lens Reflex) A camera that directs the image projected through the lens to the viewfinder using a reflex mirror.

Spot metering A metering pattern that places importance on the intensity of light reflected by a very small portion of the scene, either at the center of the frame or linked to a focus point.

Standard lens A lens with a focal length that is approximately the same as the diagonal measurement of the sensor. This results in an angle of view that is similar to the way we see.

Telephoto lens A lens with a large focal length and a narrow angle of view.

TIFF (Tagged Image File Format) A universal file format supported by virtually all relevant software applications. TIFFs are uncompressed digital files.

TTL (Through The Lens) metering A metering system built into the camera that measures light passing through the lens at the time of shooting.

Underexposure The result of allowing too little light to reach the digital sensor during exposure. Typically, the highlights in an underexposed image will appear muddy and the shadows will be dense and lacking in detail.

USB (Universal Serial Bus) A data transfer standard used by most cameras when connecting to a computer.

Viewfinder An optical system used for composing and sometimes for focusing the subject.

White balance A function that allows the correct color balance to be recorded for any given lighting situation.

Wide-angle lens A lens with a short focal length and, consequently, a wide angle of view.

Zone focusing A technique that relies on presetting the aperture and manually setting the focus point to enable the depth of field to create a specific zone of focus. This enables you to shoot without looking through the camera's viewfinder.

Zoom A lens with a variable focal length.

Useful Websites

Photographers

Brian Lloyd Duckett www.streetsnappers.com; www.brianduckett.com
William Eggleston www.egglestonartfoundation.org
Bruce Gilden www.brucegilden.com
Magnum Photos www.magnumphotos.com
Vivian Maier www.vivianmaier.com
Joel Meyerowitz www.joelmeyerowitz.com
Daido Moriyama www.moriyamadaido.com
Martin Parr www.martinparr.com

Useful Resources

Equipment reviews www.dpreview.com
Online depth of field calculator www.dofmaster.com
Websites for photographers www.squarespace.com

Photographic Equipment

Artisan & Artist (straps) www.artisanartistglobal.com
Billingham (bags) www.billingham.co.uk
Canon (cameras and lenses) www.canon.com
Domke (bags) www.tiffen.com
FujiFilm (cameras and lenses) www.fujifilm.com
Leica (cameras and lenses) www.leica-camera.com
Nikon (cameras and lenses) www.nikon.com
Olympus (cameras and lenses) www.olympus-global.com
Pentax/Ricoh (cameras and lenses) www.ricoh-imaging.com
Samyang (lenses) www.samyanglensglobal.com
Sigma (lenses) www.sigma-photo.co.jp
Sony (cameras and lenses) www.sony.com
Tamron (lenses) www. tamron.com
Tiffen (filters) www.tiffen.com
Wotancraft (bags and straps) www.wotancraft.tw
Zeiss (lenses) www.zeiss.com

Photography Publications

Ammonite Press www.ammonitepress.com
Black & White Photography Magazine www.gmcsubscriptions.com
Outdoor Photography Magazine www.gmcsubscriptions.com

Printing

Epson www.epson.com
Fotospeed www.fotospeed.com
Hahnemühle www.hahnemuehle.de
Harman www.harmantechnology.com
HP www.hp.com
Ilford www.ilfordphoto.com
Kodak www.kodak.com
Lexmark www.lexmark.com
Lyson www.specialistinks.com
Marrutt www.marrutt.com
Permajet www.permajet.com

Software & Actions

Adobe www.adobe.com
AlienSkin www.alienskin.com
Apple www.apple.com
Capture One Pro www.phaseone.com
DxO www.dxo.com
Photomatix www.hdrsoft.com
PhotoPills www.photopills.com
Silver Efex Pro (plug-in) www.nikcollection.dxo.com
Topaz Labs (plug-ins) www.topazlabs.com

Index

A

abstract images 92–93
accessories 26–27
Adams, Ansel 41, 45, 117
Adobe Bridge 158
Adobe Lightroom 157
Adobe Photoshop 156
    Black & White tool 165
    reducing/adding noise 168
    Unsharp Mask 166–167
    vignettes 169
Adobe Photoshop Elements 156
Alone (assignment) 62–63
anticipation 127
aperture 32
    Aperture Priority mode 32
Apple Aperture 157
Arbus, Diane 43
articulated viewing screens 118
assignments
    Alone 62–63
    It's all a Blur 64–65
    Juxtaposition 104–105
    Objects 106–107
    Up Close & Personal 130–131
    Where I Live 132–133
Atget, Eugène 8
autofocus 36, 37

B

backpacks 27, 119
batteries 28
black and white
    film 20
    or color? 74–75
postproduction conversion
    164–165
    shooting for 52, 56–57
blur, intentional 64–65, 86, 95
body language 115, 127
buildings, legal issues 139,
    142–143
buses 97

C

cafés 95
camera bags 27
camera straps 26, 114
cameras
    compact system (CSCs) 17–18
    digital 16–18
    film 20
    single lens reflex (SLR) 20
    "toy" 20
    twin-lens reflex (TLR) 20
Capa, Robert 122, 123
Capture One 157
Cartier-Bresson, Henri 6, 8, 9, 38,
    45, 68, 126
challenges
    from the police 138
    from the public 100, 121
chamois leathers 28
children
    images of 87
    legal/ethical issues 144
"chimping" 118
city centers 94–95
close-ups (people) 76–77, 122,
    130–131
clothing 28, 116
color
    or black and white? 74–75
    shooting for 54–55
    as subject 92
commuters 94
compact system cameras (CSCs)
    17–18
composition 40–51
    cropping 45
    figure-to-ground ratio 50–51
    landscape format 42
    layering 49
    leading lines 46, 94
    portrait format 42
    pre-visualization 41
    quick technique 41
    rule of thirds 46–47
    square format 43–44
    symmetry 48
contemporary street scenes
    80–81
context 24, 77, 122
Cooper, Martha 24, 82
copyright
    of buildings 142
    of images 147–151
counterterrorism legislation 138
crop factor 24
cropping 45
    postproduction 160–161
CSCs (compact system cameras)
    17–18
cultural issues 145
curiosity 115

D

Daguerre, Louis-Jacques-Mandé 8
dappled light 90
decisive moments 80, 126
defamatory images 148
demonstrations 100–101
depth of field 32
desensitization technique 124
digital equipment
    cameras 16–18
    or film? 14–15
digital noise 14, 15
    reducing/adding 168
Doisneau, Robert 6, 43
DSLR cameras 16, 18

E

earphones 116
equipment 12–29
Erwitt, Elliott 68
exhibitions 72
expectations, managing 111
exposure 32–35
extreme street photography 100
eye contact, avoiding 60, 114,
    118

F

fear, conquering 120–125
festivals 102–103
figure-to-ground ratio 50–51
film 14–15, 20
"fishing" 80, 119
flash 26, 50
focal length 24, 25

focus 36–39
    low light 60
Frank, Robert 9, 24, 68
Friedlander, Lee 9, 43, 68, 91
funfairs 98

G
galleries 72
Gilden, Bruce 6, 9, 10, 68, 76
"golden hour" 112
grain 14, 15
Grant, Ted 57
Gruyaert, Harry 68

H
hats 28, 116
hesitation 128
hip, shooting from the 116
history 8–9
horizontal format 42

I
image browsers 158–159
inspiration 66
Instagram 18, 43
invisibility, achieving 116–119
iPhones 18
ISO settings 32
It's all a Blur (assignment) 64–65

J
JPEGs 52–53
    converting to monochrome 165
juxtaposition 84, 104–105

K
Karlovac, Olga 68
keywording 158
"KISS" principle 30

K
Karlovac, Olga 68
keywording 158
"KISS" principle 30

L
landscape format 42
layering 49
leading lines 46, 95
legal/ethical issues 136–139
    buildings 139, 142–143
    children 144
    cultural issues 145
    people 140–141
    private property 136–139
    red lines 146
    see also copyright
Leibovitz, Annie 110
Leiter, Saul 9, 49, 54, 68, 74
lens cloths 28
lenses 22–25
    crop factor 24
    focal length 24, 25
    prime 22
    wide-angle 24
    zoom 22
Levitt, Helen 68
licensing work 149
light
    dappled 90
    low 29, 58–61
    shafts of 90
Lightroom 157
locations 94–103
    city centers 94–95
    festivals, carnivals, and events
        102–103
    markets 96, 139
    protests and demonstrations
        100–101

public transportation 97
    seaside 98
    shopping areas/malls 99,
        137, 139
low light 29, 58–61

M
McLaren, Stephen: *Crash* 70
McCullin, Don 82
McCurry, Steve 76
magazines 72–73
"magic hour" 112
Maier, Vivian 9, 24, 68, 74
manual exposure 35
markets 96, 139
Martin, Paul 8
memory cards 28, 114
Mermelstein, Jeff 74
metadata 150
Meyerowitz, Joel 9, 68, 74, 116
mirrorless cameras 17–18
model release forms 28, 148
monochrome *see* black and white
music festivals 102

N
neck straps 26
newspapers 72–73
night photography 29, 58–61, 95
noise 14, 15
    reducing/adding 168
notebooks 28, 95

O
objects 91, 106–107
observational skills 115
Outerbridge, Paul 55
overshooting 111

P
Parr, Martin 9, 54, 68, 74, 98
patience 127–128
people
    challenges from 121
    close-ups 76–77, 122,
        130–131
    legal issues 140–141
    shooting past 118
    street portraits 78–79
    see also children
Photo Mechanic 158
Photoshop 156
    Black & White tool 165
    reducing/adding noise 168
    Unsharp Mask 166–167
    vignettes 169
Photoshop Elements 156
planning a shoot 110–113
plug-ins 158
police officers
    challenges from 138
    photographing 100, 136, 139
portrait format 42
posed shots 78–79
postproduction 162
    converting to monochrome
        164–165
    cropping 160–161
    editing Raw images 162–163
    and image integrity 154
    software 156–159
    see also Photoshop
"pre-production" editing 154
pre-visualization 41
prime lenses 22
privacy laws 140–141
private property 136–139
projects 70–73, 76

protests and demonstrations 100–101

public transportation 97

publishing images 72

R

race meetings 102

rain 49, 112, 113

rangefinder cameras 20

Raw files 52–53

    converting to monochrome 75, 164–165

    postproduction editing 162–163

reflections 95

rubber bands 28

rule of thirds 46–47

S

safety

    on location 114

    night photography 60

    protests and demonstrations 100

Salgado, Sebastião 82

seaside images 98

security guards 99, 137–138

self-publishing 72

shadows 88–89, 95

sharpening images 166–167

shooting from the hip 116

shopping areas/malls 99, 137, 139

shoulder bags 27

Shutter Priority mode 32

shutter speed 32–34

    low light 60, 61

    silent shutter mode 119

signs 95

silhouettes 85

Silver Efex Pro 164

SLR (single lens reflex) cameras 20

SmartFrame 150, 151

smartphones 18

snow 49, 112, 113

social documentary images 82–83

Soho Life project 71–73

Sontag, Susan 11

sporting events 102

square format 43–44

Stuart, Matt 68

style, developing 68

subways 97

success, characteristics for 129

sunglasses 116

sunscreen 28

symmetry 48

T

Terrorism Act (UK, 2000) 138

thirds, rule of 46–47

timing 126–129

tourists 95

"toy" cameras 20

trains 97

tripods 26–27, 29

twin-lens reflex (TLR) cameras 20

U

Unsharp Mask 166–167

Up Close & Personal (assignment) 130–131

V

vertical format 42

vignettes 169

W

watermarking 150, 151

weather 112

Webb, Alex 68, 74

websites 72

    and copyright 150

Where I Live (assignment) 132–133

wide-angle lenses 24

windows, shooting through 49

Winogrand, Garry 9, 68, 121

wrist straps 26

Z

zone focusing 36–38

zoom lenses 22

Acknowledgments

This book is dedicated to two people: firstly to my wife, Johannah, for her love, motivation, patience, and terrific proofreading skills. Secondly to my son, Alex, for his ideas and encouragement during the development of this book. You've both been great. Thank you.

I must also mention my late parents, who I hope are still watching, and who proudly followed my career and supported me come rain or shine. They always said I had a book in me!

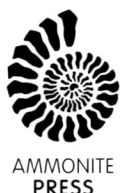

AMMONITE
PRESS

To place an order, or request a catalog, contact:
Ammonite Press
GMC Publications Ltd, Castle Place, 166 High Street, Lewes, East Sussex, BN7 1XU, United Kingdom
Tel: +44 (0)1273 488006
www.ammonitepress.com